France after
Hegemony

A VOLUME IN THE SERIES

Cornell Studies in Political Economy

EDITED BY PETER J. KATZENSTEIN

A full list of titles in the series appears at the end of the book.

France after Hegemony

International Change and Financial Reform

Michael Loriaux

Cornell University Press

Ithaca and London

First published 1991 by Cornell University Press.

International Standard Book Number 0-8014-2483-6
Library of Congress Catalog Card Number 90-55721

Printed in the United States of America

*Librarians: Library of Congress cataloging information
appears on the last page of the book.*

⊗ The paper in this book meets the minimum requirements
 of the American National Standard for Information Sciences—
 Permanence of Paper for Printed Library Materials,
 ANSI Z39.48-1984.

parentibus meis

Contents

Acknowledgments

This book began innocently enough as a term paper on French foreign monetary policy written for Miles Kahler, who offered guidance and encouragement. My debt to Robert Gilpin, who directed my dissertation, is great; he has taught me most of what I know about international relations. Ezra Suleiman, with his knowledge of France, was an inexhaustible source of ideas and support, especially "ground support" in the field. Kenneth Oye and Kent Calder drew on their expertise in monetary and financial matters to criticize, prod, and enlighten. Other Princeton faculty, James DeNardo, Leon Gordenker, Fred Greenstein, Robert Liebman, and Thomas Rochon, offered reactions and gave welcome advice.

The French-American foundation supported my initial research in France with a Tocqueville grant. Raphaël Hadas-Lebel of the Conseil d'État patiently guided my steps through the corridors of the French ministries. While in Paris, I benefited from discussions with Harold van B. Cleveland and David Calleo. Calleo directed me to Paul Fabra of *Le Monde*, who drew my attention to France's peculiar financial structures and practices and thus reoriented my research considerably. I also benefited from conversations with senior French diplomats and monetary officials who asked to remain anonymous. Their desire is granted, but not without my expressing gratitude for their patience and generosity.

My dissertation was co-awarded the Gabriel Almond Prize, and for that honor I thank the committee—Lewis A. Dexter, Ronald Inglehart, and Jorgen Rasmussen—as well as the American Political Science Association. Research funds from the University of Utah made it possible for me to complete the dissertation, make a second trip to Paris to begin following leads, and hire the editorial assistance of Mary Cascallar.

ACKNOWLEDGMENTS

On all trips to Paris, I exploited the goodwill of friends—Rhonda Boaglio, Mathieu Boaglio, Madeleine Denis, Christian Denis, and Geneviève Milesy—for crucial logistical assistance.

Valerie Bunce, Harvey Feigenbaum, John Goodman, Donald Hanson, Rand Smith, John Stephens, and Jung-En Woo surpassed the expectations of professional courtesy by reading drafts and offering comments. François Mitterrand intervened by implementing reforms in French financial structures and practices that provided welcome backing for my position. Research support from Northwestern University, provided through the good offices of Jay Casper, Department Chair, and Benjamin Page, Fulcher Professor of Decisionmaking, made it possible to hire the assistance of Kimberly Morgan, Valerie Blin, Shoma Chatterjee, Naomi Soffa, Stephen Bates, Kathy Powers, and Leslie Meeks.

Peter Katzenstein made numerous helpful suggestions; Roger Haydon ushered the manuscript through the daunting process of publication; Kay Scheuer and Peggy Hoover made editorial order out of chaos. And parts of the argument have appeared in two articles in *Comparative Politics:* "States and Markets: French Financial Interventionism in the Seventies" (volume 21, January 1988), and "Comparative Political Economy as Comparative History" (volume 29, April 1989).

Finally, I owe a great debt to members of my family. Alain, Paul, and Dominique endured countless long flights across the Atlantic. And my wife, Peggy, not only gave up a promising career to follow me to graduate school but made homes out of sparsely furnished apartments that all seemed to lack a kitchen, and did so without once asking when the dissertation, and then the book, were going to be finished. The book is dedicated to those to whom my debt is greatest, Maurice and Susan Loriaux, *sine quibus non.*

M. L.

Evanston, Illinois

*France after
Hegemony*

Introduction

In 1984, the Socialist government of France undertook the wholesale liberalization of its domestic financial structures. The Bastille of French financial policy, *encadrement du crédit*—that is, the imposition of selective credit restrictions on individual banks—was stormed and dismantled. In its place the French Socialists instituted a money market that was designed to function much like its American and British counterparts. They also established a financial futures market to rival that of Chicago, phased out exchange controls, and cut back dramatically on the allocation of loan subsidies to industry (including export industries) by public and parapublic financial institutions, all the while overseeing one of the most dramatic bull markets ever to hit the Paris Stock Exchange. In their foreign relations, French officials, once among the capitalist world's most jealous guardians of national sovereignty, argued for the creation of a European central bank and the restoration of a system of fixed exchange rates. Because the French state was, by reputation, one of the more interventionist among the industrialized democracies, because France had already established itself as a staunch defender of national sovereignty in the face of encroachments by international organizations, and because at the time of the reforms it was governed by a Socialist party that enjoyed an overwhelming parliamentary majority, one wonders what motivated the French to liberalize institutions that had hitherto given the state significant discretionary control over the allocation of credit. The question becomes more absorbing when liberalization in France is placed in the context of global liberalization, as manifested by reforms in countries as disparate as the United States, Great Britain, the People's Republic of China, and the Soviet Union.

The argument of this book is that international change, set in motion

1

by the United States' abandonment of monetary leadership in the 1960s, is the root cause of French financial liberalization in the 1980s. Though analysis of the global trend toward greater economic liberalism is beyond the scope of the present study, it is my contention that an understanding of French reforms can help one better grasp the challenge that international structural change presents to the industrialized world and how the efforts of individual nation-states to deal with that challenge are affecting the evolution of the post-hegemonic international political economy. Why France was moved to liberalize is thus of interest not only to the comparativist, who must account for the trend toward liberalism in widely disparate political societies, but also to the student of international politics, for whom the future evolution of the liberal international economic order is at the epicenter of theoretical debate.

France provides a particularly good place to look for international constraints on policy because the French have tried so hard over the years to resist them. More than any other industrialized democracy, France earned a reputation for its energetic, interventionist reactions to external shocks. John Zysman wrote in 1978 that the case of France suggests "that domestic resources can be mobilized effectively to neutralize or accommodate international constraints. . . . In fact, the capacity of the national government to respond has increased along with domestic sensitivity to the international market."[1] France's interventionist reputation was such that the world reacted with skepticism when Raymond Barre, prime minister from 1976 to 1981 as well as economics professor to the nation, made clear his liberalizing ambitions. Zysman, for example, argued that French policymakers, whatever their commitment to the canon of economic liberalism, frequently fell victim to an "interventionist temptation."[2] Institutional power was such that it enticed even liberal-minded elites, such as Barre and his staff, to pursue a path of least resistance—interventionism—when confronted with complex economic problems. In collaboration with Stephen Cohen and James Galbraith, Zysman argued that Barre's liberalism in fact masked a coherent effort to sharpen and modernize France's interventionist policy tools. The authors wrote: "Adaptation [to conditions imposed by France's increasing exposure to world markets] has not been pursued by reducing the role of the state. On the contrary, the French strategy

---

[1] John Zysman, "The French State in the International Economy," in Peter Katzenstein, ed., *Between Power and Plenty* (Madison: University of Wisconsin Press, 1978), p. 258.

[2] John Zysman, "The Interventionist Temptation: Financial Structure and Political Purpose," in William Andrews and Stanley Hoffmann, eds., *The Fifth Republic at Twenty* (Albany: SUNY Press, 1980). See also John Zysman, *Government, Markets, and Growth* (Ithaca: Cornell University Press, 1983).

has been to transform and modernize the role of the state in the economy, in an effort to make that role compatible with success for French producers on world markets."[3]

Not until the Socialists themselves began to originate and implement liberalizing reforms did observers take seriously the possibility that something was very wrong with the interventionist structures and practices that characterized the French political economy. Jack Hayward claimed, for example, that interventionist policy orientations and institutional structures had not proved themselves well adapted to a world of slow growth and changing patterns of international trade. The French state's marked predilection "to act as though it is sovereign" in economic matters set it up for the bitter lesson that its interventionist powers were limited. For Hayward, power over policy formulation and implementation had become dispersed among "semi-autonomous sub-systems," each of which pursued policy objectives of its own. "Each economic policy—trade, industrial, energy, monetary, prices and incomes, employment, regional, and so forth—has its own particular state-society sub-system so that attempts to coordinate them by the Finance Ministry or either its Budgetary or Treasury Division, by the Planning Commissariat, by the Interministerial Economic Committee or by the Prime Minister or President of the Republic, are illusory." In its dealings with French society, the state was handicapped by the "enduringly fragmented nature of the very state machine that aspire[d] to impart unity to a pluralistic whole."[4] The French political economy was not and never had been one in which the state proposes and society disposes.

According to Hayward, these structural limits on the state's interventionist capacity did not become apparent until the inadequacies of *dirigisme* (interventionism) were unmasked by a decade of global crisis. During the 1950s and 1960s, French officials had successfully pursued policies designed to accelerate the modernization of France's industry. Such policies succeeded in speeding industrial growth—but at the price of creating an industry that was indebted, overmanned, and unable to adjust easily to a world of slower growth, greater international competition, and global monetary instability. They also gave rise to policy-

---

[3]Stephen S. Cohen, James Galbraith, and John Zysman, "Rehabbing the Labyrinth: The Financial System and Industrial Policy in France," in Stephen S. Cohen and Peter A. Gourevitch, eds., *France in the Troubled World Economy* (London: Butterworth, 1982), p. 73. See also John Zysman, *Political Strategies for Industrial Order* (Berkeley and Los Angeles: University of California Press, 1977), p. 200. This argument is echoed in the report of the finance committee of the Eighth Plan, in Commissariat Général du Plan, *Préparation du Huitième Plan* (Paris: La Documentation Française, 1980), p. 5.

[4]Jack Hayward, *The State and the Market Economy: Industrial Patriotism and Economic Intervention in France* (Brighton: Wheatsheaf Books, 1986), pp. xiii, 23–25, 13.

making subcommunities that were unwilling to give serious considera-
tion to generating well-ordered strategies of industrial retrenchment.
Efforts "to teach the ministries new administrative tricks and to modify
their traditional behavior would seem to have made little headway."
Policy-making communities resisted the need for retrenchment. "The
many specific sub-programmes, each with their own little policy subcommunity, provide a plurality of rallying points for the members of
particular fragments of the national expenditure community, as they
strive to protect their medium-term priority from the depredations of
inflation-preoccupied budgetary officials." Hayward reproves an
"institutionalized, systematic, congenital optimism that the main problem is securing public funds for an ambitious investment programme,
rather than in tackling the fundamental problems."[5]

Peter Hall, like Hayward, argues that the French state has run up
against the limits of its capacity to invent interventionist solutions to
economic problems. For Hall, France's history of interventionism reflects the heritage of a relatively underdeveloped, noncompetitive industrial base, an industry dependent on lending institutions that in
turn were subject to state control, and finally a Ministry of Finance that
has power over both monetary policy and industrial policy. The French
state's characteristic ability to promote investment through control over
the supply of credit enabled the French to achieve rapid industrial
development and industrialization in the 1950s and 1960s. But as the
international economic constraints of the 1970s overloaded the state
with contradictory demands, interventionism met with fewer and fewer
successes. The state's efforts to promote industrial modernization, to
ease readjustment and decline in certain sectors, and to regulate the
distribution of income between labor and capital resulted in a "state
divided against itself," a state "faced with multiple tasks and well-
defined conflicts of interest among the social classes it governs, or
among sub-groups within them."[6]

As global demand diminished, French policymakers were forced to
become increasingly selective in allocating credits and subsidies. The
predictable consequences were slower growth, increased unemployment, and eroding political support for the government. The Socialist
attempt to reflate the economy in 1981–82 only confirmed the futility
of trying to return to the policies of the past. Consequently, the
Socialists resurrected the restrictive monetary policies of the conserva-

---

[5]Ibid., pp. 183, 189, 101.

[6]Peter Hall, *Governing the Economy: The Politics of State Intervention in Britain and France*
(New York: Oxford University Press, 1986); quotation from p. 176. Note, however, that
Hall finds a certain Machiavellian virtue in a state that can credibly promise to defend all
social categories against one another and against itself.

tives, while (prior to liberalization) bolstering efforts to enhance the competitiveness of French industry by imposing greater state control over investment decisions.

Both Hayward and Hall assert that French interventionist practices were rendered ineffectual by changes that took place in the international economic environment. Though both excel at showing how international challenge was met by institutional paralysis, neither analyzes in detail the impact of international economic change on the domestic political economy. If one asks as a counterfactual question what would have happened had there been no change in the international economic environment, no unambiguous response is suggested by their investigations, so successfully do they convey the impression that the French state was on the verge of implosion with or without a shove from the international system. But this international aspect of the question is of central interest to the student of international political economy. It is apparent that the domestic political economies of advanced industrialized states have undergone significant change as a result of structural transformations that have occurred in the international political economy. Conversely, it is equally apparent that the future of international economic relations depends to a significant degree on the capacity of individual states to adapt to change in the system. Such concerns amply warrant the effort to assess the meaning of liberalization in France, its chances for success, and the impact it is likely to have on international economic relations.

The principal change that occurred in the international political economy in the last two decades was occasioned by U.S. abandonment of its leadership role in the world economy and its consequent adoption of a number of self-regarding policies, notably (and of particular importance to the present book) the suspension of the dollar's convertibility into gold. The question that drives debate in the field of international political economy is, in effect, that of the impact of American "hegemonic decline" on global economic and political relations.[7] The notion of "hegemonic leadership" has enjoyed prominence

[7]There is no consensus on the degree to which the hegemon has "declined." The United States is still a price-maker in many areas, notably in the area of finance. It can still use control over access to its market as a tool of power, and it is still quite active in the management of certain international economic problems, such as the debt crisis. Nevertheless, in the area that interests us specifically—international monetary relations—the United States has abandoned responsibilities it once assumed, those of managing international monetary stability on a global level by sustaining the system of fixed but adjustable exchange rates and buying compliance with this system with adjustment assistance. Where monetary relations between the United States and Europe are concerned, we have clearly entered the post-hegemonic era. For discussion see Robert Gilpin, *The Political Economy of International Relations* (Princeton: Princeton University Press, 1987); Robert Keohane, *After Hegemony* (Princeton: Princeton University Press, 1984); Bruce Russett,

in the field of international political economy for more than a decade. Though its origins can be traced to E.H. Carr's classic, *The Twenty Years Crisis,* the concept was revived and elaborated in the early 1970s by Charles Kindleberger and Robert Gilpin. In *The World in Depression,* Kindleberger attributed the depth and duration of the Great Depression to the inability of Great Britain and the unwillingness of the United States to assume leadership in international economic relations. Just as the domestic market economy depends on the accomplishment of a number of necessary political tasks by the state, such as protection and regulation of the market, implementation of countercyclical economic policies, and provision of public goods such as currency, the international market requires that some powerful nation be able and willing to assume a role that on a global scale approximates the role the state fulfills domestically. The hegemonic power polices the thoroughfares of international commerce, assures—countercyclically—access to its market by distressed economic sectors of other countries, and supplies the world with a universally acceptable medium of exchange. In the absence of such leadership, the international market economy risks closure as sovereign nations, applying the self-help logic of survival under anarchy, promote their interests at the expense of the collective interests of the global community. For Robert Gilpin, the internationalization of the market that occurred after World War II—as manifested by greater trade openness, the rise of the multinational corporation, and the development of global financial markets and international economic organizations such as the International Monetary Fund (IMF) and the General Agreement on Tariffs and Trade (GATT)—was made possible by the active role the United States assumed in international economic relations. The task of liberalizing the world economy was taken on under American leadership and was facilitated not only by the military security the United States provided but also by the ability and willingness of the United States to discriminate against its own immediate commercial interests in order (1) to field an international currency, and (2) to absorb foreign goods into its domestic market in a way that promoted economic reconstruction and growth among its European and Pacific allies and clients, and (3) to build and underwrite international organizations that structured and consolidated international economic relations in a manner consonant with its fundamental liberalizing ambitions. Gilpin writes: "Just as the *Pax Britannica* provided the security and political order for the expansion of

---

"The Mysterious Case of Vanishing Hegemony," *International Organization* 39 (Spring 1985); Susan Strange, "The Persistent Myth of Lost Hegemony ," *International Organization* 41 (Autumn 1987); Imanuel Wallerstein, *The Politics of the World Economy* (Cambridge: Cambridge University Press, 1984).

transnational economic activity in the nineteenth century, so the *Pax Americana* has fulfilled a similar function in the mid-twentieth century."[8]

The issue confronting us now is whether economic openness will survive as America's power and willingness to exercise hegemonic leadership declines. Stanley Hoffmann once remarked, "Whoever studies contemporary international relations cannot avoid hearing, behind the clash of interests and ideologies, a kind of permanent dialogue between Rousseau and Kant."[9] In the field of international political economy, that dialogue remains particularly lively and vigorous as the two philosophers pursue their debate through the intercession of such modern-day mediums as Gilpin and Robert Keohane. Both Keohane and Gilpin have addressed the question of how the post-hegemonic order is evolving, and though both have formulated answers that one might call "guardedly optimistic," Gilpin's optimism, it turns out, is far more guarded than Keohane's. Indeed, in reading Gilpin's book, one cannot help but hear the repressed echoes of a thoroughly Rousseauian despair behind the expressions of hope that the advanced industrialized democracies will work together to sustain the benefits of openness. As early as 1975, Gilpin wrote: "The decline of American power and the erosion of the political base upon which the liberal world economy has rested suggest that we are entering an era of grave uncertainty." He claimed that the international economy was moving "from a liberal to a negotiated system" and argued that "it will require wise statesmanship and self-restraint to prevent the breakdown of this system into hostile economic nationalisms and antagonistic economic blocs."[10] More recently he has written: "By the mid-1980s the economic and political differences among the three major centers of economic power [Europe, the United States, and Japan] have made it highly unlikely that pluralist management and policy coordination could save the liberal world economy of the past. Each center is exploiting the system for its own parochial ends and none is interested in subordinating its national objectives to the larger goals associated with policy coordination."[11] Compounding the challenge is the uneasy coexistence between openness in trade and policies of demand management that assume a closed economy. The coexistence between "Keynes at home and Smith abroad"

---

[8]E.H. Carr, *The Twenty Years Crisis* (New York: Harper and Row, 1964); Charles Kindleberger, *The World in Depression, 1929–1939* (Berkeley and Los Angeles: University of California Press, 1973); Robert Gilpin, *U.S. Power and the Multinational Corporation* (New York: Basic Books, 1975), quotation from p. 111.

[9]Stanley Hoffmann, "Rousseau on War and Peace," *American Political Science Review* 57 (June 1963).

[10]Gilpin, *U.S. Power*, pp. 261–62.

[11]Gilpin, *Political Economy*, pp. 378–79.

was made viable only by international activism on the part of the United States.[12] Faced by mounting unemployment, the Europeans, if forced to choose, indicate a strong preference for "Keynes at home" at the expense of "Smith abroad." Gilpin writes:

> As one of France's most distinguished economists has stated, because of Western Europe's severe economic problems "internationally planned and orderly introduction of some import restrictions in selected countries that have structural deficits in their foreign trade has been proposed." Whereas the Americans had begun to speak of "fair trade" in response to the Japanese and NIC trading challenge, the West Europeans had begun to think in terms of "planned trade." For them, international policy coordination has meant the displacement of liberalism by cartelization of world markets and market-sharing agreements negotiated by the three major centers of economic power.[13]

Robert Keohane, on the other hand, develops an institutional interpretation of international relations that rings with a certain Kantian faith in the power of human reason to preserve the species from self-destruction. Keohane claims that there are grounds for believing that post-hegemonic international politics will be spared a return to self-help economic nationalism on a scale sufficient to threaten the world economy with closure. Statesmen are increasingly aware of the benefits their nations reap from economic cooperation, but are inhibited in their efforts to foster cooperative policies by the residual fear of exploitation. In an anarchical system noncooperation is a strategically rational course of action. International regimes, however, diminish the fear of exploitation and thereby enhance the willingness of states to enter into cooperative ventures. Thus, international regimes created under American hegemonic leadership will in the post-hegemonic era continue to promote the sort of cooperation among sovereign nations that is needed to diminish the threat of closure in the absence of hegemonic power.[14]

Given the importance of this debate, one looks to the French experiment for more than a glimpse of how the advanced industrialized democracies are responding to international change. The difficulties and successes the French experience in their efforts to adapt their political economy to the post-hegemonic order provide us with an

[12]See ibid., pp. 354–63.

[13]Ibid., p. 375. The reference is to Edmond Malinvaud, *Mass Unemployment* (Oxford: Basil Blackwell, 1984).

[14]Keohane, *After Hegemony*, chap. 4. For discussion of the concept of international regimes, see Stephen Krasner, ed., *International Regimes* (Ithaca: Cornell University Press, 1983).

indication of how successfully advanced industrialized democracies can be expected to preserve an international economic order founded on the principle of openness in the post-hegemonic era. Do French efforts to "take the state back out" of the financial market indicate that the contradiction between internal activism and external liberalism is disappearing? Are the forces and constraints that have hastened the implementation of liberalizing reforms in France global in scope and therefore at work in other countries? Finally, does domestic liberalization have a corresponding foreign economic policy, or in other words, have liberal reforms diminished the appeal of France's "mercantilist temptation"?

This book develops the following arguments:

1. Floating exchange rates denied the French the possibility of achieving adjustment in external payments through devaluation or depreciation. Conversely, the domestic political economy, characterized here as an "overdraft economy," was not responsive to adjustment efforts that relied solely on internal policies and mechanisms. Floating rates therefore necessitated financial reforms to rid France of its overdraft economy and render the economy more responsive to internal adjustment policies.

2. The overdraft economy revealed the existence of "moral hazard" in the French political economy, manifested by the expectation, broadly shared among French economic agents, that their power to borrow from public or parapublic institutional lenders was assured, even in times of financial crisis. It was moral hazard that, by fortifying both economic and political resistance to policies of monetary stabilization, weakened the power of monetary officials to control monetary growth using internal instruments and mechanisms.

3. Moral hazard in the domestic political economy arose from opportunities for expansionist monetary growth provided by U.S. monetary leadership, notably though the provision of an international monetary regime that facilitated adjustment through devaluation. The change of course in U.S. monetary policy—above all, the withdrawal of its support for a system of fixed but adjustable exchange rates—caused those opportunities to disappear.

4. Current reforms must not be interpreted "too liberally." The French state is seeking through reform to regain control over its monetary and exchange rate policy rather than to deliver the economy entirely to the discretion of market forces.

5. Neither should France's interest in building and strengthening international monetary regimes be read "too liberally." That interest is similarly inspired by the desire to regain stronger state control over

monetary policy. If French monetary interests are not satisfied at the global level, France could seek regional or even bilateral solutions that would jeopardize global openness.

The term "overdraft economy" denotes a political economy that has become dependent on the allocation of credit by institutional lenders and subsequently highly resistant (for reasons that are both structural and behavioral) to the government's efforts to control the growth of credit. Dependence on institutionally allocated credit generates patterns of economic behavior, characterized by a presumption of assured borrowing power, that differ markedly from those encountered in textbook models. Moreover, the overdraft economy is supported by institutional structures that were designed not to control monetary growth but to facilitate "mercantilist" policies of industrial development. (The French refer to such policies as "*volontariste*," because they pursue political goals in the face of resistance by market forces.) Structures and patterns of behavior combine to render monetary policy-making a difficult task—first by depriving monetary policymakers of effective policy tools, and second by rendering the economy economically vulnerable and politically resistant to policies of monetary rigor.

The term "moral hazard" refers to the impact of "insurance," broadly defined, on the perception of risk by economic agents. It is used to explain patterns of behavior that can be understood only if one assumes the agent has become unaware or indifferent to risk. A person insured against theft, for example, might be less concerned about locking his or her front door than one who is not. The U.S. hegemonic order, I argue, gave rise to moral hazard in the international political economy. Moral hazard became internalized in the structures and in the patterns of behavior that together comprised the French overdraft economy. Businessmen became less concerned about the financial viability of their firms than they would have been had they not been conditioned to perceive that credit was so readily and cheaply available. French policymakers would not have been as unaware of the dangers and weaknesses inherent in the financial structures of the overdraft economy if payments adjustment had proved to be a harsher challenge. Financial liberalization became imperative in the 1980s in order to rid the French political economy of moral hazard once U.S. hegemonic "decline" effectively rendered the international political economy less tolerant of it.

This interpretation of the effects of U.S. economic leadership is not intended to be revisionist. On the contrary, it is perfectly consonant with analyses of U.S. hegemony found in the works of Charles Kindleberger, Robert Gilpin, and Stephen Krasner. It does, however, draw attention to an aspect of the U.S. hegemonic order which is often overlooked and which contributes significantly to making plain current developments in the international political economy. I refer to the tolerant environment that U.S. economic and particularly monetary leadership created for nationalist policies of economic development.

To grasp fully the nature of this international environment, one must recall the politics that drove the United States to fashion the hegemonic order. Benjamin Cohen, in *Organizing the World's Money*, portrayed the history of America's leadership in international monetary affairs as one of gradual subordination of an economic goal—that of establishing an international monetary system that would promote economic openness— to a political goal, that of containing Soviet influence in Europe.[15] Although the Bretton Woods agreement as originally formulated was designed to facilitate payments adjustment, it failed to meet the de- mands of the war-torn nations of Europe as they struggled to recon- struct their economies. With the widening of the U.S.–Soviet rift, the political importance of Europe increased. In order to anchor what would one day be a strong, reconstructed Western Europe firmly within its sphere of influence, the United States began to assume a more active managerial role. It initiated a relatively generous flow of long-term loans and grants through such aid programs as the Marshall Plan, it facilitated European borrowing on the New York financial market, it encouraged the use of the dollar as a reserve currency as well as the principal means of payment in international transactions, it established a relatively liberal lending policy for the provision of short-term funds in times of monetary crisis, thus reinforcing the already overtaxed International Monetary Fund, and it tolerated and even encouraged trade and monetary relations that discriminated against its own immediate (if not long-term) commercial interests by giving support to such institutions as the European Payments Union and the European Coal and Steel Community. In other words, after promoting a certain vision of an international liberal economic order, the United States gave its blessing to state involvement in the task of economic recovery and accompanied that blessing both with material support and with a willingness to amend its global liberalizing ambitions in a way that facilitated interventionist or "mercantilist" policy in Europe. The monetary leadership of the United States helped sustain an interna- tional order that has been characterized as one of "embedded liberal- ism."[16] The values and ambitions that originally gave birth to the new

[15]Benjamin Cohen, *Organizing the World's Money: The Political Economy of International Monetary Relations* (New York: Basic Books, 1977).

[16]See John Ruggie, "International Regimes, Transactions, and Change: Embedded Liberalism in the Postwar Economic Order," in Krasner, ed., *International Regimes*.

economic order were informed by a liberalism that was largely imposed on the world economy "from the outside" as the United States, acting as hegemon, pursued its reformist ambitions. As the cold war received greater attention, however, ample provision was made for unilateral domestic responses to economic and social stress on the part of smaller countries in a manner that was more sensitive to domestic constraints, values, and expectations.

After Europe's economic recovery, the United States continued to be active in international monetary affairs, principally to contain the threat that monetary crisis or devaluation in one country—France in 1958 and 1969, Italy in 1964, Great Britain in 1967—might precipitate a cascade of crises or devaluations in other countries and thus threaten the world economy with the same monetary disorder that so delayed recovery in the 1930s. In so doing, the United States made devaluation a viable tool of adjustment and thus continued to sustain an international environment that was relatively tolerant of expansionist policy.

Peter Gourevitch introduced the expression "second image reversed" to refer to the influence of international systemic factors on domestic political structures and processes. "The international system," he wrote, "is not only a consequence of domestic politics and structures but a cause of them. Economic relations and military pressures constrain an entire range of domestic behaviors, from policy decisions to political forms. International relations and domestic politics are therefore so interrelated that they should be analyzed simultaneously, as wholes."[17] There is no better illustration of Gourevitch's thesis than the rise and reform of the French overdraft economy. Much of what passes for distinctively French—indicative planning and state control over the allocation of credit to industrial firms and consumers—is incomprehensible without taking into account the constraints and opportunities that were generated by the international system as reordered by U.S. hegemony. Similarly, France's current reform efforts can be understood only in the light of changes that are occurring in the structure of that international system. The reforms in financial structures and practices implemented by the Socialists, not to mention the convergence that one observes in economic policy between Right and Left, is largely explained by the existence of international constraints that have deprived French policymakers of options.

Gourevitch goes on to argue that the "second image reversed" is pertinent to the study of foreign policy and international politics. The "second image reversed" is a two-way street. International factors

---

[17]Peter Gourevitch, "The Second Image Reversed: The International Sources of Domestic Politics," *International Organization* 32 (Autumn 1978), 911.

influence domestic politics, which in turn influences foreign policy and therefore international politics. To study international politics is to study the interplay between domestic and international forces. Gourevitch's conceptualization thus becomes instrumental to efforts to foresee and to describe the general contours of the post-hegemonic order. It is not irrelevant to the analysis of the evolving post-hegemonic international political economy to assess the degree to which France was shackled by the legacy of policies, institutions, patterns of behavior, and economic expectations that evolved under conditions created by the *Pax Americana*. During this period, America's monetary leadership facilitated French efforts to use the state's power to regulate the allocation of credit both in order to promote industrial growth and modernization and to allay the political stress of modernization in declining sectors. Credit was made available to the French economy in plentiful supply and at interest rates that were often negative in real terms. Though this policy caused the French economy to become one of the more inflationary economies of the developed world, the international environment remained tolerant. Trade was expanding (in part because of American trade and monetary policies, which favored European exports), the European Payments Union allayed for a while the need for urgent action to balance trade, three series of deep devaluations of the franc (one in 1948, one in 1958, another in 1969) brought temporary balance to France's payments situation, and finally, the inflow of American capital lessened France's payments imbalances.

The French took advantage of this international environment by evolving, opportunistically and in piecemeal fashion, a "strategy" for economic development. As this "strategy" evolved, change occurred not only in the structure of the economy but in financial structures, monetary institutions, and patterns of economic behavior as well. France secured its position among the highly industrialized nations, but burdened itself in the process with an overdraft economy that was dependent on the continued existence of a tolerant "environmental niche": the overdraft economy was unusually resistant to policies of internal monetary adjustment and thus depended on the facility of external adjustment proffered by the international order.

Beginning in the mid-1960s, the international environment was subjected to a sort of climatic change. United States policy became more self-regarding. It began to feed global inflationary pressures against which the overdraft economy was comparatively defenseless. In 1971, the United States ceased altogether to support the Bretton Woods system of fixed but adjustable exchange rates. For all practical purposes, this deprived the French of the option of achieving adjustment through devaluation (as will be explained in Chapter One). The

French confronted a radically altered monetary environment, deprived of their principal means of achieving adjustment and burdened not only by the legacy of inflationary habits but also by an economy that was more resistant than most to policies of monetary rigor. In this context, as Peter Hall writes, the French confronted the challenge of taming "the inflationary habits of a nation that had always depended on them in order to generate growth."[18] It was the need to retool the French political economy, to "adapt" it to the post-hegemonic monetary order that explains the liberalizing reforms of 1984–85. In an environment purged of moral hazard, the French state had to regain the power to implement policies of internal monetary adjustment, and thus to purge the domestic political economy of the moral hazard that deprived it of that power. The French state sought through liberalization to regain control over its monetary policy and not, as one might be tempted to think, to surrender the future evolution of the French political economy to the laws of the marketplace.

This book is primarily a work of historical analysis, although it is informed by theoretical debate as it currently structures the field of international political economy. It begins with an analysis of the difficulties and frustrations that policymakers experienced in the 1970s, which revealed the need for financial reform. In Chapter Two, those difficulties are explained by delving into the peculiar mechanisms and behavior patterns that constitute France's overdraft economy. Chapter Three pursues the analysis at a higher level of abstraction, laying bare the skeletal mechanisms that explain the development of an overdraft economy in France with reference to the moral hazard generated by U.S. monetary leadership. After having disassembled the French political economy in the analytical chapters, we proceed to its historical reconstruction in Chapter Four through Chapter Eight, ending with an analysis of the liberalizing reforms of 1984–85. Chapter Nine assesses the impact of crisis and reform on French foreign economic policy, principally as manifested by monetary cooperation within the European Community.

As a work of historical analysis, this book advances no nomothetic claims. Though it proposes an explanation of liberalization in France that, because it privileges international factors, can allege at least partial applicability elsewhere (comparisons are drawn in the Conclusion), it does not pretend to provide a theoretical model of liberalization that can be lifted wholesale from France and made to "travel" in "sartorian"[19] fashion from country to country. Nor is a new theory of hegemonic

[18]Hall, *Governing the Economy*, p. 201.
[19]See Giovanni Sartori, "Concept Misinformation in Comparative Politics," *American Political Science Review* 64 (December 1970).

leadership or post-hegemonic cooperation advanced to rival those that already exist, though analysis of financial liberalization in France can, I argue, be usefully introduced into the discussion of such theories (again, these theories are discussed in the Conclusion). Nor is the concept of overdraft economy meant to signal the existence of yet a new type of political-economic system with its own peculiar structural and behavioral logic. The French overdraft economy is too much the consequence of the encounter between a unique national political and economic structure, endowed with its own specific and nonreplicable history, with an unmatched effort on the part of a major power to refashion the international economic order to provide the literature with a new polity-type. Though France's was not the only overdraft economy in postwar history, it becomes apparent from comparisons proposed in the Conclusion that differences among such countries are as great as the similarities. At best, the more abstract concepts developed here—overdraft economy and moral hazard—can only be suggestive of forces at work elsewhere.

By asserting that this is a work of historical analysis, I do not mean to circumscribe its ambitions. On the contrary, it entertains a claim of a "metatheoretical" nature that is of crucial importance to the analysis of the evolution of the post-hegemonic order. One cannot grasp the evolution of the international political economy in our time without according historical and contextual factors their due importance. The U.S. hegemonic order arose under specific historical conditions. The politics and the economics of that order were driven by ambitions and conflicts that set apart the *Pax Americana* from its predecessor, the *Pax Britannica*. The international environment fashioned by American leadership manifested those specificities, and therefore efforts by smaller nations to adapt their domestic political economies to that environment also reflected those specificities. Consequently, it should be expected that the capacity of smaller nations to readapt to the post-hegemonic world will be constrained by institutional and behavioral legacies of past efforts to adapt to an environment that, in spite of our ability to categorize it as "hegemonic," was in many ways unique. Nothing like it had been seen before, and it is quite likely that nothing like it will be seen again. The task of the student of politics thus becomes one of looking to the past to identify forces and constraints that bind in the present our efforts to construct the future. Kent Calder has likened the study of political economy to a "form of political archeology, in which detailed historical examination of both preexisting social structure and newly arising pressures for change during periods of crisis is crucial."[20]

[20]Kent Calder, *Crisis and Compensation* (Princeton: Princeton University Press, 1989), p. 27.

In contrast, the theorist who, driven by the ambition to build a social science bereft of the unpredictable and thus the contextually contingent, blinds himself or herself to a number of important factors that influence the evolution of the post-hegemonic international political economy.

Let us pursue this idea by contrasting the British and American hegemonic episodes. Great Britain exercised hegemony at a time when its principal rivals for power in world politics were either hopelessly isolated, like France throughout the Bismarckian era, or had ambitions that were almost entirely continental rather than global, like those of Bismarck's Germany. Though Russia rivaled Great Britain in Southern Asia, it did not compete with Great Britain for global influence. In contrast, hegemonic America was engaged in constant competition for influence in Europe, the Middle East, and Southeast Asia with a rival power, the Soviet Union, that also harbored ambitions of world leadership. Great Britain was able to combine hegemonic leadership with a policy of "splendid isolation," refusing to participate in alliances or intervene in continental politics. The "high politics" of British leadership was largely confined to efforts to assure the security of maritime commerce and to open new markets to British goods, either through persuasion or through force.[21] The "high politics" of the *Pax Americana*, in contrast, was dominated by the competition for influence over world politics with the Soviet Union. Its liberal aspirations notwithstanding, American hegemony was affected to no insignificant degree by America's efforts to create systems of alliances that contained Soviet power.

The competition for power and influence which pitted the United States against the Soviet Union, and which drove American policy in the postwar period, was aggravated by the ideological contest that pitted communism against capitalism, another element specific to America's hegemonic experience. The United States and the Soviet Union competed not only for the loyalty and deference of statesmen, but also for the hearts and souls of voting men and women. In the years following the war, Communist parties in France, Belgium, and Italy were capturing the support of about one-fourth of the electorate. Communist parties in Czechoslovakia and in Hungary acceded to power in part through electoral means. In China, the popular support of the victorious Red Army was apparent to all observers. It is true that intense ideological competition between Left and Right had already begun to drive the domestic politics of a number of industrialized states before the war, pushing them to adopt policies that bettered the economic

---

[21]See, e.g., Paul Kennedy, *The Rise and Fall of the Great Powers* (New York: Random House, 1987), pp. 151–70, 224–32; Pierre Renouvin, *Histoire des relations internationales* (Paris: Hachette, 1955), 6:24–26, 33–35.

welfare and security of their populations. But as the Soviet Union and international communism emerged from World War II martyred and victorious, ideological competition became intense indeed, increasing the pressure on the United States to demonstrate that the capitalist system could "deliver." Great Britain, in its years of hegemonic leadership, never confronted challenges of this order.[22]

In sum, efforts to theorize about hegemony and its aftermath too frequently ignore the uniqueness of the international political context in which the *Pax Americana* evolved. The contextual specificity of the terms of political discourse and the degree of international and domestic political tension that assisted at the birth and early formation of the *Pax Americana* are of significance to us because they help to explain the generation of moral hazard and its effect on efforts to reconstruct the international economic order in the post-hegemonic era. The United States did more than provide public goods in a game-theoretical setting to secure international cooperation and economic openness. Rather, the United States provided direct and indirect economic aid to allied governments that joined in its efforts to halt the advance of Communist influence, both within and beyond their national frontiers. The United States amended its liberalizing aspirations by recognizing that European nations had to be given leeway to pursue their own nationalist (or mercantilist) inclinations if the Western alliance was to cohere. It was the exercise of hegemony, thus defined, that created conditions conducive to the development of expectations, processes, and institutions that generated moral hazard. In France, moral hazard became embedded in the institutions, processes, and patterns of economic behavior that comprised the overdraft economy. The purpose of liberalization in the 1980s was to rid France of the moral hazard that was the financial and monetary legacy of the *Pax Americana*. France's success, or lack of it, in dealing with this legacy will affect the evolution of the European Community and the global economic order. The evolution of the international political economy "after hegemony" will be determined to a significant degree by the manner in which the industrialized democracies respond to the purge of moral hazard from the international system.

[22]In addition to political and ideological competition between the United States and the Soviet Union, other important contextual distinctions separate the two hegemonic experiences. For example, as Great Britain began to withdraw from its hegemonic responsibilities at the end of the nineteenth century, the world economy experienced renewed growth and vitality, partly as a result of the monetary stimulus to the economy provided by the discovery of gold in South Africa and in the Klondike, and perhaps also a result of the generation of a new "long" productive cycle by technological innovation in the chemical industries, electricity, and transportation. The United States, by contrast, began its retreat from hegemony in a context of global economic crisis. But some observers contend that we have embarked on a new "long cycle" driven by innovation. See Charles R. Morris, "The Coming Global Boom," *Atlantic Monthly* 264 (October 1988).

CHAPTER ONE

Dilemmas of the 1970s

One can trace the root cause of France's decision to liberalize financial structures and practices to the abandonment by the United States of responsibilities that it had previously assumed with regard to the management of an international monetary system of fixed but adjustable exchange rates. The immediate consequence of that event was the inception of the regime, or more appropriately the "non-regime" of floating rates. At about the time when the industrialized economies were being rocked by the oil crisis, the system based on fixed parities gave way to a system in which exchange rates fluctuated on the currency market like stocks on the stock market. Although the new system initially gave monetary authorities much freedom to deal with the oil shock, it proved over time to be a source of new and complex constraints. It modified the basic monetary mechanisms that conditioned external adjustment, and policy instruments that once were effective worked no longer. For a highly open economy like that of France, the system of flexible exchange rates soon required that greater efforts be expended to stabilize the currency and to avoid currency depreciation.

Although France's response to the challenge posed by floating rates was highly imaginative and showed the interventionist capacity of the French state to great advantage, it was not adequate over the long run to meet that challenge. French economic indicators actually declined, slightly though noticeably, relative to those of other OECD (Organization for Economic Cooperation and Development) countries. Investment and employment in France, which was excellent in the 1960s, fell to average in the 1970s. French inflation, average in the 1960s, was worse than average in the next decade. When crisis once again gripped the oil market in 1979, the French economy ushered up less resistance than other OECD economies. Indeed, the French economy displayed less resilience in the face of the 1979 shock than it did to the shock of 1973. By the end of the decade, pessimism concerning the domestic economy and disillusionment with interventionist tools of monetary and financial policy was pandemic in France. Disillusionment gave rise to calls for reforms to liberalize the political economy and bring it into conformity with other industrialized countries, notably France's more robust partner and neighbor to the east. This chapter documents and analyzes the difficulties confronted by French policymakers in the aftermath of the oil crisis and the demise of the regime of fixed but adjustable exchange rates.

THE IMPACT OF THE SUPPLY SHOCKS ON THE FRENCH ECONOMY

The change that occurred in the international political economy in the early 1970s was radical and expeditious. Before the oil crisis of 1973, France, like the rest of the industrialized world, had enjoyed a decade of rapid and relatively stable economic growth. The seven dominant OECD economies[1] grew at an annual average rate of 5.1 percent (see Table 1). The French economy grew at the faster-than-average rate of 5.5 percent. Among these seven countries, growth in France was topped only in Japan, and equaled only in Italy and Canada. In the aftermath of the oil shock of 1973, however, growth in the same seven economies was halved. Some countries experienced negative growth in 1974–75 and again in 1980. As for France, its average annual growth rate fell to 2.8 percent. After a struggle to delay the inevitable downturn in economic activity in 1974, France actually succumbed to near-zero growth in 1975.

The effects of the oil crisis, however, must be carefully distinguished from those that were produced by the change in the monetary system. The oil crisis did not so much create new difficulties for France as unmask economic rigidities that were already deeply entrenched within the structures of the French political economy. On the other hand, the new monetary regime rendered policy tools obsolete that had allowed

Table 1. Average annual growth rates, selected countries, 1960–1980

	France	U.S.	Japan	Germany	U.K.	Italy	Canada	Avg.
1960–67	5.5	4.6	10.2	3.9	2.9	5.6	5.6	5.1
1967–73	5.6	3.6	9.5	5.3	3.4	5.0	5.6	4.9
1973–80	2.8	2.3	3.7	2.3	0.9	2.8	2.8	2.5

Source: OECD, *Economic Outlook—Historical Statistics, 1960–1981* (Paris: OECD, 1983), p. 40

[1]United States, Japan, Germany, France, Italy, the United Kingdom and Canada.

policymakers to manage the encumbrances engendered by those rigidities. In the first place, the supply shocks of 1973–74 aggravated France's trade imbalance, but did not create it. This is not to belittle the impact of the supply shocks. The fourfold hike in the price of imported oil that occurred in 1973 created severe payments problems for all OECD countries. The impact of the price hike was particularly harsh for a country like France, for which imported oil was the primary source of energy. For France, the bill for imported oil increased from 16 billion francs in 1973 to 49 billion in 1974, remaining at that level until 1979, when it climbed to 112 billion francs.[2] Moreover, oil was not the only commodity to undergo a dramatic price rise. The price of copper increased from 57 cents a pound to $1.40; tin from 1.6 cents to 4 cents; zinc from 69 cents to $1.10 before settling at 80 cents.[3] The increase in France's bill for oil and other commodities contributed to a string of current account deficits. France's current account achieved only a small surplus in 1975 and 1978 and fell steeply into deficit in other years. In 1978, France's trade deficit in raw materials other than energy resources amounted to 2.1 percent of its gross domestic product (GDP), while its deficit in energy resources equaled 3.4 percent of its GDP. By 1980, the deficit in the trade of raw materials remained at 2.1 percent, but the deficit in the trade of energy resources had risen to 5.4 percent.[4]

But one must put France's trade difficulties in historical context. France's trade balance suffered chronic deficits throughout the 1950s, showing improvement only when tariffs and export subsidies were increased, as in 1954, or when the franc was devalued, as in 1949, 1958, and 1969 (see Table 2).[5] A fragile equilibrium was maintained between 1963 and 1967 by imposing policies of austerity on the French that contributed to the general strike and political crisis of May 1968.

Inflation is a second phenomenon that the supply shocks aggravated but did not create. France displayed definite inflationist tendencies throughout the postwar period. The year 1973 marked a watershed

[2]Commission du Bilan, *La France en mai 1981, Forces et faiblesses*, Rapport au premier ministre (Paris: La Documentation Française, Collection des Rapports Officiels, May 1981), p. 103.

[3]Christian Stoffaës, *Leçons sur la politique industrielle de la France*, part 1, vol. 1. of *La Politique économique de la France* by André de Lattre and Michel Pébereau (Paris: Les Cours de Droit, 1982–83), p. 11.

[4]Christian Rolen, "Les importations de matières premières," *Économie et Statistique* 138 (November 1981), 81–92. See also G. de Ménil and U. Westphal, "Le déficit pétrolier et la balance commerciale: France–Allemagne," *Revue Économique* 31 (March 1980); Serge Domard, "Dépendence entre nations et importations françaises de matières premières," *Revue d'Économie Politique* 90 (March–April 1980). Domard attempts to model France's dependence on foreign suppliers of raw materials.

[5]Following the devaluation of 1969, France's current account returned to surplus, thanks largely to progress in services and other "invisibles." The trade of goods remained in deficit even after this devaluation (see Table 2).

only to the extent that French inflation became significantly worse than in neighboring countries. Prior to that year, France kept good compa-

Table 2. France's trade balance and the parity of the franc, 1945–1980

Year	Trade balance (billion francs)	Value of dollar in francs
1945	−301.4	111.11
1946	−534.8	111.11
1947	−508.1	111.11
1948	−499.9	264.00
1949	−163.7	350.00
1950	−27.4	350.00
1951	−269.6	350.00
1952	−216.5	350.00
1953	−118.5	350.00
1954	−62.8	350.00
1955	30.3	350.00
1956	−283.1	350.00
1957	−323.3	350.00
1958	−103.4	431.00
1959	2.8[a]	4.90[a]
1960	0.5	4.90
1961	2.4	4.90
1962	2.3	4.90
1963	0.8	4.90
1964	−0.5	4.90
1965	1.8	4.90
1966	−0.1	4.90
1967	0.8	4.90
1968	−1.5	4.94
1969	−6.4	5.55
1970	−4.7	5.55
1971	−1.5	*
1972	−1.5	*
1973	−2.2	*
1974	−16.9	*
1975	6.8	*
1976	−20.9	*
1977	−11.5	*
1978	2.2	*
1979	−13.6	*
1980	−61.8	*

Source: 1945–73, adapted from Jean-Pierre Patat and Michel Lutfalla, *Histoire monétaire de la France au XXᵉ Siècle* (Paris: Economica, 1986); 1974–80, Commission du Bilan, Report to the Prime Minister, *La France en mai 1981* (Paris: La Documentation Française, 1982). The exchange rate indicated in the table is that which obtained at the end of the year.

*The currency crises of 1971–73 effectively put an end to the concept of fixed parities. Beginning in 1973, all European currencies floated relative to the dollar. The franc oscillated generally between four and five francs to the dollar. See *L'année politique, économique, et sociale en France, 1983* (Paris: Éditions du Moniteur, 1984), p. 499.

[a]The currency reform of 1959 defined the "new franc" (franc nouveau) to be equal to 500 "old francs."

ny. Though inflation in France averaged 3.5 percent between 1960 and 1967, and increased to 5.9 percent following the settlement of the strikes of 1968 and the devaluation of 1969, it nevertheless remained only slightly above the OECD average throughout the 1960s. More important, before 1973, inflation in France was only slightly higher than that of its neighbors and principal trading partners. After 1973, however, inflation in France grew worse, a problem that was compounded by the fact that France's neighbors were combating inflationary pressures successfully. Inflation in France averaged over 11 percent between 1974 and 1979, a level exceeded only in Italy and Great Britain. During the same period, inflation averaged 4.8 percent in Germany, 4.0 percent in Switzerland, 8.1 percent in Belgium, and 7.1 percent in the Netherlands. As inflation in France outpaced that of its northern European neighbors, the prices of imported goods became more competitive on the French market, while French goods lost competitiveness on foreign markets, thus contributing to France's trade imbalance.[6]

The oil shock did give rise to one new and unfamiliar challenge, that of economic stagnation. Throughout the 1970s, the rate of formation of fixed capital in France decreased, just as it did in other OECD countries.[7] The fall of productive investment was somewhat more precipitous in France than it was elsewhere, however. Between 1960 and 1973, the annual rate of growth of gross fixed capital formation (including construction) was higher in France than in all other large OECD countries except Japan. Thereafter France fell behind Germany, Italy, and Canada, when fixed capital in France grew at an average annual rate of only 2.8 percent. Though the average of the seven largest OECD countries together was still lower, at 2.5 percent, the drop in investment in France was proportionately somewhat greater.

But the resultant growth in unemployment was not a new phenomenon and could not be attributed entirely to the oil crisis. Though it is true that, as in the case of productive investment, the trend was one of decline from excellence prior to 1973 to mediocrity thereafter (unemployment throughout the 1960s averaged only 1.2 percent in France, compared with 3.0 percent among the seven largest countries and 5.1 percent in the United States, but in the next decade climbed to 4.8 percent in France, uncomfortably close to the 5.1 percent average for

[6]See *Tendances de la conjoncture* cahier 2, January 8, 1982, p. 10; André de Lattre, "L'investissement en période de croissance ralentie," *Journal des Caisses d'Épargne* 100 (August 1981); P. Artus, C. Bisart, and M. Debonneuil, "La pénétration étrangère sur le marché français: Vingt années plus une," *Économie et Statistique* 135 (July–August 1981); Anonymous, "France, cinquième importateur mondial," *Moniteur du Commerce International*, July 14, 1975; J. Baron, "Nous importons trop," *Nouvel Économiste*, May 7, 1979.

[7]See *Tendances de la conjoncture*, 44; OECD *Economic Outlook—Historical Statistics, 1960–1981* (Paris: OECD, 1983), p. 49.

all seven), the crisis nevertheless only made more apparent a problem that already existed, that of the comparative rigidity of the French labor market. French unemployment, by starting from a very low level and growing inexorably, evolved in a peculiar fashion, compared with other countries. During the 1960s, unemployment was already increasing at an annual rate of 6 percent, as opposed to less than 2 percent in the European Community as a whole. It doubled during that decade in France, whereas it actually declined over the decade in the United States and Japan.[8] After 1973, though unemployment grew everywhere, in France it grew at an annual rate of 14 percent, far higher than the 9.2 percent of the largest seven OECD countries.

Rigidity in the French labor market revealed itself with particular clarity in the relentlessness of growth in unemployment. Whereas unemployment everywhere grew on trend as a result of the crisis, variations around this trend were typically great. France, however, never experienced the ample variations in unemployment that were common in other OECD countries. After 1960, unemployment in France fell only once—in 1973. In other years it progressed by 5, 10, even 15 percent annually. In contrast to Germany, where unemployment grew at an annual rate of nearly 100 percent in 1967 but declined the following three years at the rates of 30 percent, 45 percent, and 17 percent, unemployment in France during the same years grew at a rate of about 10 percent per year. Similarly, unemployment in Germany shot up by more than 100 percent in 1974 and 1975 but receded in each of the following four years. In France, it increased by 47 percent in 1975 and then continued to grow by about 10 percent annually throughout the rest of the decade.[9]

In sum, though the oil crisis gave rise to new challenges for the French policymaker, notably by discouraging new investment, more typically it merely revealed already existing rigidities in foreign trade, price adjustment, and the labor market. Some indication of those rigidities is furnished by attempts to calculate the slope of the Phillips curve for France, which is intended to represent the trade-off that obtains between unemployment and inflation. Though one must treat with caution the notion that there is such a trade-off, it is nevertheless interesting that calculations for France reveal no trade-off whatsoever. In fact, one study shows unemployment and inflation in France to be covariant.[10] This contrasts intriguingly with France's Marshall-Lerner

[8]See OECD, *Historical Statistics*, p. 37.
[9]Ibid., p. 28.
[10]J. R. Presley and Geoffrey E. J. Dennis, *Currency Areas: Theory and Practice* (London: Macmillan, 1976), pp. 62–69. Great Britain, the Netherlands, and Ireland also show no trade-off but there is evidence of such a trade-off in Germany, Italy, Belgium, and Denmark.

coefficients, which are intended to indicate how readily an economy's trade balance responds to change in the external value of its currency. Calculations of France's Marshall-Lerner coefficients suggest that the French economy was, throughout the 1950s and 1960s, not only highly responsive to adjustments in the exchange rate but also more responsive than any other European economy.[11] Both observations suggest that France was an economy in which adjustment through internal policies and mechanisms was difficult to achieve, but one that was highly responsive to adjustment through external policies—that is, primarily through currency devaluation.

The Impact of Floating Exchange Rates

While the oil crisis acted primarily to make old problems worse, new and baffling challenges were generated by change in the monetary regime. Rather than free policymakers from the burden of defending currency parities, as many of its advocates argued it would, floating rates actually placed greater pressure on the policymakers of Europe to stabilize their currencies. The European economies, for which international trade represents a large fraction of gross domestic product, simply could not tolerate the degree of price and currency instability that the new exchange rate regime introduced. In this section, flexible exchange rates are examined in theory and then in practice.

In August 1971, the Nixon administration suspended the convertibility of the dollar into gold and announced that the United States would cease to intervene on the currency market to defend the dollar's parity. Because the dollar had hitherto furnished the standard relative to which the parities of other currencies were defined, the world's currencies, deprived of that standard, now floated freely. The system of exchange rate flexibility was born of a series of currency crises, affecting first the pound and then the dollar, which by 1969 had made devaluation of the dollar inevitable. Authorities in the United States, however, wishing to avoid devaluation for both economic and political reasons, sought instead to secure the revaluation of other currencies relative to the dollar. They scuttled the system of fixed exchange rates only after it became clear that other nations were not about to comply with American wishes. Although an attempt was made in December

---

[11]See Charles Kindleberger and Peter Lindert, *International Economics*, 6th ed. (Homewood, Ill.: Irwin, 1978) pp. 286–95; see esp. table p. 288. Trade interdependence and dependence on imports of commodities and oil have rendered the French economy decreasingly responsive to exchange rate changes.

1971 to return to fixed parities, renewed disorder forced a second devaluation of the dollar in February 1973, subsequent to which governments abandoned the effort to restore a fixed parity system. The fate of the international monetary system was sealed when the energy crisis temporarily rendered attempts to stabilize exchange rates futile. Exchange rate flexibility was legitimized by the Jamaica agreement of 1975, which stipulated that fixed rates would be restored only on approval by 85 percent of the International Monetary Fund's voting members. Moreover, in tribute to the spirit of economic nationalism that characterized the times, it was added that fixed parities would not be compulsory even if approved. Henceforth, governments were free to allow their currencies to float on the exchange or, if they preferred, to participate in joint floats by defining a parity relative to some other currency.[12]

Though born of crisis, exchange rate flexibility had long had a number of advocates who contended that flexibility had real advantages:

First, flexibility—at least theoretically—freed the world of the economic and political stress that was generated by undervalued and overvalued currencies. It eliminated the observed tendency of pegged rates to become rigid and thus to perpetuate currency misalignments that were left to be corrected only by major currency crises. This was the principle criticism directed against the system of fixed rates as it had functioned during the 1960s. Under floating rates, by contrast, adjustment in currencies and in foreign transactions was, theoretically, automatic. For example, if a country's prices were high relative to those of the rest of the world, begetting trade deficits, depreciation brought export prices down automatically and restored equilibrium to foreign trade.

Second, flexibility freed currencies from the destabilizing effects of speculation. In the words of one advocate of floating rates, "under the regime of floating exchange rates, speculation becomes a zero sum game in which some speculators must of necessity lose what others gain."[13] In contrast, under fixed rates, which pitted speculators against the central banks, speculation was riskless. As events gave rise to doubts concerning a government's ability to defend its exchange rate, speculators unloaded the currency on the market, causing the country's reserves to be depleted. If the doubts were borne out, the speculators

[12]See Leland B. Yeager, *International Monetary Relations; Theory, History, and Policy*, 2d ed. (New York: Harper and Row, 1976), p. 595; Joan E. Spero, *The Politics of International Economic Relations*, 2d ed. (New York: St. Martin's Press, 1981), pp. 51–69; Jean Denizet, *Monnaie et financement dans les années 80* (Paris: Dunod, 1982), chap. 12.

[13]Paul Coulbois, *Finance internationale*, vol. 1: *Le change* (Paris: Éditions Cujas, 1979), p. 196, quoted in Denizet, *Monnaie et financement*, 275.

profited; if they were amiss, the speculators lost little if anything. The worst that could happen to speculators was that nothing happened. But speculation frequently forced the issue of devaluation, turning rumors into self-fulfilling prophecies. Under floating rates, in contrast, currencies resemble stocks on the stock market, alternately gaining and declining and thus rendering speculation a riskier business.

Finally, and most relevant to our present concerns, monetary officials were no longer required to assign policy instruments to the defense of the exchange rate. Monetary policy was freed to pursue purely domestic economic goals. For flexibility's monetarist advocates, this meant that monetary officials were free to fight inflation at home without having to absorb the currency overhang of less disciplined countries into their money supply.[14] Conversely, flexibility's Keynesian advocates argued that, for countries suffering from persistant or "structural" inflation, the system tendered the possibility of achieving adjustment in trade and prices without incurring the social and political costs of deflation or devaluation.[15]

If one turns from theory to practice, the performance of the new regime has been mixed at best. On the one hand, there is little doubt that it helped countries deal with the supply shocks of the early 1970s. On the other hand, the new regime confronted monetary officials with new and unfamiliar phenomena that were sufficiently hazardous to

[14]"Virtuous" countries, as they intervened on the currency exchange to buy up and thus shore up the currency of "negligent" countries, both increased their monetary base of foreign currencies and gold and introduced more of their own currency into circulation.

[15]Monetarism is commonly associated with advocacy of flexible exchange rates, but one must exercise caution when attaching labels to economists, especially when not an economist oneself. It is true that Milton Friedman supplied one of the most influential defenses of flexibility; see "The Case for Flexible Exchange Rates," in *Essays in Positive Economics* (Chicago: University of Chicago Press, 1953). On the other hand, H. Johnson and R. Mundell, originators of the "monetary approach to the balance of payments," cannot be labeled monetarists. Mundell was an advocate of the discretionary use of monetary policy as part of his assignment rule and, moreover, tended to be critical of flexibility, favoring monetary union among highly interdependent economies. See R. Mundell, "Theory of Optimum Currency Areas," *American Economic Review* 51 (September 1961). Johnson tended to view flexibility in a favorable light, although his thinking contains more political fatalism than economic enthusiasm. See Harry G. Johnson, *Money, Balance of Payments Theory, and the International Monetary Problem*, Essays in International Finance, 124 (Princeton: Princeton University Press, November 1977). Conversely, J. E. Meade argued for flexibility from a Keynesian perspective. Observing that some economies were subject to structural disequilibria, he advocated flexibility in an effort to free the domestic economy from the balance-of-payments constraints. For an overview, see Kindleberger and Lindert, *International Economics*, chap. 20. See also Assar Lindbeck, "Experiences with Floating Rates," Address to the Third Paris-Dauphine Conference on Money and International Monetary Problems, in E. Claassen and P. Salin, eds., *Recent Issues in International Monetary Economics* (New York and Amsterdam: North-Holland, 1974).

provoke one prominent economist to claim, "Flexible exchange rates are an area where the economics profession was simply wrong."[16]

The most visible consequence of floating rates was the gradual though remarkable divergence over time between strong and weak currencies. Between 1971 and 1980, the effective exchange rate of the Swiss franc nearly doubled, that of the mark climbed 50 points, and that of the lira fell to less than half its value of 1971. During this same period, the effective exchange rate of the franc remained remarkably stable, a stability the French were able to achieve through policies that are explored below.[17]

Long-term variations in exchange rates were of less moment to the policymaker, and therefore of less relevance to our concerns here than the rapid and destabilizing variations in exchange rates that took place over the short term.[18] The exchange rate of the dollar relative to the franc frequently varied by as much as 20 percent over a semester, and even 5 percent within a week.[19] Such variability in exchange rates generated a number of annoyances, all more or less related to one another, of which three are considered here: "overshooting," the "ratchet effect," and the threat of vicious circles of currency depreciation and domestic price inflation.

Exchange rate flexibility gave rise to a phenomenon known as "overshooting," which occurs not because the market fails to return a currency to an exchange rate that restores equilibrium to foreign trade, but because the market pushes the currency beyond (whether above or below) that value. This is generally not a long-term phenomenon.

[16]Lester Thurow, "America, Europe, and Japan: A Time to Dismantle the World Economy," in Jeffry A. Frieden and David A. Lake, *International Political Economy* (New York: St. Martin's Press, 1987), 393. See also Jacques-Henri David, *La monnaie et la politique monétaire* (Paris: Economica, 1986), p. 258.

[17]OECD, *Economic Surveys: France, 1980* (Paris: OECD, 1981), p. 33; see also the surveys for 1981–82 (p. 29) and for 1983 (p. 30).

[18]Theoretically such long-term fluctuations should not cause difficulties for policymakers, at least if the doctrine of purchasing power parity (PPP) holds. Nevertheless, the doctrine's validity remains controversial among economists. Some have argued that a currency's ability to maintain itself at its PPP in the long term is easily threatened by shocks in either the capital market or the market for real goods. Others have claimed that historically observed departures from PPP are merely warranted sanctions on undisciplined monetary policies. See Peter Bernholz, "Flexible Exchange Rates in Theoretical Perspective," *Princeton Studies in International Finance* 49 (Princeton: Princeton University Press, July 1982); Louka T. Katseli-Papaefstratiou, *The Reemergence of the Purchasing Power Parity Doctrine in the 1970s*, Princeton Special Papers in International Economics 13 (Princeton: Princeton University Press, December 1979); Dominique Lacoue-Labarthe, "Les changes flexibles," in *Cahiers Économiques et monétaires* 9 (Paris: Banque de France, Direction Générale des Etudes, 1979).

[19]For discussion of "currency instability," see Richard E. Caves and Ronald W. Jones, *World and Trade Payments*, 3d ed. (Boston: Little, Brown, 1981), p. 469 and passim.

Currencies fluctuate above or below a longer-term trend in response to some policy-induced or real shock for three, six, or even twelve months. During this period, however, continued currency depreciation (to stick with the eventuality that is most relevant for the study of French policy) causes exports to earn less and imports to cost more, aggravating rather than alleviating the trade imbalance.

Overshooting owes its existence not only to floating rates but also to the rapid increase in international financial interdependence. Throughout the 1950s and 1960s, the expectations of devaluation that fed speculative crises were generated primarily by trade imbalances. Today a currency's exchange rate is no longer determined by a country's trade balance alone. In today's financially interdependent world, foreign currencies, bonds, and other assets denominated in foreign currencies are held in financial portfolios, which are adjusted and readjusted constantly as expectations of return fluctuate. The trade balance is only one of a number of factors that affect such expectations. Other factors include interest rates, inflation, political events, and policy expectations.[20] In other words, the locus of exchange rate determination has shifted from the market for what economists call "real goods" under fixed rates, to the market for financial and monetary assets under floating rates. This is an important development. Prices in the market for financial assets adjust almost instantaneously—the time it takes to make a telephone call. Prices in the market for goods, by contrast, adjust over a period measured in months or quarters. Because currencies are now greatly affected by events on the financial market, the exchange values of currencies fluctuate widely and rapidly. The market for "real goods" cannot react with this kind of speed to changes in relative prices provoked by currency variations, which in turn are caused by movements in the financial markets. Thus currency variations under floating rates do little or nothing to promote equilibrium in foreign trade over the short to medium term.[21]

The problems created by overshooting were compounded by what some economists dubbed the "ratchet effect." To understand the ratchet effect, one must begin once again with the difference between the market for financial assets and the market for real goods. Prices on the financial market adjust both up and down, but prices in the market for real goods have a greater tendency to adjust upward only. In strong

[20]See Jacques Waitzenegger, "Les déséquilibres courants et l'harmonisation des politiques conjoncturelles," in *Cahiers Économiques et Monetaires* 9:97–104, esp. pp. 101–2.

[21]Lacoue-Labarthe, "Les changes flexibles," pp. 79–81; Katseli-Papaefstratiou, "Reemergence," pp. 10–16; Peter Kennen, "International Monetary Relations after Jamaica: An Overall View," *Essays in International Economics* (Princeton: Princeton University Press, 1980), pp. 359–66.

currency countries, prices tend to be stable and rarely fall, whereas in countries with weak currencies prices tend to rise. Hence, the consequence of exchange rate instability on world price levels tends to be inflationary.[22] In 1976, Henri Bourguinat surveyed French business responses to changes in the exchange rate of the franc and found that among businesses that denominated the price of their traded goods in foreign currencies, more than 90 percent held their prices constant in the event of a change in the exchange rate of the franc, thereby preventing relative prices from adjusting.[23] Among businesses that denominated the price of their traded goods in francs, about 20 percent increased their prices when the franc depreciated and lowered them when the franc appreciated, again inhibiting adjustment in relative prices. Inflationary pressures, which are often generated by depreciation, are aggravated by this ratchet effect.[24] Although Bourguinat observes that variations in the exchange rate do, over the long term, become integrated into the domestic price structure, he concludes: "This happens only after a rather long delay, and for changes in the exchange rate that cause a decrease in prices and profit margins it is probably a longer and more partial process than for changes that push prices and margins upward."[25]

Because overshooting and the ratchet effect forestall adjustment, some economists have theorized that exchange rate instability actually sets off a destabilizing "vicious circle" or destabilizing spiral of variations in exchange rates and prices. Depreciation, they theorize, feeds back into the domestic economy, not only through the medium of the ratchet effect but also through that of higher import prices. Higher import prices, caused by depreciation, worsen domestic inflation; domestic inflation in turn worsens depreciation. For vicious circles to arise, however, foreign trade must be relatively inelastic. Trade elasticities measure the responsiveness of demanders and suppliers of traded goods to changes in relative prices. For countries in which demand for imports and exports is very inelastic, depreciation translates merely into a higher bill for a volume of imports that refuses to diminish, and lower income from a volume of exports that refuses to increase. A

---

[22]Sometimes referred to as the Mundell-Laffer hypothesis. See Jude Wanniski, "The Case for Fixed Exchange Rates," *Wall Street Journal*, June 14, 1974; Henri Bourguinat, *Le flottement des monnaies* (Paris: Presses Universitaires de France, 1977), p. 106.

[23]About 40 percent of invoices were drawn up in foreign currencies. Half of these were established in dollars, one-third in marks, and the rest essentially in sterling and Belgian francs. See Bourguinat, *Le flottement*, p. 31.

[24]Depreciation provokes inflation by increasing import prices and creating opportunities to increase prices of exported goods.

[25]Bourguinat, *Le flottement*, p. 109.

depreciation in the currency of such a country means little more than greater payments deficits, the threat of a vicious circle of import-induced inflation, and further depreciation. The French economy, in which the demand for certain imports, such as oil, was relatively incompressible (at least over the short term), was far from immune to the threat of such vicious circles. Awareness of the French economy's vulnerability to vicious circles informed monetary policy from the mid-1970s on.

Though economists still consider vicious circles to be a topic of debate, the experiences of Great Britain and Italy with high inflation and depreciation in the mid-1970s, and of Germany and Switzerland with low inflation and strong currency appreciation during the same period, suggest that such vicious and virtuous circles do exist.[26] Some economists have dismissed the importance of vicious circles, however, contending that they are simply the well-deserved consequences of ill-inspired policy rather than the ineluctable outgrowth of faulty trade structures. It is true that such countries as Belgium were able to extricate themselves from vicious circles by adopting rigorous monetary policies designed to contain inflation and by intervening on the exchange in order to arrest the depreciation of their currency. Responding to this argument, however, the French economist Jean Denizet argued that the threat of such vicious circles nevertheless confronts the policymaker with a sizable constraint, sufficient to deprive floating rates of much of their theoretical allure. "If the central bank lost control over the money supply, even for only a short period, one is at a loss to identify a mechanism whereby the rise in the price of foreign currencies would reduce the excess supply of money. *The whole theory of floating exchange rates seems to hang on a limitless confidence in the ability of the central bank to contain the money supply.*"[27] Denizet's objection assumes particular importance in the case of France, where, as will be shown below, the power of the central bank to control the money supply through any means but direct administrative control over bank activity was very weak indeed. Denizet concludes:

[26]See Bank for International Settlements, *Annual Report, 1978*, p. 122.

[27] Denizet, *Monnaie et financement*, p. 274 (emphasis added). See also M. Mussa, "The Exchange Rates, the Balance of Payments, and Monetary and Fiscal Policy under a Regime of Controlled Floating," in J. Herin, A. Lindbeck, and J. Myhrman, eds., *Flexible Exchange Rates and Stabilization Policy* (Boulder, Colo.: Westview, 1977); H. G. Grubel, *Domestic Origins of the Monetary Approach to the Balance of Payments*," Essays in International Finance 117 (Princeton: Princeton University Press, June 1976); Caves and Jones, *World and Trade Payments*, p. 470; Sylviane Guillaumont-Jeanneney, *Pour la politique monétaire* (Paris: Presses Universitaires de France, 1982), pp. 89–94; International Monetary Fund, *Annual Report, 1978*, pp. 37–43; Bank of International Settlements, *46th Annual Report, 1975–1976*, p. 31, and *47th Annual Report, 1976–1977*, pp. 37–41.

Who can deny that the successive appreciations of the deutschmark have made the fight against inflation difficult [in France]? They have aggravated the deterioration in the terms of trade that was provoked by the increase in the price of oil. Under fixed exchange rates, France and Germany were already vulnerable to price instability to different degrees, but fixed rates had the virtue of moderating the consequences of this fact. In 1965–66, inflation in France was lower than in Germany. This was of course the result of the stabilization plan of 1963–65, but it was possible only within a regime of fixed rates. Similarly, from the end of 1969 to the beginning of 1973, the price indexes of France and Germany can be superimposed on one another perfectly. It is only after generalized flexibility comes into effect that the two indexes begin to diverge more and more importantly. This is more than a coincidence.[28]

THE REORIENTATION OF FRENCH MONETARY POLICY UNDER FLOATING RATES

Proceeding from this general discussion of floating rates to the more specific examination of the impact of floating rates on French policy, we learn first, without surprise, that floating was not a welcome innovation. One monetary official lamented, "The foreign constraint has not been eliminated, and monetary officials in all countries are somewhat disappointed at not having been able to enjoy the sweet independence they were promised, since exchange rates, if left to their own devices, would fluctuate intolerably."[29] It became apparent that the constraint

---

[28]Denizet, *Monnaie et financement,* p. 279. A number of econometric models have tried to assess the vulnerability of the French economy to such vicious circles. In the 1960s and 1970s the National Institute for Statistics and Economic Studies (INSEE) developed three models for forecasting economic trends. The first, called FIFI, was used for preparing the Fifth and Sixth Plans. It was replaced by the Dynamique Multi-Sectoriel (DMS) Model in 1976, which had the advantage of describing economic trends from one year to the next, whereas FIFI could see only the end-point of the five-year plan but nothing in between. In 1978 the Metric Model was devised. This model takes into account certain peculiarities of France's financial structures (see Chapter Two). The DMS Model predicts that a drop of 10 percent in the exchange rate of the franc would aggravate inflation, but that the economy would benefit from gains in price competitiveness and that the inflationary effects of depreciation would taper off after one year. The Metric Model predicts that the gains in competitiveness one might expect from depreciation would almost be annulled by a compensating rise in prices within a year. According to this model, inflationary repercussions are still felt two years after depreciation. See Commissariat Général du Plan, *Crédit, change, et inflation, Rapport du groupe d'économie monétaire appliquée: Annexes* (Paris: La Documentation Française, 1979), p. 163. For another interpretation, see Christian Bordes-Marcilloux, "Monnaie, taux de change, et compétitivité," *Revue d'Économie Politique* 92 (May–June 1982).

[29]Robert Raymond, "Les politiques internes de caractère conjoncturel," in *Cahiers Economiques et Monétaires* 9:114. After a decade of experience with floating rates, American economists have come to something resembling a consensus which holds that

on policy imposed by currency instability was such that floating deprived the French of the capacity to promote economic adjustment by manipulating the par value of the franc. "The 'perverse effects' that result from a drop in parity," concludes one study of French foreign trade in the 1970s, "are difficult to control in a system of floating currencies, and are all the more important when the proportion of imported raw materials in the current account is very great."[30] The same sentiment was expressed in 1980 by the finance committee of the Eighth Plan, which observed: "Because of the disorder in the international monetary system, it is no longer possible to control the amplitude of a devaluation as it was until the end of the 1960s. The variation in a country's inflation rate, its balance of payments deficit, the depreciation of its currency—all are excessively subject to speculative expectations.... Hence, the 'spiral' of inflation and depreciation is very difficult to avoid and to control."[31]

Exchange rate instability was now perceived to be a serious policy challenge. Prior to 1973, the French had executed a number of successful devaluations in order to achieve adjustment in relative prices and foreign trade, some of which, such as the devaluations in 1958 and 1969, earned France a reputation for manipulating the exchange rate for commercial gain.[32] Now, under floating rates, the defense of the

---

flexibility is not as good as it was supposed to be or as bad as some people had feared. On the one hand, it is admitted that flexibility requires that certain conditions be met in order to confer the promised benefits. It shelters countries fairly well against shocks occurring in the trade of real goods and services. On the other hand, it fails to protect against shocks in the international financial markets, which are often policy-induced. Flexibility confers greater benefits on the country that can exert global influence over the level of interest rates than on the country that has little or no influence. See Kindleberger and Lindert, *International Economics*, pp. 371–82, Guillaumont-Jeanneney, *Pour la politique monétaire*, pp. 66–77; Johnson, "Money, Balance of Payments Theory, and the International Monetary Problem," p. 21; Caves and Jones, *World and Trade Payments*, pp. 468–71; Morris Goldstein, *Have Flexible Exchange Rates Handicapped Macro-economic Policy?* Princeton Special Papers in International Economics 14 (Princeton: Princeton University Press, June 1980). See also Weir M. Brown, *World Afloat: National Policies Ruling the Waves*, Essays in International Finance 116 (Princeton: Princeton University Press, May 1976).

[30] J. P. Broclowski and R. de Villepin, "La mutation des échanges extérieurs de la France depuis 1970," *Économie et Statistique* 94 (November 1977).

[31] Commissariat Général du Plan, Report of the Finance Committee, *Préparation du Huitième Plan* (Paris: La Documentation Française, 1981), p. 26.

[32] France's devaluations differed markedly from that of, say, Great Britain in the 1960s. With the exception of 1968, France offered little resistance to speculative crises. The financial necessity of the 1969 devaluation is generally disputed. See P. Armand-Ameller, "Pourquoi la dévaluation de 1969?" *Revue d'Économie Politique* 81 (September–October 1971); R. Mossé, "La dévaluation du Franc: A-t-elle réussi?" *Revue Politique et Parlementaire* 73 (January 1971); Anonymous, "La 13ème dévaluation du franc," *Actualités Industrielles Lorraines* 122 (October 1969); Paul Coulbois, "Dévaluation et désinflation," *Défense Nationale* 25 (October 1969); "La dévaluation," *Moniteur du Commerce International*, August 21–25, 1969. See also J. Mistral, "Vingt ans de redéploiement extérieur," *Économie et Statistique* 71

franc was assuming greater importance than it had at any time since 1934.

Policy instruments, notably interest rates, were assigned to the defense of the franc.[33] Prior to the crises of the 1970s, interest rates had frequently been negative in real terms as successive French governments sought to promote investment, but now interest rates became "the principal weapon...to sustain the external value of the franc," a policy that the 1974 annual report of the National Credit Council (Conseil National du Crédit) qualified as "new, in certain respects."[34] Floating rates imposed this reorientation in policy at a time when the rise in the price of oil and other commodities was discouraging new investment and fostering severe trade deficits (the first serious estimates of the impact of the oil shock on the French economy predicted accumulated trade deficits of at least 200 billion francs by the end of 1980), and at a time when economic crisis was revealing rigidities in the French economy that hampered adjustment. One econometric analysis suggested that interest rates would have to be increased by 4 percent to counter a 1 percent drop in the exchange rate.[35] Given constraints of such dimensions, the prospect of deflation seemed inevitable.[36] Before

---

(October 1975); "Les changements de parité depuis 1956," *Rapport de Conjoncture* 3 (March 1976); J. Mistral, "Changement de parité et croissance économique," *Revue de Science Financière* 67 (July–September 1975). See further development of this argument in the historical chapters, Chapters Four through Eight. See also M. Obradovitch, *Les effets de la dévaluation de 1958* (Paris: Éditions Eyrolles, 1970), p. 189, which hailed the 1958 devaluations as a "turning point in the evolution of the postwar economy," because by giving French exporters a competitive edge they allowed France to liberalize its trade in accordance with the Treaty of Rome and to assure a successful return of the franc to full convertibility.

[33]Central bank intervention on the currency exchange and exchange controls were no longer particularly helpful. The volume of international financial transactions far surpassed the resources of the central bank. During the month of March 1976, the Banque de France spent more intervening on the currency exchange than the entire nation spent on imports. See *Crédit, change, et inflation: Annexes*, p. 139. As for exchange controls, after having been tightened in 1971 to prevent the revaluation of the franc and the loss of advantages procured by the devaluation of 1969 (nonresidents were barred from holding short-term securities, bank deposits of foreign currencies were subjected to reserve requirements, and residents were severely limited in their ability to borrow abroad), they were lifted in 1973–74 to facilitate foreign borrowing by French firms, as explained below. See *Crédit, change, et inflation: Annexes*, p. 136; Jean-Yves Habérer, *La monnaie et la politique monétaire* (Paris: Les Cours de Droit, 1979), chap. 17; and Louis-Georges Teyssier, *Le contrôle des changes en France de 1932 à 1972* (Paris: Librairie du Commerce International, 1973).

[34]Conseil National du Crédit, *Rapport Annuel, 1974*, pp. 41, 33. Concerning interest rate policy in subsequent years, see the annual reports for 1978, p. 65; 1979, p. 70; 1980, p. 48; and 1981, p. 53. See also Chapter Eight of this book.

[35]*Crédit, change, et inflation: Annexes*, p. 232. See also Bourguinat, *Le flottement*, p. 87.

[36]"L'endettement externe de la France," in *Avis et rapports du Conseil Économique et Social, 1980; Journal Officiel*, July 4, 1980.

confronting that cold and gray prospect, however, French policymakers experimented with gentler policy responses to the crisis, foreign borrowing and selective credit restrictions.

POLICY INNOVATIONS OF THE 1970S: FOREIGN BORROWING

Fearing deflation, French policymakers fell victim to the "interventionist temptation" so well characterized by John Zysman, and they set out to devise policies that would "'filter' the effects of a trade deficit before it could have a repercussion on the currency market," and thus mitigate the need for monetary rigor.[37] The "filter" was foreign borrowing. The state had the capacity to control foreign borrowing by French firms, and it made use of that capacity to dull the impact of the external shocks. The state did not borrow directly on foreign markets, but "invited" French enterprises, principally public enterprises, to borrow from foreign banks and to issue bonds on foreign financial markets. Between 1974 and 1976, foreign borrowing became the principal means whereby France financed its current account deficit.[38]

Borrowing on foreign markets offered a number of real advantages. First, borrowing procured funds for a number of large public projects that the French held dear, such as the nuclear power program, modernization of France's notoriously antiquated telecommunications system, and construction of new superhighways. Projects such as these made large demands on France's narrow financial market. Moreover, because of the turnabout in interest rate policy, interest rates on foreign loans were now 2 to 3 percent lower than those available on the French market. The French power company, Électricité de France, for example, obtained an eight-year loan in 1977 at the six-month Eurodollar rate of 7.25 percent. The best it could have obtained on the French market was 11.3 percent.

Second, and more important, investment levels were sustained and dramatic increases in unemployment avoided. France was given a "breathing space" during which it could try to improve the export competitiveness of its industry in a way that might ultimately ease the stress of adjustment. The 1977 report of the National Credit Council disclosed:

---

[37]On the "interventionist temptation," see John Zysman, "The Interventionist Temptation: Financial Structure and Political Purpose," in William Andrews and Stanley Hoffmann, eds., *The Fifth Republic at Twenty* (Albany: SUNY Press, 1980).

[38]Bourguinat, *Le flottement,* pp. 135–47.

Because it prolongs the process whereby the current accounts return to a satisfactory balance, France's policy of foreign borrowing gives some leeway to pursue measures designed to adapt our economic structures to the new economic order. This adaptation can be only gradual. Moreover, it obliges certain industrial sectors to seek out a great deal of financial support...Such needs could not be satisfied on the national market without grave tensions, because it is too narrow, nor could they be satisfied by appropriate development of bank credit.[39]

Finally, and most important, foreign borrowing strengthened the franc. The sale of financial assets—in this case, interest-bearing bonds—has, over the short term, the same buoyant effect on the currency as the sale of real goods, even assuming that funds raised in this manner are used entirely to import goods and services from foreign suppliers. In effect, under the new monetary regime, currencies borrowed abroad were no longer handed over to the central bank for conversion, but were exchanged directly on the currency market. Borrowing, therefore, even when done through a foreign bank or lending institution, had the effect of increasing the demand for francs on the currency exchange and thus of bidding up their price relative to other currencies. That buoyant effect is reinforced when, as was the case for France, part or all of those funds are used to buy goods and services on the domestic market.

Foreign borrowing, both on the market and through foreign institutional lenders, provided a panacea that addressed nearly all the problems that the monetary and energy crises had aggravated or created. Not only did it hold at bay the specter of deflation, but it helped finance the trade deficit and sustain the value of the franc. It follows, of course, that France's foreign debt grew rapidly. The increase was especially striking when compared with the years 1971–72, when the government was encouraging foreign investment rather than foreign borrowing.[40] Though opinions differ on just how rapidly the debt grew, one study claims that medium- and long-term foreign loans increased from 14.8 billion francs in 1974 to 21.8 billion francs in 1976.[41] Other studies

[39]Conseil National du Crédit, *Rapport Annuel, 1977*, p. 37.

[40]Pompidou encouraged foreign investment to help prevent the franc, newly devalued, from appreciating relative to the dollar. See also Claudine Cortet and Michèle Debonneuil, "La balance des paiements depuis 1973," *Économie et Statistique* 119 (February 1980); Jean-Claude Papillon, "Évolution de la balance française des paiements (1945–78)," *Profils Économiques* 7 (January–March 1982); Jean-Louis Masurel, "Financements internationaux des sociétés par l'intermédiaire des banques"; Bernard Gaultier et al., "Utilisation des financements internationaux et stratégie financière des firmes," Papers presented to the colloquium "Monnaie et Finance Internationales," organized by the École Nationale d'Administration, Paris, November 14 and 15, 1979, Mimeographed.

[41]See "L'endettement externe de la France."

point to the absence of viable statistics on foreign borrowing and estimate that total foreign borrowing was much greater than official statistics suggest. Though there is much uncertainty regarding the importance of foreign indebtedness at the aggregate level, some indication can be obtained by noting the increase in foreign indebtedness at the level of the individual enterprise. There the increase in borrowing, as documented by Paul Turot, was dramatic.

> According to the report of the Commission de Vérification des Comptes des Entreprises Publiques (November 1976), foreign loans to the eight largest [state-owned] enterprises (EDF, GDF, Charbonnages de France, Commissariat à l'Énergie Atomique, Compagnie Nationale du Rhône, RATP, Aéroport de Paris, Air France), increased from 370 million francs in 1973 to 5,538 million francs in 1974 (a factor of 14.5), falling to 3,661 million in 1975. However, these figures are very incomplete. Other financial and nonfinancial public enterprises borrowed heavily these past few years on the Eurobond market (the only market for which statistics exist...), as well as from foreign banks....Between 1974 and 1976, the Banque Française de Commerce Extérieur borrowed $340 million; ERAP, $80 million; la Caisse Nationale des Autoroutes, $140 million; la Caisse Nationale des Télécommunications, $225 million; the SNCF, $230 million and 135 million Dutch guilders.... Not mentioned were the loans to the nationalized banks, to Renault (400 million francs), or to regional development societies guaranteed by the state (300 million francs)....Private firms, in contrast to public firms, were more conservative and increased their foreign borrowing by a factor of only 4 or 5.[42]

The advantages of foreign borrowing, however, turned out to be shortlived. Critics of the policy were not long in pointing out that inflows of capital would soon have to be compensated by outflows going to service the debt. As *Le Monde*'s influential financial columnist, Paul Fabra, argued in other circumstances, for the nation to confront adjustment difficulties by borrowing means that ultimately "tomorrow it will have to work more to export, forgo consumption of a larger part of the fruits of its labor, or give up some portion of its wealth."[43] Other critics objected that the sought-after stabilizing effects of borrowing on the exchange rate would rapidly be counteracted by the expansive impact of the inflow of capital.[44] In the words of Henri Bourguinat, "in the end, 'borrow today in order to adjust better tomorrow' does constitute a rather opportune philosophy in the beginning. However,

---

[42]Paul Turot, "L'endettement extérieur occidental: Le cas français," *Eurépargne* 7 (February 1977).

[43]Paul Fabra, "Endettement et équilibrage de la balance des paiements," *Le Monde*, May 17, 1983, p. 21.

[44]"L'endettement externe de la France," p. 361.

the threat of runaway inflation that such a policy implies is never far away."[45] Nor, as other critics contended, could it simply be assumed that industry would find the means through foreign borrowing to adapt to new international conditions. According to an interim report of the finance committee for the Planning Commission (Commissariat du Plan), "excessive reliance on foreign borrowing could provoke a reappearance of the internal and external imbalances created by the oil shock: the decrease in real income and the reorientation of production would be delayed once again."[46] Moreover, borrowed funds had to be repaid in the currency in which they were borrowed, exposing the borrower to the risk of an unfavorable evolution in exchange rates.[47]

Even as a short-term solution to the payments problem, foreign borrowing was not without its dangers. Its effectiveness depended largely on the domestic demand for capital, but the demand for capital often evolved in unpredictable ways. When monetary policy was relaxed in 1975 in order to stimulate activity and to fight unemployment, foreign borrowing was encouraged in order to finance the growing current account deficit that was the predictable result of the less rigorous orientation of monetary policy. Because of the economic downturn induced by the oil crisis, however, business demand for capital was slack. Firms found all the capital they required on the domestic market. Consequently, borrowing on foreign markets fell far short of the anticipated level and thus conditioned a dramatic fall of the franc on the exchange. On other occasions, the desired effects of foreign borrowing were negated by speculation. Elections, for example, given the prospects of a leftist victory, provoked large outflows of funds that frustrated attempts to balance the account through long-term borrowing.[48] For all these reasons, Raymond Barre, upon becoming prime minister in 1976, put a damper on foreign borrowing. The government turned more restrictive in granting authorizations to borrow abroad and for all practical purposes ceased using foreign borrow-

[45]Bourguinat, *Le flottement*, p. 147.

[46]*Crédit, change, et inflation*, p. 33.

[47]Some observers were not troubled by the riskiness of the policy, contending accurately that France's debts were no greater than its credits. Indeed, in an effort both to help their industries expand abroad and, above all, to promote exports through granting export credits to foreign nations, especially developing nations, France had become a major exporter of capital. See Papillon, "Évolution de la balance," p. 102; "Les investissements français à l'étranger et les investissements étrangers en France," *Avis et rapports du Conseil Économique et Social, 1981: Journal Officiel*, February 25, 1981. But, critics responded, France was borrowing in strong currencies from rich countries and lending in francs to poorer countries. There is no doubt that France was exposing itself to an exchange rate risk.

[48]See OECD, *Economic Surveys: France, 1980*, p. 33. See also the surveys for 1981–82, p. 29; and for 1983, p. 30.

ing as a tool of payments adjustment. One government analysis explained: "Recourse to foreign borrowing is not totally suppressed, but is measured out in order to keep it within limits compatible with national independence and the stability of the franc."[49] After 1976, the level of French indebtedness remained stable at about 4.5 percent of the GDP, up nevertheless from 2.5 percent in 1974.[50] Foreign borrowing would not be used again on a comparable scale until the early years of the Socialist government.

POLICY INNOVATIONS OF THE 1970S: QUANTITATIVE CREDIT RESTRICTIONS

By providing capital and sustaining demand for the franc on the currency exchange, foreign borrowing provided a panacea that effectively postponed the need to achieve adjustment in foreign payments. But adjustment could not be postponed indefinitely. In 1976, after having suffered two serious currency crises as well as diplomatic humiliation when, on both occasions, the franc was forced out of the joint European currency float, the French had to face the prospect of greater monetary restrictions. Nevertheless, they did not do so without assuring themselves of the means to intervene selectively in the economy, both in order to sustain France's export performance and to decrease the stress of restrictions in sectors that were politically sensitive. To do so, the French placed their hopes in the state's capacity to intervene administratively to restrict and to direct the allocation of credit by banks and other financial institutions to the rest of the economy.

This administrative or coercive aspect of French monetary policy as practiced during the 1970s effectively distinguished it from monetary policy as practiced in Great Britain or the United States. In the latter, the central bank intervenes to regulate the quantity of reserve assets that is supplied to the banking system on the open market. By affecting the supply of bank reserve assets, the central bank influences the price of those assets, and thus the cost to the banks of lending money. In this way, the central bank exercises some control over bank activity. In contrast, French monetary officials began in 1972 to place direct limits on the volume of credit that individual banks could accord to households and firms. In other words, rather than intervening between the market for monetary assets and the banking system, monetary authori-

---

[49]"L'endettement externe de la France," p. 358.

[50]Yves Guihannec, "Rigueur: Ça dérape," L'Express, May 4, 1984. France's medium- and long-term foreign debt stood at 12 percent of GDP in 1984.

ties in France intervened between the banks and the rest of the economy.

This technique, known as *encadrement du crédit*—quantitative credit restrictions—required that French officials agree each year on a desirable volume of credit growth. This global target in turn defined the "norms," or targets assigned to individual banking and financial institutions, expressed as a percentage of that institution's volume of outstanding loans. If the bank exceeded those norms, it had to pay a penalty in the form of increased reserve requirements.[51] *Encadrement* had already been used as a weapon against inflation on three previous occasions: first during the currency crisis of 1957, then as part of the stabilization plan of 1963, and finally following the strike settlements of 1968. It is, however, significant that only in 1972—that is, in the context of the currency crisis that accompanied the modification of the Bretton Woods system—did *encadrement* become a permanent part of France's panoply of policy instruments.

As an instrument of policy, *encadrement* offered a number of advantages. First, it allowed the government to control the growth of the money supply very effectively.[52] In 1977 the Barre government began to define monetary growth targets, thus adopting a practice that had been put to use in other industrialized countries during the early part of the decade, but that the French had resisted because of its deflationary implications. Beginning in 1975, however, in a context characterized by growing fears of monetary disorder, monetary officials began to advocate the use of such targets.[53] *Encadrement* facilitated this policy, enabling the French to come within 1 percent of the desired target (an accomplishment that can be properly appreciated when compared with the efforts of the Federal Reserve).[54] Second, and more important, credit restrictions freed interest rate policy from the task of defending the exchange rate. In effect, it allowed the government to ease pressure on interest rates actually charged to industrial borrowers (through specialized loan programs) without fear of runaway growth in the

---

[51]See M. Chazelas, J. F. Dauvisis, and G. Maarek, "L'expérience française d'encadrement des crédits," *Cahiers Économiques et Monétaires* 6 (Paris: Banque de France, Direction Générale des Études, April 1977); Jacques Masson, "Le rôle des banques dans la gestion de la masse monétaire," *Banque* 425 (February 1983); Guillaumont-Jeanneney, *Pour la politique monétaire*, pp. 217–32. See esp. Jean Truquet, "La quatrième expérience française d'encadrement du crédit," *L'Analyse Financière* (3ᵉ trimestre 1976), and David, *La monnaie*, pp. 273–75.

[52]See Masson, "Le rôle des banques."

[53]See Claude Bourillon, "Les problèmes financiers du gouvernement," *Revue des Deux Mondes*, August 1977. See also H. Bussery, "Les echéances du plan Barre," *Projet* 113 (March 1977).

[54]See Conseil National du Crédit, *Rapport Annuel, 1981*, pp. 13, 25.

money supply, and inversely, to keep interest paid on monetary assets high to defend the franc without fear of an adverse impact on investment and employment. In other words, because credit was allocated administratively, interest rates charged to industrial investors could be "disconnected" from the rates charged to the nonindustrial borrower. As one observer remarked, by using credit restrictions the government was "able to act at the very source of monetary creation while regulating interest rate levels independently."[55]

The third and most important advantage of *encadrement* lay in the power it gave policymakers to achieve a high degree of coordination among the various components of both monetary and industrial policy. How this was accomplished can be understood by considering the following equation:

money supply growth = credit growth + net foreign earnings (including net foreign investment) + budget deficit
(to the extent that it is monetized)

Money supply growth is determined not only by the expansion of bank credit, but also by deficit spending and the balance of foreign transactions.[56] Using *encadrement*, the government exploited this interdependence among the different components of money supply growth to coordinate domestic monetary policy, exchange rate policy, and even—though to a lesser extent—industrial policy. Coordination was achieved in several sequential steps. The first step consisted of determining a desirable target for monetary growth.[57] Between 1976 and 1981, officials selected

[55]J. C. Chouraqui, "L'expérience récente de la politique monétaire en France," *Banque* 359 (February 1977), 161. See also Antoine Coutière, "Le rationnement du crédit en France," *Économie Appliquée* 30 (4ᵉ trimestre 1977); *Crédit, change, et inflation*, p. 32; J. Chardonnet, *La politique économique intérieure française* (Paris: Dalloz, 1976), p. 112; Gilbert Dolletaz and William Marois, "L'analyse des relations dynamiques entre variables: Une application aux taux du marché monétaire français," *Revue Économique* 32 (January 1981).

[56]The open market was not a factor of money supply growth in France for the simple reason that there was no open market in France in the American sense. Public debt was not auctioned by the central bank in an effort to influence the market for credit and consequently interest rates. The term "money market" as employed by the French at this time applied only to an interbank market for commercial paper. The price of money on this market affected but did not determine the price of credit to some but not all borrowers. See J. Aulagnier, *L'open market en France*, Annales Économiques 2 (Clermont-Ferrand: Faculté de Sciences Economiques de l'Université de Clermont-Ferrand, 1971); Antoine Coutière, *Le système monétaire français* (Paris: Economica, 1981). The French money market has recently been the object of reforms (see Chapter Eight).

[57]The money supply was defined as M_2 in France, the definition of which, for statistical purposes, had a peculiarly bureaucratic character. It encompassed interest-bearing liquid savings and short-term bonds but excluded liquid savings deposited in postal accounts and treasury bonds, which were included in M_3. See J.-P. Patat, *Monnaie, institutions financières, et politique monétaire* (Paris: Economica, 1982), pp. 155–64.

targets that were slightly lower than anticipated nominal GDP growth. By choosing modest targets, the French sought to procure a gradual reduction in the volume of excess liquidity in the economy, their prudence reflecting the persistent desire to find ways to prolong the process of adjustment in the wake of the supply shocks.[58] Once the target was determined, the government tried to forecast as precisely as possible how much the budget deficit would contribute to monetary growth and how much foreign transactions would contribute.[59] The remainder then determined the limit to be imposed on credit growth (as seen in the above equation). This in turn defined the base figure with reference to which "norms" for credit expansion were assigned to individual banks and financial institutions.

The government's "prediction" concerning deficit spending and foreign transactions was not entirely passive. After all, the government exercised some control over budget expenses. It also exercised discretionary control over foreign financial transactions because of its power to authorize foreign borrowing by public and private firms and because of its ability to "invite" public enterprises such as Électricité de France and the SNCF to borrow from foreign lenders. Therefore, if (for example) foreign transactions deviated from the government's forecast, the government had the power to bring the actual balance closer to target by encouraging or discouraging borrowing on the international financial market.[60] This capacity to influence the final balance in foreign transactions rendered the government's hypothesis concerning the evolution of foreign transactions part "hypothesis" and part "target." And, because foreign transactions had an impact on the exchange rate, the government, in making its "forecast" regarding foreign transactions, also was committing itself to a "target" exchange rate for the franc.

Barre's economic policy has frequently been called monetarist. Although it is true that the practice of assigning money supply growth targets is associated with monetarism, the definition of targets in the

---

[58]See Conseil National du Crédit, *Rapport Annuel, 1980*, p. 35.

[59]The success of this technique supposed that bank credit contributed significantly to the expansion of the money supply. In France this was certainly the case. Bank credits to the economy were generally reckoned to contribute about 80 percent of the increase in money supply growth in any given year (see Chapter Two).

[60]Trade policy and industrial policy also were designed with an eye on the balance of payments, but they did not constitute a short-term conjunctural policy instrument. Foreign borrowing, however, supplied a policy instrument that could be used to achieve results over the short term. See "L'endettement externe de la France"; H. Bourguinat, "L'endettement externe et le VIIe Plan," *Banque* 358 (January 1977); Turot, "L'endettement extérieur occidental"; Fabra, "Endettement et équilibrage." It also assumes that the government targets a desired level of deficit spending, although budget deficits were negligible in France before 1978.

manner just described hardly fits the monetarist mold.[61] Raymond Barre, moreover, never claimed the monetarist label. His policies were the product of constraint, not theory. "If I wanted to define in a short statement the government's economic policy after 1976, I would say that it has tried to be practical and coherent. It was not the translation of any economic dogma, but evolved out of the facts—that is, out of a situation defined by certain tendencies and constraints."[62] By implementing money supply growth targets, policymakers did not intend to subject the French economy to the rigor and discipline of the marketplace, but rather to stabilize monetary growth while easing the process of adjustment by spreading it over a period of years, during which investment could be promoted in high priority sectors. The concerns that inspired the use of *encadrement* to achieve coherence in economic policy were the same as those that had inspired recourse to foreign borrowing. Bourguinat explains, "The goal . . . was one of a return to equilibrium in the current account by 1980. . . . Adjustment was sought, but in a prolonged fashion."[63] This becomes clearer when it is seen how industrial policy goals were addressed by monetary policy.

POLICY INNOVATIONS OF THE 1970S: GREATER SELECTIVITY IN FINANCIAL SUPPORT FOR INDUSTRY

Industrial policy completed this elaborate circle of interdependent policy components. "Once the volume of authorized foreign borrowing is determined," explains one government publication, treasury officials "analyze the long-term financial needs of the economy: given the needs of the public sector and the private sector, how much will be furnished respectively by the French financial market, the international market, the Caisse des Depôts [Deposit and Consignment Bank], the banks, and the specialized financial institutions."[64] *Encadrement du crédit* was put into effect in part to funnel credit to priority industrial uses, and notably to export sectors that could, by enhancing their export performance, help to balance foreign payments either in the short run or over the long term. Thus, just as one of the goals of foreign borrowing, in conjunction with stabilizing the franc, had been that of promoting

---

[61]Monetarists advocate limiting money supply growth to a rate that is in harmony with real rather than nominal GDP growth and leaves to the market all adjustments in the external balance and in public finances. Because monetarists tend to favor exchange rate flexibility, it is assumed that external payments will take care of themselves.

[62]Raymond Barre, "L'économie française quatre ans après," *Revue des Deux Mondes,* September 1980, quoted in Guillaumont-Jeanneney, *Pour la politique monétaire,* p. 140.

[63]Bourguinat, *Le flottement,* p. 141.

[64]"L'endettement externe de la France," p. 359.

investment in strategic sectors of the economy, so one of the goals of *encadrement* was to spare the same strategic sectors from the rigors of deflation. This was easily achieved: strategic sectors had only to be exempted from the quantitative restrictions that *encadrement* imposed. Export industries naturally were the principal beneficiaries of this exemption.[65]

Inversely, the government tried to use *encadrement* to restrict the allocation of credit to industries that were not contributing to external adjustment. In doing so, the government was reacting to criticisms of industrial policy that had been growing since the late 1960s, when critics began to charge that industrial policy resulted in the indiscriminate distribution of aid among both growth and declining sectors, as well as in the distribution of aid among a number of firms that was so large that financial aid was diluted and ineffectual.[66] For Jean-Pierre Patat, writing in the 1980s, French growth had been "wasteful with money."[67] Comparative studies of France and Germany revealed the inefficiency of industrial policy as practiced throughout the 1960s. Germany had achieved a level of labor productivity that was higher than that of France with a per capita level of investment that was at least 10 percent lower, despite higher wages and social costs.[68] Industri-

---

[65]Similar measures were enacted in favor of investments that helped conserve energy. As an instrument of industrial policy, *encadrement* was merely one part, though of central importance, in a whole arsenal of new industrial initiatives that benefited, most notably, exporting industries. Insurance arrangements were improved, generous credit was extended to LDCs and Soviet bloc countries to finance purchases of French goods, and the state subsidized industrial innovation and took a number of specific sectoral actions in certain industries that promised to cut import dependence and increase exports. The government continued to facilitate bank lending to exporting industries by promoting medium-term loans that were discountable at the Banque de France. The state also invested directly or promoted investment in the telecommunications, nuclear energy and other alternative energies, civil aeronautics, and computer technology. On French industrial policy, see Stoffaës, *Leçons sur la politique industrielle*; Chardonnet, *La politique économique*, chap. 12; Suzanne Berger, "Lame Ducks and National Champions: Industrial Policy in the Fifth Republic," in William Andrews and Stanley Hoffman, eds., *The Fifth Republic at Twenty* (Albany: SUNY Press, 1981); John Zysman, *Government, Markets, and Growth* (Ithaca: Cornell University Press, 1983), chap. 3; and Zysman, "The Interventionist Temptation: The French Case." French energy policy is described in Daniel Deguen, "Problèmes de structure," in de Lattre and Pébereau, *La politique économique de la France*, part 3, chap. 5; Philippe Rossignol, "Régler la facture pétrolière," *Économie et Statistique* 84 (December 1976); Paul Turot, "Comment l'État aide les entreprises privées," *Revue Politique et Parlementaire* 77 (January–February 1975). See also René Monory, "De nouvelles relations entre l'État et les entreprises," *Bulletin de liaison et d'information de l'administration centrale du Ministère de l'Économie et du Budget* 83 (October 1978–March 1979); David, *La monnaie*, pp. 309–19.

[66]See Lionel Stoléru, *L'impératif industriel* (Paris: Seuil, 1969). Stoléru was economic adviser to Giscard d'Estaing.

[67]Patat, *Monnaie*, p. 346.

[68]See André de Lattre, "L'investissement en période de croissance ralentie," *Journal des*

al policy was also criticized for having contributed to inflation by diminishing the overall productivity of French industry.[69] Critics demanded greater selectivity as well as greater submission to market discipline.[70]

Thus, with the onset of the new decade and the new challenges that accompanied it, industrial policy was assigned a new goal: the "redeployment of activities in order to adjust them to the new conditions of the world economy and to the new trends in the international division of labor."[71] In this more parsimonious spirit, the government sought after 1976 to confine its aid to growth sectors and exporting industries, leaving the others to struggle with the rigors of the marketplace.[72] In pursuit of this policy, the government drew up a list of industries and other sectors of the economy that were to be exempt from *encadrement*. In 1976, this list included all credits destined to facilitate exports (including those intended to augment "export production capacity") and credits destined to finance energy conservation.[73] In addition to using credit policy to support the export effort by exempting certain loans from *encadrement*, the government also encouraged the rediscounting of medium-term loans at privileged rates to purchasers of French goods who did not belong to the European Community and also subsidized interest payments on export loans.[74]

Though credit policy had always been a mainstay of France's industrial policy, in the 1970s monetary and industrial policy became more integrated and more inseparable than before. Cohen, Galbraith, and Zysman write:

> The evolution of financial and credit policy under the Barre government goes far beyond the introduction of monetary targets and the institution of a monetarist anti-inflation program. There has been in addition, or

---

Caisses d'Épargne 100 (August 1981). See also Groupe d'Études sur les Perspectives de la Balance Commerciale Française au Cours des Dix Prochaines Années, "Les perspectives du commerce extérieur français," *Économie et Statistique* 106 (December 1978).

[69] See P. Roux-Vailland and J. Vignon, "Les conditions d'un ralentissement de l'inflation," *Économie et Statistique* 84 (December 1976).

[70] Stoléru's complaints were echoed in 1978 in two well-publicized books by French officials which were equally critical of the indiscriminate character of previous industrial policies (Christian Stoffaës, *La grande menace industrielle* [Paris: Calmann-Lévy, 1978], and Alain Cotta, *La France et l'impératif mondial* [Paris: Plon, 1978]). They reiterated the demand that state aid be made more selective and parsimonious.

[71] Stoffaës, *Leçons*, p. 157.

[72] See Monory, "De nouvelles orientations."

[73] The list also included credits allocated in foreign currencies and activities not directly related to export performance, notably housing and agriculture. See Chazelas et al., "L'expérience française." See also Conseil National du Crédit, *Rapport Annuel, 1979*, p. 59.

[74] In the mid-1970s the rediscount rate on discount loans was 4.5 percent in nominal terms, or about a negative 5 or 6 percent in real terms. See Guillaumont-Jeanneney, *Pour la politique monétaire*, p. 221; and Coutière, "Rationnement du crédit."

perhaps instead, a substantial strengthening of selective mechanisms to affect the flow of credit on two levels. First, the *encadrement* and associated instruments have been perfected to assure state control over the aggregate quantity and composition of capital formation and over the broad sectoral outlines of bank lending. Second, an array of specific selective credit institutions, under Treasury control, have been developed to facilitate intervention in microeconomic planning and decision making in a virtually comprehensive range of contexts.[75]

In 1976, French officials could reasonably hope that credit rationing by the state held the key to adaptation to a changed and more hazardous economic environment. Credit rationing contributed to monetary rigor and a fairly strong franc yet kept credit available to industries that might use it to increase their foreign sales and thus help France to achieve equilibrium in foreign transactions.

DISILLUSIONMENT WITH INTERVENTIONISM

The power to control the allocation of credit in a way that at least theoretically allowed the French to pursue incompatible monetary and industrial policy goals—those of slowing monetary growth while simultaneously promoting investment in key industrial sectors—has been portrayed as the hallmark of the strong, interventionist state that France historically has exemplified.[76] The state as actor was highly visible, and it acted in almost hermetic isolation from society. Monetary policy in France was set by a powerful troika consisting of the prime minister, the minister of finance, and the Treasury. The latter is aptly described by John Zysman as "the sanctuary inside the temple of the Ministry of Finance, the economic apex." He continues: "A remarkable range of policy responsibilities concentrate here, including a concern with the money supply, bank regulation, and the control of government lending or grants to industry."[77] Though monetary policy does not typically elicit an aesthetic reaction, one is struck by the exotic alliance between brutality and elegance that characterized the French system as it functioned between 1976 and 1986. It was brutal in its heavy-handed

---

[75]Stephen S. Cohen, James Galbraith, and John Zysman, "Rehabbing the Labyrinth: The Financial System and Industrial Policy in France," in Stephen S. Cohen and Peter Gourevitch, eds., *France in the Troubled World Economy* (London: Butterworth, 1982), p. 65.

[76]See John Zysman, "The French State in the International Economy," in Peter Katzenstein, ed., *Between Power and Plenty* (Madison: University of Wisconsin Press, 1978).

[77]Zysman, *Governments, Markets, and Growth*, p. 114. On the peculiar role and powers of the French treasury, see esp. François Eck, *Le trésor* (Paris: Presses Universitaires de France, 1982).

interventionism yet elegant in its theoretical power to achieve a high degree of coordination among a large number of policy goals.

Given such elegance, however, the growing number of voices, very much in evidence by the end of the decade, that were calling for liberalizing reforms is puzzling. The reformers had several complaints. First, as a tool of monetary regulation, *encadrement* proved to be uncommonly difficult and awkward to implement. The two missions that *encadrement* was supposed to fulfill—that, in the long term, of contributing to industrial redeployment, and that, in the short term, of managing money supply growth, were difficult to coordinate. In the words of Jacques-Henri David, one of the central participants in the monetary policy-making process, "the definition of a serious selective policy obviously requires much time (because of the studies and the verification that it implies). Hence, it is difficult to manipulate in the short term, and because of this, there is a certain contradiction between the idea of applying a policy of selective allocation of credit on the one hand and the desire to use credit policy to influence the economic conjuncture on the other."[78]

Second, there was considerable confusion concerning how credit policy, as a tool of industrial modernization, could best be used. Industrial policy had already come under criticism in the late 1960s, and it remained a topic of intense debate and confusion throughout the next decade. There was little agreement on what was ailing French industry or on what to do about it. According to some critics, French industry was particularly weak in sectors that international trade had singled out for growth: capital goods and consumer durables, especially household electrical goods. Was it preferable, in order to balance the external account, they asked, to lend to exporting enterprises even if they were less competitive than firms that produced only for the domestic market, or was it not more advisable to lend to the most competitive firms, even though, rather than export, they nevertheless produced goods that would otherwise be imported?[79] Other critics maintained that the more parsimonious orientation of industrial policy

---

[78]J.-H. David, "Quelques réflexions sur la politique sélective du crédit," *Banque* 330 (June 1974).

[79]Sylviane Guillaumont-Jeanneney, "Synthèse des travaux," in *Cahiers Économiques et Monétaires* 9:161. See also Chazelas et al., "L'expérience française," pp. 112–15; J. M. Bertrand, M. Guy, and M. de Rose, "Le système bancaire et le financement déséquilibré de la croissance, 1960–1975," *Banque* 359 (February 1977); J. M. Lévèque, "Contre l'encadrement du crédit," *Revue Politique et Parlementaire* 80 (July–August 1978); Guillaumont-Jeanneney, *Pour la politique monétaire*, pp. 217–32. For a synopsis on credit allocation at preferential rates, see the report of the finance committee in "Commissariat Général du Plan," *Préparation du Huitième Plan: Annexes* (Paris: La Documentation Française, 1980), pp. 117–46.

was making unemployment worse. If parsimony's advocates could respond by applauding the fact that productivity was rising, its critics pointed out that this was happening principally in noncompetitive, labor-intensive industries, which in the long term held no promise of improving the export competitiveness of the French economy.[80] Finally, industrial policy and the credit policy that sustained it were criticized for discriminating against a number of viable but overlooked small and medium-sized firms. The report of the finance committee of the Eighth Plan stated: "Credit restrictions inconvenience only the small borrower, especially the small business, since banks have no desire to upset their principal clients."[81] In 1979, the government established a commission to investigate the financial difficulties encountered by small and medium-sized firms. The resultant *Mayoux Report* designated bank centralization and selective credit restrictions as the two principal threats to the health of smaller firms, and advocated the abandonment of *encadrement du crédit* as an instrument of policy.[82]

The most important criticism of France's activist credit policy, however, stemmed from the perceived powerlessness of officials, though armed with impressive policy instruments, to prevent financial resources from making their way to declining sectors. Restrictions were difficult to impose on industries that had, over the past decades, forged strong ties with government offices. Selectivity in industrial policy was jeopardized, argues Christian Stoffaës, by the "clientelistic effects" that had developed as the result of decades of state involvement in industry. Stoffaës concludes that in "a context in which pubic expenditure is to be reduced rather than continue to grow, redeployment into priority programs is both difficult and essential."[83] It is the existence of such clientelistic effects that Jack Hayward has so thoroughly documented and analyzed.[84] As Hayward demonstrates, there is no one industrial policy, but rather a plurality of policies, each elaborated by some specific policy subcommunity and embodying the efforts of those subcommunities to protect their priorities from the depredations of budgetary officials who are preoccupied with inflation. Suzanne Berger, writing contemporaneously, had already found that French industrial

---

[80]See "L'investissement industriel en France: Son évolution, son financement," *Bulletin du Crédit National* (2ᵉ trimestre 1980); de Lattre, "L'investissement," pp. 24–26; Stoffaës, *La grande menace industrielle*.

[81]*Crédit, change, et inflation*, p. 32.

[82]See J. Mayoux, *Le développement des initiatives financières locales et régionales*, Report to the prime minister (Paris: La Documentation Française, 1979).

[83]Stoffaës, *Leçons*, pp. 157, 189.

[84]See Jack Hayward, *The State and the Market Economy: Industrial Patriotism and Economic Intervention in France* (Brighton: Wheatsheaf Books, 1986); for a discussion of Hayward, see the Introduction and Conclusion of present volume.

policy, far from pursuing its alleged goal of greater selectivity, was being used primarily to salvage declining or bankrupt firms: "The *dirigisme* of the seventies would commit the state far more extensively than ever before in the Fifth Republic to the survival of particular enterprises and particular jobs."[85] Although the government did treat steel, textiles, and shipbuilding with uncharacteristic parsimony, one must agree with Berger that French policy overall did not provoke the rationalization it sought to achieve.[86]

Berger's and Hayward's analyses suggest that the state, though it undertook to discipline the banks, was incapable of disciplining itself. That impression is confirmed by the evolution of credit allocations by the state and by public and semipublic financial institutions controlled by the state. As the state clamped down on the supply of bank credit, it intervened more systematically with the help of the semipublic financial institutions to provide capital to certain industries and industrial sectors (Table 3). Long-term and medium-term loans from banks grew quickly in the wake of the oil crisis, and then diminished almost as quickly after 1976 as the government tightened restrictions. Long-term and medium-term loans by public and semipublic lending institutions, in contrast, increased on trend throughout the 1970s (though they were also reduced after 1976). By the end of the decade, public and semipublic lenders were providing the economy with more long- and medium-term credit than the banking system.

Credit policy, moreover, was diverted from the task of facilitating investments that would make the French economy more competitive on the world market in the long term to that of promoting export contracts that addressed more immediate payments difficulties. Although this diversion of credit policy provided short-term fixes, it

Table 3. Sources of long- and medium-term financing for nonagricultural, competitive firms, 1970–1979 (billion francs)

	1970	1971	1972	1973	1974	1975	1976	1977	1978	1979
Semipublic and public sources	2.0	3.0	4.0	5.5	5.5	9.0	10.0	7.5	7.0	8.5
Banks	4.5	6.0	17.0	6.5	14.5	19.0	19.0	10.0	6.0	7.0

Source: "L'investissement industriel en France: Son évolution, son financement," *Bulletin du Crédit National* (2ᵉ trimestre 1980), p. 26.

[85] Berger, "Lame Ducks." See also OECD. *Economic Survey: France 1979*, p. 46; P. Papon, "The State and Technological Competition in France, or Colbertism in the Twentieth Century," *Research Policy* 4 (July 1975).

[86] See Stoffaës, *Leçons*, p. 150; David, *La monnaie*, pp. 236–38.

harbored long-term costs. First, to the extent that policy favored large contract items, such as infrastructure and industrial plant, it failed to promote the reallocation of capital toward sectors for which the market was expanding, and instead privileged sectors that were dependent on the state's ability to negotiate interstate contracts, primarily with less-developed countries. Moreover, by relying on large contractual transactions with non-Western nations, capital was drained into a sector in which France had no real comparative advantage: capital goods. France indeed depended on other developed countries for the capital goods used in its own industries, and so found itself in the ironic position of having to import capital goods for its own industry while manufacturing capital goods to be sold abroad.[87]

Credit policy introduced distortions not only into the French economy's productive base, but into its financial structures as well. *Encadrement* created incentives for banks to lend generously to firms that were exempted from controls. Unrestricted credits (that is, credits exempt from *encadrement*) accounted for more than one-fourth the volume of credit distributed to the economy in 1979, as opposed to only 14 percent in 1972 (see Table 4). By 1976, rapid expansion of unrestricted credit was threatening to undo with the left hand what credit restrictions were trying to achieve with the right: to slow the growth of the money supply. Writing in 1975, Jacques-Henri David complained that credit policy "has been the source of a number of disappointments; first, it limited very significantly the global impact of monetary policy

Table 4. Unrestricted credits as percentage of all credits to the economy, 1972–1979

Year	Percent
1972	14.1
1973	17.9
1974	14.8
1975	18.1
1976	21.5
1977	n.a.
1978	20.9
1979	27.7

Sources: Commissariat Général du Plan, *Crédit, change, et inflation: Annexes* (Paris: La Documentation Française, 1979), p. 208; Sylviane Guillaumont-Jeanneney, *Pour la politique monétaire* (Paris: Presses Universitaires de France, 1982), p. 225.

[87]See "Les grands contrats d'équipement," in *Moniteur du Commerce International*, April 26, 1982; M. Galy, "Les échanges de biens d'équipement entre la France et l'extérieur," *Bulletin Trimestriel de la Banque de France* 14 (February 1975). Conversely, sales of agricultural products, a sector in which France was expected to enjoy a significant comparative advantage, actually regressed. See Bourguinat, *Le flottement*, pp. 137–141.

on the French economy, in part because it prevented credit restrictions from affecting a growing volume of bank operations and in part because it contributed to maintaining the price of credit at abnormally low levels."[88] Though the government tried at one point to control the supply of credit to sectors that were exempt from *encadrement*, persistent fears of deflation caused credit restrictions to these sectors to be defined liberally. In 1979, credits to exempt sectors were restricted to 20 percent growth relative to the previous year. In 1980, after the second oil shock, this limit was increased to 50 percent.[89]

The impact of *encadrement* on the banking system's dynamism and competitiveness was another source of concern. One critic of *encadrement* wrote: "Since credit restrictions were instituted, the very outlook of the banking profession has been altered. Before, the primary objective of the banker was to develop his credits to the utmost, since the banker's profit was derived from the interest payments that he received.... Now, on the contrary, the primary concern of the banker [at least vis-à-vis nonexempt sectors] is to stay within the limits defined by his restrictive norms, to limit credits to the utmost, to refuse clients, and even to send his own clients to his competitors."[90] Because the demand for credit addressed to any given bank was greater than the volume of credit the bank could supply, banks no longer had to compete for business. This had an anesthetic effect on some banks, while creating opportunities for others. Banks with large reserve assets were able to increase their lending by dealing more heavily in export loans that were not subject to credit restrictions, but this introduced distortions into the banking system, causing credit restrictions to hurt some banks more than others.[91]

Finally, as banks scouted the market for lending opportunities that were not subject to *encadrement*, they began to shower the Banque de France with rediscountable medium-term export loans. Because of the narrowness of the financial market in post–World War II France, successive governments sought to promote the use of liquid deposits in banks and savings institutions to fund medium- and long-term loans for industry and housing. One of the instruments devised to facilitate this transformation of short-term liabilities into longer-term assets was the medium-term loan accepted for rediscount by the Banque de France (under specifiable conditions). Because this was the monetary

---

[88]David, "Quelques réflexions."

[89]See Coutière, *Le système monétaire*, p. 183.

[90]See Masson, "Le rôle des banques," p. 133.

[91]See Chazelas et al., "L'expérience française," pp. 135–38. See also Raymond Penaud and François Gaudichet, *Sélectivité du crédit, financement, politique monétaire* (Paris: Economica, 1985), chap. 3.

Table 5. Medium-term (M.T.) loans in Banque de France assets, 1968–1985

Year	Total Banque de France assets (billion francs)	M.T. loans for export promotion (billion francs)	M.T. loans for housing (billion francs)	M.T. loans for other purposes (billion francs)	M.T. export loans as % of total Banque de France assets
1968	91.2	5.2	4.8	4.3	5.7
1969	96.5	6.8	4.7	6.6	7.0
1970	96.6	8.0	4.8	4.3	8.3
1971	100.5	9.6	0.0	1.5	9.6
1972	136.9	11.4	0.0	7.3	8.3
1973	160.5	12.9	0.1	13.4	8.0
1974	164.1	14.0	0.1	10.8	8.5
1975	182.8	18.3	0.0	3.9	10.0
1976	191.3	26.1	0.1	3.1	13.6
1977	210.4	34.1	0.1	0.1	16.2
1978	269.0	41.4	0.0	0.1	15.4
1979	387.9	48.8	0.0	0.1	12.6
1980	566.0	59.8	0.0	1.5	10.6
1981	542.2	72.8	0.0	2.2	13.3
1982	697.4	86.0	0.0	1.1	12.3
1983	732.3	86.1	0.0	1.3	11.8
1984	771.4	87.8	0.0	0.8	11.4
1985	729.3	83.6	0.0	1.4	11.5

Sources: Table compiled by author from data contained in annual reports (Comptes-rendus) of the Banque de France. Figures rounded off to the nearest 0.1 billion francs.

equivalent of playing with matches, Treasury and bank officials had to be vigilant. With the imposition of credit restrictions in 1972 and the export push that accompanied the oil crisis, however, more and more medium-term loans to exporters were addressed to the central bank for rediscount until they accounted for 16 percent of Banque de France assets in 1977, displacing all other categories of rediscountable medium-term loans (Table 5). The inflationary threat was apparent to everyone, and the practice was thereafter more tightly regulated.

The French Economy in 1980: Voices for Reform

France's policies, for all their virtuosity, yielded disappointment. Efforts to "finesse" the challenge of adjustment in hard times by "prolonging" the adjustment process through interventionist means ultimately gave way to demands for wholesale reform. But one should not paint too monochromatic a picture of gloom. Growth in the 1970s was equal to and even slightly higher than the average for the seven largest OECD economies, and unemployment was slightly lower. On the other hand, trade deficits and inflation were somewhat worse than those experienced by most OECD economies, and the French economy began to show signs of stress brought on by its failure to adjust fully to the external shocks of the first half of the decade.

First, inflation still threatened to jump the fence of monetary rigor and run rampant. The 1980 OECD survey observed: "Despite a marked slowdown in demand and the existence of considerable spare capacity, the inflation rate has hardly ever been below 10 percent for any length of time since 1974."[92] Policy was certainly not innocent in this regard. Foreign borrowing, though it dampened imported inflationary pressures by helping to keep the exchange rate high, sustained domestic inflationary pressures by maintaining investment and consumer demand at artificially high levels. Bourguinat describes the "pernicious effects of foreign borrowing, which has 'anesthetized' the deflationary effects that a trade deficit should have had on the money supply."[93] Even *encadrement du crédit*, to the extent that it was riddled with loopholes, helped nurture inflationary pressure. Lacoue-Labarthe attributes French inflation to the ambivalence of a credit policy that was not only supposed to slow monetary growth, but also contribute to the "mercantilist objective" of a commercial surplus.[94] A similar conclusion is found in the report of the finance committee of the Eighth Plan: "Monetary conditions (refusal of monetary deflation and more difficult control over the money supply) as well as external financial conditions (indebtedness and commercial credits) render inflation more difficult to reduce in France than elsewhere. That seems to be the price to pay for a policy that from the outset refused to allow any brutal reduction in the real income of economic agents, notably households."[95]

Policy ambivalence prevented the French economy from adjusting to the external shocks of the early 1970s. By the decade's end, France found itself saddled with an economy in which inflation was higher and unemployment greater, and in which the policies of foreign borrowing and export promotion were at the limits of what they could supply in the way of a short-term panacea. The French economy was thus left weaker and more vulnerable when the second oil crisis struck in 1979. In 1980, the annual growth rate of industrial production fell from +4 to -4 percent. French industrial growth matched the OECD average at the beginning of the year but lagged behind it by 3 percent at the end of the year. Inflation remained fairly constant at 13.5 percent, but

[92]OECD, *Economic Surveys: France 1980* (Paris: OECD, May 1980), p. 52.

[93]Bourguinat, "La dette extérieure et le VIIe Plan."

[94]Lacoue-Labarthe, "La politique monétaire extérieure française: L'expérience de flottaison contrôlée des taux de change," *Vie et Sciences Économiques* 71 (October 1976).

[95]*Crédit, change, et inflation: Annexes*, p. 185.

this was more than 1 percent higher than the OECD average at the end of the year, compared with 2 percent below that average at the beginning of the year. And whereas the balance of payments was showing clear signs of recovery in Great Britain, Japan, and Germany by September 1980, it was showing no signs of recovery in France as late as December.[96] The OECD survey of 1982 noted that the second oil shock had revealed the existence "of a certain number of profound structural inadaptations" in the French economy.[97] Economist François Meunier tried to measure the aggregate "external levy" that the oil and commodity shocks of the 1970s had exacted on the French gross domestic product, not only by increasing the cost of imports but also by affecting France's capacity to export. According to his calculations, the first shock extracted nearly 3 percent of France's gross domestic product and transferred it to other economies. On the other hand, the third commodity shock (the second oil shock) claimed nearly 3.5 percent of the GDP. While the first shock was compensated for somewhat by an increase in the value of exports and a sharp decrease in domestic demand for imports, no such compensation was forthcoming after the third shock. Meunier concludes: "The response was weaker and more delayed after the [third commodity] shock than after the first two..., especially because there was no reduction in the volume of imports. This inertia, along with the failure of export prices to react, resulted in the French economy's experiencing much more difficulty overcoming the third external shock than overcoming the two that preceded it."[98]

It was in this context that talk of fundamental reform in economic structure and policy grew loud. Reformers demanded that *encadrement du crédit* be eliminated, that the use of *encadrement* to hold certain interest rates artificially low be discontinued, that fiscal and technical reforms to encourage the issue and purchase of bonds (in preference to borrowing from financial intermediaries subject to *encadrement*) be elaborated, and that privileged access to lending institutions be abolished.[99] Reformers voiced other complaints about the complexity of French financial institutions and the related weakness of the French financial market and proposed that financial practices be liberalized. They suggested that the privileges of the semipublic financial institutions,

[96]Conseil National du Crédit, *Rapport Annuel, 1980*, pp. 30–31.
[97]OCDE, *Études économiques: France, 1982–1983* (Paris: OCDE, 1983), p. 8.
[98]François Meunier, "La deuxième crise pétrolière plus éprouvante que la première," *Économie et Statistique* 149 (November 1982). The "second" external shock was the commodity shock of mid-decade. The second oil crisis is referred to as the "third" external shock.
[99]*Préparation du Huitième Plan*, pp. 5, 48.

which facilitated state intervention in finance, be suppressed, and the institutions themselves dismantled and replaced by a more unified financial market. In the France of 1979, there clearly existed a reformist *élan*. Though the idea of reform was shelved pending the outcome of the presidential elections of 1981, many of the liberalizing reforms advocated by the conservatives were reformulated and implemented by the Socialists in the 1980s (see Chapter Six). Similar constraints bred similar policies, in spite of ideological differences.

CONCLUSION

The demise of the monetary system of fixed but adjustable exchange rates deprived the French of the possibility of achieving adjustment in foreign payments through currency devaluation. Financial interdependence brought a high degree of short-term instability to the currency market, while the openness of the French economy, to which one must add the inelasticity of demand for certain imported commodities such as oil, rendered the French economy particularly vulnerable to currency instability. This caused monetary officials to alter a well-established pattern of French exchange rate policy and to place a premium on strengthening the franc and avoiding depreciation.

Simultaneously, the oil crisis revealed rigidities in the French economy that inhibited economic adjustment through internal mechanisms and policies. This helps explain why French officials went to such lengths to find ways to prolong and to ease the process of adjustment, first by borrowing heavily on foreign financial markets, then by using the state's control over the allocation of credit to pursue a highly complex and sophisticated policy designed both to slow monetary growth and to promote investment in exporting industries. However impressive, that effort ultimately failed. By the end of the decade, not only was inflation still high, but the economy displayed even greater vulnerability to the oil crisis of 1979 than it had shown with the crisis of 1973. The attempt to find an interventionist solution to the challenge brought about by change in the international political economy clearly had failed, and this strengthened the sentiment that radical reform was required.

In the next chapter I consider the hypothesis that the economic rigidities revealed by the oil shock, the government's preference for a prolonged and managed process of economic adjustment, and the resistance shown by economic agents to credit restrictions all spring from the same source: the existence in France of an "overdraft economy."

CHAPTER TWO

The Overdraft Economy

The resistance of the French political economy to policies designed to promote internal monetary adjustment can be explained with the help of the concept of the "overdraft economy." An overdraft economy is characterized by a high degree of dependence on institutionally allocated credit. Some French economists have claimed that such dependence creates patterns of economic behavior that differ significantly from those encountered in textbook models, and that this, given that such dependence is typical of the French political economy, accounts for the imperfect fit between textbook models and economic behavior as observed in France. However, the behavior patterns posited by the overdraft economy model depend in turn on the existence of institutional structures that were designed to ensure that French economic agents had access to adequate financial resources, not to control monetary growth. Thus, if one were to ask why monetary policy proved ineffectual in France, one might alternately point to the high level of indebtedness of French banks vis-à-vis the Banque de France, or to the nonexistence of a money market, or to the Byzantine structures of the French financial market, or to the loopholes in *encadrement*, or to the rather casual cash-flow management of French firms, or finally to the government's basic unwillingness to tackle the political legacy of a growth-oriented industrial policy. All these explanations are correct. They are all, moreover, inextricably—structurally and conceptually—bound up with one another and together constitute the French overdraft economy. Structures and the patterns of behavior they induced together compounded the challenge of achieving monetary stabilization in France, first by depriving monetary policymakers of effective policy tools, and

55

second by rendering the French economy relatively more vulnerable to policies of monetary rigor than other leading industrial economies.

THE OVERDRAFT ECONOMY IN THEORY

The concept of the overdraft economy owes its existence to the British economist John Hicks. In a discussion of the uses and abuses of monetary policy,[1] Hicks observed that textbook economic theory assumes a large and active financial market, an economy in which firms and banks, when faced by liquidity shortfalls, sell securities previously purchased and held in reserve in order to confront monetary emergencies. Thus one finds in such an economy a "precautionary demand" for financial assets that can be liquidated in case of need. The financial market brings the supply and demand of money and interest-bearing assets into equilibrium by varying their price, as expressed in bond yields and interest rates.

This ideal type economy, Hicks argued, does not exist universally, and therefore the textbook explanation of the demand for monetary assets is not universally applicable, but rather applies only when agents address their demand for money to the market for monetary and financial assets. What would happen, Hicks asked, in an economy in which agents tended to bypass the market because they felt their power to borrow from institutional lenders, banks, or other lending institutions was assured, and therefore that the need to set assets aside for monetary emergencies did not exist? It is precisely this presumption of assured borrowing power that defines the overdraft economy. Given this presumption, Hicks reasoned, economic behavior and the effects of monetary policy in the overdraft economy are significantly different from that encountered in the asset-based economy, if only because, under such conditions, the precautionary demand for monetary assets disappears.

The concept of the overdraft economy generated considerable interest among French economists during the latter half of the 1970s. Introduced into the literature by Vivien Lévy-Garboua and Gérard Maarek, the concept found its way into numerous studies of French monetary policy.[2] It seemed to account for some of the unusual

[1] See John Hicks, *The Crisis in Keynesian Economics* (Oxford: Blackwell, 1974), pp. 51–56.
[2] See Vivien Lévy-Garboua, "Le taux de change et la politique monétaire dans une économie d'endettement," *Annales de l'INSEE* 32 (October–December 1978); and Gérard Maarek, "Monnaie et inflation dans une économie d'endettement," *Revue d'Économie Politique* 88 (January–February 1978). See also C. Toullec, "Économie de marché, économie

characteristics of France's political economy—its high degree of indebtedness vis-à-vis banks and other lending institutions, the high level of
bank indebtedness vis-à-vis the Banque de France, the comparative
narrowness of the French financial market, and the comparative difficulty of defining and implementing monetary policy—that could not be
explained by commonly accepted theoretical models. Because of the
predominance of Anglo-American scholarship in economic theory, the
existence of a large and active financial market is assumed, reflecting
the experience of economists living in the United Kingdom and the
United States. French economists argued, however, that the mechanisms described and the policies recommended by "Anglo-Saxon" theorists, whether Keynesian or monetarist, were ill-adapted to a country
like France, in which the financial market was very weak and in which
money supply growth was fed largely by bank credit. In the words of
Maarek:

> A theoretical effort must be made to free oneself from the traditional
> concept of "token money," which is injected into the economy in mysteri-
> ous ways. . . . If the monetary financing of the public deficit resembles in
> certain ways a discretionary injection of the means of payment, it is not
> the same for money that is created by the distribution of credit by banks.
> Contrary to the situation in the Anglo-Saxon countries, this form of
> monetary creation has dominated in France since the war. This situation
> reflects a specific financial structure that the Keynesian or monetarist
> models (which originated across the Channel or across the Atlantic)
> describe inadequately.[3]

The intellectual history of the concept was marked by renewed
interest in pre-Keynesian economists, such as Böhm-Bawerk, Wicksell,
Myrdal, and Hayek.[4] The work of the French economist Jacques Rueff,
for whom the main problem confronting the modern economy was
indebtedness and the creation (primarily by the state) of what he called
"false money," was accorded particular attention by theorists of the
overdraft economy.[5] This revival of interest in the works of Rueff was

d'endettement, et politique monétaire," *Banque* 382 (March 1979); Sylviane Guillaumont-
Jeanneney, *Pour la politique monétaire* (Paris: Presses Universitaires de France, 1982), pp.
254–57; Jean-Pierre Patat, *Monnaie, institutions financières, et politique monétaire* (Paris:
Economica, 1982), pp. 223–48; Dominique Lacoue-Labarthe, *Analyse monétaire* (Paris:
Dunod, 1980), chap. 10.
[3]Maarek, "Monnaie et inflation," p. 96.
[4]See ibid., p. 99.
[5]See Jacques Rueff, *L'ordre social* (Paris: Plon, 1981); Rueff, *Combats pour l'ordre financier*
(Paris: Plon, 1972); V. Lévy-Garboua and G. Maarek, "La théorie monétaire de Jacques
Rueff," *Cahiers Économiques et Monétaires* 11 (Paris: Banque de France, Direction Générale
des Études, c. 1980). One can also consult the numerous articles written by Paul Fabra for
Le Monde, as well as his *L'anticapitalisme: Essai de réhabilitation de l'économie politique* (Paris:

of significance, for Rueff had been a champion of classical liberalism in a country where Keynesianism and the cult of technocracy had come to dominate economic thinking. There is a distinctly classical tone to the literature on the overdraft economy, which anticipated the current revival of interest in economic liberalism. One could of course dismiss all this as merely another scholastic debate—so characteristic of the France of Anglo-Saxon imagery—if it were not for two facts that were indicative of an important intellectual trend. First, concern about France's financial structures was widespread, extending far beyond the circle of these theoretical innovators. Jean Denizet, one of France's authoritative voices in economic matters as well as a confirmed Keynesian, welcomed the efforts of the younger economists to assess the impact of institutional indebtedness on the French economy.[6] Though his own prescriptions differed markedly from those that theorists of the overdraft economy were advancing, he shared their concern about the long-term impact of indebtedness on the economy. Second, and more important, the concept of the overdraft economy penetrated official thinking and influenced reformist ambitions. This was evident not only in the preparation of the Eighth Plan[7] but also in the elaboration of the Metric Model, one of the econometric models developed by the National Institute of Statistics and Economic Studies (Institut National de la Statistique et des Études Économiques, INSEE), whose description of financial and monetary behavior closely paralleled the behavior of the overdraft economy.[8]

FRANCE AS AN OVERDRAFT ECONOMY

The concept of the overdraft economy accurately describes France's political economy prior to the reforms of the mid-1980s. French economic agents, especially industrial investors, showed a marked preference for institutional borrowing. In the France of the mid-1970s, 85 percent of all credits allocated to firms and households were accorded

---

Flammarion, 1982). Pierre Salin, *L'ordre monétaire mondial* (Paris: Presses Universitaires de France, 1982), is a supplementary example of a French economist who turns to the classical continental tradition for criticism of expansionist monetary policy, in his case to the economic philosophy of Friedrich Hayek.

[6]Jean Denizet, *Monnaie et financement dans les années 80* (Paris: Dunod, 1982), pp. 288–90.

[7]See Commissariat Général du Plan, *Crédit, change, et inflation, Rapport du Groupe d'Économie Monétaire Appliquée: Annexes* (Paris: La Documentation Française, 1979), pp. 219–22.

[8]P. Artus et al., *Présentation et multiplicateurs du modèle Métric base 71* (Paris: INSEE, Service de la conjoncture, Division des Comptes Trimestriels, 1979), note 341.

Table 6. Sources of credit to the economy, 1976 (% of all credit)

	France	Germany	U.K.	Netherlands	Japan	U.S.
Institutional lenders	85	86	58	80	68	51
Financial market	15	14	42	20	32	49

Source: Jean-Pierre Patat, *Monnaie, institutions financières, et politique monétaire* (Paris: Economica, 1982), p. 223. Used by permission of the publisher.

by banks or some other financial institution (see Table 6), as opposed to 51 percent in the United States.[9] Although Germany also showed a high level of intermediation by financial institutions, German banks themselves acquired nearly one-fifth of their capital on the bond market and another 10 percent on the stock market, but in France banks acquired only a small percentage of their capital on the financial market. For this reason, the role of the financial market is much greater in Germany than Table 6 suggests. It is not surprising that the French financial market was among the narrowest in the Western world. The value of bonds and stocks as a proportion of gross domestic product was 28.5 percent in 1980, compared with 116 percent in the United States and 144 percent in Great Britain.[10] In Sweden, a country that exhibited some similarities with France, this proportion, at 36 percent, was nevertheless higher.

Numerous and closely interrelated factors explain the importance of financial intermediation by lending institutions in France. First, the financial position of French firms was weak. Business savings, as a proportion of gross fixed capital formation, was 73 percent in 1970–72 and fell to 62 percent in 1975–77.[11] Second, institutional investors, such as insurance companies, retirement funds, and banks, did not play the active financial role in France that they played in other countries. Insurance companies, though purchasers of 18 percent of newly issued stock in 1980, were still in a state of relative financial underdevelopment in France.[12] As for retirement funds, they generally redistributed the funds they collected without investing them. Banks, which one would

[9]On the other hand, the level of indebtedness in France is not excessive in absolute terms. See *Crédit, change, et inflation*, pp. 155–63. See also Robert Raymond, "Strutture finanziare, stabilità economica e allocazione delle resorse: Il caso della Francia," *Bancaria* 37 (October 1981).

[10]See Patat, *Monnaie*, p. 224.

[11]C. Gros, "L'investissement industriel en France: Son évolution, son financement," *Bulletin du Crédit National* 8 (2ᵉ trimestre 1980).

[12]Patat, *Monnaie*, p. 142.

Table 7. Bonds as percentage of total bank balances, 1979

	France	Germany	Italy	U.K.	U.S.	Japan
Bonds held by banks	0.3	9.3	27.1	2.6	22.4	18.0
Bonds issued by banks	3.1	17.1	0	0.5	0.5	11.1

Source: Jean-Pierre Patat, *Monnaie, institutions financières, et politique monétaire* (Paris: Economica, 1982), p. 230. Used by permission of the publisher.

expect to have played a more active role in bringing together the financial market and the notoriously suspicious French investor, remained comparatively aloof. Table 7 reveals the sharp contrast that existed at the end of the 1970s between the banks of France on the one hand and those of the United States and Japan (net buyers of bonds) on the other hand, as well as the contrast with German banks, important issuers of bonds. French banks traditionally confined their activity to the collection of liquid savings and the distribution of credit. Though the government promoted the creation of investment clubs and trust funds managed by the banks in an effort to breathe life into the financial market, these accounted for only 5 to 10 percent of bond and stock purchases by the end of the decade.[13]

Third, French savings, though abundant, were highly liquid. At 20.4 percent, France's rate of consumer savings in 1978 (the proportion of disposable income not spent on consumer goods) was, at the end of the decade, surpassed only by that of Japan (20.8 percent) and Italy (29.2 percent) among the largest OECD economies, and was significantly higher than that of the financially more powerful economies of Great Britain (12.6 percent) and Germany (12.0 percent). On the other hand, nearly three-fourths of household and business savings in France was liquid,

Table 8. Savings of households and firms deposited in liquid accounts and invested in stocks and bonds, as percentage of total savings (average flows, 1973–1977)

	France	U.S.	U.K.	Germany
Deposited in liquid accounts	72.2	42.7	45.5	46.7
Invested in stocks and bonds	27.8	57.3	54.5	53.3

Source: Jean-Pierre Patat, *Monnaie, institutions financières, et politique monétaire* (Paris: Economica, 1982), p. 234. Used by permission of the publisher.

[13]See Maurice Laure, "Différences, y compris de fiscalité, entre les systèmes financiers britannique et français," *Banque* 312 (November 1972).

as opposed to about half in the other countries (see Table 8). Because of the liquidity of French savings, banks were called on to mediate between savers and investors by "transforming" short-term savings into longer-term credit, complicating the process of adjustment between savings and investment.[14] The simple fact that "the banks [in an overdraft economy] place a screen between lenders and borrowers complicates the adjustment between savings and investment," argued Maarek, because the banks must "anticipate upon a level of savings that is not yet constituted."[15]

Fourth, fiscal and monetary policy both contributed to the comparative atrophy of the French financial market—fiscal policy by being too conservative, and monetary policy by being too liberal. In the mid-1960s, there reigned in France a spirit of fiscal orthodoxy that caused the state's budget deficits to be cut to next to nothing (see Chapter Six). This had the effect of depriving both the financial market and French firms of an easily redeemed and potentially widely demanded asset, the treasury bill. The finance committee of the Eighth Plan complained that "the policy of reducing the public debt [had] led to a significant decline in the treasury's contribution to the creation of money. This evolution, of praiseworthy appearance, had an important consequence. ... It weakened the market for treasury bonds and public bills."[16] The state's own liquidity needs were satisfied by the Banque de France, which monetized the debt, and by the Deposit and Consignment Bank (Caisse des Dépots et des Consignations), which, because it managed the accounts of local government, state savings institutions, and other public and parapublic collectors of savings, could supply funds to the state taken from real constituted savings (see Chapter Five). Bonds were rarely issued to the public. Though banks bought treasury bills, they generally redeemed them at the Banque de France and rarely held them as a portfolio asset.[17]

Interest rate policy also conspired to inhibit the growth of the French financial market, not because it was conservative but because it was generous. By using its pervasive power over financial activity to keep interest rates low and credit plentiful and thus promote investment, the French government had, prior to the 1970s, given industry little cause to concern itself over money. Bank loans at low rates were easy to come

[14]See M. F. Masféty-Klein, "Quand les français épargnent," *Regards sur l'Actualité* 30 (April 1977); J. -F. Akar, "L'épargne pour l'investissement industriel," *CNPF Patronat* 361 (July 1975). See also P. Berger, "Les problèmes de l'épargne," *Bulletin Trimestriel de la Banque de France* 13 (November 1974).

[15]Maarek, "Monnaie et inflation," p. 111.

[16]*Crédit, change, et inflation: Annexes*, p. 241. See also Guillaumont-Jeanneney, *Pour la politique monétaire*, p. 225; Maarek, "Monnaie et inflation," pp. 95–96.

[17]See Antoine Coutière, *Le système monétaire français* (Paris: Economica, 1982), p. 118; *Crédit, change, et inflation: Annexes*, p. 241.

by, and firms had little incentive to address their needs to the financial market by issuing bonds or stocks.

MONETARY POLICY IN THE OVERDRAFT ECONOMY, IN THEORY

The concept of the overdraft economy was used by Hicks to theorize that monetary policy could under certain conditions be an effective instrument for regulating aggregate demand. The contrary argument, that monetary policy was relatively ineffective ("the lesson that fiscalists have so largely drawn from Keynes"), was, Hicks contended, valid only in the case of asset-based economies. In the asset-based economy, declines in the level of interest rates often failed to incite businessmen to exchange liquid assets for nonliquid assets (that is, to make a real investment) because they occurred at times when doubts about the future availability of liquidity were widespread, encouraging firms to hold tight to whatever liquid assets they possessed. Conversely, restrictive monetary policies, designed to discourage investment, also failed when firms held assets in their reserves that were readily exchanged for cash, allowing firms to maintain a tolerable level of liquidity over a long period of time and thus to test the government's commitment and patience by obliging it to pursue its restrictive policy for many months. On the other hand, Hicks reasoned, monetary policy could be used with great effectiveness in the overdraft economy.[18] Because agents expect that liquidity can by definition be had for the asking, the only significant variable affecting the demand for money is its price. If the government were to force the level of interest rates below that of expected returns on investment, then real investment would increase and the economy would expand (and vice versa).

Ironically, France's experience with the overdraft economy led most French theorists to quite the opposite conclusion. The overdraft economy, they argued, made it relatively more difficult, rather than less difficult, to regulate economic activity through monetary policy. We examine this theoretical argument first and then identify more concretely the constraints that the overdraft economy imposed on policy.

The French economists who introduced the concept of the overdraft economy into the literature did so chiefly because they believed it explained the French economy's susceptibility to inflation, especially under floating exchange rates. The concept of the overdraft economy had ramifications that Hicks's brief treatment did not explore. Textbook theory depicts the money supply as basically an exogenous,

[18]Hicks, *Crisis*, pp. 50–54.

policy-dependent variable. If demand for credit increases in the asset-based economy because of an increase in overall economic activity, the price of credit is eventually bid up to levels at which demand levels off—at which point the market for credit, in the venerable imagery of the economist, is presumed to "clear." In the overdraft economy, however, the money supply grows at a rate that varies directly as a function of economic activity. Because the overdraft economy is characterized by the presumption that borrowing power is assured, a rise in the price of credit induced by accelerating economic activity only provokes economic agents to meet the higher cost of credit by incurring more debt. In other words, the institutionally based overdraft economy lacks a market mechanism to slow monetary expansion. Borrowers, since they are not discouraged from borrowing by the higher cost of credit, must be turned away from the bank window by administrative fiat if credit expansion is to be stopped.[19] In the absence of administrative rationing of credit, the supply of money becomes an endogenous rather than an exogenous variable—that is, the supply of money becomes a positive function of nominal economic activity, and a negative function of the desire to save.[20] An economy that corresponds to this model is, of course, threatened with a chronic overabundance of money.[21] "In an overdraft economy," writes Gérard Maarek, "monetary

[19]There is evidence that interest rates in France may have varied *inversely* with the level of activity. Because credit supply was an administered and not a market-determined quantity, its cost depended, as mentioned above, on what it cost the banks to supply it to the rest of the economy, which in turn depended on the price at which the central bank refinanced loans and on the operating costs of the banks. It is reasonable to assume that the unit operating costs of supplying credit decreased as the volume of credit increased, if only because the costs of bank administration, assumed to remain constant, were spread over a larger number of loans. In other words, when the central bank's intervention rate was held constant, the unit cost of supplying credit increased as demand sagged. In that case, banks may have raised their interest rates as demand for credit fell in order to maintain their profit margin, and may have lowered their rates as demand picked up. Empirical studies of France indicate that such economies of scale did exist and that this perverse movement in interest rates could have come into play. Under this hypothesis, there was nothing in the system to prevent a vicious circle whereby adjustments in interest rates would have exacerbated rather than allayed an upward or downward evolution in the level of economic activity unless monetary authorities intervened. See Lacoue-Labarthe, *Analyse monétaire*, pp. 406–17; Louis and Vivien Lévy-Garboua, "Les coûts opératoires des banques françaises: Une étude statistique," *Revue d'Économie Politique* 85 (January–February 1975); V. Lévy-Garboua and F. Renaud, "Structures et rentabilité des banques," *Banque* 365 (September, 1977). See also Pierre Coupaye, *Les banques en France* (Paris: La Documentation Française, 1984).

[20]See Lacoue-Labarthe, *Analyse monétaire*, pp. 412-13. Because the demand for money is satisfied by credit, it results in no portfolio decisions by firms and households, in contrast to the stipulations of most models. Models of the overdraft economy dispense with the demand function for money altogether.

[21]See Patat, *Monnaie*, p. 235.

equilibrium is obtained only if the money created by the banks as they distribute credit is accepted as part of real balances—in other words, if the intention of firms to invest coincides with the desire of households to save."[22]

Building on this simple representation of monetary growth, theorists of the overdraft economy developed an explanation for France's endemic inflationary bias that privileged monetary factors and conversely downplayed the importance of supply-side factors, such as wages and the cost of resources.[23] Of singular importance among these monetary factors was the aggravation of currency instability under the system of floating exchange rates, as described in the previous chapter, to which, it was claimed, the overdraft economy was more vulnerable than the asset-based economy. In both the overdraft and asset-based economies, if the currency depreciates because an increase in domestic demand for imports has resulted in a commercial deficit, and domestic consumers

[22]Maarek, "Monnaie et inflation," p. 111.

[23]Their arguments are found in *Crédit, change, et inflation*. The causes of inflation in France were, it goes without saying, subject to intense debate. Jean Denizet argues that inflated interest rates were a principal cause of inflation in France. Though his interest in indebtedness echoes that of the overdraft economy theorists, his analysis led to radically different prescriptions. The former sought to reform financial structures and practices to increase the effectiveness of monetary policy, but he would like to see monetary policy play a more passive role. Given the indebtedness of French firms, Denizet argues that monetary policy should be supportive, a prescription that makes him very critical of the current exchange rate regime, which requires most countries to pursue restrictive monetary policies in order to avoid currency depreciation. See Denizet, *Monnaie*, pp. 176–82, and rebuttal in *Crédit, change, et inflation: Annexes*, p. 240. For other interpretations of inflation in France, see J.-P. Mockers, *L'inflation en France, 1945–75* (Paris: Éditions Cujas, 1975), pp. 257–91; Guillaumont-Jeanneney, *Pour la politique monétaire*, pp. 148–57, M. Déméocq and S. Guillaumont-Jeanneney, "Les relations entre monnaie et salaires dans l'économie française," *Annales Economiques* 2 (June 1974). Michel Crouhy and Jacques Mélitz, "Faut-il rejeter les thèses traditionnelles de l'inflation?" (Centre d'Enseignement Supérieur des Affaires de Jouy-en-Josas, contrat no. 72/1977, Mimeographed), and A. Fourçans and M. Fratianni, "Cost Push vs. Excessive Demand: Explanations of Inflation in France, 1960–1973," in *European Financial Association, Proceedings, 1975* (New York and Amsterdam: North Holland, 1975), emphasize the importance of supply-side factors such as wages, the cost of resources, and interest rates. See also colloquium, "Approches de l'inflation," organized by the Centre d'Études Prospectives d'Économie Mathématique Appliquée (CEPREMAP), March 22, 1978 (Mimeographed); and *Économie et Statistique: Inflation* 77 (April 1976). A monetarist interpretation of inflation in France can be found in A. Fourçans, "Le dynamique inflationniste et les impulsions économiques: Une analyse de l'expérience française," in CEPREMAP, "Approches de l'inflation," and in Fourçans, *La politique de la monnaie* (Paris: Economica, 1976). Overdraft economy theorists would consent to aspects of the monetarist explanation but underscore the importance of financial structures in explaining monetary growth itself. As for supply-side explanations, overdraft economy theorists would argue that one of the principal supply-side factors of inflation—wage inflation, abetted by the inflationary expectations of workers and their unions—has existed only because rapid monetary growth, typical of the overdraft economy, has allowed it to exist.

must therefore pay higher prices for imported goods, the demand for money increases. In the asset-based economy, however, this produces an increase in the volume of securities offered for sale on the financial market, which in turn provokes a fall in yields and a rise in interest rates, which in turn increases demand for interest-bearing assets and dampens consumer demand and therefore investor demand, returning the economy to equilibrium. In the overdraft economy, the resulting increase in the domestic prices of imported goods does not lead as readily to a reduction in consumer or investment demand, because, barring administrative intervention, the increased demand for money is satisfied by an increase in the supply of credit. Indeed, if the fall in the exchange rate of the currency increases foreign demand for domestic goods, this can further stimulate investment and thus further increase the demand for money. Describing the results of his initial efforts to simulate the behavior of the French overdraft economy under the system of flexible exchange rates, Lévy-Garboua concludes:

> Every simulation reveals a tendency toward instability under floating exchange rates. The results are robust when specifications of the numerical value of the parameters are modified. They do not stem from the "real" components of the model and cannot be observed under the hypothesis of a closed economy or fixed exchange rates. It does not depend on the hypothesis made for the "critical" elasticities—that is, the sensitivity of the trade balance to factors of competitiveness. In other words, in an overdraft economy, one sees cumulative effects develop which are due to the interaction of the specificities of the exchange rate regime and the financial system.[24]

THE OVERDRAFT ECONOMY AS PRACTICAL POLICY
CONSTRAINT

The theoretical claim that the overdraft economy is inherently more vulnerable to currency instability than the asset-based economy is a controversial one. It is important to the argument developed here to the extent that it acquaints us with the debate surrounding French finance and thus invites us to examine more thoroughly French financial structures, institutions, and practices as they existed prior to reform. In doing so we can observe how poorly tooled the French political economy actually was when it came to combating the monetary instability induced by floating rates, and how real were the constraints

---

[24]*Crédit, change, et inflation*, p. 232. See also V. Lévy-Garboua, H. Sterdyniak, G. Oudiz, and P. Villa, "Change, inflation, et intérêt: Un modèle," *Revue Économique* 29 (September 1978).

on policy that the theorists of the overdraft economy described and tried to capture in their models. The French overdraft economy, with its characteristic pyramid of credit extending from the Banque de France to the individual firm, its atrophied market for financial and monetary assets, and its institutional and behavioral legacy of having encouraged, through an ambitious and generous industrial policy, unrealistic expectations on the part of firms regarding the availability of credit, effectively tied the hands of the monetary policymaker. For the purposes of this book, the concept of the overdraft economy refers to no mere abstract model susceptible to discussion only by economists, but rather to a concrete and well-documented set of institutions, processes, and expectations that invite political analysis.[25]

The constraints the overdraft economy imposed on French policy become apparent when one compares how policy was implemented in France and how it is implemented in asset-based economies, such as one finds in Germany or the United States. Take, for example, the use of rediscount policy, and compare French practice with German practice. The German Bundesbank uses rediscount policy effectively to target the rate of growth of the economy's monetary base (the sum of all currency in circulation and the reserves of the banks). Such targeting, however, assumes that growth in the money supply varies directly as a function of growth in the monetary base. This function is called the multiplier of credit and is thought to be relatively stable. In other words, the financial activity of the banks should increase in a predictable manner as their reserves increase and should diminish as their reserves decrease. Hence, the volume of money injected into the economy can be controlled by regulating the reserves available to individual banks. The Bundesbank, as "banker of last resort," extends loans to individual banks, in general against some form of collateral such as public securities or commercial paper. By placing limits on its assistance, it regulates the growth of bank reserves and thus effectively constrains the ability of banks to accord new credits to firms or to individuals.

Compare this with France, where rediscount policy, as practiced throughout the 1950s and 1960s, encountered two fundamental problems. First, it could not be assumed that the multiplier of credit in France was stable. It was not even certain whether the multiplier of credit existed. In the French overdraft economy, the banks were structurally indebted to the central bank and did not dispose of free

[25]See Thierry Chauveau and Henri Pagès, "Une économie d'endettement, est-elle instable?" *Cahiers Économiques et Monetaires* 21 (Paris: Banque de France, Direction Générale des Études, 1986), who conclude that the asset-based and overdraft economies display instability under similar conditions and that consequently the thesis that the overdraft economy is somehow "unique" is overstated.

Table 9. Composition (in %) of central bank assets, c. 1979

	France	Germany	U.S.	U.K.
Reserve operations (gold and currency)	32	67	12	36
Treasury financing	13	13	81	64
Bank refinancing	45	17	—	—

Source: Jean-Pierre Patat, *Monnaie, institutions financières, et politique monétaire* (Paris: Economica, 1982), p. 269. Used by permission of the publisher.

reserves. In contrast to the central banks of the United States and Great Britain, whose assets are composed primarily of public debt, and in contrast to the central bank of Germany, whose assets are composed primarily of foreign debt, the assets of the Banque de France are composed primarily of debt owed by French banks (see Table 9). This is no accident, but rather the logical consequence of the importance that institutionally allocated credit assumed in the overdraft economy. Bank indebtedness vis-à-vis the Banque de France constitutes the mirror image of the indebtedness of the economy as a whole vis-à-vis the banks and other credit institutions. "Once bank credit is—as in France—the source of 80 percent of monetary creation," explains Lévy-Garboua, "the banks are of necessity indebted to the central bank.... The larger the proportion of bank credit, the less difference there is between liquidity held by nonfinancial agents and the volume of credit that is distributed. Because bank deposits are only a fraction of this liquidity (if only because agents want to hold some currency, and banks must respect their reserve requirements), it becomes inevitable that they distribute more credit than they can cover, and hence that they will come to require refinancing."[26] Given this level of bank indebtedness, an increase in the supply of reserve assets was typically used to pay off a part of the banks' debts to the Banque de France. There was thus no guarantee that an increase in reserve assets would result in increased lending activity by the banks, and consequently provide a monetary stimulus to the economy. Conversely, restricting the supply of central bank money to the banks (for example, by limiting central bank interventions on the money market, on which see below) merely incited the banks to increase their level of indebtedness.[27] Hence, within the

[26]*Crédit, change, et inflation*, p. 241.

[27]See Michel Pébereau, "Les instruments de la politique économique," in André de Lattre and Daniel Deguen, *La politique économique de la France*, part 1, vol. 2 (Paris: Les Cours de Droit, 1982–83), p. 247. For a survey of attempts to calculate the credit multiplier for France, see Guillaumont-Jeanneney, *Pour la politique monétaire*, pp. 234–54. See also P. Frochen and G. Maarek, "Réflexions sur le concept de base monétaire en France," *Cahiers Économiques et Monétaires* 11 (Paris: Banque de France, Direction Générale des Études, 1980) and Jacques-Henri David, *La monnaie et la politique monétaire*, 2d ed. (Paris: Economica, 1986), pp. 137–41; esp. pp. 140–41.

constraints determined by rediscount policy, it was the banks alone that determined the volume of refinancing that they required, and consequently the level of their lending activity. The use of credit policy to stimulate growth in certain sectors of the economy, such as housing and exporting, aggravated the problem. Medium-term credits to such sectors were frequently exempted from discount ceilings altogether.

Bank indebtedness not only played havoc with the multiplier of credit, but also prohibited the Banque de France from using rediscount policy to impose effective discipline on French banks. Rediscounting is an individualized sort of assistance that the central bank makes available to the banking system. In the French system, however, banks were more dependent on this type of individualized assistance than in Germany. The reason for this higher degree of dependence resided in the relatively atrophied state of the market for financial and monetary assets in France, as a consequence of which bank reserves were composed primarily of nonmarketable private paper (short-term commercial debt) that could by law be sold only to other banks or be rediscounted at the Banque de France. The Banque de France, one imagines, could have exploited bank dependence very effectively to implement a monetary policy of its choosing. However, bank dependence did not translate into central bank power. Again, the comparison with Germany is instructive. German banks, because they support their lending activity with reserves composed of anonymous marketable assets, are not as dependent on central bank refinancing as their French counterparts. Subsequently, the Bundesbank has fewer scruples about holding a German bank to its rediscount ceiling. Because the German bank's financial health is not as dependent on Bundesbank policy, the Bundesbank bears less responsibility for a bank's failure than its French counterpart would, and subsequently is less reticent about putting a delinquent bank in peril. The Banque de France, in contrast, assumed greater responsibility for the well-being of France's banks and for this reason was held accountable. The dependence of French banks on rediscounting was such that any credible use of ceilings threatened them with failure. In France's overdraft economy, the more active and restrictive use of rediscount policy was a political liability. "It is rather a paradox," writes Antoine Coutière, "that the central bank, too powerful if it refuses to intervene, never has the possibility to use this power."[28] Coutière's sentiment was echoed by a senior banking official who stated candidly, "The Germans, to keep their banks in line, do not hesitate to sink one now and then. In France, this simply would not be tolerated."[29]

[28]Coutière, *Système*, pp. 81, 173. See also Patat, *Monnaie*, pp. 271–72.

[29]Personal interview conducted in June 1983. A final complaint concerning rediscount policy was that it was not very flexible. See Patat, *Monnaie*, pp. 298–99, Commissariat

Turning now to the comparison with central bank practices in the United States, one discovers other constraints on the ability of the French to impose monetary rigor on their economy. The Federal Reserve Board regulates money supply growth by buying and selling monetary assets on the money market, thus affecting the price the banks pay for reserve assets and consequently the price banks charge for credit. Such a policy is possible in the United States, where there is a large and flourishing money market on which treasury bonds and other instruments of public debt can be bought and sold by banks, other financial institutions, households, and businesses as their short-term needs for liquidity fluctuate. If the Federal Reserve Board seeks to slow the growth of the money supply or to dampen aggregate demand by pushing interest rates higher, it reduces the volume of its bond purchases, thereby occasioning a fall in the price of bonds and a rise in their yield. Buyers shift from money to bonds in anticipation of higher yields. This causes bank reserves to fall, thus inciting the banks themselves to sell bonds at disadvantageous prices in order to reconstitute their reserves and to compensate for the higher cost of money by raising the interest rates they charge on loans. Thus, by varying its purchases of public debt, the Federal Reserve System exercises significant leverage over aggregate demand in the economy.

In France, by contrast, because of the atrophied state of its market for financial and monetary assets, there simply did not exist an equivalent open market for public bonds and titles until the reform of the money market in 1984. The term "money market" applied only to an interbank market for commercial paper. Though the Banque de France did intervene on this market in order to influence bank activity, the form that intervention assumed differed little from rediscount policy and thus displayed the same limitations. Intervention on this money market occurred as follows: as banks extended credit to particulars, they had to ensure that their own reserves of liquidity were adequate to meet newly created claims. Therefore, subsequent to an increase in credit outlays, banks sought to increase their reserves of liquid assets by exchanging commercial paper with other banks (as well as some public debt, the circulation of which was limited by law to financial institutions). But because the interbank market was insufficient to meet their

---

Général du Plan, *Préparation du Huitième Plan: Annexes*, pp. 180–81. Rediscount policy could not be used, for example, to react effectively to events on the currency market. Discount ceilings gave the central bank little discretionary control over monetary growth, for as long as a bank did not exceed its ceiling, the central bank could not refuse its collaboration. In the 1960s, mounting external pressures on monetary policy caused the French to supplement rediscount policy with a more flexible "money market" policy, described below. See David, *La monnaie*, pp. 261–63.

needs, banks were obliged to address some of their demand for liquidity to the Banque de France. In its efforts to control bank activity, the Banque de France, employing a technique called the *mise en pension* (repurchase agreement) intervened on this interbank market somewhat in the manner of a pawnshop, buying commercial paper and other rediscountable bills from the banks, leaving the banks with the option of repurchasing them on demand.[30] Like the pawnshop, the central bank set the price at which it accepted bills for rediscount. The banks were left either to acquiesce and accept the central bank's offer, or to withhold their bills in anticipation of a rise in the central bank's offered price.[31] The *mise en pension* was designed not so much to influence aggregate demand by influencing the price of money as to complement rediscount policy with an instrument that gave monetary policy greater flexibility and responsiveness. It allowed the central bank to vary the price of its purchases more easily and to time its purchase offers in a way that fostered greater bank discipline by periodically withholding reserve assets. The *mise en pension* was a more flexible instrument than rediscount policy, but not a conceptually different instrument. Money market policy as practiced in France was subsequently quite unlike open market policy as practiced in the United States. Moreover, as a more sophisticated form of rediscount policy, it labored under the same burden of bank indebtedness that crippled rediscount policy and that denied it the power to place rigorous restrictions on bank activity.

In addition to the absence of an open market, there were other structural obstacles that prevented French officials from using interest rates to influence aggregate demand or money supply growth. The Byzantine structure of the French banking system was one of these, and one of the most frequently cited by advocates of financial reform. Credit was allocated not only by banks but also by a whole array of relatively specialized semipublic financial institutions that operated under special statutes and that benefited from a diversity of legal privileges. While the banking system became deeply indebted to the Banque de France, these specialized institutions, such as the Crédit Agricole and the Crédit Mutuel, were able to accumulate important liquid balances. At the other end of the spectrum, business banks and financial institutions that did not manage sight deposits were burdened by the threat of overextension. The large nationalized deposit banks

---

[30]In this case, rediscountable medium-term debt was the more typical collateral.

[31]Banque de France, Service de l'Information, "Le marché monétaire en France," *Problèmes Économiques,* July 31, 1974; Patat, *Monnaie,* pp. 147–54. See also Claude Chérief, "Il mercato monetario in Francia," *Bancaria* 30 (July 1974); Jacques Mélitz, "Une tentative d'explication de l'offre de monnaie en France," *Revue Économique* 24 (September 1973). David, *La monnaie,* pp. 155–65.

were in an intermediate position—sometimes in deficit, sometimes in surplus. Consequently, French financial institutions displayed unequal levels of dependence on the money market and on rediscounting by the central bank, and thus displayed varying degrees of vulnerability to shifts in interest rates. French monetary officials shied away from pursuing a more active interest rate policy, in part because of the distortion it would introduce into financial structures, and through them into the economy as a whole. Certain privileged sectors would have gained, while others would have lost.[32]

The final obstacle to a more active interest rate policy was the vulnerability of the French firm to policies of monetary rigor. Although Hicks originally theorized that the overdraft economy would prove more responsive to interest rate policy than the asset-based economy, a number of observers contended that the high level of indebtedness of French firms, coupled with their lack of reserve assets, made them so vulnerable to monetary policy that the more rigorous use of interest rate policy was perilous.[33] "The considerable degree of indebtedness of French firms to banks," the finance committee of the Eighth Plan observed, "creates fears concerning the repercussions of a substantial and prolonged rise in the basic rate (several percentage points over several months) on their costs and on their financial situation. In fact, this rise would apply not only to new credits but also to debts accumulated in the past (for example, an overdraft in a bank)."[34] Concern for the financial health of French firms was justified not only by the firms' position at the base of an immense pyramid of credit, extending

---

[32]Literature on this subject is voluminous. See Patat, *Monnaie*, pp. 39–58, 71–98, 148–49, p. 238–46; J.-H. David, "Les limites du contrôle monétaire," *Banque* 366 (October 1977); *Préparation du Huitième Plan: Annexes*, p. 182; "Banques: Comment ils exercent leur pouvoir," *Nouvel Observateur*, September 18 and 25, 1978; Vivian Lewis, "The Sleeping Giant of French Banking," *The Banker* 129 (May 1979). A complete analysis of the French banking system would take into account the treasury's contribution to money supply growth. See P. Biacabe, "Quelle réforme pour le système monétaire français?" *Banque* 396 (June 1980); Patat, *Monnaie*, pp. 102–8; Guillaumont-Jeanneney, *Pour la politique monétaire*, p. 236; François Eck, *Le trésor* (Paris: Presses Universitaires de France, 1982).

[33]More faithful to Hick's thesis, however, are Guillaumont-Jeanneney, *Pour la politique monétaire*, pp. 257–64; and Lacoue-Labarthe, *Analyse monétaire*, p. 426.

[34]*Préparation du Huitième Plan: Annexes*, p. 183. On the indebtedness of French firms and the constraint indebtedness imposes on monetary policy, see Françoise Bourdon and Hach Sok, *Tableaux des opérations financières et endettement des entreprises par secteur, 1959–1976* (Paris: Economica, 1983); R. Brocard, S. Ghesquière, and B. Micha, "La place et le rôle du crédit bancaire dans le financement des entreprises industrielles françaises," *Cahiers Économiques et Monétaires* 12 (Paris: Banque de France, Direction Générale des Études, 1981); Raymond Penaud and François Gaudichet, *Sélectivité du crédit, financement, politique monétaire* (Paris: Economica, 1985), pp. 96–104; Michel Pébereau, *La politique économique de la France: Les instruments* (Paris: Armand Colin, 1985), pp. 195–200; David, *La monnaie*, p. 248.

upward through the banking system to the Banque de France itself, but also by the firms' strategic position as purveyors of social welfare. During the 1960s, French firms had replaced the state as principal contributors to a whole host of social insurance programs—for example, health insurance programs, unemployment funds, retirement programs, adult education programs, and public housing programs (see Chapter Six). *Prélèvements obligatoires*—that is, public levies on business earnings—are thus higher in France than in any other major OECD country. To provoke the bankruptcy of a firm is therefore equivalent to diminishing financial support for social policy.

It might seem that the fear provoked by the firms' vulnerability to policies of rigor would contradict the hypothesis that, in the overdraft economy, incremental adjustments in policy had little impact because of the agent's presumption of assured borrowing power. The contradiction is one of appearance only, for together the two observations suggest that interest rate policy, if used with caution, accomplished nothing, but that if it was used with authority it threatened the economy with collapse. The two observations are complementary, not contradictory.

The concept of the overdraft economy, when made concrete by incorporating observations of the institutions and structures that sustained it, explains why payments adjustment through internal policies and mechanisms was so difficult to achieve in France.[35] Bank indebtedness, the absence of an open market, compartmentalization of financial structures, and the aggregate level of indebtedness of the economy as a whole tied the hands of the monetary policymaker. Given the constraints that the overdraft economy placed on monetary policy, France's preference for a more interventionist and administrative form of monetary regulation becomes understandable.

THE OVERDRAFT ECONOMY AS EXPLANATION OF FRENCH POLICY

One can now understand better why the French were so attracted to the prospect of using the state's interventionist powers to "prolong" the process of adjusting to the supply shocks. Even ignoring the structural

[35]The French were able to overcome some of these difficulties by supplementing interest rate policy with a reserve requirement policy. See Patat, *Monnaie*, pp. 284–87. By varying the volume of reserve assets banks were required to keep on account with the central bank, officials were able to influence the cost to the banks of refinancing their operations. This gave them a greater degree of liberty in setting interest rates. Nevertheless, reserve requirements ultimately suffered from the same limitations as the other policy instruments. After 1976, reserve requirements were liberalized to the point of

obstacles that the French financial system placed in the way of monetary rigor, the prospect of subjecting the French economy to such a policy could not have been an appealing one, given the indebtedness of French firms and their lack of precautionary savings. Foreign borrowing offered a temporary haven, enabling the state to finance the economy while maintaining upward pressure on the exchange rate. Unfortunately, the advantages of foreign borrowing were short-lived. *Encadrement du crédit*, on the other hand, seemed to offer a more promising way out of the policy dilemmas of the 1970s. Here, it was thought, was an instrument that gave policymakers the power to regulate the growth of the money supply effectively and, moreover, to assign interest rate policy entirely to the task of stabilizing the exchange rate because it unlinked the supply of credit from its price.[36] Finally, by exempting export industries from *encadrement*, French officials could assure them they would have the capital they needed to invest in ways that would improve their competitiveness and yet respect the exchange rate constraint. The constraints imposed on policy by the overdraft economy were such that policymakers hesitated to return to the more orthodox policy of managing aggregate demand through a more active interest rate policy even when financial interventionism began to reveal its drawbacks and weaknesses. The reflections contained in the report of the finance committee of the Eighth Plan are revealing in this regard. Though the financial experts concurred that it was desirable to suppress *encadrement du crédit*, such a move depended on the possibility of implementing "substitution techniques immediately that would be just as effective [in containing the rate of growth of the money supply]. However, given the present state of our financial structures, recourse to such techniques would be hazardous."[37]

The policy of prolonged adjustment was doomed to fail. Despite the implementation of sophisticated interventionist techniques, France was, with the exception of Italy, the country in which liquidity continued to grow at the fastest pace.[38] Credit expansion remained the principle source of rapid liquidity growth. Though the policies adopted by Raymond Barre did succeed in slowing the growth of liquidity somewhat, there was nevertheless growing awareness that France's peculiar financial structures placed real limits on the power of the government to achieve the sort of internal monetary stability that external condi-

---

becoming nonexistent. The burden of regulating activity and the money supply fell almost entirely on administrative restrictions on the growth of credit.

[36]See *Crédit, change, et inflation*, pp. 239, 234. See also *Préparation du Huitième Plan: Annexes*, pp. 173–77.

[37]*Préparation du Huitième Plan*, p. 33.

[38]Ibid.

tions required. "The expansion of liquidity," one reads in the report of the finance committee of the Eighth Plan, "is all the more difficult to halt or to slow because, given the insufficiency of long-term savings, a tightening of the money supply can cast doubt on the financing of the firm's investment plans, the greater fraction of which is supplied by bank credit."[39] Because of the financial fragility of France's industry, the state intervened through its network of semipublic financial institutions to provide it with more financial support while it required simultaneously that the banks restrict the growth of credit. It is hard to find a more graphic illustration of the dilemma that confronted French policymakers.

Dissatisfaction with *encadrement* fueled growing interest in reform, but talk of reform was temporarily silenced by the electoral defeat suffered by Valéry Giscard d'Estaing in 1981. When the Socialist government acceded to power, it was confident that *dirigiste* solutions to France's economic difficulties could still be found.[40] Its ambition was to restore planning to a position of preeminence and use it to solve economic problems. The Socialist experience, however, confirmed the existence of policy constraints so overwhelming that the government eventually sought to eliminate them even if it meant sacrificing much of the state's discretionary power over the allocation of credit. Within only a few years, the Socialists were themselves implementing liberalizing reforms that resembled those that had been examined by the previous government—and were doing so after having already pursued for nearly three years a restrictive monetary policy even more rigorous than that of Raymond Barre. Commenting on the fate of the Socialist's *dirigiste* ambitions, Jack Hayward wrote, "Despite the scorn poured on the still-born Eighth Plan [of the conservatives], its Socialist successor was forced to follow it closely, in substance and even in form."[41] Similar constraints had elicited similar responses—in spite of the differences in ideology and constituency that distinguished the two governments.

CONCLUSION

In Chapter One I argued that rigidities in the French political economy hampered the capacity of policymakers to stabilize the economy through internal policies of monetary adjustment, at a time when

[39]Ibid., p. 34.

[40]See Michel Ozenda and Dominique Strauss-Kahn, "French Planning: Decline or Renewal?" in Howard Machin and Vincent Wright, eds., *Economic Policy and Policy-making under the Mitterrand Presidency, 1981–1984* (New York: St. Martin's Press, 1985).

[41]Jack Hayward, in Machin and Wright, eds., *Economic Policy*, p. 114. See also the comment by Diana Green in ibid., pp. 141–42.

change in the international monetary system deprived policymakers of the option of devaluation. If those rigidities cannot be entirely explained by the overdraft economy, it is nevertheless clear that the overdraft economy contributed to their existence. Not only was the overdraft economy biased toward inflation, but it left policymakers ill-tooled to combat the inflationary pressures it tended to generate. Not only did its inherent inflationary bias contribute to trade imbalances, but it hampered efforts to render the French economy more competitive internationally by preventing the Schumpeterian process of "constructive destruction" from taking place, because it slowed the net flow of capital to competitive firms and prolonged the life of noncompetitive firms. Finally, a credit system that assured firms of the cash they needed to retain redundant labor helps explain rigidities in the labor market, which were aggravated by the fact that viscosity in the net flow of capital slowed job creation in rising industries. The following chapter likens French credit policy to a sort of economic insurance program and equates the overdraft economy with "moral hazard." This allows us to understand the overdraft economy's political significance and ramifications, both domestic and international.

CHAPTER THREE

U.S. Hegemony and Moral Hazard

The French overdraft economy, though it had always imposed constraints on policymakers (as will be seen in subsequent chapters), did not become unmanageable until the shift to floating exchange rates deprived the French of the facility of achieving adjustment in trade through devaluation. This suggests that there must be some relationship between the French overdraft economy and the ambient international political economy as structured by U.S. hegemonic leadership in general and by Bretton Woods in particular. The concept of "moral hazard," can describe the nature of that relationship.

"Moral hazard" describes a condition that obtains when economic agents are insured against risk. Under moral hazard, economic behavior is altered by the fact that the agent's incentive to exercise care is diminished. "The very existence of . . . insurance," writes Yair Aharoni, "may reduce the incentives to avoid carelessness and, in extreme cases, create incentives to increase loss."[1] The overdraft economy was the product of credit policies designed to extend a type of financial insurance to certain sectors of the French economy. In other words, "financial insurance" gave rise to the "presumption of assured borrowing power" that characterized the overdraft economy. It is precisely this presumption of assured borrowing power that betrays the fact that moral hazard existed in the French political economy.

This orientation in French credit policy was a response both to the

[1]Yair Aharoni, *The No-Risk Society* (Chatham, N.J.: Chatham House, 1981), pp. 173–91, esp. 173–77; quotation from p. 174. See S. Shavell, "On Moral Hazard and Insurance," *Quarterly Journal of Economics* 93 (November 1979); J. Cassing, "Alternatives to Protectionism," in Irving Leveson and Jimmy W. Wheeler, eds., *Western Economies in Transition* (Boulder, Colo.; Westview Press, 1980).

challenge of rapid change in postwar economic relations and to the opportunity for monetary expansion that American monetary leadership held forth. The international political economy, as ordered by U.S. hegemonic leadership, fostered the generation of moral hazard in the domestic political economy of France. Though moral hazard hampered the capacity of the French political economy to adjust to external shocks, that handicap became a source of preoccupation only when the United States ceased to provide the underpinnings for the system of fixed but adjustable exchange rates that rendered the French overdraft economy viable. This retreat from leadership on the part of the United States compelled the French to liberalize financial structures and practices in order to rid the French economy of moral hazard.

Moral hazard is a condition that describes individual economic behavior. By advancing the claim that there is a link between the structures of international political economy and individual behavior, one is committing to navigate the narrow straits of economic theorizing and rational choice. To avoid sinking on the shoals of abstraction, it is necessary here to recall my claim that this is primarily a work of historical analysis grounded in the metatheoretical conviction that patterns of behavior evolve in historically specific narrative contexts. Consequently, the ambition of the following analysis is not to hypothesize first principles of political conduct, but rather to capture the timeliness of new patterns of behavior, encountered in the overdraft economy, and to explain them with reference to a specific historical event: the construction of the *Pax Americana*. Rational choice is exploited in this analysis for the conceptual clarification it provides. As Russell Hardin observed, "how limited is the value of many of the most technical developments [in rational choice theory] in directly resolving problems and [yet] how great is the conceptual clarification that we have gained from the theories."[2]

THE BASIC FRAMEWORK: MAKING DECISIONS UNDER UNCERTAINTY

The conceptual framework elaborated here builds on the work on economic uncertainty accomplished by the British economist G. L. S. Shackle more than a generation ago.[3] Shackle's work is not frequently

[2]Russell Hardin, "Rational Choice Theories," in Terence Ball, ed., *Idioms of Inquiry: Critique and Renewal in Political Science*, (Albany: SUNY Press, 1987).

[3]See G. L. S. Shackle, *Uncertainty in Economics and Other Essays* (Cambridge: Cambridge University Press, 1955); idem, *Expectation in Economics* (Cambridge: Cambridge University Press, 1949).

evoked today, but it has two characteristics that render it particularly appropriate for the task at hand. First, it conceptualizes decision-making as an activity that occurs within a specific historical context of ambient beliefs and expectations, and second, it conceives of uncertainty in a manner that applies meaningfully to the many one-shot decisions economic agents must make—such as choosing one's profession, making a large fixed investment, or, as Shackle suggested, Napoleon's decision to engage his troops at Waterloo.[4]

Shackle begins with the concept of the "crucial decision." Every person is confronted by a number of critical life decisions concerning such things as the choice of career goals, educational goals, or even place of residence.[5] Such decisions generally involve some rudimentary estimation of cost and benefit. The rationality of that estimation is tempered by the fact that it requires projection into a future that is of course uncertain, and so engages one in a good deal of guess-work. Shackle theorized that individuals, when confronted by uncertainty, base their decisions on two factors: the believability of a given outcome and the attractiveness (or adverseness) of that same outcome. His representation of this calculus is shown in Figure 1, which depicts the economic decision as yielding an infinity of possible outcomes, some of which are more believable than others (believability decreases at extreme values of both loss and gain) and some of which are more attractive, or more unattractive, than others (both characteristics in-

[4]Rational choice models often employ a frequency-ratio concept of probability, a concept based on the mathematical probability that a given outcome will repeat itself in a specifiable number of events and that therefore is more appropriate for analyzing risk (as in the risk of holding a financial asset) than analyzing uncertainty. Shackle's interpretation of decision-making may be of great value for the study of politics because it allows the student to extend some of the insights of portfolio analysis to situations in which outcomes are noniterative and not easily quantifiable.

[5]Modern economics supplies us with a suggestive way to define "crucial decisions." Economists have developed the concept of "expected-lifetime earnings" in an effort to shed light on a well-circumscribed puzzle: the failure of temporary tax increases to alter consumer behavior. If it is assumed that expectations of lifetime earnings rather than current earnings determine consumer behavior, it follows that temporary changes in the tax burden will have little impact on consumer spending because they will have only a small impact on the individual's perceptions of his or her lifetime earnings. This concept also accounts for the fact that individuals maintain a more or less constant level of consumption over the years, even though during their middle years their earning power is much greater than during their youth or old age. People live beyond their means and go into debt when they are young, but they restrict their consumption during their middle years in order to amass the savings needed to see them through retirement. In sum, the propensity to consume or to save is determined by what the individual expects to earn, in real terms, over his or her lifetime. The life-cycle hypothesis of consumption provides the basis for defining "critical choices." Critical decisions, as understood here, are decisions that affect expected real lifetime earnings. See William Branson, *Macroeconomic Theory and Policy* (New York: Harper and Row, 1979), pp. 190–95.

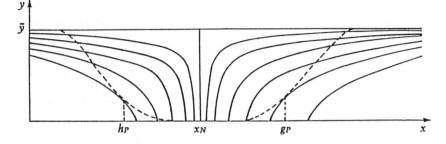

Figure 1. Shackle's representation of decision-making under conditions of uncertainty. Adapted from G. L. S. Shackle, *Uncertainty in Economics and Other Reflexions* (Cambridge: Cambridge University Press, 1955), p. 46, by permission of the publisher. The x-axis represents varying degrees of pleasure produced by different outcomes of some action, such as investing in an asset. Pleasure increases to the right of x_N and decreases to the left. The y-axis represents the degree of potential surprise produced by all possible outcomes, the limit $\bar{y}$ being absolute disbelief. The curve indicated by the discontinuous line represents the actor's assessment of all possible outcomes of a given action, both in terms of the likelihood of a given outcome—its "believability"—and the pleasure that that outcome would procure. This curve intercepts indifference curves indicated by solid lines which represent the *anticipated* pleasure or displeasure of all possible outcomes of all possible actions (anticipated pleasure varying as a positive function of pleasure [x] and a negative function of potential surprise [y]). Shackle reasoned that actors, when deciding whether to pursue a given course of action, focus on those outcomes that produce the greatest degree of anticipated pleasure and displeasure. He refers to these outcomes as "focus loss" (hp in the figure) and "focus gain" (gp in the figure).

crease at extreme values). Outcomes at which the combination of believability and attractiveness (or adverseness) yield optimal values constitute what Shackle calls "focus points." There is a focus point for gain, called "focus gain," and one for loss, called "focus loss." Focus points, he reasoned, are the hypothetical outcomes to which the individual refers while pondering his or her decision.[6]

For example, the young Frenchman of the Jura who is about to make a more or less binding career choice, might be attracted by the potential income offered by the briar pipe industry, yet be concerned about the economic future of such artisanal industries and therefore (depending on his degree of aversity to risk) decide to enter the watchmaking industry—which, though it offers lower wages, seems to provide greater security. During times of significant economic change, however, such as might be occasioned by radical change in international trade patterns, our Frenchman's focus gain and focus loss might suffer a rude shock. New trade agreements might result in a flood of cheap imported watches, threatening the survival of the watchmaking

[6]There is some similarity to Herbert Simon's conceptualization. See Herbert Simon, *Reason in Human Affairs* (Stanford, Calif.: Stanford University Press, 1983), p. 20.

industry in France. In order to adapt to economic change, our subject must therefore shift his focus points to the left and admit that what had earlier been a reasonable job choice was now turning sour. He must realize that if he does not alter his life-style he may face insolvency. Several alternative courses of action suggest themselves. He might, for example, place a greater percentage of his take-home pay into savings in case of a layoff, or he might accept his employer's offer of guaranteed employment at a lower wage. The most attractive course of action, however, is to find a way to break into the briar pipe industry, where incomes are higher and security is now perceived to be greater. But the critical step in all cases is the revision of expectations of gain and loss in response to change. If he is blind to change, he cannot take steps to confront it.

UNCERTAINTY, INSURANCE, AND POLITICAL ACTIVISM

Such responses to change might well occur in the world of the economist, but they are unlikely to occur in France. Though economics has been described as the "dismal science," it is frequently less dismal than the world it seeks to describe. In the event of radical change in the patterns of trade affecting an individual's expectations of lifetime earnings, political struggle is a far more credible response than economic adjustment. Our subject might well choose to participate in an industry-wide strike demanding that the government intervene to save the industry. Factories might be occupied by the striking workers. The workers might even continue to produce watches and sell them on their own, defying the most elementary laws of property and thus challenging the government to intervene and inflict just enough violence to render the whole affair a cause célèbre that sullies its prestige.[7] Economic change takes on a political dimension when individuals, instead of altering their living standard in accordance with new conditions, demand that the state intervene to preserve their focus gains through such policies as trade protection, subsidies, public purchases, or price supports. In other words, the individual frequently demands that the state intervene to provide some form of *insurance,* the function of which is to provide sufficient compensation for economic loss to ensure that his focus points do not depreciate.

What is insurance, and how does the state provide it? In Figure 2, the individual's situation is likened to that of holding a risky asset, A. Insurance diminishes or negates the material risk incurred by holding

[7] The storyline is inspired by the "affaire Lip" of the early-1970s.

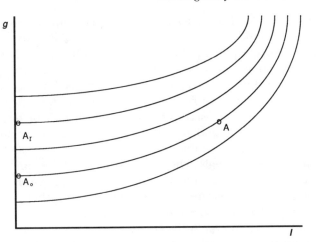

Figure 2. A figurative representation of insurance. The g-axis represents focus gain and the l-axis focus loss. Indifference curves represent the attractiveness ("utility") of various courses of action (investment in asset A, for example) characterized by their combinations of focus gain and focus loss. That attractiveness varies as a positive function of focus gain and a negative function of focus loss. The curves become steeper at high values of focus loss because of the risk-averse actor's insistence that higher values of focus loss be compensated by proportionately higher values of focus gain. Because insurance provides compensation in the event of loss, it has the effect of shifting the "utility" of a given course of action upward (from A to A_I). The actor is willing to pay a premium for this insurance, the cost of which varies as a positive function of the difference, expressed monetarily, between the utility of the original "asset" or course of action and that of the insured asset or course of action (or $A_I - A_O$).

that asset by promising compensation in the event of loss. In so doing, insurance diminishes the individual's "focus loss." Accordingly, insurance causes the individual's perception of the "utility" or "attractiveness" of holding asset A to shift upward, that is, to A_I. Because insurance is typically a service, bought and sold on the marketplace, the individual will have to pay for his insurance, the price of which will include not only the insurer's fee for making this service available, but also the cost of creating an adequate pool of resources from which to finance compensation. The price, or premium, that the individual is willing to pay for this service varies as a positive function of the attractiveness, expressed monetarily, of shifting from an "asset" of utility U(A) to an "asset" of utility $U(A_I)$—that is, a positive function of the value $A_I - A_O$. In plain English, the premium cannot be so costly that the utility of the insured asset is equal to or lower than that of the uninsured asset.

The provision of insurance, thus portrayed, depends on the willingness of an entrepreneur to assume the risk that the insurance pool may not suffice to meet commitments. Hence, when uncertainty concerning the future worth of an asset is great, the consequent risk of insuring that asset becomes great. For this reason, many entrepreneurs are willing to insure a person's life, but few are willing to insure a person's livelihood. Actuarial tables minimize uncertainty for the purveyor of life insurance, but no such divining rod exists for the entrepreneur who might want to insure income.[8] In this event, the demand for insurance can be addressed to the state, which may or may not choose to provide insurance and to act as entrepreneur. If it does, it might proceed to constitute a pool of resources, composed of the insurance premiums of individuals who voluntarily subscribe to the insurance plan, upon which it will draw to finance compensation. But it might do something that the private entrepreneur cannot—that is, *use its powers of coercion and/or monetary creation to constitute a pool of resources by appropriating them principally from uninsured individuals.*[9] Trade protection or price supports supply insurance to certain sectors by taxing consumers with artificially inflated prices for imported goods. As for the overdraft economy, it accomplishes a similar task by using credit policy to make available to firms in certain sectors a type of insurance that lessens the risk of investment. To the extent that insurance is supplied through monetary expansion, however, it effects a transfer of wealth from savers (because the real interest they earn is diminished by inflation) to borrowers (because the real interest they pay is diminished by inflation). And to the extent that it inhibits expansion of the financial market, it deprives investors of investment opportunities.

The state's power to provide insurance in this fashion has the unwelcome effect of inviting greater political activism to promote the creation of ever new programs of insurance. As the state steps in to finance insurance through coercive, redistributive means, it does away with part or all of the individual's insurance premium, giving rise to the perception that the state can provide insurance without requiring payment of premiums. This perception *frees up the countervalue of the premium to fund political action designed to promote the enactment of new insurance policies.* The "insurance premium," in other words, can now be spent on lobbying, campaign financing, graft, or the creation of strike funds. The amount of money the individual will be willing to spend on such activity will be, like the insurance premium itself, a positive function of the monetary value of the projected shift in "utility" of his "asset," once insured.[10]

---

[8]Or, more accurately, expected lifetime earnings.

[9]See Aharoni, *No-Risk Society*, p. 111.

[10]Other factors will influence how much the individual wants to spend to lobby for his "insurance policy." One such factor might be his or her expectation of success, as mediated, for example, by collective action constraints.

What does the government do when confronted by demands for insurance? If we make the simplifying assumption that the primary goal of government is to retain power,[11] it follows then that the government will respond by seeking, above all, to prevent resources generated by the demand for insurance from going to benefit its opponents. This response can take three forms, the first of which is leadership. Because one is dealing with *perceptions* of expected gain and risk, it is possible, through argument and rhetoric, to alter those perceptions. In the example of our young Frenchman from the Jura, the government might argue that the demise of the watchmaking industry, though tragic, will in fact free resources for new and more promising industries that hold out even greater opportunities for the worker, on condition that he consent to what can be a trying period of economic adjustment. If the worker is convinced, the resources needed to promote insurance legislation are no longer generated. For present purposes, we need make note of leadership only to the extent that we observe how so remarkably absent it was in postwar France. Perhaps the intense ideological conflict that was so characteristic of French politics before and after the war diminished the effectiveness of rhetoric as a means for opposing demands for insurance. One could convince neither the worker nor the small shopkeeper to accept the need for adjustment when the political opposition of the far left and the far right objected effectively that the word "adjustment" in fact hid the transfer of wealth to a dominant class that was abusing its power over policy to enrich itself. Thus it was that French officials, even when confronted by the imperious need to impose monetary rigor, were nevertheless driven by the fear of unleashing a wave of opposition that could threaten the very existence of republican institutions to prefer policies that postponed rather than pursued the elusive goal of monetary adjustment. In so doing, successive French governments missed a number of opportunities to reform the overdraft economy. The overdraft economy was not fated to be. It was allowed to develop by politicians who lacked the leadership, as understood here, to deny the French people the economic insurance they demanded.

The second possible response is coercion. The government can act to discourage lobbying, strikes, or political competition by increasing the cost or riskiness of such activity. Again, the concept is of interest to us principally to the extent that it was encountered so infrequently in France. This is not to say that there was no social strife, no long and violent strikes, no violent actions by farmers and shopkeepers to defend

---

[11]In this case it is more appropriate to speak of the "incumbent," as John DeNardo, *Power in Numbers* (Princeton: Princeton University Press, 1985), does.

a way of life that economic development threatened, and no equally violent episodes of repression by the police. It is to say, however, that the principal victims of coercion were those who suffered from the extension of insurance through monetary and credit mechanisms, rather than those who gained. Savings in financial assets were taxed by inflation, and opportunities for investment were curtailed by regulation and exchange controls at a time when savers essentially were deprived of political power. During the years immediately following World War II, the forces that would have assumed the defense of finance capital were supplanted by the more progressive forces associated with the Resistance—that is, Communists, Socialists, and Christian Democrats. There was no coherent opposition to policies that subjected the allocation of credit to the state, even though those policies resulted in the quasi-elimination of finance capital as an economic and political entity.

The final response consists of satisfying the demand for insurance. This was in fact the typical response of most governments of postwar France. This pattern of acquiescence clashes with France's reputation as a state endowed with great strength and policy-making autonomy, as defined by the capacity to pursue some coherent national purpose in the face of societal opposition and as manifested in the high level of development of its institutions and its power to intervene in economic life. Institutional development, however, does not clearly denote state capacity to implement policies that impose costs on society.[12] Institutional development and the power to intervene in economic life can in fact reflect the existence of constraints on policy that actually deprive the incumbent of autonomy. Because many interventionist or regulatory institutions evolved primarily to dispense insurance, their existence reveals that there are economic expectations that constrain the government's power to impose costs on society. In France, the institutions and techniques of credit allocation grew increasingly sophisticated, just as the government's power to impose the discipline of the marketplace on its population declined. The history of French financial and monetary policy suggests that, though the state's power to intervene in the economy to redistribute income was remarkable, its ability to use that power to pursue any recognizable "national purpose"[13] was rather tenuous, and certainly when measured against the claims of primitive state theory. Far from living up to its image of regal autonomy, the French state showed unusual readiness to accede to societal demands for protection from economic risk.

[12]See Michael Loriaux, "Comparative Political Economy as Comparative History," *Comparative Politics* 21 (April 1989).
[13]With the exception of arms development and procurement policy.

MORAL HAZARD, ECONOMIC ADJUSTABILITY, AND
NATIONAL POWER

The notion of insurance developed here does not differ markedly
from the concept of "rent-seeking," which has received so much attention in recent literature.[14] The term "insurance," however, does make
clearer the link with the notion of "moral hazard," which is vital to
present purposes. It is not, after all, the activity of rent-seeking per se
that we seek to understand, but rather the changes in the definition
of individual self-interest and the subsequent changes in patterns of
economic and political behavior that rent-seeking (in the form of
insurance-seeking) induced. It is the change in perception and behavior
that occurs because of moral hazard that elucidates the logic of the
overdraft economy and exposes the constraints that confront the policymaker in his efforts to adapt the French political economy to the post-
hegemonic world. French credit policy, I argue, caused change in
economic behavior. The state's efforts to assure the supply of credit to
industrial investors, in pursuance of its "industrial policy," precipitated
the decline of the financial market and increased the reliance of firms
on lending institutions. French firms grew dependent on institutionally
allocated credit and came to perceive it as a quasi-entitlement. The
"presumption of assured borrowing power" that came to characterize
economic behavior in the overdraft economy clearly manifested the
existence of moral hazard.

By equating the overdraft economy with moral hazard, one can more
easily identify the articulations that linked the domestic political economy of France to certain structural features of the international political economy. The key articulation is that which exists between moral
hazard and economic power. This link is in turn mediated by the
national economy's capacity to adjust to external change.

Because of its impact on perceptions, moral hazard inhibits economic adjustment. It does so in several ways. First, moral hazard weakens
the individual's capacity to adjust, since individuals are, by the very
definition of moral hazard, less cognizant of economic risk and thus
less quick to take steps to prepare for shocks. In France, the absence of
a precautionary demand for money and the noninterest of French
firms in holding redeemable financial assets weakened the firm's capacity to respond to changing economic conditions and placed it at the
mercy of lending institutions. Second, under moral hazard, individuals
are conditioned to react to economic shocks by demanding insurance

[14]See esp. John Conybeare, "The Rent-seeking State and Revenue Diversification,"
World Politics 35 (October 1982).

rather than by accepting the need for adjustment. There was considerable expectation in France that the state could and would prevent the collapse of an industrial firm or sector, and its failure to do so often had serious political repercussions. Third, because moral hazard inhibits adjustment in individual firms, it causes resources, capital, and labor to be retained in economic activities that do not prosper under changed conditions, while it withholds resources from growth sectors that might facilitate adjustment.[15] As Aharoni explains, "too much insurance and risk-reduction does not allow the Schumpeterian 'constructive destruction' to operate; there is much less incentive for innovation either in new products or in cost-cutting methods."[16] We recognize in this criticism of moral hazard as obstacle to economic rationalization a more abstract version of the criticisms that were being addressed to industrial policy toward the end of the 1970s.

By inhibiting adjustment, moral hazard aggravates an economy's "vulnerability" to external shocks. The term "vulnerability" holds specific meaning for students of international political economy.[17] A country is said to be vulnerable to an external economic event, or shock, if that event imposes costs on the country that cannot be allayed through any imaginable shift in policy. By comparison, a country is said to be merely sensitive to an event if policies that diminish the cost incurred can be devised. If one accepts this distinction, then it follows that the country in which the costs of adjustment are accepted by the population will experience greater success in trying to foster shifts in resources between sectors in such a way that it can, over time, reduce the costs that some shock (e.g., the internationalization of the market for watches) has imposed on its economy. Such an economy is sensitive but not vulnerable to external shocks. Peter Katzenstein, in his provocative analysis of economic policy-making in Switzerland and Austria, attributes successful economic performance in those countries to the consensual acceptance of the need for policies of economic adjustment, allowing political actors to focus debate on the modalities of adjustment.[18]

[15]The impact of moral hazard on behavior is even greater when insurance is financed through redistributive politics. For the individual who confronts risk by consenting to pay an insurance premium, there is of necessity some perception on his part of the precariousness of his situation. By contrast, the individual whose insurance premium is paid by society at large may have no sense whatsoever of the risks he confronts. The misperception generates greater resources with which to oppose policy.

[16]Aharoni, No-Risk Society, p. 106.

[17]See Robert Keohane and Joseph Nye, Power and Interdependence (Boston: Little, Brown, 1977), pp. 11–15.

[18]Peter Katzenstein, Corporatism and Change: Austria, Switzerland, and the Politics of Industry (Ithaca: Cornell University Press, 1984). One might object that insurance, rather than being an impediment to adjustment, could be used to diminish the costs imposed by change. For example, it could be argued that subsidizing hard-hit sectors might be more

In contrast, the country that, because of moral hazard, has difficulty promoting resource reallocation will prove to be more vulnerable to external shocks. In France, economic adjustment is harder to achieve and policies of adjustment are more vigorously resisted. This helps to explain why the French economy displayed increasing vulnerability to the energy and commodity shocks of the 1970s. International change, as manifested by the change in patterns of trade that resulted from the oil crisis, necessitated adjustments that the French political economy, fallen prey to moral hazard, could not achieve through internal policies. The state tried to restrict financial support to French firms because of the new exchange rate constraints, but monetary rigor threatened the government with mounting political opposition as it shifted the individual's focus points to the left (to recall Shackle's terms). This gave rise to demands for insurance that caused the government to look for methods to allay and to prolong the adjustment process, thereby preventing the economy from adjusting at all. Because it adjusted to none of the shocks, it encountered each successive external shock from a position of diminishing resilience. Growing economic uncertainty, coupled with the growing inability of the French state to provide economic insurance through credit policy, contributed to the resurgence of a united Left opposition in the 1970s.

The link between moral hazard, the capacity to adjust to external shocks, and economic vulnerability suggests in turn that there is a broader relationship between moral hazard and national economic "power." The idea that such a relationship exists was advanced by Charles Kindleberger:

> The capacity to adjust to change is a significant dimension of economic power.... A vital aspect concerns the responsiveness of the economy to macro-economic stimuli—its ability to expand expenditure, employment, and income when money is increased and budget deficits are run in

---

economical than providing for an increasing number of unemployed, that insurance might be in the form of an industrial policy designed to encourage rather than discourage the shift of resources into less vulnerable sectors. The validity of such objections is not disputed, but insurance, however warranted by economic factors and considerations, will always create conditions that are conducive to the generation of moral hazard. Hence, to propose policies of insurance at a particular time as a useful tool of adjustment does not preclude the possibility that at some later date adjustment in the industry may be hindered because of patterns of economic behavior conditioned by moral hazard. For instance, one can reasonably defend the proposition that protection is warranted in the case of infant industries. It is commonly observed, however, that it is economically and politically difficult to wean such industries away from protectionism once they have reached adolescence. In sum, although providing insurance can occasionally be justified economically, there is always the danger that it will encourage patterns of economic behavior that may hinder adjustment later.

depression, and to curb inflation and balance-of-payments deficits in response to higher interest rates and higher taxes in boom. In an adaptive economy, economic decisions are taken with minimal delay after changes in conditions supervene, and take hold without extended lags. The country is not impaled on a Phillips curve...so placed that there is only the choice between depression and inflation, with no middle ground of fairly full employment and broad price stability.[19]

What is this putative relationship between adjustability and economic power, and how does it relate to the concepts of political activism and moral hazard explored above? A good jumping-off point from which to explore this relationship is offered by Jeffrey Hart, who, defining a state's power as its "control over outcomes," sees international politics as the encounter between nations endowed with varying degrees of "concern" and "control" over particular policy issues. According to Hart, the power of one country over another can be conceived as the product of the first country's degree of control over outcomes of interest to the second country, and the second country's degree of concern over those same outcomes. For example, the oil producer that depends little on the sale of its oil to achieve balance in trade (high degree of control, small degree of concern—the United States in the 1950s, for example) can, if it likes, use its power over the oil market (and relative invulnerability to similar attempts on the part of other countries) to influence the policies of the oil producer that depends greatly on oil exports to finance its imports (high degree of control, high degree of concern). This country, in turn, enjoys potential leverage in its relations with the oil consumer that is suffering from payments problems (low degree of control, high degree of concern).[20]

The notions of adjustability and vulnerability can usefully be introduced into Hart's analysis. The country that is not vulnerable to events within a specified issue arena can be said to possess greater power than other states, because it by definition displays less concern over those events. Other countries cannot use the issue arena as a fulcrum point from which to leverage desired policy choices. Inversely, the country that does not adjust easily, and is therefore relatively more vulnerable to external shocks, possesses less power, ceteris paribus, than countries

[19]Charles Kindleberger, *Power and Money* (New York: Basic Books, 1970), p. 66.

[20]Jeffrey Hart, "Three Approaches to the Measurement of Power in International Relations," *International Organization* 30 (Spring 1976). It must be recognized that the above analysis does a disservice to the efforts of a number of scholars—foremost among whom is David Baldwin—to refine and enrich our understanding of power. Consequently, this analysis does not claim to exhaust the definition of power, but rather seeks merely to explore the relationship between economic flexibility, economic size, and the ability to exert influence in the world economy and to demonstrate that both economic size and adjustability help rather than hinder that ability.

that do adjust easily.[21] Therefore, a country's power can be said to vary as a function of its ability to adjust to change in the pattern of international transactions, and therefore in inverse proportion to the degree of moral hazard that characterizes its political economy. In time, the country whose political economy generates moral hazard runs the risk of losing power to other countries.

This analysis is suggestive of the reasons for financial reform in France. The post–Bretton Woods crisis of the overdraft economy assumed an international dimension as the French were made to endure a loss of power primarily in the form of growing French vulnerability to German policy. This relative loss of power was made apparent by France's unsuccessful efforts to participate in the joint European currency float. The joint float, which pegged currencies to the deutschmark, was regarded with reluctance by the French but was made necessary by the economy's vulnerability to floating rates. Internal economic weakness, due to moral hazard, made it impossible for the French to sustain the franc's participation in the joint float, while the Germans remained unsympathetic to French demands that the float be rendered less rigorous and less affected by German policy. The franc was forced out of the float on two occasions, rendering the French economy vulnerable to the monetary shock induced by the franc's depreciation in relation to the mark, Germany being France's principal trading partner. French power, as understood here, declined relative to German power. This evolution manifested itself in Germany's more visible leadership role in European economic affairs.

The French government was thus caught in the grip of crisis on two fronts, domestic and external. Increasingly cognizant of the French economy's underlying weakness, the government finally decided to attack moral hazard through structural reform. The "descendants of Colbert" energetically embraced the cause of liberalism in the late 1970s, a cause that was embraced again by the "descendants of Jules Guesde" in the mid-1980s. But France's rediscovery of liberalism had less to do with the robustness of liberalism as an economic system than it did with the fact that the post–Bretton Woods world of floating rates had revealed the constraints moral hazard had placed on the government's ability to define and to implement monetary policy. If the French government now sought to rid the economy of moral hazard, it did so in order to retrieve its policy-making capacity and to regain power vis-à-vis other states, most notably the German Republic. The logic of liberalization should therefore not be misconstrued: state

---

[21]The measure of adjustability is a relative one, not an absolute one. If all countries experienced adjustment difficulties equally, there would be no power differential.

strength and national power, not abdication to the marketplace, was the goal that liberalizing financial reform pursued.

MORAL HAZARD AND U.S. HEGEMONY

Although the United States as hegemon has not yet been brought into this analysis, one can guess the role it plays, for the domestic political economy of France, suffused by moral hazard, could not have endured long if the environment created by the international political economy had been hostile to it. For the student of international political economy, the principal interest of French financial reform resides precisely in what it reveals about the nature of the hegemonic order and the clues it furnishes concerning the evolution of the post-hegemonic international political economy. It is to this question that we now turn, exploring the link between moral hazard, as it manifested itself in the French political economy, and the efforts of the United States to refashion the global economic order.

The characterization of the postwar economic order as "hegemonic" is no longer controversial, nor is it disputed that the United States was able to promote trade openness in international affairs by exploiting the power that its large economy gave it. Questions relating to the how and why of hegemonic leadership, however, are still intensely debated by students of international political economy. What is "economic" power, and what does it allow a state to do?

First, let us recall from our previous discussion of adjustability that the powerful country is one that achieves adjustment easily. For Robert Gilpin, adjustability is a sine qua non of hegemonic power: "The ultimate basis of the economic strength of the hegemon is the flexibility and mobility of its economy. . . . In the long term, economic power is neither the possession of particular monopolies and/or technologies nor economic self-sufficiency, but rather the capacity of the economy to transform itself and to respond to changes in the global economic environment, such as shifts in comparative advantage or price changes."[22]

Adjustability alone, however, does not a hegemon make. Switzerland has an adjustable economy, but Switzerland has not been and is never

---

[22]Robert Gilpin, *The Political Economy of International Relations* (Princeton: Princeton University Press, 1987), p. 77. He continues, "The inflexibility of the British economy in the late nineteenth century in response to the rise of new industrial powers was an important cause of its decline. Similarly, the difficulties experienced by the United States during the closing decades of the twentieth century in adjusting to profound shifts in the global location of industry and the revolution in the price of energy have undermined its power and international position." Gilpin cites Ralph G. Hawtrey, *Economic Aspects of Sovereignty* (London: Longman's, 1952).

likely to be a hegemon. To be a hegemon, one must also have a "large economy." For the economist, who makes frequent use of the distinction between "large countries" and "small countries," the large country is that which, by modifying its demand or supply of specifiable goods, affects the price of those goods on world markets—it is a "price-maker."[23] The "small country," which has no comparable influence on world prices, is a "price-taker." Prices of traded goods on the small country's market are world prices, and no shift in domestic supply or demand of those goods affects those prices. For purposes of modeling economic behavior, economists treat large economies as closed economies. These are economies in which, for example, fiscal policy has the effect Keynesian theory attributes to it, because policymakers are able to pursue policies that generate domestic investment without too much concern for the policy's impact on foreign transactions. Such policies fail in small, open economies because they result so readily in current account imbalances. Relating this distinction to the definition of power proposed above, one concludes that the large country has a larger fraction of control over events than the small country, both because of its influence over world price levels and because it behaves like a closed economy and is therefore less vulnerable to external shocks.

Powerful countries, as defined by their economic size and adjustability—whether the United States, Germany, or Japan—can and occasionally do play a distinct and significant role in the international political economy. First, large countries, as price makers, can be a significant source of external stress that challenges the capacity of smaller states to adjust. This characterization applies, for example, to the "predatory hegemon" one encounters in the work of John Conybeare, Susan Strange, or Riccardo Parboni.[24] French hostility to U.S. policy after about 1965 can be understood as France's reaction to the adoption of more "predatory" U.S. policies in monetary affairs. On the other hand, large countries can also use their power over world prices to foster stability on international markets. This more benevolent activity corresponds to the benign leadership described and advocated by Charles Kindleberger and practiced by the United States during the 1950s and early 1960s. Third, however, and most important to the argument developed in this book, the large country can assume a fraction of the smaller country's costs of providing insurance to its economy, principal-

---

[23]See Branson, *Macro-Economic Theory,* pp. 332–35.

[24]John Conybeare, *Trade Wars: The Theory and Practice of International Commercial Rivalry* (New York: Columbia University Press, 1987); Susan Strange, "The Persistent Myth of Lost Hegemony," *International Organization* 41 (1987); Riccardo Parboni, "The Dollar Standard," in Jeffry A. Frieden and David A. Lake, eds., *International Political Economy* (New York: St. Martin's Press, 1987), p. 285.

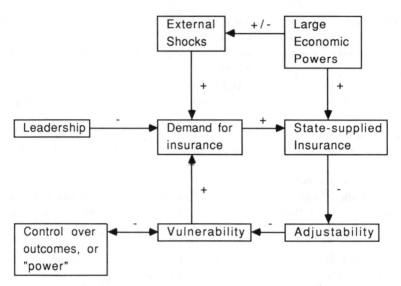

Figure 3. Large economic powers, insurance, and economic adjustment in smaller states.

ly because of its capacity to sustain the cost of doing so while achieving adjustment in foreign payments, either through internal adjustment or manipulation of world prices. This conceptualization of hegemony is represented graphically in Figure 3.

This insurance function has received little attention in the hegemonic literature, and yet, as one contemplates the French overdraft economy, it is this aspect of leadership that was most in evidence throughout the 1950s and 1960s. The French overdraft economy depended on external currency manipulation to achieve adjustment. The United States rendered such manipulation viable by sustaining the costs of managing the "*n*th" currency—that is, the stable monetary standard with reference to which the parities of all other currencies were defined—by assuming the opportunity costs of forgoing more "predatory" policies and by fostering international institutions and rules of international monetary relations that prevented devaluation in France from giving rise to a cascade of retaliatory devaluations that would have deprived the French of any benefit from devaluation. United States monetary leadership legitimated and rendered viable French monetary policies that gave rise to the overdraft economy and to moral hazard.

Why would the United States, or any large country, choose to do this? Recall that the domestic political system can be conceived as a set of materially sustained demands for insurance, addressed to an incumbent who, to preserve its power, has either to repress them, to exorcise them through leadership, or to satisfy them. Demands for insurance, however, are important not only to the government of the state in which they arise, but to foreign governments as well. The economic interests of a nation are endangered if demands for insurance arising in a neighboring nation threaten, say, greater protectionism or market interventionism that could alter patterns of trade. Or the security interests of neighboring states may be affected if demands for insurance benefit political groups, such as the Communist party, that advocate closer association with an adversary.

In the case of U.S.-French relations, the United States was both the source of the stress that provoked French modernization policy and the mainstay of an international environment that made such policy possible. The United States did not set out to underwrite the cost of insurance in smaller countries. On the contrary, when it emerged from World War II as the predominant economic power, it took advantage of European dependence on financial aid for economic reconstruction to impose liberalizing reforms in the rules and institutions that regulated international trade, both out of self-interest and out of an ideological vision of how the postwar world should be ordered. For France, this meant the eventual breakdown of its colonial empire and the integration of its economy into a European free-trade bloc, and thus a pressing need to adapt its political economy to radically new circumstances. These challenges, coupled with the trauma of defeat in 1940 (which the French attributed in part to the sclerosis of the prewar economy), drove the French to adopt a policy of rapid industrial modernization by giving the state the power to allocate credit in a way that diminished the riskiness of industrial investment.

The United States showed little sympathy for this policy orientation prior to the outbreak of the cold war. Beginning in the late 1940s, however, fears provoked by the strength of the Communist party in France and by a growing political polarization that threatened the very institutions of the Fourth Republic caused the United States to become more sympathetic to French policymakers who sought both to hasten industrial modernization and eschew the rigors of economic adjustment. The overdraft economy would not have arisen if the United States had not provided the opportunity to pursue such policies. That opportunity was forthcoming when the United States, in an effort to help the governments of such countries as France defuse social and political tensions that were perceived as threatening to its political and economic interests, amended its blueprint for global economic reform in ways that facilitated the adoption of policies designed to speed industrial modernization and to elude the necessity of adjustment in trade and prices. The overdraft economy could not have survived the

93

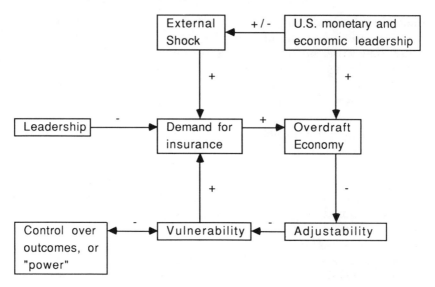

Figure 4. U.S. hegemony and the French overdraft economy.

initial postwar reconstruction of the French economy had not the United States been willing to discriminate against its own immediate monetary and commercial interests. This argument is depicted in Figure 4.

All this suggests that France's political economy, though considered rather idiosyncratic among Western industrialized democracies, in actuality reflected constraints and opportunities that the French encountered in the international system. Students of French politics too readily interpret French economy policy as a mere series of footnotes to the work of Colbert. This is a selective vision of the history of the French political economy. There is simply no historical precedent for the overdraft economy. Throughout the nineteenth century and up to the outbreak of World War II, France was one of the chief financial powers of the globe. Throughout this period, observers commonly alluded to the contrast between France's banks and Germany's steel mills. Even after the reconstruction of their economy following World War I, the French returned to the very orthodox monetary policy orientation that had been characteristic of French policy throughout the nineteenth century. After World War II, on the other hand, no such return to orthodoxy occurred. The break with the past was abrupt and profound, as France not only ceased to be a major financial power, but indeed allowed its financial market to wither into insignificance.

To understand reform in the 1980s, one need only observe that present constraints are the legacy of past opportunities. Changes that one now observes in the French political economy have their source in changes that occurred in the international political economy. By the end of the 1960s and the beginning of the 1970s, the international environment that had rendered France's overdraft economy viable began to change dramatically. Trade interdependence, which had grown significantly, caused the French economy to become "smaller" in economic terms, while the overdraft economy continued to render adjustment by means short of currency devaluation increasingly problematic. Within this changing context, the monetary regime of fixed but adjustable rates was abandoned as the United States shed the onus of managing a stable international currency. The U.S. retreat from leadership gave rise first to the Franco-American monetary conflict of the 1960s, when inflation in the United States aggravated inflationary pressures in France's overdraft economy. It gave rise also to the monetary crises of the late 1960s and early 1970s, when the Bretton Woods system of fixed exchange rates was finally scuttled altogether. Liberal financial reforms are the product of French efforts to regain the monetary control they had relinquished after World War II. They are the product of efforts to regain power in a world in which the United States evolved from being a benign hegemon that shared the cost of extending insurance to French economic agents, thus shoring up the fragile institutions of the French republic, to the more self-regarding and "predatory" hegemon of the late 1960s, 1970s, and 1980s.[25]

CONCLUSION

Equating the overdraft economy with moral hazard sheds new light on the nature of the hegemonic order, the meaning of hegemonic decline, and the ramifications of that decline for smaller states. Hegemony is generally defined and analyzed from the perspective of structural realism. According to that perspective, the international system is conceived as an anarchical assemblage of self-regarding, unit-like, rational states that coexist in a strategic relationship to one another which resembles the game of "prisoner's dilemma." Within this system, a liberal order can obtain only if there is a hegemonic power that allows itself to be exploited (by "playing C" while other nations "play D") by assuming unassisted the onus of supplying the collective goods that are necessary if that order is to endure. The structural realist perspective, however, offers only insufficient understanding of the how and the why of the hegemonic order. John Conybeare, for instance, has argued

[25]One might speculate that the predatory hegemon has been tamed by the Plaza monetary agreement, though this is unlikely.

cogently that, given this perspective, there is no reason for the hegemon to allow itself to be exploited when its true interests lie in exploiting others ("playing D" while others are obliged, by their smaller economic size, to "play C"). Moreover, Robert Keohane, drawing on the work of Robert Axelrod, has suggested that cooperative outcomes can be achieved under anarchy. By looking at the hegemonic era through the lens provided by the notion of the "second image reversed," one gains greater purchase over the how and the why of hegemonic leadership and one sees more clearly how economic power confers the ability to allay the threat of domestic political strife in allied countries that may be harmful to the hegemon's political interests by facilitating the extension of economic insurance in those countries.

The structural perspective similarly fails to give a firm sense of what is meant by hegemonic decline. Because it deals with a world of actors that differ from one another only in the amount of power they can bring to bear in interactions with one another, the structuralist is faced with the impossible task of defining the power "threshold" above which one begins to act like a hegemon and below which one ceases to act like a hegemon. By linking hegemony with moral hazard (at least in the case of the *Pax Americana*), one can easily date the end of the hegemonic era: early in the Johnson administration, the United States began to pursue more inward-oriented and less international policies, which had the effect of depriving insurance programs in such countries as France of their monetary support. After that date, America's power no longer made the task of achieving economic adjustment in France easier. Instead, by adopting more "prɛdatory" policies the United States made that task harder, giving rise to more than a decade of intense Franco-American disputes over economic issues.

Finally, structural realism offers only ambivalent hints concerning the probable evolution of the international political economy in the aftermath of hegemony. Though one cannot project from the study of a single country to the international political economy as a whole, the French case is nevertheless suggestive of the forces that drive that evolution. Discussion of this must be postponed to the Conclusion, however. In the intervening chapters, the development and decay of the overdraft economy are explored in historical detail. After analyzing the overdraft economy and laying bare its elemental logic, it is time to gain a greater contextual understanding of both the overdraft economy and the reforms that sought to put an end to it.

CHAPTER FOUR

The Birth of the Overdraft Economy

Having documented the rigidities in the French political economy, attributed their existence to an overdraft economy, and argued that a tolerant international monetary environment underpinned by American leadership made that overdraft economy possible, I can now reconstruct the history of the French overdraft economy. Having "dismantled" the French political economy into its elementary components—insurance and moral hazard—we are ready to put it back together, retrace its structural and institutional development, and put that development in its political context, both domestic and international. I contend that France's overdraft economy developed under conditions generated by U.S. efforts to contain the influence of its principal rival in international affairs, the Soviet Union. That rivalry is responsible for the hiatus that one observes in the history of French finance. Before World War II, France was one of the world's great financial powers. During the nineteenth century, the French financial market had experienced a vast expansion that saw savings shift rapidly away from land into interest-bearing bonds and stocks. Whereas in the mid-nineteenth century two-thirds of French wealth was still held in land, on the eve of World War I less than half of France's wealth was held in land. During the same period, French businesses tended to finance their investments out of business savings rather than, as after 1945, through credit accorded by institutional lenders, and activity on the Paris Stock Exchange was quite lively.[1]

France as a financial power suffered greatly from the destructions

[1] See François Caron, *An Economic History of Modern France* (New York: Columbia University Press, 1979), pp. 58–62, 87.

and monetary shocks of the two world wars, but war does not explain the decline of the French financial market in modern times. Although after World War I the financial market was restored once the franc was stabilized in 1926, the period following World War II witnessed no similar financial renaissance, primarily because the French chose to forgo monetary stabilization. In contrast to their neighbors—the Belgians, Italians, and Germans, who pursued rather rigorous stabilization policies— the French avoided stabilization for fear of discouraging investment and compromising recovery, industrial growth, and political stability. As a consequence of policy choices made as early as January 1945 and replicated in subsequent years, confidence in fixed-interest-bearing bonds never recovered from the shock of war. The money supply, which had grown at an annual rate of 14 percent during the years of the Popular Front, grew by 30 percent annually under the governments of Vichy and the Fourth Republic and sustained a rate of inflation that negated yields offered by interest-bearing assets.[2] One critic of postwar policy complained that inflation had caused fixed-interest-bearing bonds purchased in 1938 to lose 95 percent of their value, and stocks to lose 43 percent of their value by 1952. Bonds bought in 1913 had lost 99.4 percent of their value, and stocks had lost 81 percent.[3] Government policy not only undermined investor confidence by unleashing infla- tion, but also freed businesses from the need to address their demand for capital to the financial market by making it easy to borrow from institutional lenders at interest rates that were typically negative in real terms. As a consequence of such decisions, bond issues fell from 5.3 percent of the gross domestic product in 1938 to only 1.7 percent of GDP in 1947, creating conditions for the generation of new patterns of economic behavior characteristic of the overdraft economy.

The importance of international factors in explaining the peculiari- ties of France's political economy cannot be overemphasized. France's reputation for interventionism is such that it is easy to overlook policy innovations that cannot be explained without some reference to changes in the international environment. The history of the French political economy is one of discontinuities. There was no smooth evolution of institutions and structures that could be traced from the present back to the origins of capitalism. In this regard, it is significant that Peter Hall, as he elaborates his institutional approach to the study of compar- ative political economy, begins his analysis of France in 1945, whereas in the case of Great Britain he reaches back to the nineteenth century.

---

[2]See Jean-Pierre Patat and Michel Lutfalla, *Histoire monétaire de la France au XXe siècle* (Paris: Economica, 1986), p. 16.

[3]Jacques Lacour-Gayet, Charles Rist, et. al., *Monnaie d'hier et de demain* (Paris: Spid, 1952), p. 39.

This is not to say that there are no elements in the history of France's political economy that bespeak some degree of continuity. The development of an overdraft economy was indeed facilitated by the prior existence in France of a number of parapublic financial institutions that could be brought together to create a state-directed system of credit allocation. A number of those institutions, however, also existed in 1926, when Raymond Poincaré returned the country to a very conservative version of financial orthodoxy. Not until 1945 could one see those institutions melded into the statist structure that we associate with modern-day France. In other words, that statist structure did not coalesce until a different international economic environment was constructed, one fashioned by U.S. leadership. Had the United States adopted a different orientation, the French overdraft economy would have collapsed.

The birth and early development of the overdraft economy—from January 1945, when the provisional government rejected monetary stabilization in favor of a path of least resistance, to 1951, when the European Coal and Steel Community was created—are the focus of this chapter.

LIBERATION AND THE REJECTION OF MONETARY STABILIZATION, 1944–1947

The French Resistance set up a provisional government that assumed power in August 1944. The challenges confronting it were immense. As if the destruction of war were not enough, the winter of 1944–45 was harsh and the economic stress the population suffered was great. Economic activity was at a standstill. Railway transportation was virtually paralyzed, and bridges, engines, and nearly half a million homes were destroyed. The output of electricity was half what it had been before the war, and coal production was one-fifth its 1938 level. Although the French farmer had not suffered as much as his Russian or Polish counterpart, he nevertheless had difficulty getting his produce to the city. Paris was placed on starvation rations, and the price of food available on the open market or on the black market was out of reach for most city-dwellers, whose purses swelled with a currency that had lost four-fifths of its prewar purchasing power.[4]

War and occupation had left the French economy highly liquid. In 1944, the stock of money (M_1) in circulation was two-and-a-half times the GDP (compared with 50 percent in 1980). Abundant liquidity,

[4]See Alexander Werth, *France, 1940–1955* (London: R. Hale, 1956), p. 225.

coupled with the restricted supply of goods on the market, caused rapid inflation. Because of monetary disorder, the government had to intervene to regulate both the supply and the demand of goods through administrative means: fixed prices, fixed wages, and rationing. With the economy awash in valueless occupation currency, some form of monetary housecleaning was imperative.

The leaders of the French Resistance had planned their policy response to the challenge of stabilizing and reconstructing the economy long before the Liberation. That response was informed by the overarching ambition to subject the whole of French society to radical economic and political renovation. The resistance to Nazi occupation was infused with a spirit of social revolution and cultural renewal. In the words of André Siegfried, "if in Vichy there reigned a spirit of national revolution, one found in London a spirit of republican renewal, which claimed to be no less revolutionary, politically or socially."[5] Conservatives, such as Charles de Gaulle and his lieutenants, René Pleven and Maurice Schuman, worked in collaboration with Socialists and Communists to draft plans to overhaul and restructure French society. If a person such as de Gaulle was able to wrench himself so radically from his traditional, familial, and professional milieu, it was because he considered that milieu hopelessly attached to the past and incapable of understanding the problems of the present. A dominant theme of the Resistance, and one that won the adherence of all political forces that composed it, was the need to overcome and eradicate the "Malthusianism" (*malthusianisme*) of prewar French society. The leaders of the Liberation were unanimous in their condemnation of traditional society less because of its injustices than because of its resistance to change and modernization, a resistance that effectively sapped France's economy and society of the dynamism that could have energized the nation to resist the Nazi invasion. In his address to the nation, broadcast from Algiers on Bastille Day, July 14, 1943, de Gaulle exclaimed: "France will choose a new path. The Fourth French Republic will abolish all coalitions of interest or privilege, having seen only too well what peril they bring. The nation will demand that its natural resources, its labor, and its technology not be exploited for the profit of a few.... If there are Bastilles still to be taken, they should prepare to open their doors of their own will."[6]

De Gaulle was joined in his flight from his traditionalist roots by an entire generation of renovators who were creating a new force in

[5]See André Siegfried, *De la IIIe à la IVe République* (Paris: Grasset, 1956), p. 111, quoted in Jacques Chapsal, *La vie politique en France depis 1940* (Paris: Presses Universitaires de France, 1969), p. 61.
[6]Quoted in Chapsal, *La vie politique*, p. 66.

French politics, that of Catholic reformism.[7] Though a Catholic movement for social reform had held on to a tenuous existence since the
middle of the nineteenth century, and had prior to World War II
experienced a dramatic rise in influence with the creation of such
professional organizations as Young Christian Workers (Jeunesse Ouvrière
Chrétienne, or J.O.C.), it met with noncomprehension and suspicion by
the Roman Catholic church establishment until the Occupation and the
Resistance discredited both the traditional Catholic Right and a number of Catholic prelates who had adopted a policy of accommodation
with the Nazi occupants. The Catholic reform movement became an
integral and important component of the Resistance and shared in its
triumph. In 1944, the Catholic wing of the Resistance organized itself
into a political Christian Democratic party, called the Popular Republican Movement (Mouvement Républicain Populaire, or MRP).[8]

The desire to reform French society gave rise to a relatively coherent
"esprit de la résistance" that facilitated collaboration between men and
women of radically different social origins and ideological commitments. Indeed, it "was believed that the routines and the divisions of
the Third Republic could be left behind and that the coming together
of bourgeois and worker, of Catholic and Communist, would be a
lasting phenomenon."[9] This "esprit de la résistance" was given expression in the Charter of the National Resistance Council (Charte du
Conseil National de la Résistance), which was composed in March 1944.
In it the resistants made clear their ambition "to destroy what they
called the *esprit bourgeois,* the power of money, the great feudal lords of
the economy, for which they would need a planned economy, renouncing traditional liberalism which was abandoned to the Right."[10] The
charter called for nationalization of major mining and petroleum
companies and insurance companies and banks, development of an
economic plan, recognition of independent trade unions, creation of a
general system of social security, and reform of education in order to
promote an elite of merit rather than birth. It became the program of
the provisional government, which was officially constituted in Algiers
on June 2, 1944, and relocated to Paris in September. Within three
months of the government's installation in Paris, major firms were

[7]See Stanley Hoffmann, ed., *In Search of France* (Cambridge: Harvard University Press,
1963), pp. 36–37. See also Jesse Pitts, "Continuity and Change in Bourgeois France," in
Hoffmann, ed., *In Search of France,* pp. 279–83; Yvon Tranvouez, "Entre Rome et le
peuple (1920–1960)," in François Lebrun, ed., *Histoire des Catholiques en France* (Paris:
Édouard Privat, 1980).

[8]See Jean-Pierre Rioux, *The Fourth Republic, 1944–1958,* trans. Godfrey Rogers, (Cambridge: Cambridge University Press, 1987), p. 51.

[9]Chapsal, *La vie politique,* p. 74.

[10]Ibid.

nationalized, the social security system was created, the Enterprise Committees (Comités d'Entreprises) were created in order to democratize the industrial firm, and the right of unionization was secured.

Pierre Mendès France, finance commissioner for the Resistance, became minister of the economy in the provisional government. While still in Algiers, he developed the broad lines of the economic policy he intended to implement. In his biography of Mendès France, Jean Lacouture writes:

> Mendès France [and others] wanted to make policy on the basis of the ... Algiers [charter]. ... They wanted to impose austerity in order to assure justice in a time of want; they wanted to deflate the money supply in order to restore balance between the production of goods and the medium of exchange. It was to obtain the realization of these principles that Mendès, very briefly as minister of finance, a little longer as minister of the economy, fought uninterruptedly against those who wished to believe that time, the regulatory effects of the market, and the excellence of human resources would always arrange things for the best.[11]

The monetary plan proposed by Mendès France faithfully expressed the "esprit de la résistance," not because it sought monetary stabilization but because it sought to use stabilization to pursue the goals of the charter. Mendès France was particularly keen on using monetary policy to impose a greater sense of the collective interest on speculators who were profiteering from the difficulties of transporting provisions to the major urban centers.[12] This proposal consisted of an exchange of currency that would have left to the bearers a uniform sum of 5,000 francs, a freeze on 75 percent of funds deposited in checking accounts, and restrictions that would have allowed the remaining 25 percent to be used only for payments by check (cash withdrawals were not permitted). Moreover, his plan required that all securities be deposited in order to prevent the development of a parallel money. Finally, the plan contained a number of miscellaneous measures that affected postal accounts, savings accounts, and treasury bonds that pursued a coherent goal: to stabilize prices and currency, to destroy the black market, and to weaken the grip of the traditional moneyed classes on the economy.[13] "One of Mendès France's principal ideas was that the black market would necessarily be paralysed, if not come to a complete standstill, if the mountains of currency in the possession of the marketeers were

[11] Jean Lacouture, *Pierre Mendès France*, trans. George Holoch (New York: Holmes and Mier, 1984), p. 157.

[12] See Werth, *France*, p. 247. A brief portrait of Mendès France that does much to make his policies comprehensible can be found in Stanley Hoffmann, *Decline or Renewal: France since the 1930s* (New York: Viking, 1974), pp. 88–89.

[13] Jacques Fauvet, *La IVe République* (Paris: Fayard, 1959), p. 37.

frozen or exchanged for new notes progressively, and subjected to various controls and checks."[14]

Mendès France's plan for monetary stabilization not only was not implemented, but was in fact roundly rejected by the provisional government for reasons that illuminate the conditions in which the overdraft economy was allowed to evolve. The provisional government feared the political consequences of the plan. The authority of the provisional government, despite de Gaulle's immense personal prestige, was far from secure. The intentions of the resistants were scrutinized with skepticism and concern not only by the classes that felt targeted by the resistants' declarations and policies, but also by political leaders whose republican credentials were secure—leaders of the Third Republic such as Léon Blum and Édouard Herriot, who, returning from exile, refused at first to collaborate with the provisional government more out of suspicion of the bourgeois general than because of disagreements with the program of the Resistance. For many members of the provisional government, however, the principal cause of fear was found within the government's ranks—that is, from the growing success and influence of the French Communist Party (Parti Communiste Français, or PCF). Though the bourgeois reformers who formed de Gaulle's entourage had rejected the traditionalist milieu that had sired them, they had not shaken the dust from their sandals, and the future of their relationship with the forces of the Left with which they now shared power was an uncertain one. The fortunes of the Communist party were at their apex in post–World War II Europe. It had been one of the most dynamic and selfless elements of the Resistance. Not only had the "party of the executed" (*parti des fusillés*) earned the respect of many, but Communist *militias* became de facto centers of power as the occupation forces withdrew. The Departmental Liberation Committees were frequently the creatures of the Communist party. Mendès France "recalled that in late 1944 and early 1945, the *commissaires de la République* were veritable viceroys of the large provincial capitals, that in cities like Lyon or Marseille, Yves Farge or Aubrac were subject to formidable pressure by the *comités de libération* and the Communist Party.... 'Farge, in Lyon, once published only articles 3, 9, and 28 of a law promulgated in Paris and recorded in the *Journal Officiel*.'"[15] In the months following the Liberation, the PCF acted swiftly and methodically to consolidate its hold on political activity at the local level by creating a number of functional groups and unions, such as the General Farmers' Confederation (Confédération Générale des Agriculteurs, formed

[14]Werth, *France*, p. 247.
[15]Quoted in Lacouture, *Mendès France*, p. 170. See also Rioux, *Fourth Republic*, pp. 46–48.

in 1945 with Waldeck Rochet, future successor of Maurice Thorez at the helm of the PCF, as its vice-president), and offered to be the spokesman for sectoral demands. It also set up committees to revive local economies and to assure the supply of goods.[16] The power of the Communist party increased rapidly. From 380,000 in January 1945, its membership rose to around 800,000 by the end of 1946. It was effectively becoming the principal political force in France.

But Communist influence did not threaten the work of the provisional government as much as it did the fortunes of the other parties that composed it. The PCF was quite attached, at least in principle, to the restoration of the Republic and parliamentary democracy. Since 1934, the PCF's strategy had been one of creating a "popular front" that would weaken the hold of the capitalist class on French politics by promoting reforms that would foster a large, broadly based anticapitalist coalition.[17] Far from being under Stalin's thumb, the French party frequently found itself having to defend its strategy against Soviet critics. The result was considerable policy ambiguity. The PCF sometimes undermined the efforts of the provisional government to reassert its authority, but at other times supported those efforts, even at the expense of the Communist-dominated departmental committees. For example, it agreed to disarm its own militias, the *francs tireurs*, despite the conflict this created within its ranks.

Although the Communist party was part of the provisional government, it used its influence among workers and within economic organizations to work separately and autonomously to promote economic reconstruction and to return the population to some semblance of economic normalcy. In September 1944, the General Confederation of Labor (Confédération Générale du Travail, or CGT, the largest labor union, in which Communist influence was great) launched "la grande bataille de la production," and the Communist party called for a "renaissance nationale" and granted absolute priority to economic recovery in its programs.[18] The PCF acted vigorously to overcome a number of economic problems besetting the French, including insufficient coal production and the lack of transportation to bring farm produce to the city. The Communist party was able to use its influence among the miners and the transportation workers effectively to overcome such bottlenecks.

The Communist party was hostile to the monetary reforms advanced by Mendès France. That hostility was the consequence not only of an

[16]See *Histoire du Parti Communiste Français: Manuel* (Paris: Éditions Sociales, 1964), p. 449. See also Rioux, *Fourth Republic*, pp. 54–56, pp. 49–50.
[17]See *Histoire du Parti Communiste Français: Manuel*, chap. 7, pp. 459, 485–501.
[18]Ibid., pp. 469–74.

economic doctrine that accorded money no real economic importance, but also of its strategy of fomenting broad opposition to monopoly capitalism. That strategy was not served by a policy that imposed the hardships of deflation on the population, even though it was designed to break the backs of profiteers. Commenting on the failure of his plan Mendès once observed, "Consider that the CGT was demanding that the minimum wage not be calculated according to official prices, but rather according to black market prices, relying on this argument: that there is no reason why only the rich, and not the people, should be able to buy on the black market!"[19] The attitude of the PCF placed real constraints on the other political forces of the provisional government who were not only the Communist party's collaborators but its competitors as well. When viewed from the perspective of a Radical Socialist or a Christian Democrat, Communist success was a source of concerned admiration that gave rise to a natural inclination to show greater solicitude for the interests of one's own social clientele. Thus, however much inspired by the "revolutionary" ambition of the Resistance to revitalize French society, many members of the provisional government feared that Mendès France's policy of monetary stabilization would create hardship for social categories that were expected to lend support to the Radicals, the Christian Democrats, or even the Socialists. After all, peasants and small merchants were foremost among the "profiteers" that were targeted by monetary stabilization. Leading the opposition against the plan, René Pleven claimed: "As a Breton, I knew how strongly our peasants were against too heavy an intervention by the administration. We risked seeing established the withholding of production and deliveries, starving Paris."[20] Subsequently, little enthusiasm for radical deflation remained among Mendès France's colleagues. As for de Gaulle, who was openly contemptuous of such partisan calculations, "the choice was not between two men, or even between two economic policies, but between two ways of establishing a hierarchy of problems. He gave preference to the minister and the policy that left him free to be, in the face of Roosevelt and Stalin, a 'full-time' General de Gaulle."[21] Only two Socialist ministers in the government, Augustin Laurent and Adrien Tixier, sided with Mendès France. The MRP ministers were divided, although Maurice Schuman was supportive of the plan. Mendès France tendered his resignation when he saw the extent of his isolation within the government. As for the Communists, they were "openly pleased by the exclusion of this troublesome figure."[22]

[19]Quoted in Lacouture, *Mendès France*, p. 168.
[20]Quoted in ibid., p. 161.
[21]Quoted in ibid., p. 169.
[22]Ibid., p. 168.

The defeat of the stabilization plan revealed the extent to which political figures had abandoned the "esprit de la résistance" to return to the normal business of political competition. The organizations that had given life to the Resistance were forgotten as political life was rebuilt around the traditional structures of a multiparty democracy. "Political life had been reconstituted along its old lines, and the parties had demonstrated their ability to absorb the new men. Those who had hoped for something different were disappointed: they had failed to appreciate the extent of the constraints, and had put too much faith in the value of a denunciation of existing political traditions and habits to open the way for an alternative."[23] The rejection of monetary stabilization in 1945 was a harbinger of the politics to come, the politics of the overdraft economy—that is, a politics of facility, a politics that sought through administrative prowess to avoid the hard choices with which not only reconstruction but also economic change confronted the nation.

THE BIRTH OF THE OVERDRAFT ECONOMY

The decision to eschew the rigors of monetary stabilization was a decision that was peculiar to France. Germany carried out a currency exchange that produced a 90 percent reduction in the liquidity of the economy, and Belgium enacted a similar policy. But in both countries, stabilization was facilitated by idiosyncratic conditions. The Belgians benefited from a vast source of currency reserves in the mines of the Belgian Congo; in Germany, monetary stabilization was imposed by an army of occupation that, for the time being, showed little concern about the political ramifications of its actions.

Too weak and too disunited to impose the costs of monetary stabilization on the population, the government of France chose to refrain from actions that might have fanned the flames of social discontent. It chose instead to place faith in its ability to accelerate economic reconstruction and to respond to the demand that excess liquidity generated by hastening production of a commensurate supply of goods. Such was the professed ambition of René Pleven, Mendès France's principal adversary. Pleven advocated a *volontariste* program of industrial investment that, he claimed, bypassed the need for monetary stabilization. His program was attractive to politicians and officials who harbored painful memories of the debilitating and ultimately ineffective deflationary policies of the 1930s.[24] "Maintaining that it was the volume of

[23]See Rioux, *Fourth Republic*, p. 53.

[24]See Jean-Pierre Patat, *Monnaie, institutions financières, et politique monétaire* (Paris: Economica, 1981), p. 202.

production that should adjust to the volume of money in circulation, and not the other way around," explained a contemporary supporter of Pleven, "the present minister places his faith in the renewal of France, exhorting it to great efforts. Thus, it has been said that the Pleven Plan is more inspired by Stakhanov than by Poincaré."[25] Such appeals to the boundlessness of the human will cannot hide the timorousness of this policy. Fearful of the redistributive implications of economic reconstruction and modernization, the French government embraced the politics of inflation. As Jean-Pierre Rioux argues, "inflation pointed up the state's failure to arbitrate between the powerful interest groups and the trade unions, its powerlessness to uphold a semblance of justice over food prices, and its inability to restore confidence in the franc. The solutions offered by inflation... prevented an invigorating shake-up of the economy's productive structures [and] mitigated the stimulative effects of the new public sector."[26]

The provisional government chose to consolidate the state's outstanding debt to the rest of the economy (as represented by the excess liquidity of the economy) with a massive bond issue made unusually attractive with fiscal dispensations (exemption from the death tax) and indexation on the "louis d'or" (that is, indexation on the market price of gold). According to its proponents, the bond issue had the virtue not only of absorbing excess liquidity in the economy but also of constituting a pool of financial reserves that could be tapped to promote investment. Moreover, it addressed the interests of sectors that Mendès France had targeted for monetary expropriation.[27] This "Liberation Loan" brought in 164 billion francs and allowed the government to consolidate past debts. On the other hand, it withdrew only 4 percent of liquid assets from circulation. In April 1945, a second attempt was made to absorb excess liquidity by giving holders of monetary assets supplementary incentives to exchange their liquid assets against treasury bills. The result was again encouraging: more than 100 billion francs worth of bonds were purchased.[28]

Nevertheless, though the bond issue was successful, its monetary effects were at best only mildly deflationary. Given the fact that the supply of liquidity was expanding at a rate of 21 percent a year, the bond issue could do little to relieve the pressure of excess liquidity on the prices of goods that remained in short supply on the market. It would have had to be three times as great if inflation were to be

[25]Pierre Lormel, *L'expérience Pleven et le contribuable français* (Paris: Éditions du Chêne, 1945), p. 31.

[26]Rioux, *Fourth Republic*, p. 68. See also Fred Block, *The Origins of International Economic Disorder* (Berkeley and Los Angeles: University of California Press, 1977), pp. 77–79.

[27]See Werth, *France*, p. 248.

[28]See Patat and Lutfalla, *Histoire monétaire*, p. 114.

contained.[29] It goes without saying that the outcome was continued inflation. The increase in the cost-of-living index, which was 22.2 percent in 1944, climbed to 48.4 percent in 1945.[30] Contemporary studies revealed a fivefold increase in most prices between 1944 and the end of 1948.[31] The decision made at the time of the Liberation to increase wages by an average 50 percent had already fanned the flames of inflation. Similar increases in family allowances had been accorded in October 1944, and in public sector wages in January 1945. To prevent such increases in worker incomes from crowding out productive investment, industrial subsidies had also been increased. On November 17, 1944, confronted by inflationary pressures that resulted in part from such policies, the government decided to freeze prices. This administrative approach to price and wage stabilization forced the government to assume the task of judging between competing claims for income.

The provisional government's fateful decision also had unwanted ramifications on its external position. Inflation worsened France's trade imbalance, which was already suffering because of the need to import to rebuild and modernize the economy, thus ushering in a long period of dependency on outside financing. Though France's reserves were already depleted in December 1944, France continued to import in 1945 more than five times the value of the goods it sold abroad. Forced to borrow in order to meet the most immediate payments problems, the French began to negotiate a series of agreements with the Swiss and the British. Although the first multilateral redefinition and stabilization of exchange rates (which occurred in December 1945, as stipulated by the Bretton Woods agreements) allowed the French to devalue their currency by a factor of more than two (the franc was devalued from 49.63 francs per dollar to 111.1 francs per dollar), persistent inflation, running at about 5 percent per month, quickly negated any commercial gain.

POLITICAL CRISIS AND MONETARY EXPANSION,
1945–1948

The history of French monetary policy in the years following World War II is one of persistent monetary expansion coupled with institutional reforms designed to funnel resources to the task of economic reconstruction. To be properly grasped, that history must be put in the broader context of growing economic and political crisis. The politics

[29]Patat, *Monnaie*, pp. 203–8.
[30]Patat and Lutfalla, *Histoire monétaire*, p. 115.
[31]See Jean-Guy Mérigot and Paul Coulbois, *Le franc: 1938–1950* (Paris: Librairie Générale de Droit et de Jurisprudence, 1950), pp. 84, 86.

of postwar France evinced growing polarization as nationalist Right and Communist Left broke ranks with the government, leaving the center isolated and fragile as well as ideologically fissured. Monetary policy was both a cause and a consequence of political crisis. The growing inability of the center to govern made monetary stabilization increasingly difficult to achieve, while the consequences of unbridled monetary growth fed social discontent that benefited the political extremes.

The first significant political shock occurred when Charles de Gaulle resigned as prime minister of the provisional government. De Gaulle's departure was the result of his growing impatience with the party politics that he considered an obstacle to the restoration of French military power and diplomatic influence. His impatience increased after the constitution of the Fourth Republic, against which he had campaigned, was adopted. In April 1947, he gave his approval to the formation of a new political group, the Assembly of the French People (Rassemblement du Peuple Français, RPF), the two dominant themes of which were anticommunism and constitutional reform.[32] De Gaulle preached resistance to the "illegitimate" regime of the Fourth Republic, and vigilance in the face of growing Communist influence within the state.[33] The RPF claimed nearly one million adherents by the summer of 1947, and its electoral success was immediate. At the municipal elections of October 1947, the RPF swept to a tidal wave victory, gathering 40 percent of the votes cast in urbanized areas, to the detriment of the centrist MRP and the SFIO, which together captured a mere 25 percent.[34]

After de Gaulle's departure, the PCF, the MRP, and the socialist party, or SFIO (Section Française de l'Internationale Ouvrière), tightened ranks by signing a tripartite nonagression treaty designed to "avoid any polemic of an offensive or insulting character and to develop a spirit of loyal solidarity for the defense of decisions made in common by the government."[35] Because of underlying ideological differences, however, "the solidarity postulated by *tripartisme* was one of convenience rather than conviction, which was clear from the painstaking attention devoted to the sharing out of the [ministerial] portfolios; the promise made by the partners to refrain from criticism and controversy pointed up rather than concealed the conflict which underlay the alliance."[36]

From the outset, the tripartite alliance was threatened by growing social conflict fed in part by the government's inability to impose

---

[32]See Chapsal, *La vie politique,* p. 163.
[33]Rioux, *Fourth Republic,* p. 124.
[34]See Chapsal, *La vie politique,* pp. 168–69.
[35]Ibid., p. 118.
[36]Rioux, *Fourth Republic,* p. 98.

monetary stability. Though the financial demands of economic reconstruction were great, it was wage policy, not reconstruction, that was the
source of inflationary pressure in 1947. In July 1946, in the face of
growing farmer and worker discontent, the government conceded a 25
percent wage increase and a 50 percent increase in farm prices.[37] Meat
prices were further increased by 20 percent in February 1947,[38] by
which time, abundant liquidity, rationing, and the black market were
contributing to an annual inflation rate that remained close to 50
percent. Though the government attempted to slow inflation by imposing a reduction of 10 percent in overall price levels, foreign trade
imbalances and a hard winter negated its efforts. Industrial output fell,
and currency reserves dwindled. American credits had to be diverted
from the task of economic reconstruction and applied to the urgent
task of paying foreign suppliers. The combined impact of inclement
weather and discouraging price structures caused food stocks to run
low. In May, bread riots broke out in some parts of the country and
worker unrest in the capital increased throughout the spring. Social
conflict aggravated political insecurity. In an international atmosphere
made heavy by fear of war between the United States and the Soviet
Union, social unrest infused the political atmosphere of the country
with suspicion and speculation of revolution and civil war. Warnings of
"a new 6th of February" were voiced.[39] General Revers, head of the
general staff, placed forces that were not suspected of Communist
infiltration on a state of alert. Though called without the approval of
the CGT, a strike in April at the Renault factories won support post
hoc from the Communist-animated trade union. The strike was widely
followed, and the PCF found itself in the uncomfortable position of
having to defend a powerful movement that was directed largely against
policies for which it shared governmental responsibility. When the
government decided to repress the strike, the Communists found
themselves forced to vote in opposition. The government, rather than
resign, took the unusual step of simply expelling the Communist
ministers from its ranks.[40] After de Gaulle's abrupt departure, the
eviction of the PCF from government was the second great political
shock suffered by the infant republic.

In the face of crisis, the MRP and the SFIO were unable to agree on
a plan to stabilize the economy. Maurice Schuman, for the MRP, argued

[37]Chapsal, *La vie politique,* p. 131.
[38]Rioux, *Fourth Republic,* p. 122.
[39]Ibid., p. 123. The reference is to a demonstration in 1934 by extreme Right groups
before the National Assembly, which was interpreted by many on the Left as an
attempted coup d'etat.
[40]Ibid., p. 125.

in favor of restoring markets. André Philip, for the Socialists, argued in favor of greater *dirigisme* and state intervention. In the absence of agreement, the government drifted. "The conditions of daily life were becoming desperate. In September, domestic coal production fell, the price of imports rose; grain was scarce after the poor harvest; a kilo of potatoes supposed to cost 9 francs typically sold for between 16 and 20; shortages of bread and sugar led to rioting at Verdun and Le Mans. Auriol noted grimly on September 15: 'The unrest is close to panic...the government appears to lack the means to get its authority respected.' "[41] Strikes multiplied as a settlement in one sector generated wage demands in another. Industrial unrest fostered fears of Communist subversion, even though the CGT and the PCF, far from fomenting social conflict, were running to keep up with spontaneous strikes. Vichy sympathizers were discovered arming themselves to resist a Communist takeover. Fears of revolution were aggravated by the violent elimination of anti-Communist parties in the countries of Eastern Europe. The polarization of French politics was reflected in the municipal elections of October, which, as stated above, resulted in a large victory for the anti-Communist RPF and revealed that the MRP and the SFIO, the mainstays of the government coalition, were a minority in the nation.

One must place the evolution of monetary practices and institutions within this context of growing political crisis. The financial market, victimized by continued inflation and political uncertainty, was abandoned to its fate of death by starvation. On the other hand, the banking sector became the object of structural reforms designed to render it a willing and able partner in the government's expansionist policy orientation by giving banks the means to supply industry with capital that was no longer forthcoming from the financial market. This constituted a real innovation. Prior to the war, French banks had shunned direct financial involvement in industry, neither participating in the capital of industrial firms nor supplying medium-term and long-term credit. Before 1945 they rarely ventured beyond the task of discounting short-term commercial paper, which at the time was the only type of asset the Banque de France accepted for rediscount. Their financial conservatism was ensconced in the legislation of 1941, which furthermore subjected the banking system to a corporatist-like system of government and surveillance. After the war, however, new legislation was adopted in order to integrate France's financial institutions into an ambitious program of industrial development that bypassed the financial market. The legislation of December 2, 1945, created new categories of banks: "business banks," which were allowed to accept

----

[41]Quoted in ibid., p. 126.

only time deposits but could participate in the capitalization of industrial firms, and medium- and long-term lending banks, which could accept only time deposits and which, though barred from extending short-term loans, could grant credit of two years maturity and longer. These took their place beside the traditional deposit banks (which were allowed to accept only sight deposits and were obliged to limit their financial activity to discounting short-term commercial paper) and were expected to play an active role in France's industrial development.

Moreover, the provisional government ratified legislation adopted in May 1944 that gave the Banque de France the power to rediscount loans of five years maturity, thus amending its prewar statutes limiting its power of rediscount to short-term loans of three months maturity or less. This facilitated the expansion of medium-term credit by business banks and medium-term credit banks that often lacked the reserves necessary to develop their activities as much as the government wished. To qualify for rediscount, a medium-term credit application had to be sponsored by one of the numerous semipublic financial institutions that were either created or restructured during this period. One such semipublic financial institution was the French Bank for Foreign Trade (Banque Française de Commerce Extérieur or BFCE), created in 1946. The BFCE not only provided seed money to promote export-enhancing investment, but also was empowered to designate certain medium- and long-term loans eligible for rediscounting by the central bank. (The central bank, however, was empowered to accept such loans for rediscount only through their seventh year; the BFCE reassumed the loan after that time.)[42] To finance its activities, the BFCE relied primarily on the sale of bonds, on loans, and on subsidies.

The creation of discountable medium-term loans involved the banks more actively in the financing of industrial investment. The banks received applications from firms for medium-term loans, which they passed on to relevant semipublic financial institutions such as the BFCE, to be underwritten and sponsored. After careful perusal by the relevant semipublic financial institutions, a loan application, if it passed muster, was granted an *accord de réescompte* (approval for discounting) by the Banque de France, making it eligible for rediscount. In this way the practice of *"transformation"* was inaugurated, whereby relatively liquid time deposits were "transformed" into medium-term credits.[43] This fateful decision was a crucial one in the development of the overdraft economy. Heavy reliance on *"transformation"* was ultimately to become one of the overdraft economy's most characteristic features. It

[42]See Patat, *Monnaie*, pp. 40–42, 50–58, 61–62.
[43]See Patat and Lutfalla, *Histoire monétaire*, p. 122.

enabled banks to extend loans of five to seven years maturity, financed either by the banking system or by the Banque de France, and consequently financed by monetary creation. Though its importance in the immediate postwar years was diminished by the fact that much investment was financed directly by the state as it redistributed Marshall Aid money, its advantages would soon prove attractive. The French people had a high propensity to save, and because of inflation and the weakness of the financial market, they were both induced and compelled to put savings in semiliquid accounts with savings institutions. This facilitated *"transformation,"* and allowed policymakers to tap this source of savings to fuel industrial investment. *"Transformation"* gave the state the power to exercise significant control over the use of capital, while sparing business the need to bid for capital on the market and thus pay market prices and satisfy market expectations.

The nascent practices and institutional structures of the overdraft economy prefigured an economy in which capital would be both abundant and cheap. The supply of credit was generous during the reconstruction years: 25 percent of the gross national product (GNP) in 1946, 12 percent in 1947 and 1948, and 8 percent thereafter. Throughout 1946, the discount rate of the Banque de France remained stable at 1.625 percent, lower than both the yield on bonds, which varied between 3.5 and 4.5 percent, and the rate of inflation, which remained near 50 percent during the years 1945–48. In order to combat inflation, however, the Banque de France increased the discount rate in January 1947 ... to 1.75 percent!

Lest it be thought that monetary expansion was the necessary consequence of economic reconstruction, it must be emphasized that the root cause of French inflation during this period was not the cost of rebuilding and modernizing French industry, but rather wage and income policy. The cost of modernization did not become a major contributor to inflation until the implementation of the Monnet Plan in 1948. Though formal wage indexation was forbidden, wage demands subsequent to the strikes of 1947 and 1948 were generally satisfied through some form of de jure or de facto indexation that was agreed on at the level of the firm or the industrial sector and that allowed wages to keep even with inflation through the remaining years of the Fourth Republic. "Money illusion" never affected the French worker. Informal indexation of wages and the development of the overdraft economy went hand in hand. The Bank of International Settlements (BIS) noted in 1949: "After each wave of increases in wages and prices, since a higher nominal sum of operating funds was required, the volume of credit accorded invariably grew. ... The businessmen, *knowing that they could count on additional credit that they needed,* may have opposed less resistance to nominal wage and price increases."[44] Wage increases contributed to the large increases in credit allocations: 41 percent in 1946 and 29 percent in 1947. The proportion of new credit allocations going to the private sector henceforth surpassed that which went to the state treasury, despite the size of the budget deficit.[45] Thus, a principal cause of the development of an overdraft economy during these years was the government's inability to resist demands by workers and independent artisans and farmers for income increases that protected them from inflation.

The constraints on monetary policy that are typically generated by the overdraft economy had already become quite visible by this time. In contrast to the prewar years, only a feeble proportion of credit came out of constituted savings. In 1928, during boom years when credit allocations amounted to 7 percent of GNP, monetary investments were quite marginal. In 1937, when, prodded by the Popular Front, credits allocated to the economy increased to 10 percent of GNP, interest-bearing bonds still accounted for two-thirds of the total. After the war, the quasi-totality of credit was funneled through financial institutions, such as banks and the semipublic financial institutions.

Growing reliance on bank credit not only contributed to inflation but also shifted the locus of monetary policy intervention from the market-place to the lending institutions whose activity could be regulated by the state. When, in 1948, the fight against inflation began to assume greater importance, policymakers, rather than raise interest rates, imposed greater selectivity in the allocation of medium-term credits by approving fewer investment projects for rediscount.[46] The discount rate was raised to a mere 2.5 percent in October 1947, and to 3 percent in October 1948. It is significant that such "stringency" was not achieved without opposition from the head of the treasury. Chronic conflict

[44]Bank of International Settlements, *La situation économique de la France* (Basel: 1949); emphasis added.

[45]Patat and Lutfalla, *Histoire monétaire*, p. 126.

[46]They also tried to deregulate wages and prices in order to contain the wage-price spiral. Administered prices of basic goods and services, such as coal, steel, electricity, and railroad transportation, were inceased significantly. This had the effect of compressing aggregate demand and thus helping inflation fall from over 50 percent in 1948 to 10 percent in 1950 (though it also caused industrial growth to fall from 14 percent to 5 percent over the same period). Moreover, they imposed a forced loan on business and withdrew large-denomination bills from circulation. Though the government imposed reserve requirements on the banks, as well as rediscount ceilings, in September 1948, these constituted "one-shot" measures designed to put brakes on the credit-allocating machinery that had been set in place after the Liberation rather than a conjunctural policy. Such policies, combined with the increase in U.S. aid and the devaluations of 1948 and 1949, contributed to bring the trade deficit down from 3.7 percent of GNP in 1948 to almost nothing in 1950.

between the treasury, whose priority it was to assure the financing of industry, and the Banque de France, which was more concerned with stabilizing prices, would become a characteristic of monetary policymaking in France for the next three decades.

Discount rates of 2 and 3 percent were of little or no use in containing inflation rates that were cruising at 50 percent. In fact, it is doubtful the government intended that they be effective. In the 1949 report of the National Credit Council, one reads that "the money supply, despite important growth during the year, doubtless remains insufficient, given the economy's need for liquid assets."[47] Further indication that the deceleration of monetary growth was low on the government's list of priorities can be found in the policies adopted in 1951, when fear of deflation caused the government to decrease the discount rate from 3 percent to 2.5 percent and to extend rediscount eligibility to medium-term loans for public housing. "All such measures," conclude Patat and Lutfalla, "undoubtedly opportune had the conjuncture been deflationary, were already debatable in a context in which demand would continue to remain unsatisfied for a number of years. Coming at a time when the Korean War was about to provoke a considerable increase in demand and in international prices, they contributed significantly to the return of economic imbalance."[48]

THE MONNET PLAN AND THE MARSHALL PLAN

The decision of January 1945 to reject deflation as a means to absorb excess liquidity generated by the war economy was motivated principally by the government's fear of the adverse social and political consequences of deflation. That decision, however, produced its own adverse consequences. Inflation rather than deflation became a source of social stress and contributed to the growing polarization of French political life. Growing governmental isolation, in turn, inclined political leaders to seek economic order through interventionism rather than through a market-driven process of adjustment.

Faith in the state's administrative powers inspired the conviction that policies could be devised that would hasten economic reconstruction and restore monetary equilibrium to the economy by increasing supply rather than by restricting demand. Political leaders were confident that if the economy could be rebuilt and modernized the monetary situation would take care of itself. That faith was bolstered by the expectation

[47]Patat and Lutfalla, *Histoire monétaire*, p. 130.
[48]Ibid., p. 133.

that France would realize some economic benefit from the Allied victory over Germany. The expectation of German reparations that informed French policy after World War II was not essentially different from that which informed policy after World War I. After the first war, the French were forced to alter those expectations because of international hostility, but after the second war it is the international system that had to bend to French demands. The outcome was an international political economy that validated French policy orientations and ultimately created trade and international monetary arrangements that rendered the overdraft economy viable.

France's plan for economic modernization was drawn up in the fall of 1945 by Jean Monnet, a member of the Resistance who had spent the war years in Washington, D.C. Though Monnet was not a Gaullist, nor even part of the government in exile in Algiers, General de Gaulle gave his modernization plan enthusiastic support and made it the foundation of French economic policy in January 1946. Conceived as the "first overall plan for the modernization and economic equipment of metropolitan and overseas France," it set forth proposals designed to develop national production and exports, to increase productivity, to ensure full employment, and to improve living standards.[49] The plan for reconstruction was extraordinarily ambitious and was intended to overcome "the constrictive *malthusianisme* that underlay France's poor economic performance."[50] France had suffered decades of demographic and economic decline relative to other European nations—above all, Germany. This decline was held responsible for France's poor trade performance, its low standard of living, and even its collapse in 1940. France's decline, it was argued, was both cause and consequence of low labor productivity, outdated technology, overcautious entrepreneurs, plethoric distribution networks, excessive administrative costs, and a too-ready recourse to protectionism.[51] Simply attending to the postwar reconstruction of such an economy was out of the question. What the French economy wanted was not reconstruction, but thorough modernization and reform. After World War I, Alan Milward explains, the "revival of the German economy had been accompanied in France by economic stagnation at a low level of output, as well as by bitter quarrels over the distribution of the national product. Avoiding a repetition of this pattern was as much a political imperative in France as full employment in Britain."[52]

[49]Rioux, *Fourth Republic*, p. 170.

[50]Ibid., p. 173. See also Herbert Luethy, *France against Herself* (New York: Meridian Books, 1960), pp. 291–315.

[51]Rioux, *Fourth Republic*, p. 173.

[52]Alan S. Milward, *The Reconstruction of Western Europe, 1945–1951* (Berkeley and Los Angeles: University of California Press, 1984), p. 51.

The financial and monetary implications of Monnet's modernization plan were prodigious. The plan called for investments over a four-year period that were the equivalent of no less than 25 percent of France's GNP as well as massive imports worth an estimated $11 billion over a three-year period.[53] To ensure success, ingredients that only the international community could provide were necessary, notably consignments of German coal and foreign financial aid. Prior to 1948, therefore, it was not at all clear that the plan was viable. The issue of French access to German resources was still pending, trade and public finances were already in severe deficit, and France's ability to pursue expansionist monetary policy was threatened by the fact that France was committed by the Bretton Woods agreement to stabilize its currency.

French policy goals were for these reasons inconceivable without U.S. aid and external accommodation. "The Modernization Plan had been based from its beginnings on the assumption that American aid was indispensable if planning targets were to be achieved and in fact it had begun its life as a one-year import program from the United States."[54] Unambiguous American support for the Monnet Plan, however, was not immediately forthcoming. The initial thrust of American foreign economic policy after the war was informed by a liberalism that showed little willingness to make compromises with the more mercantilist thrust of policies adopted by the Europeans. Jacob Viner wrote in 1944: "The United States is, in effect, as concerns leadership, very nearly single-handedly trying to reverse the whole trend of policy and practice of the world at large in the field of economic relations since 1914, and especially in the ill-fated years since 1929."[55] Cordell Hull defended a vision of a free-trade world that would, it was claimed, maximize economic welfare, promote world prosperity and foster peaceful international relations. "Universal access to foreign supplies, markets and investments would neutralize that competitive territorial imperative which lay at the base of the modern imperial scramble."[56] The economic goals of the United States were clearly stated in a 1944 State Department memorandum:

> The development of sound international economic relations is closely related to the problem of security. The establishment of a system of international trade which would make it possible for each country to have

[53]See Rioux, *Fourth Republic*, p. 114.

[54]Milward, *Reconstruction*, p. 99.

[55]Quoted in Fred·L. Block, *The Origins of International Economic Disorder: A Study of United States International Monetary Policy from World War II to the Present* (Berkeley and Los Angeles: University of California Press, 1977), p. 9.

[56]Quoted in David P. Calleo and Benjamin M. Rowland, "Free Trade and the Atlantic Community," in Jeffry A. Frieden and David A. Lake, eds., *International Political Economy* (New York: St. Martin's Press, 1987), p. 340.

greater access to world markets and resources would provide a firm basis for political cooperation. Conversely, if such a system is not established, the international frictions which would result in the economic field would be certain to undermine any international security organization which might be created. Past experience makes it clear that close and enduring cooperation in the political field must rest on a sound foundation of cooperation in economic matters.[57]

Harry Dexter White, the U.S. representative to the Bretton Woods conference, defended vigorously the concept of an International Monetary Fund that, though designed to facilitate trade adjustment, nevertheless imposed disciplinary action on countries in balance-of-payments deficit.[58] He insisted that countries in deficit be permitted only a minimum of restrictions on convertibility and only limited access to international credit. This position created a number of difficulties, for France was not the only European country to have opted for expansionist reconstruction policies. European concerns were voiced by John Maynard Keynes, who at Bretton Woods argued for a more permissive system that would be endowed with sufficient credits to allow deficit countries to achieve equilibrium without deflation.[59] For the first several years after the war, the United States tried to counter European opposition to global liberalization by tying its financial aid to liberalizing reforms. Financial aid to Great Britain, both in 1945 and 1947, was conditioned by such reforms as the early return of the pound to convertibility.[60] Similarly, a loan of $550 million extended by the Eximbank to the French in 1945 was accompanied by the demand that France, "under its Article VII obligations, reduce trade barriers, restore trade to private channels, and generally lessen governmental interference in the domestic economy."[61]

In 1947, however, U.S. policy began to undergo revision in response to growing conflict with the Soviet Union and growing economic and political instability in the countries of Western Europe where communist influence was strong. The change in American policy became

---

[57]Robert A. Pollard, *Economic Security and the Origins of the Cold War, 1945–1950* (New York: Columbia University Press, 1985), p. 13.

[58]See Block, *Origins*, pp. 42–55.

[59]See Calleo and Rowland, "Free Trade," pp. 342–343: In Great Britain, for example, the Labour party, which acceded to power in June 1945, was determined to build a domestic economy based on full employment and the welfare state. Above all, it was determined not to return to the deflationary policies and massive unemployment of the interwar years. The British workingman, it was said, was no longer to be sacrificed to the interests of the City and the liberal international system." See Pollard, *Economic Security*, p. 75. See also Block, *Origins*, pp. 55–68.

[60]See Block, *Origins*, pp. 84–86.

[61]Pollard, *Economic Security*, p. 75.

manifest in response to crises in Greece and Turkey. The idea of a financial crusade against communism began to resonate in the spirits of American legislators. Without renouncing the philosophical tenet that an open and integrated world economy would promote peace and world prosperity, as well as American interests, American policymakers became more sympathetic to the need that European problems and policies made apparent, the need to show greater tolerance for the more mercantilist economic policy orientations of the Europeans. "Congressmen returning from Europe were often skeptical about the extent of European distress, but not the Communist threat. Members of the influential Herter Committee commented that they had observed no real starvation during their travels, and, that if it were not for the communist menace spreading its poisonous tentacles across western Europe the Committee's interest in [increased financial aid] would be anything but enthusiastic."[62] In March 1947, President Harry Truman announced that significant financial, diplomatic, and military aid would be made available to Greece and Turkey to combat a takeover by forces loyal to the Soviet Union, and suggested that such measures would be considered for other nations similarly threatened by "totalitarianism." France was a strong candidate for membership in this club. Growing concern over political instability and the power of the Communist party in France softened the U.S. position on financial aid conditionality.[63] The American analysis of the situation in France was summed up by Under-Secretary of State Dean Acheson on February 22: "with four Communists in the government, one holding the vital Defense portfolio; with one-third of the electorate voting for the Communist Party; with the trade unions, factories, and military either controlled or infiltrated by Communists; and with a worsening economic and social climate—a Soviet takeover could occur at any moment."[64] The American ambassador to France, Jefferson Caffery, relinquished the hard line he had initially adopted in financial aid negotiations and prior to the French elections of 1946 pressed the U.S. government to assess France's loan request "in terms of its political importance." And as the crisis in France grew more threatening, he reported in February 1947:

> Posing to the average Frenchman as the strongest defender of his fatherland, especially against the German "menace" and "international capital," the Soviet Trojan horse in France is so well camouflaged that millions of Communist militants, sympathizers, and opportunists have been brought to believe that the best way to defend France is to identify French national interests with the aims of the Soviet Union.... The

[62]Ibid., p. 147.
[63]See ibid., pp. 73–77.
[64]Quoted in Rioux, *Fourth Republic*, p. 113.

Comintern "brain trust" here is more active and bolder than at any period since the liberation.[65]

One outcome of this turnabout in U.S. policy was American support for the Monnet Plan, made explicit in March 1947. Reacting to the proximity of legislative elections in France, as well as to the balance-of-payments and currency crisis in Great Britain, the United States made financial aid available on an interim basis during the summer of 1947 in order to help the countries of Europe stay afloat until a more systematic plan for financial assistance was prepared.[66] France received approximately 60 percent of this interim aid, to which were added loans from the Import-Export Bank, treasury advances, and restituted Nazi loot.[67] The promise of greater aid bore its most delectable fruit in the proposal made by George Marshall in June for a vast program of financial assistance for all European countries to hasten the reconstruction effort. Though the plan was bereft of the heavy conditionality that had tainted previous offers of aid, attached to it was the inchoate ambition of using aid to foster both the economic and the political integration of Europe in a way that would stabilize democracy and secure the "free world" from forces that were threatening it both internally and externally. To this end, the Marshall Plan proposed the creation of an Organization for European Economic Cooperation (OEEC).[68] As the OEEC was being established, the French and the Americans signed a bilateral treaty that provided for future collaboration.

The Economic Cooperation Administration (ECA), which administered Marshall Plan aid, was highly supportive of Jean Monnet and his modernization plan. The sheer magnitude of American aid, more than $2.5 billion between 1948 and 1952, was impressive. The French received more than 20 percent of Marshall Plan aid—less than the British but twice as much as either the Italians or the Germans. Because the principal weakness of the Monnet Plan was financial, U.S. support was crucial. Whereas, only a short time before, France's effort to rebuild and reform its economy had been threatened by the monetary instability and the trade imbalance it generated, U.S. support allowed the French to stay their *volontariste* course without concerning themselves unduly with the monetary consequences. Indeed, "inflation was now actually welcome, giving buoyancy to the money supply and easing liquidity problems."[69] The state supported investment with subsi-

[65]Pollard, *Economic Security*, pp. 75, 77.
[66]See ibid., pp. 146–48; Milward, *Reconstruction*, pp. 86–89.
[67]Rioux, *Fourth Republic*, p. 115.
[68]See Pollard, *Economic Security*, pp. 73–74; Milward, *Reconstruction*, pp. 53–55.
[69]Rioux, *Fourth Republic*, p. 175.

dies and tax reliefs, and it enrolled the nationalized banks and an array of semipublic financial institutions in the effort. Beginning in 1948, the newly created Capital Modernization Fund (Fonds de modernisation de l'équipement) funneled resources, largely drawn from Marshall Aid, to sectors that the Marshall Plan identified for priority treatment. Thus, by coordinating the efforts of the Treasury, the banks, and the semi-public financial institutions, the Monnet Plan was able to impart strategic coherence to a scheme of investment, contributing significantly to the success of reconstruction.[70]

It is true that the United States, having made peace with French mercantilist policy, nevertheless tried to link aid to the stipulation that the French work to promote financial stability, that they protect American firms seeking to invest in France, and that they curtail sales of strategic goods to the Soviet Union. American intervention in the formulation of domestic economic policy and administration was undeniable, and indeed there were complaints of "colonization" that met with something of an imperial response in the United States.[71] Senator Henry Cabot Lodge, during an executive session of the Committee on Foreign Relations on Interim Aid, exclaimed, "I don't think we need to be too sensitive about interfering in the internal affairs of these countries. We are in it up to our necks, and almost everybody except a few political leaders will be damned glad to see us interfere."[72] It is true that MRP leaders such as Georges Bidault and Robert Schuman, whose influence in government was great after the break with the Communist party, were vocal defenders of Atlanticism. On the other hand, the Communist party decried France's subjugation to U.S. imperialism and qualified France's foreign policy as nothing short of unpatriotic. Similar sentiments were voiced by leaders of the RPF, although their opposition to Atlanticism was tempered by their anticommunism.

On the whole, however, the ECA's power to intervene was far from commensurable to the quantities of aid being furnished. Although the United States was able to impose currency realignment, a multilateral decrease in intra-European trade barriers, and abandonment of certain unacceptable currency practices such as the dual exchange rate employed by the French and the Belgians, the very existence of the Marshall Plan signified a compromise with European, and notably French, mercantilism. Moreover, the opportunities to use aid as leverage over French policy were significantly diminished by two factors. First, chronic ministerial instability deterred the Americans from overplaying their hand. A visible American role would only have contributed to aggravate

[70]Ibid., p. 177.
[71]Ibid., 134.
[72]Quoted in Pollard, *Economic Security*, p. 156.

political instability and threaten the hold on government by the MRP, the closest political ally of the United States. This was particularly apparent when the United States threatened in 1948 to withhold aid unless a more sustained effort were made to contain inflation. The threat of a ministerial crisis led the U.S. government to increase the supply of funds. Second, the existence of the Monnet Plan preempted many opportunities for American interference. The ECA mission to France was largely restricted to funding Monnet Plan projects that could not be included in the French budget, and as for direct American participation in the elaboration of the Monnet Plan, it was for all practical purposes nonexistent.[73]

Thus, the expansionist economic policy orientation that gave life in France to an overdraft economy was validated and financially underwritten as a result of the change in U.S. foreign policy goals that occurred at the outset of the cold war. But the world was to be rendered even safer for the French overdraft economy when regional economic institutions were developed, such as the European Coal and Steel Community and the European Payments Union, which struck a compromise between the liberalizing ambitions of the United States and the mercantilist policy orientations of the French.

FRANCE AND EUROPEAN INTEGRATION

It was argued above that French political weakness, the threat of political turmoil, and growing Communist power incited the United States to adopt a more sympathetic attitude toward French policy goals. France, however, brought more than political fragility to the bargaining table. It held the key to the success of an enterprise to which the United States became increasingly attached as East-West tensions mounted— that of integrating a unified West Germany into some form of cooperative and pro-Atlantic European community. The French displayed real skill in using leverage over this issue to fashion regional institutions that were conducive to their program of economic renewal. Jean-Pierre Rioux writes:

> The German question and moves for European unity were the two, complementary, bases of an original and positive French diplomacy conducted by the MRP. With a right to a major say in the future of Germany acknowledged by her partners, France was strongly placed to influence the making of alliances and to mold the future of Europe. Whatever the claims of their opponents, the governments of the Third

[73]See ibid., pp. 156–59. See also Milward, *Reconstruction*, p. 120.

Force took full and sometimes far-sighted advantage of this privileged position.[74]

Immediately after the war, France's German policy was driven by fear of the security threat a unified Germany would recreate on its eastern frontier.[75] France proposed to turn Germany into a weak confederation of states with no central institutions, such as it had been prior to unification in 1871. One of these regions, "Rhénanie," which contained the coal-producing region of the Ruhr, was to be placed under the supervision of the French, the British, and the Low Countries and its resources made accessible to the other national economies of Europe.[76] The Monnet Plan assumed the success of this effort.

France's policy was initially similar to the policy it had pursued after World War I, when its efforts to thwart the reconstitution of a unified Germany were frustrated by American and British opposition. French policy seemed doomed to suffer the same fate after World War II. Though the Potsdam agreements (from which the French had been excluded) did respond to some French concerns—the four occupation zones that were established were administered as sovereign and independent economies, thereby precluding the economic reunification of Germany for the medium term—the principle was established that Germany would eventually be restored as a unified economic if not political entity. After Potsdam, de Gaulle worked hard to avoid a repetition of the post–World War I experience by multiplying the obstacles in the path of German reunification. The Soviet Union, a country the French assumed was capable of understanding the security benefits of German dismemberment as well as of responding with hostility to the idea of economic reunification, was seen as a natural ally in this endeavor. French policy tilted toward the Soviets as France courted Soviet support, notably by becoming the first Western country to recognize the pro-Soviet government in Poland.[77]

Security, however, was not the only animator of France's German policy. Economic recovery was predicated on access to German resources, especially coal and steel, and on the opportunity for French steel firms to replace German firms in key European markets (one is reminded of the reparations debate following World War I).[78] Indeed, the Monnet Plan presumed that France would have access to German

[74]Rioux, *Fourth Republic*, p. 139. See also Pollard, *Economic Security*, p. 160.
[75]See Roy C. Macridis, ed., *De Gaulle: Implacable Ally* (New York: Harper and Row, 1966), pp. 99–103.
[76]Milward, *Reconstruction*, pp. 127–28.
[77]See Luethy, *France against Herself*, pp. 342–51.
[78]See Milward, *Reconstruction*, p. 129.

resources, and thus depended on French diplomatic success in securing for France some sizable guarantee concerning that access. "Far from being based on a liberal internationalism," Alan Milward writes, "the Monnet Plan was based on the crudest possible expression of mercantilist principles. It was aimed at seizing German resources in order to capture German markets." Economic and security concerns were tightly intertwined as the French urged internationalization of the Ruhr "so as to guarantee French national security in the future, of which guaranteeing the success of the Modernization Plan was one crucial aspect."[79]

The attitude of the United States toward Germany had been one of ambivalence, alternately favorable and unfavorable to the idea of economic reconstruction, but the growing tension caused U.S. policymakers to revise that attitude. The idea soon prevailed that a politically reunified and economically reconstructed Germany, now the "front line" state in the struggle against the Soviet Union, was indispensable to the success of U.S. political goals. The United States, it was argued, had to take steps to foster economic prosperity in Germany. It was not merely that the United States wanted to restore a prosperous market, but, even more important, it was the growing awareness that an economically strong Germany was destined to play a key role in the increasingly virulent competition between the United States and the Soviet Union, coupled with the awareness that an economically strong Germany would hasten achievement of a level of prosperity in Europe that would secure it against the threat of communism.[80]

In order to speed German economic recovery, the United States now urged that steel production in Germany be allowed to increase and that trade be permitted between the American zone and the British zone, which contained Germany's industrial heartland.[81] The French objected strenuously to both proposals, not only because they revived French fears for their security but also because they increased German demand for German coal and coke, sorely needed in France, and threatened to deprive French industry of markets. France could not prevent the economic reunification of the British and American occupation zones and the consequent creation of the "bi-zone," but it did have veto power over integration of the French zone into the new reunified German market, and more important, it had veto power over the proposal that production levels of German steel be increased. French fears had to be allayed if American objectives in Germany were to be realized. Americans were thus made to understand that German reconstruction and reunification were European, not simply German prob-

[79]Ibid., pp. 137, 467.
[80]See Pollard, *Economic Security*, pp. 82–84.
[81]Ibid., pp. 94–99.

lems and that no solution to the problem of German reconstruction could be found without addressing the needs and concerns of France and other countries and winning their support.[82]

It was in this context that the London conference met to discuss the German question in April 1947. During the conference, the United States and Great Britain made substantial concessions to the French position. They acquiesced to the creation of an International Authority of the Ruhr to oversee and control German economic reconstruction, and they gave France control over the Saar steel-producing region, and thus the opportunity to use the franc rather than the dollar to purchase Saar coal and steel. (The U.S. also committed troops to a prolonged occupation of Germany).[83] The United States was willing to bargain to get French support for its policy of reunifying Germany (economically if not politically) and of integrating Germany into an as yet vaguely defined European Community.

The Marshall Plan was informed by this political goal. In pursuit of one avowed ambition of the Marshall Plan, Marshall Aid was made contingent on elaboration of a common program of European recovery, in an attempt to force the issue of European economic and political integration. The Organization for European Economic Cooperation, ostensibly set up to coordinate the use of Marshall Aid money, was actually intended to provide the supranational institutional framework within which the goal of integration could be pursued. The need for French collaboration, therefore, was urgent. "The CEEC [Committee for European Economic Cooperation] report to Congress, on which the Marshall Aid legislation depended, could not have been produced unless the United States had made a substantial concession to France, namely to support in some form or another the French policy of internationalization of the Ruhr."[84]

French acquiescence was not so easily bought. Despite the overwhelming financial power of the United States, and five years' worth of efforts, the OEEC was never much more than an international consulting firm. Its weakness was apparent from its inception, when the French threatened to boycott the inaugural ceremonies if German representatives were included on the guest list. Milward quotes French representative Hervé Alphand: "German technical advice was not needed and German politicians were not wanted."[85] Because it was part of the Marshall Aid plan, the OEEC was inaugurated before agreement was reached on its constitutional structure. It turned out to be far less supranational than

[82]See Milward, *Reconstruction*, pp. 75, 142, 54.
[83]Pollard, *Economic Security*, pp. 140–44.
[84]Milward, *Reconstruction*, p. 467.
[85]Ibid., p. 178.

the United States had intended, and it gave far more influence to the representatives of the larger economic European powers—Great Britain, France, Holland, and Italy—than the United States wanted. During the constitutional debates, de facto collusion between the French and the British placed effective obstacles in the path of any form of European integration that went counter to their perceived interests. For the French, this meant vigilance with regard to the German question, and for the British it meant vigilance concerning the fate of the "sterling zone." In the OEEC, the United States had unwittingly created a forum that facilitated the sealing of ad hoc alliances among European governments that, in the end, effectively thwarted attempts to foster the liberal and supranational interpretation of multilateralism desired by the United States.[86]

Divergent national ambitions were such that the OEEC was unable to do the one thing it was ostensibly designed to do—allocate Marshall Plan financial aid. Its efforts to coordinate recovery plans were frustrated by British unwillingness to coordinate policy with the more conservative governments of France, Italy, and, later, West Germany, as well as by their ambition to promote the use of sterling as the principal currency for European transactions. The Low Countries were reluctant to open up their newly created customs union to outsiders. Finally, the attempt by the United States to promote multilateralism within the OEEC clashed with its new avowed tolerance for the expansionist policies being pursued by France, the Netherlands, and Great Britain. The OEEC became a battleground between expansionist countries and other countries, such as Italy and Belgium, that feared Marshall Aid would merely reward financial indiscipline. Alan Milward observed: "Should a country such as France, which planned for substantial trade deficits and where high inflation rates increased the propensity to import still further, have its balance of payments deficit funded in the same proportion as a country such as Italy where deflationary policies were aimed at reducing imports? How many dollar imports should be allowed for Belgium where recovery had been so rapid and where imports fueled exports to Western Europe which were becoming increasingly difficult to sustain?"[87] It is therefore not a surprise that in 1949 it was decided to lift the burden of distributing Marshall Aid monies from the OEEC and transfer it to the ECA, administered directly by the United States.[88]

It would be false to conclude that throughout all this France was not obliged to reorient its own foreign policy drastically. With American aid

[86]Ibid., p. 168.
[87]Ibid., p. 185.
[88]See Rioux, *Fourth Republic*, p. 135; Block, *Origins*, p. 95.

came the bipolarization of world politics and adherence to an Atlantic bloc and the U.S. policy of containment.[89] De Gaulle's German policy had to be entirely abandoned. The idea of an internationalization of the Rhineland and the Ruhr was overturned when the French were forced to accept a joint Anglo-American zone in Germany. It is true that, as payment for its dramatic shift in diplomacy, France was given the largest share of free Marshall Aid grants (almost one-fourth), "a compensation no doubt for her diplomatic concessions over the German question and in recognition of her efforts in favor of European reconstruction."[90] Nevertheless, the French, having reoriented their foreign policy toward the Atlantic, now had "to devise a different policy in Western Europe which would none the less support the national economic objectives of the Monnet Plan."[91] They dropped their demands for German dismemberment and began to elaborate a plan for a Franco-German economic association that would satisfy both American demands for a unified West Germany and French demands for assured access to the resources of the Ruhr. Milward explains:

> Before the Monnet Plan had achieved its ultimate objective of making the French economy internationally competitive, France would be left exposed to the free play of comparative advantages against an economy which seemed in the circumstances of 1947 to be likely to emerge with a great many such advantages. From the moment the Marshall Aid was offered and the CEEC met, therefore, French policy towards Germany had also to be conceived in the light of an alternative Western European economic framework to that which the United States now wished to impose through the ERP [European Recovery Program].[92]

The mutual adjustment of French and American policies was slow and trying. However great the modifications in the foreign policies of both France and the United States before and immediately after the London conference, differences between the two regarding German reconstruction remained great. The United States continued to give strong support to German efforts to rebuild their steel industry, and it remained hostile to efforts to contain German industrial reconstruction. Thus, the United States gave only grudging support to the International Authority of the Ruhr, the creation of which it had accepted in

[89]See Rioux, *Fourth Republic*, p. 115. See also Guy de Carmoy, *The Foreign Policies of France, 1944–1968* (Chicago: University of Chicago Press, 1970), pp. 16–20; Michael M. Harrison, *The Reluctant Ally: France and Atlantic Security* (Baltimore: Johns Hopkins University Press, 1981), pp. 8–15; Pollard, *Economic Security*, pp. 94–99.

[90]Rioux, *Fourth Republic*, p. 134.

[91]Milward, *Reconstruction*, p. 468.

[92]Ibid., pp. 468–69.

London.[93] France, on the other hand, remained just as adamant in its opposition to German economic reconstruction as presently conceived. Franco-American differences concerning the fate of the Ruhr thus continued unabated even as European foreign ministers arrived in Washington to negotiate the creation of a North Atlantic Treaty Organization in March 1949. The U.S. "high" political goal of uniting the countries of Europe into a defensive alliance against its principal adversary was effectively being held hostage by the "low" politics of the coke trade. Dean Acheson, U.S. Secretary of State after 1949, found the road to a negotiated settlement of the German question so long and arduous that at last he acquiesced in the realization that the United States was incapable of achieving its ambitions in Europe alone. "It was in the end," Milward writes, "only France which had the power to fulfill America's ambitions."[94] Acheson decided to put the task of finding a feasible path to European economic integration almost entirely in the hands of the French. He appealed directly to Robert Schuman: "I believe that our policy in Germany, and the development of a German Government which can take its place in Western Europe, depends on the assumption by your country of leadership in Europe on these problems."[95]

The French seized this diplomatic opening with energy and proposed in 1950 the creation of a European Coal and Steel Community. The author of the proposal, the indefatigable Jean Monnet, recommended that the entire French and German outputs of coal and steel be placed under a single European High Authority, which would be open to other European steel producers as well. The proposed European Coal and Steel Community (ECSC) would thus create a common market for coal and steel products, but the market would be an administered one, a sort of "common cartel" for coal and steel products. For France, it would assure French access to the resources of the Ruhr and guarantee the "competitiveness" of French firms on European markets. Moreover, it would facilitate planned economic modernization, as called for by the Monnet Plan, and render the ideal of economic integration compatible with the *volontariste* thrust of French economic policy. For the United States, the plan laid the foundation for European integration and opened the door to German participation in a Western European economic and political community. Though the plan was denounced as anti-Soviet by the Communists, as unpatriotic by the Gaullists, and as too costly by the steel industry, the ECSC was nevertheless established in August 1952 and became operational in 1953.

[93]Ibid., p. 382.
[94]Ibid., p. 391.
[95]Quoted in ibid., p. 392.

The ECSC embodied France's conception of a more closely knit European economic community founded on "regulated and controlled markets." Fearful of confronting German industrial competition within a liberalized common market, the French rejected a broad integrationist approach in favor of one more compatible with French economic interests as defined by the Monnet Plan. By limiting the initial integration of the European market to the strategic items of coal and steel, the French restricted the process of integration by surrounding it with complex regulations. Milward explains: "The market would be regulated more in the French than in the German interest, because the Federal Republic would have to make economic sacrifices in return for so dramatic an acknowledgement of its equal political status. And in those sacrifices France would achieve a better guarantee of access to German resources than by any other policy now conceivable. The Schuman Plan [which proposed the ECSC] was called into existence to save the Monnet Plan."[96]

The European Payments Union (EPU) like the ECSC, created external conditions that facilitated France's modernization policy while promoting the vision the United States had of a Europe that was both economically integrated and politically resistant to the threat of Soviet expansion. Though French diplomacy weighed less in the creation of this regional monetary arrangement than British diplomacy, the EPU nevertheless needs at least brief examination, both to see how European interests were instrumental in the construction of the burgeoning hegemonic order and to see how that order, though predicated on liberalism, was rendered tolerant of French mercantilism.

Like those of the Marshall Plan and the ECSC, the origins of the EPU go back to the political and economic crises of 1947, when the failure of the British pound to sustain the rigors of its return to convertibility spelled the de facto demise of the Bretton Woods agreement. The pound crisis convinced American policymakers that liberalization on a regional scale was required before the more global ideals embodied in the Bretton Woods agreement could be achieved.[97] But efforts to construct a regional monetary regime were plagued by serious trade deficits in a number of European countries. Some economists began to call those deficits "structural," suggesting that some European economies were fundamentally ill-adapted to a world of strict currency convertibility.

Moreover, the proposal to create a regional monetary arrangement encountered sizable obstacles in British unwillingness to abandon its ambition of recreating the "sterling zone" and in growing American

[96]Ibid., p. 475.
[97]See Pollard, *Economic Security*, p. 165.

reluctance to grant the Europeans yet another opportunity to stay their expansionist and mercantilist course. Even America's staunchest advocates of a European payments system believed it was time to temper the expansionist thrust of European policies.[98] The subsequent inability to reconstruct a monetary regime, whether global or regional, slowed trade liberalization. Bilateral arrangements were the rule as a series of payments agreements "clawed their way painfully forward to multilateralize tiny percentages of intra-western European trade while the basis of Europe's trade remained even more restrictive and protective than in the 1930s."[99]

Meanwhile, the French attempted to address their own currency difficulties by adopting unilaterally a number of policies that had the effect of worsening distortions between exchange rates. After the inflated wartime franc was devalued to 111.11 francs to the dollar in 1945, inflation in France and the deficit in trade with the United States nevertheless continued to feed a black market for foreign currency, depriving the state of foreign currencies at a time when the need for them was great. The French devalued the franc a second time by a dramatic 80 percent in January 1948, bringing the dollar to 214.39 francs. The French decided at that time, however, to create a dual market. Exporters were allowed to redeem up to half their dollars and pounds earned through the export of real goods and the totality of foreign currencies earned through the sale of financial assets and other invisibles on a free market, on which currencies were allowed to float. Policymakers claimed that their intention was to let the market determine the optimum par value for the franc, but unavowed was the intention to favor French exports with a disguised subsidy, equal to the difference between the value of the floating dollar and that of the official dollar.[100]

The dual market depressed the value of sterling relative to the dollar on one of the few existing open currency markets. Because the United States had, since 1947, recognized dollar-sterling stability as the condition sine qua non of a return to international monetary convertibility as advocated in the Bretton Woods agreement, American officials were ruffled. The United States objected strenuously to the dual exchange rate, and the IMF refused to approve it and even disbarred the French

[98]Paul Hoffman, general administrator of the Marshall Plan and a staunch advocate of a European payments structure, wired his opinion to the embassy of Paris: "Present investment programs no longer sufficient justification for continuation present levels overall deficits, particularly when contribution to attaining viability by 1952 doubtful." Quoted in Milward, *Reconstruction*, p. 324.

[99]Ibid., p. 282.

[100]The Italians had instituted a similar policy the previous summer. See ibid., p. 308.

from access to IMF facilities. In October 1948, the French compromised by subjecting all commercial transactions to a fixed exchange rate that was defined halfway between the official parities and the floating rates of the dollar and the pound. They made no commitment, however, to honor the official exchange rates.

A second French initiative complicated American efforts: creation in France of a public market for gold—especially for gold coins, a favorite savings instrument in France. The market was instituted to dispel fears among French investors that their capital was threatened by inflation and heavy-handed state intervention in the economy. For the United States, however, this constituted a unilateral policy decision that had multilateral implications for the reconstruction of international monetary unity. The United States would have preferred that the question of gold's status and the creation of a public market be settled by international agreement. Despite its objections, the United States was unable either to persuade or coerce the French to close the market. France henceforward boasted one of the few markets where the public could buy gold for monetary purposes.

In September 1949, the devaluation of sterling provoked a general realignment of currencies and created the conditions for establishing a multilateral monetary union. The French participated in this generalized currency realignment by devaluing the franc for a third time to 350 francs to the dollar, a parity at which it remained until 1957, and put an end to the dual exchange rate pending the outcome of multilateral negotiations.[101] Further compromise, however, had to come from the United States, which though skeptical of the need to facilitate European reconstruction in a way that might discriminate even further against its short-run commercial interests, was nevertheless concerned that "[if] there were a second collapse in Europe as a result of our inability to figure out the technical aspects of recovery, Europe once more would become an easy prey for Communist propaganda."[102] Thus, the United States agreed again to an international economic arrangement that placed only moderate restraints on European policy and included no conditions at all concerning the integration of European markets. The resultant European Payments Union was "realistic, practical and durable," but only "because it fell so far short of ambitions on the American side."[103] It established a central clearinghouse that made use of currency deposits by European central banks to create

[101]Maurice Niveau, *Histoire des faits économiques contemporains* (Paris: Presses Universitaires de France, 1970), p. 342.

[102]Quoted in Milward, *Reconstruction*, p. 323. Agreement was facilitated by the currency realignment of 1949; see ibid., pp. 323–26.

[103]See ibid., p. 326.

credit lines that could be used to finance payments deficits. A small deficit could be covered entirely by a credit line, though larger deficits required currency payments. The EPU thus introduced a sliding scale that increased the ratio of cash to credit as the deficit increased, thereby discouraging large chronic trade deficits. Because European deficits were so high to begin with, however, U.S. participation was imperative. Without the United States, the proposed credit lines would not have been adequately funded.

The ostensible purpose of the European Payments Union was to facilitate the return to currency convertibility and to lay the corner-stone of European economic integration. However, the EPU fell well short of this goal. Though it placed constraints on national policies, it did not foster the sort of discipline that would have made possible real economic integration or even a rapid return to convertibility. It failed even to solve Europe's payments disequilibriums. On the contrary, it put off the return to convertibility for almost a decade and introduced a distinct measure of discrimination against non-EPU economies, with which bilateral payments arrangements, exchange controls, and quanti-tative import restrictions remained the rule.[104] Says Alan Milward, "What the United States had to settle for was the highest common factor of agreement which would preserve one trade and payments system in the western world, a limited form of multilateralism, contin-ued dollar aid to make that possible, and the persistence throughout the 1950s of discrimination by powerful economies against the dollar." And concerning the way in which the ECSC and the EPU effectively refashioned the international political economy, Milward concludes: "In place of a liberal unified Europe came a closely regulated Little European common market whose twin purposes were to provide for French national security by containing West Germany and to permit its members to continue to pursue a very limited range of common economic policies in a few specific sectors of the economy, which would otherwise have become impossible." On the other hand, "[the] conclu-sion of the EPU agreement . . . , representing as it did a major policy retreat by the United States, together with the agreement on a coal and steel community, laid the foundations of an effective reconstruction of Europe, closing one period and inaugurating another."[105] For the present, one notes that this more pragmatic approach to integration had the effect of preserving the opportunity for the French to continue their forced march toward industrial modernization—at the end of which the overdraft economy lay in ambush.

[104]Pollard, *Economic Security,* p. 166.
[105]Milward, *Reconstruction,* p. 333.

CONCLUSION

In Chapter Three it was argued not only that governments on occasion extend economic insurance to specific sectors of the political economy in order to defend their hold on power, but also that economically powerful neighbors sometimes share the cost of implementing those insurance programs because they fear the local opposition as much as the government does. It was also advanced that cost-sharing, conceived in this manner, was one of the characteristics of the American hegemonic order. The history of French-American relations in the years following World War II confirms this characterization of U.S. leadership. The hegemonic order first took the form not of an elaborate and game-theoretically elegant international regime, but rather of a series of inelegant compromises between the United States' ideologically informed ambition of global liberalization and the efforts of European governments to strengthen their economies and to assure social peace through sustained economic growth. U.S. leadership was asserted not so much through the creation of an international economic order as through the destruction of one. The policy reversal that occurred in 1947 destroyed the Bretton Woods system almost at birth. In the pointed imagery of Alan Milward, the Bretton Woods system "died in 1947 of infant mortality, or, if a harsher view is taken, of infanticide by its European parent."[106]

The change in the U.S. policy was provoked by the crises—both economic and political—of 1947. The economic crisis, as it manifested itself both in France and in Great Britain, was characterized by a seemingly unmanageable payments imbalance. The political crisis, as it manifested itself chiefly in France, was characterized by severe labor unrest coupled with growing Communist influence in public opinion. The United States intervened with financial support to ease the pressure the payments imbalance placed on policymakers, and thus freed the governments of France and other European countries from the need to attack that imbalance with a politically risky deflationary policy. In so doing, however, the United States in effect ratified the mercantilist policy orientation the French embraced after the war. After all, the payments imbalance, despite the concerns that Keynesian economists were voicing concerning "structural imbalances," was the product chiefly of expansionist monetary policy. The government of France, like other European governments, seized on economic policies that promoted growth, because they "could find no other basis for political consensus."[107] It was not the imperatives of reconstruction that pro-

[106]Ibid., p. 466.
[107]Ibid.

voked expansionist policy in France, but rather the mercantilist desire to hasten the process of industrial modernization, to lift France to the economic level of the principal world powers, and to break the trammels of the social and economic "malthusianisme" that was held responsible for the country's collapse in 1940. The redistributive implications of France's ambitions, however, were never squarely faced. On the contrary, they were cast aside along with Mendès France's plan for monetary stabilization. By extending state control over the allocation of financial resources, the French government hoped that modernization could be achieved without sacrificing the economic expectations of whole sectors of the population. For this reason, it is important to note, as Milward has perceptively argued:

> The economic crisis of 1947 which ended dollar-sterling convertibility and produced the European Recovery Program was not caused by the deteriorating domestic economic situation of the western European economies. [It] was, on the contrary, attributable to the remarkable speed and success of western Europe's economic recovery. It was caused by the widening gap in the first six months of 1947 between increasing imports and increasing exports in some European economies, particularly Britain, Italy, and the Netherlands, and the failure of that gap to continue to narrow in others, notably France.[108]

By 1947, it had become apparent that this policy orientation would collapse unless it received U.S. support. Though the United States had initially sought to use financial aid as leverage to discourage mercantilist policy in Europe, it now not only feared the possible political consequences of economic policy failure in Europe but also confronted a France that was able to use the German question as leverage to discourage American efforts to press the theme of liberalization too hard. The United States shifted gears, and after 1947, U.S. policy had the effect not of combating "economic nationalism," or mercantilism, as hegemonic theorists frequently claim, but rather of rendering mercantilism viable. It not only supported French modernization efforts financially, but also fostered the creation of binding international trade and monetary arrangements, the ECSC and the EPU, without which French mercantilist modernization efforts would have failed. "It was out of [the] expression of French national interest," argues Milward, "that the first real steps towards 'supra-nationality' in Europe were taken."[109] It was U.S. policy that made possible the implementation of the egregiously mercantilistic Monnet Plan of industrial modernization. And by the same token, it was U.S. "leadership" that created the conditions that

[108]Ibid.
[109]Ibid., p. 167.

facilitated the development of the overdraft economy, the general contours of which were clearly visible by the end of the 1940s.

The debate over monetary stabilization that opposed Mendès France and René Pleven has, even now, not been entirely laid to rest. Economists and policymakers have lamented the ability of inflation in France to resist an array of remedies and, looking back to the fateful decision made before the guns of war were even silenced, have asked aloud if the right path was taken.[110] French economists and political leaders, without seeking to tarnish the mythological aura that surrounds the Monnet Plan, readily admit that monetary inspiration was not one of its characteristics. Indeed, the inability to think through the monetary and financial consequences of modernization was, in the words of Patat and Lutfalla, "one of the great weaknesses of the first plan, in which the monetary and financial orientations occupied a very modest position."[111] One senior monetary official reminisced, "We may have missed the train."[112]

[110]See Patat and Lutfalla, *Histoire monétaire*, p. 118.
[111]Ibid., p. 121.
[112]Personal interview, Paris, June 1983.

CHAPTER FIVE

The Institutionalization of the Overdraft Economy under the Fourth Republic

The overdraft economy was born of the fear of confrontational politics. Instead of securing economic modernization on a foundation of monetary stability, as Mendès France proposed, the government chose to promote modernizing investment by injecting new monetary resources into the economy, resources that for the time being remained without counterpart in the form of real goods. The consequences of that policy for France's balance of payments, it was hoped, would be addressed by modifications in France's external economic environment: increased financial aid, a favorable solution to the German question, and the implementation of lenient rules governing international transactions. Once such modifications were won, it was hoped that the state's power to regulate prices would suffice to keep the lid on the kettle until such time as a new and revitalized economy would produce real goods in sufficient quantity to absorb excess liquidity.

The consequences of that fateful choice for the development of the French political economy in the 1950s are related in this chapter. By adopting a policy path that obfuscated the redistributive implications of economic modernization, the state in effect provided a type of economic insurance to whole sectors of the population. It provided insurance to rising sectors by freeing them from the capital risk of new investment. It provided insurance to wage earners in the form of de facto wage indexation that promised to guard workers' real incomes against the effects of inflation. It provided insurance to declining sectors— artisans and shopkeepers—both in the form of inflation itself, which slowed or halted the unfavorable evolution in relative prices that modernization brought, and through price freezes that validated inflationary gains.

136

Once France committed itself to this path there was no turning back. Efforts to define and implement more rigorous policy by the likes of an Antoine Pinay bred political contestation and polarized French politics. Fourth Republic leaders thus chose repeatedly to eschew the confrontational politics implicit in monetary stabilization, preferring to refine and to perfect the instruments of administrative control over credit, money, and prices that gave them some discretionary power to manage the overdraft economy in a manner that ratified the economic expectations of the population. In this way the overdraft economy became ensconced in the financial institutions and processes of the French political economy.

Monetary Stabilization under Antoine Pinay

It is useful to examine in some detail Antoine Pinay's efforts to stabilize the monetary situation, because however moderate his policies they show up the difficulties and the limits of stabilization in the nascent overdraft economy. The government of Antoine Pinay was in effect the first to mount an attack on monetary disorder. His government inaugurated a period of two-and-a-half years (January 1952–June 1954) of government by the Right. After the exclusion of the Communists from government in 1947, France was governed by a tripartite coalition that included Socialists on the left and Christian Democrats (the MRP) on the right. Because of ideological incompatibilities, however, the coalition was not long-lived. Differences over economic policy forced the Socialists into opposition in January 1952. This created the political conditions for a return to greater financial orthodoxy and greater monetary stability.

Antoine Pinay was a leather manufacturer from the provinces, a provincial political "notable" who ran for office on the Independent list (and thus not a member of the tripartite alliance) with nothing of the technocrat about him. Though he had some Gaullist support, he owed neither his success nor his political views to the Resistance. In fact, he spoke of the policies of the resistants with disdain and expressed open hostility toward the concept of *dirigisme* and the technocrats who implemented it. His economy policy was inspired by the common sense of the businessman and consisted of nonprogrammatic, pragmatic measures, the chief ambition of which was to put an end to inflation.

Pinay attacked inflation by reducing government spending by about 3 percent and temporarily suspending the inflationary practice of asking the Banque de France for cash advances. The centerpiece of his policy of stabilization, however, was the "emprunt Pinay," or Pinay loan.

137

Issued in May 1952, it carried an interest of 3.5 percent on a capital that was not only indexed on the price of gold but also exempt from taxes, including inheritance taxes. It was designed to lure savings away from gold and liquid accounts into longer-term treasury assets. Such attractive features made it an immense success, instilling the habit in both the great and small, because of its exemption from inheritance taxes, "de mettre en Pinay avant de mettre en bière (to place in Pinay before placing in the coffin)."[1]

While they had a slight deflationary impact on the economy, Pinay's policies hardly constituted an armored assault on monetary instability. Like the Liberation loan, the "emprunt Pinay," rather than douse inflationary expectations with real monetary austerity, actually ratified underlying inflationary expectations by creating a savings instrument that was immune to inflation. Pinay's other policies shared this comforting feature. Typical was the refusal to increase (and occasionally the decision to decrease) prices that were controlled by the government, notably those of coal, steel, wheat, and electricity. Because truth in prices required an increase rather than a decrease in most government-controlled prices, however, Pinay's effort represented a transfer of wealth from the state to the consumer, rather than an assault on the root cause of inflation.

However great his conviction that inflation had to be stopped, Pinay did not supply the kind of political leadership that was required to stabilize the monetary situation in France. He proved responsive to the same political constraints that had discouraged his predecessors from tackling the problem of monetary instability head on. His response was typical of politics under the Fourth Republic to the extent that it sought solutions to economic disequilibria that left the expectations of economic agents essentially unaffected. As Jean-Pierre Rioux remarked, Pinay learned and taught his successors "the value of wooing public opinion with moderate policies and an assiduous attention to the cult of higher living standards":

> For it was this question which remained at the forefront of popular preoccupations until 1954. Were the French people in fact prepared to reopen old wounds and make painful choices? Or could a Cassandra-like figure have persuaded them to face up to the inevitable? The questions are perhaps futile; for in 1952, when opinion did express itself clearly, it opted simply for the safeguard and improvement of its well-being.[2]

But one might object that Pinay's policies did in fact inaugurate a period of price stability that lasted until 1957. The index of wholesale

[1] Jean-Pierre Rioux, *The Fourth Republic, 1944–1958* (Cambridge: Cambridge University Press, 1987), p. 198.
[2] Ibid., p. 200.

prices actually fell by 8 percent in 1952 and by another 2 percent in 1953.[3] Price stabilization, however, owed more to the downturn in the international economy than to the success of Pinay's policies. The Korean War came to an end, and with it the global inflationary pressures the war had generated. Aggregate demand fell, price levels dropped, and industrial investment contracted. The impact on world price levels was severe—the Reuter index of raw material prices fell 15 percent. Credit allocation in France, which fell from nearly 800 billion francs in 1951 to less than 500 billion francs, was the consequence of slack demand rather than governmental parsimony. Price stabilization in France and worldwide recession, coupled with a drastic reduction in demand for imported goods (capital goods and industrial commodities among them), produced a dramatic turnabout in France's external balance, which in 1954 and 1955 was in surplus.

The real measure of Pinay's policies is in the evolution of the money supply, where growth continued strong, not in the evolution of prices. Although M_2 growth fell from over 18 percent in 1951, it remained high at 13.6 percent in 1952, declined to a little less than 12 percent the following year, and climbed again to 14 percent in 1954 as reflationary measures came into play (see Table 10). Despite the success of the Pinay loan, the ratio of liquidity (M_2) to GDP hardly varied. At 29.5 percent in 1950, it declined only to 28 percent in 1952, and thereafter climbed steadily until it reached 34 percent in 1955. As for the budget deficit, it was reduced but not eliminated. It dropped from 769 billion francs in 1952 to 346 billion in 1954, and began climbing again thereafter.[4] The government was soon renewing its appeal to the Banque de France for cash advances.

Price stabilization, though it owed little to government policy, had

Table 10: Evolution of selected economic indicators, 1952–1955

	1952	1953	1954	1955
GNP (%)	2.6	2.9	4.8	5.8
Trade balance (billion francs)	−216.5	−118.5	−62.8	30.3
Retail prices (%)	11.9	−1.7	0.4	0.9
M_2 (%)	13.6	11.8	14.0	12.9
Credit (%)	15.9	12.8	11.0	8.0

Source: Adapted from Jean-Pierre Patat and Michel Lutfalla, *Histoire monétaire de la France au XXe siècle* (Paris: Economica, 1986), pp. 140, 143. Used by permission of the publisher.

[3]The impact of this fall in prices was all the more dramatic as the government chose this moment to make official the practice of wage indexation.

[4]Note that between 1950 and 1954 U.S. aid to France for the war in Vietnam totaled $3.6 billion, 80 percent of the cost of the war. See Rioux, *Fourth Republic*, p. 214.

unwanted consequences that illustrate the politics of the overdraft economy.[5] Widespread economic discontent was fomented by slumping farm prices, poor salaries in the civil service, and the end of inflation-generated profits for the small shopkeeper. Among workers, though unemployment rose only to 100,000 by the spring of 1953, discontent was nevertheless great in the public sector, where the government tried to compress public sector salaries in order to reduce the budget deficit. In August 1953, postal service workers went on strike. The strike spread rapidly to the national railways (Société Nationale des Chemins de Fer Français, SNCF), the Parisian urban transportation system (Régie Autonome des Transports Parisiens, RATP), and the national power company (Électricité de France—Gaz de France, EDF-GDF). By the middle of August, 4 million workers were on strike. Retreating from the anti-inflationary thrust of its policies, the government acquiesced to the demands of the strikers, reversing policies of budgetary rigor that had been enacted only a few months earlier. The social crises of 1953, compounded by reversals in the colonies, caused political crisis at home and bared the impotence of government for the public to see. The revelation fostered popular alienation vis-à-vis the regime and gave rise to a sense of impending disaster in the second half of 1953 that caused Pierre Mendès France to exclaim, "Nous sommes en 1788."[6]

Growing political discontent caused the "deflation" of Pinay to give way to the reflation of Joseph Laniel. Although Laniel was no less than Pinay a representative of the conservative right, he did not continue on the path of monetary stabilization, but rather acted to reflate aggregate demand. His policies included a muffling of the relatively "rigorous" monetary policies of his predecessor, a relatively generous wage policy, and an attempt to stimulate productive investment. The minimum salary was increased by a generous 21.5 percent in 1954, and salaries above the legal minimum were increased by an average of 10 percent. Laniel's monetary policy consisted of a series of reductions in the discount rate, bringing it from 4 percent in 1953 to 3 percent by the end of 1954. In other initiatives, the cost of credit was reduced for exporters, farmers, and all borrowers of medium-term loans that were eligible for discount. Furthermore, regulations facilitating the allocation of consumer credit were enacted, thus sustaining demand through the creation of what was in fact a new type of credit instrument.[7] It is also under the Laniel government that the state's control over the

[5]Pinay's personal popularity never suffered.

[6]See Rioux, *Fourth Republic*, pp. 210, 223 (Mendès France quoted on p. 218).

[7]Banks could lend no more than ten times the value of their reserves for a period not to exceed eighteen months and with the requirement that the borrower pay 20 percent down on whatever was being credited.

allocation of credit was used to facilitate lending to local housing authorities in order to promote the construction of new homes and apartment buildings.

Pinay's short-lived experiment showed that monetary rigor, however adulterated by efforts to defend real purchasing power and however unsuccessful in slowing the undercurrent of monetary growth, could nevertheless not be sustained. However moderate, it gave rise to social conflict. In the long run, it even provoked the alienation of the traditional sectors of the French political economy in such a way that Fourth Republic governments were deprived of their last vestiges of authority.

MONETARY DISEQUILIBRIA AND NEW COMPLAINTS OF *MALTHUSIANISME*

Monetary policy during this period must be placed in the context of the social and political conflicts of which it was both cause and consequence. The expansionist thrust of policy in the immediate postwar period provoked defensive reactions and adaptive efforts on the part of economic agents that rendered the return to more orthodox modes of monetary regulation highly problematic. First, inflation and price freezes brought about a revival of "corporatism" (in the French sense of the word, to be explicated below) that aggravated the French political economy's newly acquired allergy to market mechanisms. Second, inflation itself fostered the development of an entire parasitic class, the existence of which was threatened by the restoration of price stability. These two aspects of the development of the postwar political economy are examined in this section.

As the French political economy evolved into an overdraft economy, in which control over monetary growth through market interventions became more and more problematic, administrative and coercive instruments of monetary regulation assumed greater importance. Administrative price controls were the principal instrument of coercive economic regulation. The legislation that instituted price controls, contained in two ordinances of June 30, 1945, was originally intended only to meet the economic urgencies of the Liberation, but in time that legislation became the legal vehicle for the imposition of at least ten price freezes over the next thirty years. Under the Fourth Republic alone, price freezes were imposed in 1948, 1952, and 1957.[8] Even

[8]See Jean Chardonnet, *La politique économique intérieure française* (Paris: Dalloz, 1976), pp. 121–33. See François Caron, *An Economic History of Modern France* (New York: Columbia University Press, 1979), p. 237.

during the intervening years, prices were not given complete liberty to respond to market forces, but rather were subjected to strict surveillance. The effectiveness of price controls, however, was doubtful. To the extent that inflation was fed by rising production costs, notably wages, price controls had little effect other than the deleterious one of squeezing profit margins. And to the extent that inflation was fed by excess consumer demand, price controls abetted rather than repressed inflationary trends because more often than not they validated underlying inflationary pressures. As one contemporary critic complained, "price controls, far from restraining price rises, tend on the contrary to accelerate them, since the administration merely endorses the rise in costs claimed by the producers."[9] Finally, because price controls left many people out in the cold, whether investors, farmers, or professionals, the practice of indexation tended to spread spontaneously through the economy with or without the approval of the government.

Price controls enhanced "corporatist" aspects of the French policymaking process as professional solidarities and associations arose to give voice to sectoral demands.[10] By "corporatism," however, I mean not tripartite negotiations between unions, government, and employer associations over wages and working conditions, but rather the atomization of French society into numerous small and specialized professional groupings, each working to enhance the prosperity of its members, with little or no regard for the prosperity of the French economy as a whole. This is how the term *corporatisme,* which refers back to the guild structure of the pre-modern economy, is understood in French.[11] Though research on this point is lacking, it is a fact that many administered prices were subject to some form of "agreement" between the government and interested professions, organized formally in associations that were given official recognition by the state (which continues to organize the election of officers in these associations even today).[12]

Corporatisme and price and wage indexation spawned economic rigidities. In 1954 the Government Accounting Commission (Commission des Comptes) complained of "structural rigidities" that hampered France's ability to compete in a more integrated European market.[13] The

[9]Caron, *Economic History,* p. 237.

[10]See Melchior Palyi, *A Lesson in French: Inflation* (New York: Economists' National Committee on Monetary Policy, 1960).

[11]For an attempt to apply the notion of corporatism to France, see Frank L. Wilson, "French Interest Group Politics: Pluralist or Neocorporatist?" *American Political Science Review* 77 (December 1983).

[12]Price deregulation in the early 1950s (although surveillance was maintained up until the late 1970s) slowed but did not roll back the evolution toward a "corporatiste" economy.

[13]See Caron, *Economic History,* pp. 233–34.

commission referred explicitly to informal ententes among producers to limit competition, to fiscal privileges, to subsidies, and to growing "corporatisme" in the liberal professions. By the mid-1950s, the notion of "structural rigidities" had become a leitmotif in official as well as academic publications. For example, the economist Jacques Le Bourva complained in 1951 that France was returning to a past it had rejected at the time of the Liberation, that inflation and monetary disorder were prolonging the survival of unproductive firms, while structural rigidities were feeding inflation by preventing adjustment in relative prices. Le Bourva concluded: "It is the existence of a conservative type of *capitalism of small coalesced units* in agriculture and in consumer goods industries that is responsible for high prices."[14]

Paradoxically, therefore, the overdraft economy, born of the desire to promote productive investment, and indeed not unsuccessful in doing so, was by the mid-1950s evolving into an economy that was being labeled once again as Malthusian. This was the ineluctable consequence of a policy orientation, validated by change in the structures and processes of the international political economy, that sought growth in a manner that tried to elude the political stress generated by growth's redistributive impact. Stanley Hoffmann, writing in the early 1960s, described it thus: "The state has promoted change by exploiting that very craving for security which had previously slowed down change. That is, the state has done its best to lower the risks of change. Having to deal with notoriously reluctant swimmers, it has warmed the water so that the swimmers would not be afraid to catch cold, and it has multiplied the incentives to convince them that swimming would not only be harmless but profitable."[15]

The threat of "corporatisme" was compounded by the impact of inflation itself. Inflation dulled the redistributive consequences of industrial modernization and prevented the Schumpeterian process of "creative destruction" from occurring. Indeed, it reinforced the numbers and prosperity of an entire class of artisans and shopkeepers who would soon become the fiercest opponents of modernization. Each year since 1940, one hundred thousand new shops opened their doors in France, numbering 1.3 million by 1954 and providing income to 2,240,000 persons.[16] The small shopkeeper owed his or her success to the fact that low turnovers could be amply compensated for by the high

[14]Jacques le Bourva, *L'inflation française d'après-guerre, 1945–1949* (Paris: Armand Colin, 1951), p. 367.
[15]Stanley Hoffmann, "Paradoxes of the French Political Community," in Stanley Hoffmann et al., *In Search of France* (Cambridge: Harvard University Press, 1963), p. 63. See also Charles Kindleberger, "The Postwar Resurgence of the French Economy," in ibid., p. 143.
[16]Rioux, *Fourth Republic*, p. 248.

profit margins generated by inflation. Price stabilization, helped by the post-Korea economic downturn and by the very prudent anti-inflationary policies of Antoine Pinay, constituted a slow-acting though imperfectly perceived threat to the prosperity of this class that by 1954 was pitting the shopkeeper against an imaginary adversary made up of nightmarish technocrats and impotent and unprincipled politicians in Paris. Alienation expressed itself as a struggle between "us" and "them," or "eux," the suspicious and scornful utterance of which was so brilliantly captured in Laurence Wylie's contemporary study of life in the Vaucluse.[17] Writing in the mid-1950s, Herbert Luethy, who with Stanley Hoffmann must be counted among the most insightful observers of French politics and society, describes this evolution in graphic terms:

> In the midst of her stagnation and sclerosis, poverty and social decay, France is the only modern country in which the numbers, influence, and share in the national income of an independent middle-class based on one-man or two-men businesses ... have increased, both absolutely and relatively—a remarkable achievement in the self-defence of a remarkably individualistic social and economic type in defiance of all the tendencies of the time. But this self-preservation was attained by the most ruthless methods. This was not the arising of a healthy bourgeoisie, but of an unhealthy, cancerous growth. These people are devoid of social or political scruples, thoroughly "class-conscious," pugnacious, and ready for the "class-struggle," and full of solidarity, because fully aware of the threatened nature of their position. ... True liberalism, real competition, public morality, and honest facing up to questions would represent a deadly danger to them; and the most important thing in the world to them is the maintenance of their control of the key positions in Parliament and the state, the distributing centre of favours, privileges, and immunities. ... The degeneration of French domestic politics into an orgy of economic pressure groups is a reflection of this "transformation in stagnation."[18]

Later Luethy concludes:

> Thus the final balance sheet is full of contradictions. The achievements in economic and physical reconstruction were all the more impressive in view of the almost superhuman difficulty of the conditions in which they took place. The Monnet plan and the Marshall plan, the tremendous effort of the post-war period, and the immense expansion in industrial potential, created the conditions for a revival, but failed to set the engine of this national economy in motion.[19]

Luethy goes on to cite a report of the French economic council of 1953 which concluded forlornly, "The decisions which appear so hard to us

[17]Laurence Wylie, *Village in the Vaucluse* (Cambridge: Harvard University Press, 1964).
[18]Herbert Luethy, *France against Herself* (New York: Meridian Books, 1960), p. 324.
[19]Ibid., p. 328.

to make today will probably be made by a younger generation which will burst the existing structures asunder and throw the leaden weight of *situations acquises* [entitlements] off the shoulders of national politics."[20] The passage reveals the mentality of policymakers struggling with the imperative of modernization while handicapped by the lack of political muscle to impose change on the population. The revolutionary spirit of the Liberation had given way to a siege mentality. Just as in the 1970s—the similarity is striking—policymakers resorted to what can only be described as financial and fiscal tricks to gain time until the cavalry might come in the form of an industry that had somehow turned suddenly vibrant and competitive. In sum, the efforts of political leaders to promote modernization in a manner that eschewed political confrontation had the ironic effect of multiplying political demands on the government and creating new sources of political stress.

The outcome was the alienation of an entire class of French society that contributed greatly to bringing down the regime. In the summer of 1953, Pierre Poujade, a small provincial shopkeeper, began to organize resistance to tax inspectors.[21] The movement was provoked, ironically, by an amnesty granted tax evaders by the Pinay government in an effort to encourage the French to bring their fortunes out of hiding and to invest in Pinay bonds. The amnesty had the perverse effect of turning tax inspectors away from the large taxpayer toward the small taxpayer, giving rise to increasingly numerous confrontations between inspectors and small shopkeepers and farmers. The conflict was aggravated in 1954 when the Mendès France government enacted a bill that threatened imprisonment for anyone who resisted tax inspection. The movement spread rapidly through the provinces, and as it spread it broadened its theme from fiscal injustice to criticism of a regime that Poujade began to decry as unpatriotic, "oppressive," and "rotten." The movement spread to agriculture and turned violent. It grew into a movement of sufficient power and influence to mark the course of French politics during the remaining years of the decade. It expressed the fears, the frustrations, and petty intolerance of a class whose growth was, to a significant degree, the unexpected side-effect of policy itself—Poujade's support came from the more than 3 million shopkeepers, artisans, and small farmers whose livelihoods, though threatened by economic modernization, had profited greatly from expansionist monetary policy.

Poujadisme gave voice to the alienation of a class that was being left

[20]Ibid., p. 330.
[21]See Stanley Hoffmann, *Le mouvement poujade* (Paris: Armand Colin, 1956).

behind by industrial modernization and was, temporarily at least, abandoned by economic policy. "Born of a powerlessness to stem the tide of modernization, Poujade's revolt was backward-looking, invoking the glories of France and the uncomplicated patriotism of the pre-1914 primary school, coming close to Vichy with its exaltation of a social life based on the family and the small community, a way of life now under attack from the technocrats, the tax inspectors, and the politicians."[22] *Poujadisme* created an intractable antiparliamentarian opposition on the right, which, coupled with the intractable though less resolutely antiparliamentarian opposition on the left, further sapped the government of its authority. This, in turn, made more remote the likelihood of monetary rigor and rendered more automatic the reflex that consisted of looking to technocratic skill rather than to political leadership to resolve political problems. The "interventionist temptation" was born of and coexisted with political timorousness in a manner depicted by the "vicious circle" described in Chapter 3, according to which the extension of economic insurance by the government gives rise to ever new constraints because it gives rise to moral hazard and to the expectation that the government has the power to assure expected incomes.

MENDÈS FRANCE, FAURE, AND THE TREASURY CIRCUIT

The "vicious circle" linked policies of insurance such as, in the early days of the Fourth Republic, inflation and income indexation, to the development of policy demands and expectations that inhibited the restoration of market discipline. It is this sort of vicious circle that gave rise to the overdraft economy in France which in the early 1950s was given institutional foundation with the development of the *circuit du trésor*, or treasury circuit. To understand the *circuit du trésor*, however, one must first understand Edgar Faure, and to understand Edgar Faure, one must first examine the ministry of Pierre Mendès France. Chosen to form a cabinet in June 1954, Mendès France assumed power with the firm intention of restoring political leadership to government.[23] He had retained the reputation for decisive, uncompromising leadership earned at the time of the Liberation, and his pro-

[22]Rioux, *Fourth Republic*, p. 249.
[23]On Mendès France, see esp. the collective study by François Bédarida and Jean-Pierre Rioux, *Pierre Mendès France et le Mendésisme* (Paris: Fayard, 1985) and, for a comparison between Mendès France and Edgar Faure, see François Bloche-Lainé and Jean Bouvier, *La France restaurée, 1944–1954* (Paris: Fayard, 1986), chap. 8. See also Pierre Mendès France, *A Modern French Republic* (New York: Hill and Wang, 1963); and idem, *Gouverner, c'est choisir* (Paris: Julliard, 1958), on the critical period 1955–58. Finally, see Georgette Elgey, *La république des contradictions, 1951–1954* (Paris: Fayard, 1968).

posed solution to the challenges that confronted France in 1954 did not belie that reputation. He confronted the National Assembly with an ultimatum rather than a program. He proposed to promote the further modernization of the French economy while liquidating the problem of Vietnam and other divisive foreign policy issues. Mendès France insisted in return that he be given the freedom to choose his cabinet without party interference and that the National Assembly give its unconditional support so he could make hard choices rather than prolong the practice of avoiding divisive issues. He received a large and enthusiastic majority on the left, extending from the Communist party (though Mendès France rejected their support) to the Radicals. The MRP abstained.

Mendès France acted decisively and successfully to clear the political stage of its most encumbering article, Dien Bien Phu.[24] He then turned to economic issues and proposed forward-looking policies that sought to modernize the French economy. Though his government survived only a few months, it enhanced his reputation as a courageous and progressive politician. In the words of Jean-Pierre Rioux, "In what came, no doubt prematurely, to be known as 'Mendésisme' was encapsulated the whole question of whether the Republic was capable of renewal, of adapting itself to the needs of a rapidly modernizing nation. The few months during which Mendès France held power were marked by optimism, when thoughts at last turned to the future. They were ended brutally by the crisis in Algeria, which brought a return to the familiar impotence."[25]

Nevertheless, whatever his reputation, when one examines the economic policy of Mendès France closely one can find no philosophical difference with politicians whose weakness he denounced. Far removed in spirit from policies he defended ten years earlier, he now prolonged the practice of asking the state to assume much of the cost and risk of modernizing investment. His policies took ample advantage of the state's mastery over the instruments of capital allocation to provide cheap loans for agricultural modernization, price supports for dairy and meat products, and investment support to encourage the planting of industrial crops such as corn and colza and to promote conversion of the vineyards of the Midi (producers of cheap, low-quality wine) to the production of rice and fruit. In industry, Mendès France relied on similar policy instruments in inaugurating the policy of fostering industrial mergers to assure competitiveness on an increasingly integrated European market, a policy that would be renewed frequently over the next three decades. By encouraging the construction of public housing

[24]Rioux, *Fourth Republic*, p. 228.
[25]Ibid., p. 224.

through the use of medium-term rediscountable loans to local housing agencies, he increased the French economy's dependence on this unusual and rather perilous credit instrument. Thus, though his policies were forward-looking, they shared with those of his predecessors the ambition to anticipate market rationalization by funneling credit to modernizing investments, thereby avoiding the impact that a market-driven process of redistribution of capital and resources would have on political stability.[26] Nothing in Mendès France's economic policies threatened the structures or processes of the growing overdraft economy, the viability of which apparently was unquestioned. Ironically, despite the moderation of his policies, they often met with a violent reception. Mendès France's suggestion that the wine growers of the Midi grow something else contributed to the spread of *Poujadisme*. When the government was beset by reverses in the colonies, opposition to Mendès France became vituperative, plunging to depths of simple poor taste not seen since the days of the Popular Front. Accused of defeatism and antipatriotism, Mendès France was branded an agent of Moscow in a campaign in which anti-Semitism and slander were an integral part.

Following the fall of Mendès France, the task of governing fell to his fellow Radical, Edgar Faure, who, in contrast to his predecessor, put together a government on the right that included MRP ministers and a number of traditional conservative notables. Edgar Faure shared the brilliance of Mendès France, but substituted consummate diplomatic skill for the latter's combativeness. Faure preferred dousing conflict in ridicule and enjoyed the rhetorical skills to do so. He sought to defuse the ideologically charged atmosphere of French politics by advocating a philosophy of managerial pragmatism. Jean-Pierre Rioux gives us a portrait of the man who, though a collaborator and in many ways the heir of Mendès France, so ingeniously and with such virtuosity put an end to the crusade to "govern" a country that one could "manage" so much more expeditiously:

> Like Mendès France, Faure realized that for the bulk of the population sharing the fruits of expansion and economic modernization, with better standards of living, improved amenities, and more social services, counted for more than questions over the Atlantic Alliance, Europe, Germany and colonial wars.... Where Faure differed from his precedessor, however, was in being ready to try to wean the politicians gradually and painlessly away from the old quarrels.[27]

[26]In the literature on Mendès France, the theme that there was a contradiction between his will to act decisively and his conception of parliamentary democracy recurs with some frequency. See Maurice Duverger, "Pierre Mendès France et les institutions républicaines"; Richard Kuisel, "Pierre Mendès France et l'économie: Une volonté de modernité," both in Bédarida and Rioux, *Mendès France.*

[27]Rioux, *Fourth Republic,* pp. 240–41.

In his memoirs, Faure described his philosophy as one of "realism and unpretentiousness, which I have called, or which has been called... 'managerial realism,' sometimes 'reformism,' or even 'managerialism,' which term has the disadvantage of appearing to lower this political concept to the level of sub-intellect." He continued: "When a man of action, who is also a man of conviction, speaks highly of managerial realism, he is considered a dimwit, incapable of reveling in the delights of ideology.... As soon as I speak of management, it is as if I have become a theoretical illiterate."[28]

Characteristically, Faure rejected Mendès France's attitude of defiance via-à-vis the political parties and reverted to the practice of negotiating directly with the parliamentary groups in the National Assembly. The government he put together was a judicious mixture of competing currents. While satisfying the collective egos of the parliamentary groups, he sought in technocracy the means to avoid the need to confront the parties with potentially divisive economic issues. Under his government some of the most enduring institutions of French economic policy were forged.[29] The Fund for Economic and Social Development (Fonds de Développement Économique et Social, FDES) was created to allocate budgetary seed money and subsidies to industry. The Mutual Guarantee Fund (Fonds de Garantie Mutuelle) was established to organize markets and exports of agricultural goods. The successor to the Monnet Plan, the Second Plan for Modernization and Equipment, was prepared and implemented. It diverted the state from its postwar obsession with heavy industry and sought to promote regional development, education, sanitation, and other essentials of the good life. Faure's economic policy was expansionist. In 1955, he increased purchasing power by consenting to a wage increase that averaged 8.5 percent (this at a time when prices had not increased in two years). The government also acted to stimulate investment by reducing the tax on the production of capital goods by half as well as by creating new subsidies to facilitate reconversion and modernization of old plant. The most important of these was the National Fund for Regional Planning (Fonds National d'Aménagement du Territoire), a subsidy designed to promote the industrialization of the provinces and the industrial deconcentration of the Paris–Le Havre axis.

Facilitating Edgar Faure's managerial approach to politics was his half-discovery and half-construction of what came to be known as the *circuit du trésor,* or "treasury circuit." The keystone of this complex structure was the administrative obligation that required a vast number of financial institutions, such as the Deposit and Consignment Bank

---

[28]Edgar Faure, *Mémoires* (Paris: Plon, 1984), 2:98–99.
[29]See ibid., chap. 20.

(Caisse des Dépôts et Consignations), the savings banks (caisses d'épargne), the Crédit Agricole, the National Credit Agency (Crédit National), and the French Mortgage Bank (Crédit Foncier de France), to deposit a part of their resources with the treasury. Also feeding into the treasury were all the funds deposited with the post office.[30] The treasury in turn kept an account with the post office. The banking system was also partially integrated into this *circuit du trésor*, as a consequence of the 1948 requirement that they retain a certain portion of their reserves in treasury bonds.[31]

The semipublic financial institutions became part of the *circuit* with the development of medium-term rediscountable loans. The legal basis was provided by a 1944 amendment to the statutes of the Banque de France that allowed the central bank to rediscount loans of up to five years maturity.[32] Because such loans were generally underwritten and partially funded by the semipublic financial institutions, they involved the latter more deeply in the treasury's expansionist financial programs. The Deposit and Consignment Bank, for example, became the principal lender to local governments, public housing authorities, and to a lesser degree, nationalized firms and other financial institutions. The National Credit Agency played much the same role for productive investment as the French Mortgage Bank did for housing. It discounted loans for industrial development, many of which were subsequently handed over to the Banque de France to be rediscounted.

The crisscrossing of liabilities between the treasury, the post office, and a number of semipublic financial institutions created the opportunity for treasury officials to draw on a multiplicity of accounts to finance the public deficit without recourse either to new bond issues or to advances from the Banque de France, much as the U.S. government draws on social security funds. Moreover, because these deposits were composed of previously constituted savings (collected by the diverse financial institutions either through the deposits of their own customers or through bond issues of their own), they could finance public deficits in a potentially noninflationary manner. The treasury circuit, however, was unlike anything found in the United States in one key respect. Because the money generated in this fashion ultimately found

---

[30]In France, as in most European countries, the post office manages sight deposits and liquid savings accounts. During the 1950s, post office accounts amounted to 18 percent of M_1.

[31]This minimum was composed of a sum equal to at least 95 percent of the bank's holdings in treasury bonds in 1948, added to which was a sum equal to at least 20 percent of the subsequent variation (growth or decrease) in credits extended to the public. See Jean-Pierre Patat and Michel Lutfalla, *Histoire monétaire de la France au XXᵉ siècle* (Paris: Economica, 1986), p. 122.

[32]See Order of the Counsel General of the Banque de France, May 11, 1944.

its way back to the banks, the post office, or one of the financial institutions that composed the circuit, a fraction of it found its way back to the treasury, thus rendering the credit multiplier inoperative, or at least ineffective.[33] In other words, the treasury, which used money deposited in post office accounts in much the same way that a bank uses its reserve assets to create money, by making entries onto the post office accounts of households (the salaries of civil servants, for example) and firms (subsidies and grants), the treasury had the unusual capacity to feed its "reserves" *with money of its own creation,* because part of the money it created found its way back into the post office network (or some other collector of savings linked to the circuit) in the form of sight deposits or savings. Properly handled, the treasury circuit offered policymakers a tool with which to redistribute money while forgoing both the political liability of having to augment state income through increased taxes and that of inflationary financing. In the words of Dominique Leca, a high treasury official of the period, "Everything that goes out should normally come back. As long as the circuit works, everything is rosy. However, when the circuit for some reason or other is obstructed, then everything you have done falls apart."[34]

Edgar Faure first became aware of the opportunities generated by the close intertwining of France's financial institutions while he was minister of finance in the government of Joseph Laniel in 1953. He saw the advantages of the circuit, the technocratic nature of which conformed to his managerial conception of government. In subsequent years, the treasury circuit would be exploited extensively, especially since the financial needs of the treasury were indeed great. Throughout the Fourth Republic, it was the treasury, with help from the banks and little from the financial market, that financed a considerable share of investment (see Table 11). In collusion with the semipublic financial institutions, the treasury accounted for almost half of all credit allocated to the French economy and almost 80 percent of investment credits. The problem of modernization was therefore largely conceived as one of discovering ever new resources for the treasury to distribute. Before the Marshall Plan, the treasury's funds were generated primarily through the inflationary creation of new money. During the four years that the United States provided Marshall Aid, the treasury was able to decrease its dependence on inflationary financing. When Marshall Aid came to an end in 1952, however (as did, in 1954, American support for France's operations in Vietnam), France was on its own, faced with growing budget deficits—hovering near 4 percent of the GDP—and

---

[33]On the credit multiplier, see Chapter Two.

[34]See Edgar Faure, *Mémoires* (Paris: Plon, 1982), 1:456–57; quoted in Patat and Lutfalla, *Histoire,* p. 141.

Table 11: Institutional sources of credit to the French economy, 1953–1959 (% of credits allocated by institutional lenders)

	1953	1957	1959
The treasury	24.6	21.5	26.1
Semipublic financial institutions	14.9	28.0	22.7
Banks	60.5	50.5	51.2

Source: Jean-Pierre Patat, *Monnaie, institutions financières, et politique monétaire* (Paris: Economica, 1982), p. 205. Used by permission of the publisher.

obliged to find the means to finance its economic policies within itself. This is where the treasury circuit came into play. The crisscrossing of liabilities that characterized the circuit allowed the treasury to accomplish veritable tours de force. For example, when the budget deficit was great and the government did not want to ask the Banque de France for a cash advance for fear of parliamentary or monetary repercussions, the treasury would instruct the Deposit and Consignment Bank to rediscount at the Banque de France some of the loans it had itself previously discounted for the French Mortgage Bank and deposit the sums it procured from this operation on its account with the treasury. In this way, the treasury procured the liquid funds it needed while preventing its account at the Banque de France from going deeper in the red. A fairly important budget deficit (6.3 percent of the GDP in 1955) could be financed without a large appeal to the bond market and without an inflationary creation of money. The undercover transfer (*transfert occulte*) of 1.12 billion francs from the Banque de France to the treasury in 1955, using the intermediary of the Crédit Mobilier (a semipublic financial institution that supplied loans primarily to small businesses) not only helped diminish the deficit but actually allowed the treasury to reduce its debt to the Banque de France.

The treasury circuit, however, had its Achilles' heel. If, because of inflationary expectations, depositors and small investors turned away from the savings institutions of the circuit (in favor of gold, for example, for which there was an open market in France), thus preventing the funds generated by the circuit from returning to the circuit, the result was pure monetary creation and inflation. The cost of waging war in Algeria ultimately caused the card castle to collapse in 1957. The onus of war caused budget deficits to increase from 630 billion francs in 1955 (3.7 percent of the GDP) to more than 1,000 billion francs in 1957 (5 percent of the GDP).[35] The inflationary impact of deficit spending did not make itself immediately felt, because the treasury circuit was able to generate 234 billion francs in 1956, and 159 billion francs in 1957, allowing the treasury to cut back inflationary financing

[35]Patat and Lutfalla, *Histoire,* p. 153.

of the deficit. Indeed, money supply growth actually slowed to about 10 percent in both 1956 and 1957, while retail prices did not begin their inflationary climb until 1958.[36] The balance of payments, however, which had been laboriously forced into equilibrium the preceding year, responded to the growing disequilibrium in public finances by registering a serious deficit, necessitating a humiliating appeal to the International Monetary Fund for help in 1957.[37]

ECONOMIC MODERNIZATION AND THE EVOLUTION OF
FINANCIAL STRUCTURES

The French political economy evokes images of heavy state intervention in pursuit of mercantilist goals—sometimes successfully, as demonstrated by France's record of rapid growth and achievements in a number of specialized fields, such as aeronautics and transportation, sometimes less so, as demonstrated by France's inability to derive commercial benefit from many of its more innovative products. I have argued thus far that this image of state-promoted growth provides a less accurate characterization of the French political economy in the 1950s than that which highlights the development of structures and processes described as the overdraft economy, a development driven by fear of the redistributive implications of modernization and validated by the elaboration of tolerant international trade and financial arrangements. Thus conceived, one can reconcile the rapid development of the French economy during this period with its endemic monetary fragility, its entrenched *corporatisme* and the renewed criticisms of *malthusianisme* to which it was subject, and the widespread perception that, by the middle of the decade, France, for all its growth, was the "sick man of Europe."

This was not to deny the dynamism of the French economy during this period.[38] The French gross national product increased by 50 percent in the eight years between 1949 and 1957, an increase that was propelled by growth in industry. Below-average growth was found only in the more traditional sectors, such as agriculture and textiles, but

[36]In part because conscription, made necessary by the widening scope of the Algerian war, buffered the impact of wage hikes on consumer demand by withdrawing large numbers of consumers from the market as well as by the fact that the government of Guy Mollet, convinced that the inflationary surge was temporary, attacked the symptoms rather than the disease by decreasing sales taxes, decreasing the price of gas, and importing foodstuffs to ease market tensions. The government was driven more by concern about the impact of the price inflation on the minimum wage (which was indexed) than about the phenomenon of inflation per se. See ibid., chap. 11.

[37]Ibid., p. 152.

[38]See Rioux, *Fourth Republic*, p. 323.

there was nevertheless strong growth even in some agricultural sectors. Dairy and cattle farming developed dramatically, as did the production of fruit and fresh vegetables. In contrast, agro-industrial products, such as wheat, flax, and beets, suffered from foreign competition. During this period, the rate of investment was high, the percentage of GDP reinvested in the economy rising to the high teens and low twenties, a figure much higher than that achieved during previous periods of rapid growth, such as the 1890s or the 1920s. Direct government investment accounted for more than one-fourth of total investment, and, in support of the statist image, capital was generally allocated according to priorities established by the plan. Thirty percent went to construction, 15 percent to industry, another 15 percent to energy, 13 percent to transportation, and 9 percent to agriculture.[39]

Industrial production more than doubled between 1938 and 1957, and it grew by more than 70 percent between 1950 and 1957. National output increased 29 percent between 1952 and 1957, some 4 percent more than the goal of the Second Plan. The index of industrial production stood at 145 rather than 130 as called for in the plan, and investment targets were generally exceeded by 10 percent. One of the most dynamic sectors of the French economy was the chemical industry. Growth in the chemical industry was fueled in part by the development of fertilizers and in part by consumer demand at a time when plastics and synthetic fibers were acquiring a position of prominence in daily life. The industry was also favored by its high level of technological development and the degree of concentration of its principal firms. Rapid growth was also apparent in metallurgy. Although metallurgy had been one of the sectors to be singled out for special treatment by the plan, consumer demand, once again, was not foreign to growth in this sector. On the contrary, demand for household appliances, such as refrigerators and to a lesser extent washing machines, combined with growing demand for agricultural machines, ships, and machine tools, to give rise to large orders for the steel industry. The most visibly spectacular component of metallurgical demand came from the automobile industry. The 1950s were the era of the great mythological griffins of the French automobile industry: the *deux-chevaux* and the *quatre-chevaux*. Consumer demand for such automotive mutants, both within and beyond France's borders, sustained a visibly impressive rate of growth in the industry, the output of which doubled in the period 1952–57. The stock of private vehicles doubled in the same period, from 1.7 million in 1952, to 4.0 million in 1958. Though considerably down-scale, it should not be forgotten that this was also the era of the

[39]Ibid., p. 336.

Solex, the Mobylette, and the Vespa, the latter made in France under Italian license.[40] There were many other visible signs of economic modernization: the dam at Donzère-Mondragon, the oil pipeline between Paris and the lower Seine, the electrification of the major railway lines, the first fruits of the new housing program which provided the French with 240,000 new homes in 1955—not to forget the graduation of the first class of technocrats from the National School of Administration (École Nationale d'Administration). Faure could indeed survey all this and conclude that Mendès France had erred in being too combative. It sufficed to leave the cause of progress to the quiet competence of the illusionists in the ministries.

This monument to modernization, however, rested on a fragile foundation. Growing dependence on institutionally supplied credit was the consequence of policies that resisted the shift of real wealth to modernizing activities. The rate of investment in France was inferior to that of countries in which the state played a less visible role, such as Italy and Germany, despite the importance of the investment effort. French growth, though high, was not extraordinary by European standards, nor did it appear to be the work of anything peculiarly and specifically French, such as the plan. On the contrary, similar and shared factors seemed to be working concurrently to promote economic growth all across Europe: (1) economic modernization in both infrastructure and in the tools and techniques of production; (2) a buoyant economic environment created both by high levels of consumer demand, unleashed after two decades of privations, and sustained high levels of growth in international trade, promoted chiefly by the gradual and prudent opening of the European market; and finally (3) expansionary monetary policies pursued to a greater or lesser extent by France and other European governments. The state's direct involvement in the economy was actually declining during this period. The treasury's contribution to the financing of industrial investment fell from 50 percent in 1950 to 35 percent in 1952 to 27 percent in 1956.[41]

As the state retreated from financial responsibilities assumed after the war, it developed institutions and techniques that enhanced the role of institutional lenders in financing economic activity, notably by promoting the use of medium-term loans rediscounted by the Banque de France. Thus, though the contribution of the stock exchange to investment financing increased from 4.4 percent in 1950 to 9.2 percent in 1956, the share of medium-term bank loans increased from 3.3 percent in 1950 to 14.2 percent in 1956.[42] Nor should one be tempted

[40]Ibid., p. 327.
[41]Ibid., p. 336.
[42]Ibid., p. 332–33.

to think that this growth in institutional financing translated automatically into modernizing investment. At the end of 1955, the demand for credit rose from an annual growth rate of 19 percent, after having fallen to 13 percent in 1954 and 1955 in response to the global downturn in economic activity as well as to the policies of Antoine Pinay.[43] Renewed demand for credit, however, was not so much fed by renewed investment as it was provoked by cash-flow problems encountered by firms in the wake of wage increases conceded by the governments of Joseph Laniel, Pierre Mendès France, and Edgar Faure. Reflation—which should be put in the context of the political crises of 1953 and 1954—saw the economy's dependence on institutional lenders increase. Table 12 reveals that as the French economy pulled out of the recession of 1952–53, bond issues increased from 181 billion francs in 1953 to 300 billion in 1955, less than the level attained in 1952. On the other hand, credit allocations by banks doubled from 217 billion francs in 1953 to 439 billion in 1955, significantly higher than their 1952 level of 332 billion francs. Stagnant bond issues and increased recourse to bank credit reinforced the overdraft economy.

There was no statist juggernaut at work refashioning the French political economy. More characteristic of its evolution was the marked preference for policies that sought to avoid the redistributive consequences of modernization, policies that conspired to piece together institutional arrangements and practices that forged an overdraft economy characterized by a high level of dependence on institutional credit. It is no surprise that such an economy experienced rapid growth, but that growth owed more to the high level of consumer demand that the overdraft economy sustained than it did to the interventionist actions of the state. The other side of the coin was endemic imbalance in foreign trade. Because consumer demand threatened the economy's balance of

Table 12: Source of financing, 1952–1955 (billion francs)

	1952	1953	1954	1955
Stock issues	71	63	88	148
Bond issues	515	181	312	300
Bank credit	332	217	334	439

Source: Adapted from Jean-Pierre Patat and Michel Lutfalla, *Histoire monétaire de la France au XXᵉ siècle* (Paris: Economica, 1986), pp. 148–49. Used by permission of the publisher.

[43]The gross national product grew by 4.8 percent in 1954 and by 5.8 percent in 1955, while prices remained stable. Most of the growth in investment and much of the growth in GNP came from the housing sector, now generously supported by the newly implemented program of rediscountable medium-term loans and by the public sector.

payments, this evolution of the domestic political economy required the existence of an international environment that facilitated adjustment without deflation. It is to the examination of this environment that we now turn.

FRENCH POLICY AND THE HEGEMONIC ORDER

Prior to 1957, France relied heavily on trade policy to achieve adjustment in its foreign trade, whereas after 1957, constrained by the Treaty of Rome, it relied more on exchange rate policy. In 1954, growing concern over the trade balance incited the government to impose temporary import duties of up to 15 percent. Export subsidies were in effect since 1952 which accorded a premium of up to 15 percent on exports. The temporary duties and subsidies together had the same buoyant effect on France's foreign commerce as a 15 percent devaluation of the franc that, moreover, did not need to be declared to the International Monetary Fund. Though import duties were reduced on many items in 1955, they were again raised to 15 percent in June 1957, when deficits reappeared. In August 1957, the tax on imports was raised to 20 percent, the revenue from which was used to fund a 20 percent subsidy for exports.

The economic crisis of 1957 finally forced France to appeal to the IMF for assistance, which responded in January 1958 with a loan for $131.25 million. The European Payments Union also extended payments facilities worth $250 million, while the United States established its own credit line of $274 million ($45 million of which was destined to be used to cover military expenses in conjunction with French's NATO commitments). The IMF did not miss this opportunity to criticize French economic policy, especially deficit spending and the byzantine intricacies of the treasury circuit. In return for its assistance, it required that France's budget deficit be reduced, that France open its market wider to foreign trade, and—significantly—that the inflationary practice of according medium-term loans be restricted.[44] Subsequently, French monetary officials placed limits on the power of the Banque de France to rediscount medium-term discountable loans and created the Medium-Term Credit Consolidation Fund (Caisse de Consolidation des Crédits à Moyen Terme). Unfortunately, the government, taking two steps forward and one step back, financed the activities of the Fund with budget subsidies—in the words of Lutfalla and Patat, "at least the principle [of containing the growth of medium-term credit] had been

---

[44]*L'année politique, 1958* (Paris: Presses Universitaires de France, 1959), pp. 166–67.

established."[45] On the other hand, neither the IMF nor the United States, though critical of certain of France's more notorious financial practices, criticized the fundamental logic of the overdraft economy. They did not, for example, criticize growing reliance on the *"transformation"* of liquid assets by financial institutions beyond objecting to the rediscounting of such loans by the central bank, nor did they criticize the meager capitalization of French firms or draw attention to the responsibility of policy for that state of affairs. The institutionalization of the overdraft economy in France is testimony to the fact that the U.S. hegemonic order was a permissive one. During the late 1940s and early 1950s, the United States' efforts to reform the nature of international economic relations ended with the delegation of much authority over the reformist enterprise to its European partners-cum-rivals, Great Britain and France. For France, "hegemonic leadership" in the 1950s brought more in the way of opportunity than constraint. Even when it found itself gripped by balance-of-payments crises, that order came forth with significant amounts of aid, which, though tied to economic reforms, left the overdraft economy intact and ready to confront a new decade.

CONCLUSION

The history of the French economy under the Fourth Republic was one of rapid economic growth, industrial modernization, and sweeping social change. By 1951, French national income and industrial production surpassed levels achieved in 1929, France's best economic year heretofore. The Monnet Plan laid the foundations for sustained economic growth throughout the decade of the 1950s and beyond. Between 1950 and 1960, the French economy grew at an annual rate of 4.5 percent, placing it fourth among the industralized nations of Europe, behind Germany (7.6 percent), Italy (5.9 percent), and the Netherlands (4.9 percent). Industrial production in France grew by 7 percent annually, facilitated by the rapid increase in French exports. It is curious that the politics that accompanied this record of unprecedented economic growth was one of compromise and even timorousness. The revolutionary ambitions of the Resistance and the Monnet Plan had, by mid-decade, given way to growing dependence on technocratic virtuosity. The overdraft economy, born of patricide as the postwar offspring of Third Republic bourgeois notables buried the old financial order under a heap of debt, revealed to perceptive politicians a number

[45]Patat and Lutfalla, *Histoire*, p. 156.

of unsuspected advantages. By bringing the lending institutions together into a more coherent institutional framework and by coordinating their activities, state officials and politicians learned that they could supply the economy with capital taken from liquid savings while absorbing the inflationary pressures that this practice generated. By exploiting the conduit that linked the coffers of the state treasury to those of the savings institutions, they discovered they had the power to make budget deficits disappear. This enabled Fourth Republic politicians to allay the redistributive impact of industrial modernization.

For the historian Jean-Pierre Rioux, the Fourth Republic's principal failing was its inability to find a solution to the conflict that opposed the reformist and modernizing spirit of *Mendésisme* to the rear-guard, antimodernist reaction expressed by *Poujadisme*.[46] One must qualify Rioux's judgment, however, by observing that the politicians conspired to strengthen the opponents of modernization when they jettisoned the policies of economic and social renewal advocated by the Resistance. *Poujadisme* was the social and political companion of the overdraft economy. *Poujadisme* and the overdraft economy lived in a symbiotic relationship, such that a threat to the overdraft economy was also a threat to the existence of sectors that fed the ranks of the *poujadistes* and such that efforts on the part of increasingly technocratic political leaders to elude the social and political implications of modernization gave rise to new practices and institutions that anchored the overdraft economy more solidly in the foundations of the French political economy.

The government let itself become ensnared in this vicious circle in part because the overdraft economy's deleterious effect on the state's power to control monetary growth was masked by the tolerance of the international political economy. The hegemonic order sustained rather than threatened the overdraft economy. The United States seemed to be acting under the illusion that French political orientations were transitory and would be abandoned once European reconstruction was achieved. It provided no opposition to the *volontariste* path on which the French persisted, even when, as during the crisis of 1957, the opportunity arose to press for reforms.

[46]Rioux, *Fourth Republic*, pp. 245–53.

CHAPTER SIX

Reform and Resistance of the Overdraft Economy under Charles de Gaulle

War in Africa was the undoing of the Fourth Republic. René Coty, president of the Republic, summoned Charles de Gaulle to form a government on June 1, 1958, with the mandate to enact constitutional reforms that would strengthen the government's power to confront the crisis. After serving as last premier of the Fourth Republic, de Gaulle became, on December 21, 1958, the first president of the Fifth Republic. The change of regime not only promised constitutional reform and an end to the Algerian conflict, but also set the stage for profound reforms in the political economy. The rise to power of a strong conservative leader, supported by the more presidential constitution of the Fifth Republic, created the opportunity to return France to financial orthodoxy. Such measures were expected. The final days of the Fourth Republic were marked by inflation and insolvency, provoked in part by the war. The first days of the Fifth Republic, in contrast, were marked by intense efforts to produce a thoroughgoing reform of the French economy.

It is ironic that the overdraft economy survived de Gaulle's presidency unreformed and even reinforced. The economic reforms of 1958–59 left financial structures basically untouched. Absence of change in the international financial environment explains the survival of the over-draft economy. French officials felt little anxiety concerning the idiosyncrasy of France's financial structures, and consequently little inclination to reform them. Indeed, devaluation in 1958 seemed to eliminate many of the most serious disequilibria that had beset the French economy during the preceding eighteen months, and even gave the illusion that the fundamental monetary reform de Gaulle's entourage had promised had been achieved. Over the next decade, however, the French economy's dependence on institutionally allocated credit was reinforced as state subsidies to industry were reduced and the burden of financing many social programs were transferred to businesses. Moreover, by reforming the banking system in a manner that facilitated bank involvement in industrial financing, the government improved the capacity of lending institutions to acquit themselves of the responsibilities that the overdraft economy had conferred on them. But because failure to reform the overdraft economy allowed endemic inflationary pressures to fester, the government had to exercise constant administrative pressure on prices and wages, giving rise to the social discontent and political opposition that exploded in the events of May 1968. Thereafter, as a result of the expansionist policies inspired by that crisis, the French overdraft economy functioned according to its ideal type.

THE NEW REPUBLIC AND ECONOMIC REFORM

Charles de Gaulle assumed power with the firm intention and mandate to restore strength—constitutional, economic, diplomatic, and military—to a France that both the French and outside observers perceived as the "sick man of Europe." The opportunity for thoroughgoing economic reform was never greater. First, de Gaulle armed himself with a new constitution that regulated the activities of the National Assembly in a way that put constraints on its sovereignty, both by transferring the power of introducing legislation to the government and by strictly regulating its power to amend and to reject legislation the government proposed. Second, de Gaulle enjoyed immense prestige and moral authority, as evidenced by the referendum of September 28, 1958, which sought approval of the new constitution establishing the Fifth Republic and which was ratified by nearly 80 percent of the electorate. The results incited the influential editor of *Le Monde*, Hubert Beuve Méry (who had given de Gaulle grudging support), to write that the general had been handed "a blank check." Third, de Gaulle was able to appeal to the "nation" above the heads of party leaders. De Gaulle's first government could almost have been characterized as one of *union nationale*, accepting within its ranks representatives of all the major parties except the Communists and the *poujadistes*. Like Mendès France and Edgar Faure before him, de Gaulle came to power to govern, to manage, to renew, and to modernize, and displayed nothing but disdain for ideological debate. Indeed, the institutions of the Fifth Republic were designed to facilitate his more "managerial" approach to government. Although this caused discontent on the left—about half the Socialist deputies, joined by deputies close to Mendès France, refused to support de Gaulle—major party leaders, including the Socialist Guy Mollet, joined the government and took an active part in elaborating the new institutions.[1] This managerial style was adopted by the Gaullist party, the Union pour la Nouvelle République (UNR), which was established in October 1958 to provide de Gaulle with party support. It was, in the words of its first general secretary, Roger Frey, "a great party of the center, a great party of management, capable of avoiding the violent clashes between Right and Left."

Finally, de Gaulle altered the electoral system in a manner that further reinforced his power by favoring the more conservative countryside over the city, the large party over the small, and the party that could enter into electoral alliances over that which could not. The new electoral regime reduced the power of the extremes, notably the Communists, and promised to reinforce the success of Gaullist candidates.[2] The legislative elections of November confirmed both the moral authority of General de Gaulle and the savant calculations that inspired the new electoral system. The big winners were the "Gaullists" (who ran principally on the UNR ticket) with 20 percent, and the Moderates, or independent conservative notables, who with 22 percent benefited both indirectly from the realignment of the French electorate to the right and directly from their lack of involvement in the successive governments of the "république des partis," the Fourth Republic. The Communist party's representation in the new National Assembly fell from about 180 to 10, and that of the Socialists from about 100 to 44, while the UNR, with 20 percent of the votes after the first round of the elections, ended up with nearly 200 deputies. Thus armed, de Gaulle was in a position to exercise the sort of political leadership that would be required if the economy was to be overhauled.

By 1958, the economic crisis was visible to all. Although the caretaker government of Maurice Bourgès-Manoury (which assumed power after the fall of Guy Mollet) had enacted some effective policies to counter the crisis, the economic situation in June remained one that justified energetic measures. De Gaulle did not disappoint the public's expectations. He quickly came up with a number of highly visible policies designed to restore balance both to the budget and to foreign trade, including spending cuts and a devaluation of the franc. In December 1958, the more radical stabilization plan, the Pinay-Rueff Plan, subjected the franc to a second devaluation and slashed another 275 billion francs of economic and social subsidies from the budget, increased tax

[1]See L'année politique, 1958 (Paris: Presses Universitaires de France, 1959), pp. 111, 135.
[2]Jacques Chapsal, La vie politique en France depuis 1940 (Paris: Presses Universitaires de France, 1969), pp. 349–55.

revenues by 200 billion francs, and put an end to indexed wages and indexed prices for a number of goods. Together these measures brought the budget deficit below 600 billion francs.[3] The Pinay-Rueff Plan was so rigorous that it inspired Jacques Chapsal to write: "One of the motivations [behind the plan] was probably the fact that General de Gaulle still experienced remorse over the decision he had made in 1945 by choosing the policies of Monsieur Pleven, that is, policies of facility, over those of Monsieur Mendès France, that is, over policies of austerity."[4]

A more detailed examination of the history of those reforms, however, reveals their limitations. That examination begins with de Gaulle's selection of Antoine Pinay, the author of the price stabilization in 1952, to be minister of finance. Pinay was a popular figure on the right, whom the French associated with the common-sense economic conservatism of the provincial businessman, the Pinay loan, and the price stabilization of 1953. Pinay, in 1958, still advocated fostering monetary confidence and encouraging savings through large—even spectacular—indexed public bond issues. Such was the remedy he proposed in 1958 to combat high inflation, currency weakness, and the severe payments deficit.

At the time of de Gaulle's accession to power, Jacques Rueff was magistrate for the European Coal and Steel Community and had held a number of high offices in the finance administration before the war, including that of vice-governor of the Banque de France. Rueff, an advocate of the strictest financial and monetary orthodoxy, believed the last thing the French economy needed was yet another large, indexed bond issue à la Pinay. So strong were his convictions that he took the initiative of writing an unsolicited letter to de Gaulle, in which he argued that the French economy needed a more thorough reform of its finances. He proposed a much more stringent policy of austerity that included the higher taxes, the second devaluation, and the budget restrictions that ultimately became the stabilization plan that was to assume his name. He also insisted, however, that French financial practices be fundamentally reformed. He proposed, notably, that the treasury's shortfalls be financed through the sale of three-month bills rather than pluri-annual securities and (echoing the IMF) that the practice of rediscounting medium-term loans be stopped. Both reforms, he argued, would keep the state out of the market for long-term financing, where he felt it was crowding out the private sector. Such bills would also help feed a real money market and thus lessen the economy's dependence on rediscounting. He maintained that his plan

---

[3]*L'année politique, 1958*, pp. 137–38, 170–73; *L'année politique, 1959* (Paris: Presses Universitaires de France, 1960), pp. xiii–xv.
[4]Chapsal, *La vie politique*, p. 368.

would strike at the roots of French inflation, which he traced to the *volontariste* credit policies of the Fourth Republic.

Rueff's proposals were grounded in his conviction that the French economy, along with the economies of other modern industrialized societies, was the victim of "false money" (*fausse monnaie*). "False money" was produced when credit was not backed up with constituted savings. According to Rueff, the disease provoked by "false money" was not only inflation but also the decay of national economic and social order, because it destroyed any incentive to exercise economic self-discipline on the part of individual economic agents. The cure for the disease was to reimpose economic self-discipline by forcing economic actors to compete for credit on an authentic financial market. Though Pinay's bond issue could not be accused of injecting false money into the economy, it failed, in Rueff's mind, to address this underlying economic disease. It did nothing to alter what we would call inflationary expectations, it did little to impose economic discipline on the state, and it did even less to reactivate a real market for financial assets. Indeed, by crowding industry out of the market, it threatened to increase industry's dependence on institutional lenders and to discourage investment, and thus to reinforce the *malthusianisme* of the French economy. In a word, what was called for was elimination of what Rueff's younger disciples would, two decades later, label the overdraft economy.

It may be that Rueff's criticism of French financial practices and structures was facilitated by his pre-Keynesian conception of economic order, but it would be unfair to claim that his perception of France's economic problems was somehow distorted by concepts and philosophies that had gone out of fashion. Rueff's accusation that credit expansion was the culprit behind monetary disorder was far from inaccurate. The French economy in 1956 and 1957 had witnessed once again a particularly rapid increase in credit expansion of 17 percent per year, creating the conditions for the inflationary crisis of 1958. Credit expansion was provoked in part by cash-flow shortages in French firms unable to honor the steep wage increases that had been granted throughout French industry between 1954 and 1956. Rueff was among the first to recognize this unstable interdependence between credit expansion and de facto indexation of revenues.

It is a reflection of the personalities of both Rueff and de Gaulle, as well as of the spirit of renewal and reform that accompanied the advent of the new regime, that Rueff was immediately invited by de Gaulle to collaborate with his minister of finance to devise a plan of monetary stabilization. The Pinay-Rueff Plan adopted many of Rueff's more stringent austerity measures, but the proposals for a more fundamental reform of financial structures and practices were rejected.[5] Indeed, the government, far from renouncing long-term bond issues, profited from the temporary return to monetary stability that was procured by devaluation to encourage a number of state-owned enterprises to borrow long on the financial market. Rueff objected strenuously to the selective hearing given his reform projects, and he inveighed against the continued issue of long-term bonds by the state and by public enterprises, demanding that a second committee be convened to map out an even more fundamental and effective reform of the French economy. De Gaulle was convinced of the need for deeper reforms and created a second committee of experts under the direction of Rueff and Louis Armand. This committee proposed yet more liberalizing reforms, including the abolition of indexation in prices, wages, and nonwage revenues, especially in agriculture.[6] As for financial reform, however, the committee was again given explicit instructions to stay away from it. Rueff wrote in his memoirs:

> One may be surprised not to find in the report any recommendations on credit policy, which, according to my letter to General de Gaulle of August 20, 1959, constituted one of the two sources of obstacles, and probably the principal one, to economic expansion. This failure is due to the fact that, from the beginning of the committee's work, I was notified that the domain of credit was expressly excluded from the field of our research, the Conseil National du Crédit... having competence in all matters relating particularly to monetary policy.[7]

Was there more involved in this refusal than a bureaucratic battle for turf? The impression Rueff left is that government officials were simply unwilling to replace a secure source of income (long-term bonds) with a less secure one (short-term bonds). Rueff, in a letter to Antoine Pinay dated February 4, 1959, wrote: "You maintain that during the period when the state is forgoing sales of long-term bonds, the treasury must find the resources it needs and will not find them without borrowing. Permit me to remind you that this is a fundamental error. You acquire no resources through borrowing that you would not acquire by issuing three-month bills."[8]

[5] Jacques Rueff, *Combats pour l'ordre financier* (Paris: Plon, 1972), pp. 460–62.
[6] See *L'année politique, 1959*, p. xiv. The attempt to introduce market mechanisms into agriculture was short-lived. As we shall see, farmers were the first to show any real resistance to the economic policies of de Gaulle.
[7] Jacques Rueff, *De l'aube au crépuscule* (Paris: Plon, 1977), p. 254.
[8] Ibid., p. 234. See also Rueff, *Combats*, p. 461. Nevertheless, the stabilization plan included the stipulation that medium-term credits for construction would no longer be discounted by the central bank and that a limit be placed on the discount of medium-term credit for productive investment, in application of IMF recommendations.

For the conservatives who assumed power under the Fifth Republic, Rueff's financial orthodoxy must have appeared radical and adventurous. Inflation and monetary weakness were thought to be caused not by the economy's weak financial foundations but by deficit spending. The first priority, therefore, was to balance the budget (see below). The treasury circuit provided a tool that finance officials could use to fund government projects in a theoretically noninflationary manner, since funds deposited with the semipublic financial institutions that made up the circuit were taken from constituted savings. Those funds were raised in part through long-term bond issues by semipublic financial institutions. Although the governments of the Fifth Republic would not activate the treasury circuit to provide "covert" funds to finance budget deficits with the abandon of their predecessors, it must have made little sense to put limits on the power of semipublic financial institutions to borrow on the financial market and thus deprive government of extrabudgetary sources of capital over which it had some discretionary control and with which it could finance politically desirable projects such as public housing and industrial modernization. Moreover, the need for an industrial policy, and therefore for some source of investment funds that could be controlled by the state, was not questioned by the conservatives who accompanied de Gaulle to power. On the contrary, the signature of the Treaty of Rome and the creation of a European Common Market had, in the eyes of many, made industrial policy more imperative.[9] The challenge was to make industrial policy compatible with fiscal conservatism. This required that the state exploit the advantages of existing financial structures rather than undertake the wholesale reform of those structures.

Opposition to Rueff's radical reformism could not have prevailed had not concern on the part of government officials about the supposedly unhealthy condition of the economy's finances been fairly weak. What was "apparent" to Rueff, given his ideological bent, was less than obvious to the government and to the technocrats who peopled the Ministry of Finance. First, the monetary situation stabilized rapidly in 1958, thanks in large part to measures enacted even before de Gaulle assumed power.[10] Second, and of greater importance to the present study, the nature and the mechanics of the international monetary

[9]See Suzanne Berger, "Lame Ducks and National Champions: Industrial Policy in the Fifth Republic"; Volkmar Lauber, "The Gaullist Model of Economic Modernization," in William Andrews and Stanley Hoffmann, eds., *The Fifth Republic at Twenty* (Albany: SUNY Press, 1981).

[10]If the monetary situation stabilized so rapidly, it is due in part to the policies enacted by de Gaulle's predecessor, Bourgès-Manoury, the Radical leader who replaced Guy Mollet at the helm of government in June 1957. Because he inherited an economic situation that by that time was visibly in crisis, Bourgès-Manoury's first initiative was to ask the Banque de France to prolong its advances to the budget—that is, to acquiesce in

system facilitated adjustment in France in a way that diminished the perceived need for fundamental reform. After de Gaulle assumed power, the franc was subjected to two successive devaluations—the first during the month of June 1958, when it was devalued from its 1949 parity of 3.50 francs to the dollar to 4.19 francs to the dollar (making official the disguised devaluation of 1957). In December of the same year, a second devaluation dropped the franc to 4.90 francs to the dollar, a parity at which it remained for the next ten years. Together, the two devaluations diminished the par value of the franc by 40 percent.

The second devaluation was part of the Pinay-Rueff stabilization plan. Rueff had been a member of the cabinet of Henri Poincaré, who was head of government when the franc was stabilized in 1926. The recollection of that event informed his approach to monetary reform in 1958. With an utter lack of guile, and in a way that sheds an especially crude light on the dependence of French policy on a lenient international monetary environment, Rueff wrote:

> In economies in which prices are determined by the market, prices tend to settle, under the pressure of prices on foreign markets, at levels that correspond to the parity of those external prices, as expressed in the local currency. But there is one crucial exception: wage levels, for which any diminution is refused by the labor unions, for obvious sociological reasons.... When the exchange rate would imply an appreciable decrease in the level of domestic wages relative to wage levels that obtain in neighboring countries, there is no other solution than to increase the parity of foreign wage levels by depreciating the currency, that is, by increasing the exchange rates of foreign currencies.[11]

By fixing the franc at a parity that many foreign critics considered unfairly low (Rueff was, as the above passage indicates, consciously

---

continued inflationary financing of the budget deficit. However, he compensated for this emergency measure with a number of rigorous policies designed to restore basic monetary equilibriums. First, he reduced the budget deficit to an expected 600 billion francs for the fiscal year 1958, essentially by eliminating a number of tax exonerations and reductions enacted by the previous government. Second, he raised the discount rate to 4 percent and raised the "enfer" and "super-enfer" rates (rates applied to bank applications for rediscounts in excess of their quota) to 8 percent and 12 percent respectively. Moreover, the Bourgès-Manoury government abandoned Mollet's efforts to cure France's economic illness by manipulating the thermometer—that is, the price index. The result was a brief period of very high inflation during which prices sought out their market levels. The most dramatic policy enacted by the Bourgès-Manoury government, however, was the imposition of an authoritative cap on credit allocation by banks in February 1958. Banks that lent in excess of the cap were penalized by having their rediscount quota reduced (forcing them to borrow from the Banque de France at the "enfer" or "super-enfer" rediscount rates). Thus it was that *encadrement du crédit* made its first appearance among the tools of monetary policy.

[11]Rueff, *De l'aube au crépuscule*, p. 60.

transferring the burden of adjustment from the French economy to foreign economies), the French were able to rid the economy of its trade deficit. France joined the Common Market with a trade surplus and was quickly able to recoup the foreign reserves lost during the crisis of 1957.

The success of the 1958 devaluation was such that observers waxed lyrical. For example:

> The [devaluation] marked the most important turning point in France's postwar economic evolution. By permitting the integration of the French economy in the world market under conditions of financial stability, it contributed to [the economy's] long-term expansion and to a rate of growth such as had not been seen in the past.... By the mechanisms it provoked, this operation has assumed the importance of a more general model.... The merit of the December 1958 devaluation is to have underscored, developed, and applied [fundamental] principles capable of assuring monetary stability while stimulating economic growth.[12]

In 1958 and 1959, therefore, when Rueff's proposals were being discussed, in circumstances in which the value of the currency was stabilized as much from without—by the multilateral effort to stabilize the currency market in the wake of devaluation of the franc as well as by direct financial help from the International Monetary Fund—as from within, how could French finance officials have been alarmed by the fragility of their financial structures and the potential weakness of their instruments of monetary policy? Indeed, it was de Gaulle's conviction, shared by those around him, that his economic reforms, in conjunction with devaluation, had assured lasting monetary stability for the French economy. The introduction of a new currency unit, the "nouveau franc" (worth 100 "anciens francs") was intended to symbolize the passing of an era of weakness, both monetary and political. De Gaulle saw himself as the Poincaré of the postwar era despite the fact that he had tied the hands of one of Poincaré's closest advisers, caught red-handed trying to tamper with financial structures and practices.

REINFORCING THE OVERDRAFT ECONOMY THROUGH "LIBERALIZING" REFORMS

The monetary stabilization of 1958 proved fragile. Whereas price stabilization in 1952 had been facilitated by a global economic down-

---

[12]Mileta Obradovitch, *Les effets de la dévaluation française de 1958* (Paris: Les Éditions d'Organisation, Éditions Eyrolles, 1970), p. 191. Obradovitch (p. 11) claims that the 1958 devaluation is a model to be followed by developing nations.

turn, global economic expansion in the early 1960s generated inflation-ary pressures against which the French overdraft economy was poorly defended. By 1966 the French government was confronting a new dilemma. To sustain price stability, it had to restrict the growth of credit through *encadrement. Encadrement,* however, discouraged investment, not by rendering it more onerous (as would the more active use of interest rate policy) but by restricting French industry's access to capital. In so doing, it jeopardized both social peace and industrial modernization, the need for which was now greater because of the Common Market. To extricate itself from this dilemma, the govern-ment decided to decrease budget expenditures, in order to fight inflation, and to deregulate the banking industry, in order to facilitate industrial investment. Though billed as "liberalizing" reforms, these had the effect of reinforcing the overdraft structures of the economy.

Encadrement du crédit was used for the first time as a stopgap measure by the caretaker government of Bourgès-Manoury. Once the economic situation was stabilized through devaluation and the policies that ac-companied it, the government lifted *encadrement* and lowered the dis-count rate from 4.5 percent to 4 percent. New credit allocations, which had fallen to 6 percent of the GDP in 1958, grew to 8.5 percent in 1959 and to 10 percent in 1962. Credit allocations after 1959 expanded by nearly 20 percent a year in response to demand emanating principally from the private sector. Rapid credit expansion caused the money supply to grow rapidly—by as much as 18 percent, for example, in 1962.

Monetary expansion was facilitated by the internal mechanisms of the overdraft economy. Although price stability restored investor confi-dence, private savings continued to prefer liquid savings accounts managed by banks and other savings institutions to financial assets negotiated on a moribund market. Investments in stocks actually de-creased from 17 percent of total financial investment in 1959 to 14 percent in 1962. By contributing to the growth of bank reserves, this preference for institutionally managed semiliquid savings accounts fu-eled the capacity of lending institutions to expand the money supply by indulging the economy with credit.[13] The liquidity of the economy, as measured by M_2 / GDP, grew from 31.7 percent in 1958 to 37.6 percent in 1962.

Monetary expansion, of course, stimulated industrial and GDP growth. Industrial output grew by 7 percent in 1960 and 5 percent in 1961; the GDP grew by 7.2 percent in 1960 and 5.5 percent in 1961. Expansion, however, could not be maintained long without generating inflationary

[13]See Jean-Pierre Patat and Michel Lutfalla, *Histoire monétaire de la France au XXe siècle* (Paris: Economica, 1986), pp. 166–70.

pressures. By the second half of 1960, the government began to fear the potential impact of rapid credit and monetary growth on price stability and by January 1961 began to reimpose restrictions on bank activity. The *coefficient de trésorerie* was instituted, requiring banks to hold at least 30 percent of their assets in the form of treasury bonds or medium-term rediscountable credits in order to restrict bank access to the rediscount facilities of the Banque de France.[14] The measure proved ineffective, however, because the banks, profiting from the increase in private sector demand for credit, enjoyed an ample supply of rediscountable assets, such that they felt little deprivation as a result of the new requirement. Even when the government raised the *coefficient de trésorerie* to 32 percent early in 1962, credit expansion still did not slow.

The French economy was once again beset by price inflation. Prices increased by 4 percent in 1962 and by almost 7 percent in 1963. Rapid growth in the money supply sustained the forces of inflation. The arrival of refugees from Algeria (granted independence in 1962) aggravated inflation by provoking a sudden and dramatic increase in consumer demand. The growing fear of inflation, combined with the inefficacy of the monetary restrictions imposed during the preceding two years, caused the government to mount a more serious attack on inflation in 1963.[15] The *coefficient de trésorerie* was raised to 36 percent, the discount rate was increased to 4 percent, consumer credit was tightened and *encadrement du crédit* was imposed for the second time. The government restricted banks to a 12 percent increase in credit allocations in 1963 and a 10 percent increase in 1964.

As a result of such policies, the volume of credit allocations as a proportion of GDP fell from over 10 percent in 1962 to 7 percent in 1964 and 1965, effectively slowing money supply growth from nearly 19 percent in 1962 to 10 percent in 1964 and 11 percent in 1965. Price inflation fell to 3 percent by the end of 1963, and France's commercial balance improved. The cost of monetary stabilization, however, was high. Industrial growth stagnated during 1964 and did not recover until spring of 1965, while annual growth in gross fixed capital formation fell from more than 11 percent in 1963 to 3 percent in 1965. On the other hand, growth in GDP remained high (6.5 percent in 1964 and 4.8 percent in 1965), thanks principally to rapid increases in agricultural productivity.

[14]Simultaneously, the *plancher de bons du Trésor* (minimum reserve of treasury bonds), adopted by the Fourth Republic in order to facilitate treasury bond issues, was decreased from 25 percent to 17.5 percent.

[15]See *L'année politique, économique, sociale, et diplomatique en France, 1963* (Paris: Presses Universitaires de France, 1964), pp. 129–33, 141–42.

Policymakers attributed endemic inflationary pressure in the economy to deficit spending and therefore sought to use fiscal policy to fight it. The Fifth Republic, in stark contrast to the Fourth, embraced the doctrine of fiscal rigor with the zeal and single-mindedness that comes with religious conversion. Though fiscal conservatism became the hallmark of French economic policy for the next decade, it was in no way preordained by the ascension of Charles de Gaulle to the office of president. Among de Gaulle's closest collaborators, Michel Debré maintained that fiscal policy should continue to be treated as an instrument of economic policy. Deficits, he argued with good Keynesian logic, were not a bad thing if they contributed to an active countercyclical policy. On the other hand, there were those, like Valéry Giscard d'Estaing, who thought that in the specific economic context of early Fifth Republic France deficit spending was "a reasonable idea gone mad."[16] The government's inability to slow inflation by any means short of *encadrement du crédit* contributed to the success of Giscard's position. Among Western nations, Fifth Republic France soon became a paragon of fiscal restraint.

France's conversion to the cult of fiscal conservatism is an important part of our story because in an economically perverse way it contributed to the persistence of the overdraft economy. Policymakers discovered the secret of reducing budget deficits without diminishing the state's "standard of living." The secret was *débudgétisation*, according to which expenses that had hitherto been assumed by the state were transferred from the state budget to those of public and private enterprises, financial institutions such as the Deposit and Consignment Bank (Caisse des Dépôts et Consignations, CDC), individual consumers, or even local government.[17] The burden of supporting highways, hospitals, and schools, for example, was placed on cities and *départements*. A greater fraction of the cost of building and running public services, such as the post office, trains, and urban transportation was borne by the consumer through increases in user fees. Industry itself was made to carry a larger proportion of the costs of French social policy as employers were required to increase their contribution to social security and other programs such as public housing and adult education. This in time caused the levy on business earnings to become the highest in Western Europe, a fact that did nothing to ease the financial problems of French firms (see Table 13).

[16]Jean Bouvier et al., *L'ère industrielle et la société d'aujourd'hui*, vol. 4, part 3, of Fernand Braudel and Ernest Labrousse, eds., *Histoire économique et sociale de la France* (Paris: Presses Universitaires de France, 1982), p. 1080.

[17]Jean Chardonnet, *La politique économique intérieure française* (Paris: Dalloz, 1976), p. 47–48; for a broader overview, see ibid., pp. 42–57.

Table 13. Fiscal and social levy on firms and households, 1970–1977 (as % of GDP)

	France	U.K.	Germany	Netherlands	U.S.
Firms	17	12	12	14	10
Households	22	24	26	32	20
Total	39	36	38	46	30

Source: Jean-Pierre Patat, *Monnaie, institutions financières, et politique monétaire* (Paris: Economica, 1982), p. 226. Used by permission of the publisher.

Nor did fiscal conservatism facilitate industry's access to capital. In the words of one analyst, "though the state competed less with the private sector for financing, it replaced itself with other competitors."[18] Table 14 traces the evolution of borrowing on the bond market by government, the public sector, and the private sector from 1963 to 1972. Recasting the figures into percentages, one observes that the fraction of the market claimed by government issues fell from 24.6 percent in 1963 to 7.2 percent by 1972. On the other hand, bond issues attributable to the public sector overall grew from 57.8 percent in 1963 to 71.2 percent in 1972. Much of this was due to borrowing by semipublic financial institutions. The private sector's share of bond issues increased very little, from 17.6 percent in 1963 to 21.6 percent in 1972.

Table 14. Bond issues by government, the public sector, and the private sector, 1963–1972 (billion francs)

	1963	1964	1965	1966	1967	1968	1969	1970	1971	1972
Government	13.3	13.9	14.1	14.8	15.3	14.5	13.8	12.6	11.1	10.6
Public sector	31.2	35.7	40.9	49.9	59.6	65.5	71.8	79.0	88.8	104.7
Private sector	9.5	10.2	11.4	11.8	12.3	13.0	14.0	17.4	23.4	31.7

Source: Adapted from Antoine Coutière, *Le système monétaire français* (Paris: Economica, 1981), p. 136. Used by permission of the publisher.

Simultaneously, *débudgétisation* reduced the volume of funds disbursed to industrial firms by the Economic and Social Development Fund. Whereas the treasury had allocated nearly 7 billion francs in credit to the economy in 1963, it disbursed less than 4.5 billion in 1965. Industry was made to contribute more while receiving less, and was forced to turn to lending institutions (and in lesser degree to the bond market) for financial support, where it competed with local housing authorities and local governments. The impact of *débudgétisation* on the

[18]Ibid., p. 48.

financing of the French economy was not immediately felt because the deflationary thrust of policy in the years following the stabilization plan of 1963 forestalled any immediate rush to the bank window on the part of industrial firms. It nevertheless helped set the stage for the investment crisis that was to characterize the French economy throughout the 1970s. The financial activities of the Deposit and Consignment Bank reflect this evolution. The importance of government debt in the CDC's portfolio diminished in both relative and absolute value, from 2.8 billion francs in 1964 to 2.3 billion francs in 1972.[19] The volume of its long-term credits increased dramatically, from 10.1 percent of total CDC credits in 1964 to 21.1 percent in 1971.[20] This increase resulted in large part from the transfer of financial burdens previously assumed by the treasury, principally in the area of public housing.

In sum, fiscal conservatism merely shuffled the financial responsibility for government programs to parapublic or private agents. The "liberalizing" effects of this transfer on the financial structure of the political economy were therefore insignificant. If fiscal conservatism had any structural impact, it was one of consolidating the overdraft economy. It did so in three ways: it weakened the financial position of industrial firms and increased their dependence on institutional credit lines, it enhanced the importance of semipublic financial institutions and confirmed the predominant role they were made to assume in financing the economy, and finally, it deprived the financial market of public bills that could have been used to help reanimate a moribund market by making available a dependable asset—which in turn could have eased the burden being placed on lending institutions by the transfer of budget expenses to industry and to local governments.

Because fiscal conservatism worsened rather than eased the financial challenges that confronted French firms, the government began to explore reforms that would assure businesses of the financial support they needed but not threaten the economy with renewed inflation. A key motivation was the desire to unlink the fight against inflation, which required financial rigor, from the effort to hasten the modernization of French industry, which required new investments. The need for modernization had become more urgent since the creation of the Common Market and concomitant decolonization had drastically altered France's trade patterns. Apart from liquid savings, no exploitable source of investment capital seemed to exist. The capital market was too narrow, and the state could no longer supply much in the way of investment support, given the thrust of its fiscal policy. As for the semipublic financial institutions, already heavy lenders, they were ill-

---

[19]Antoine Coutière, *Le système monétaire français* (Paris: Economica, 1982), p. 77.
[20]See Braudel and Labrousse, *Histoire économique,* p. 1081.

suited without thorough deregulation to meet the more diverse and complex financial needs of the modern industrial economy.[21] The quest for new, noninflationary sources of capital that could be used to facilitate industrial investment culminated in the reforms of 1966 and 1967, which partially deregulated the banking industry. Deregulation, it was hoped, would make the capital amassed in deposit and savings accounts more accessible to industrial investors.

The reforms essentially facilitated the *"transformation"* of liquid savings deposited in banks into pluri-annual loans suitable for investment. Before the war, the contribution of the banking system to the financing of industry had been small. Though that contribution was strengthened by the reforms of the postwar period, which restructured the banking system and created the rediscountable medium-term loan, banks still lagged behind the state and the semipublic financial institutions in contributing to industrial growth. By the mid-1960s, as state support for industry dried up and as the burden of social policy was increased, the need for more active bank participation in industrial financing became great. The state could not simply abandon its financial responsibilities toward industry and expect it to respond to the multiple challenges the French economy was facing. Efforts to lure savings into bonds and stocks through fiscal incentives proved insufficient. Consequently, after much debate, principally about the inflationary consequences of the proposed policy, the French government decided in 1965 to develop the practice of *"transformation"* and make it the principal source of financing for the economy.

This required two types of reform. First, bank deregulation was needed to decrease the degree of bank specialization. Three decrees promulgated in January and December 1966 and in September 1967 put an end to the distinction between deposit banks and business banks, as defined by the legislation of 1944. Deposit banks were given the power to extend loans of longer maturities to businesses, as well as to buy into industrial firms, and business banks were authorized to manage deposit accounts. Second, because the banks were to lend more, and because this involved the *"transformation"* of short-term assets into medium-term and long-term credits, the banks had to be given the means to augment their reserves.[22] In 1965, the government abolished the fiscal privileges attached to treasury bonds as well as to savings

[21]See Jean-Pierre Patat, *Monnaie, institutions financières, et politique monétaire* (Paris: Economica: 1982), pp. 211—20; J. M. Levesque, "Economic Planning: The Experience of the French Banking System" (International Banking Summer School, Paris, 1968), pp. 105–6; Peter Coffey, *The Social Economy of France* (New York: St. Martin's Press, 1973), pp. 93–97.

[22]*"Transformation"* defined in this manner had been going on since 1945, but was of secondary importance and was underwritten by the state.

accounts in certain types of savings institutions. This modest reform put the banks on a relatively equal footing in their competition with savings institutions for household savings. In December 1965, the government created an attractive savings instrument called "épargne logement." This home-savings plan doubled interest paid on savings accounts not drawn on for at least four years, then matched the amount accumulated in the account with a low interest mortgage. This new and innovative savings plan proved very attractive. In the same year, the government validated and reinforced the practice of making certain medium-term loans for investment eligible for rediscount by the Banque de France by increasing the maturity of such loans from five to seven years. In order to counteract the expansionary impact this reform would have on the growth of credit, the government tightened the conditions medium-term loans had to meet to qualify for rediscount. Tighter conditions, combined with the *coefficient de trésorerie*, actually reduced the volume of medium-term loans that was being presented to the Banque de France for rediscount, at least for the time being.

In September 1966, the government set up a financial network that allowed banks and semipublic financial institutions to discount mortgages with a number of institutions endowed with stable resources, such as retirement accounts and the CDC, thus further augmenting the discount facilities available to banks. In order to increase bank reserves, the National Credit Council in January 1967 gave banks permission to open branches without prior authorization, and indeed encouraged deposit banks to multiply their branches in order to increase their deposits. The government also encouraged bank mergers. In addition, the government continued to develop financial and fiscal incentives to lure savings from sight deposit accounts into more stable longer-term savings accounts. In July 1967, as part of this effort, the government prohibited the payment of interest on sight deposit accounts and suppressed regulations that limited interest rates that could be offered on less-liquid accounts.[23]

Finally, in order to respond to the banks' increased needs for refinancing, reforms were introduced into the money market. Because there was no French equivalent to the "money market" in the U.S. sense of the term—there was a small interbank market for short-term assets and government bonds, which helped banks and other financial institutions manage their reserves—bank refinancing typically took the form of rediscounting by the central bank. Within this system, treasury bonds, instead of being auctioned off on a money market, were offered for sale at a price and interest rate determined by the government. As part of its reform effort, the government created a market for treasury

[23]See Patat and Lutfalla, *Histoire*, pp. 176–81, 167.

bonds whereby the state auctioned off short-term securities at conditions determined by supply and demand. The CDC and the Crédit Agricole were given permission to invest funds on this money market, thereby increasing the volume of very short-term funds available to the banks. Though it is true that only banks and financial institutions were admitted to this auction, the reform nevertheless allowed the government to introduce some market discipline into a system founded almost entirely on the allocation of credit through institutional intermediaries by forcing banks to bid for assets to add to their reserves, while freeing the financial system from its dependence on the Banque de France. The efficacy of the reform was reinforced in January 1967 by imposing reserve requirements that obliged banks and other financial institutions to manage an account with the Banque de France, the amount of which varied in proportion to their sight and savings deposits. These measures placed some constraints on the activities of banks and other financial institutions, in anticipation of the rapid increase in credit allocation that was expected to result from the increase in bank deposits and the deregulation of their activities.

Compared with Fourth Republic financial structures, based on a treasury circuit that linked specialized financial institutions to the treasury, these reforms created a "revised circuit" that linked the banks to the specialized financial institutions and, to a lesser extent, to the Banque de France. The importance of the treasury circuit was diminished. By entrusting the financing of the economy to the practice of "*transformation,*" however, the reforms of 1966–67 validated the structures of the overdraft economy, as manifested by the increasing dependence of France's industry on bank financing. In the words of Patat and Lutfalla, "a structure such as this is not neutral, the high indebtedness of firms failing to help moderate inflationary expectations; moreover, when, some ten years later, would come a time of crisis, the addition of the state's demand for financing, once again in augmentation, to an indebtedness on the part of industrial firms that had become structural would create a fearsome disequilibrium for the French economy."[24]

The peculiarity of France's financial structures did not go unnoticed by contemporary observers. Sima Lieberman, in his *Growth of European Mixed Economies* (1977), wrote of France:

> Private firms strove to finance their modernization, made now imperative by conditions of unrestricted free trade within the area of the EEC, by means of bank credit. Bank finance allowed productive investment to rise in 1966. In terms of constant 1963 francs, private productive investment

[24]Ibid., p. 163.

rose from 47 billion francs in 1965 to 52 billion in 1966 and 60 billion in 1968. This investment expansion was almost entirely based on an increase in the indebtedness of firms.... Compared with the existing situation in rival nations, private investment in France suffered from an excessive recourse to indebtedness and from inadequate self-finance.[25]

The curious triangle that linked the financial structures and practices of the overdraft economy to industrial modernization on the one hand and to the survival of backward economic sectors on the other also failed to go unnoticed. In the 1960s, as in the 1950s, fear of a market-driven redistribution of capital between rising and declining sectors was still very much part of the politics of the overdraft economy. Lieberman, for instance, cited both the "rising trend in the yearly number of mergers and consolidations in France" and the government's efforts to assure the survival "of the traditional industrial structure by giving tax advantages to the small or medium-size firm instead of favoring the large establishment, by granting reimbursements of paid taxes and social security contributions to small exporters and by maintaining tax laws which made the process of merger quite costly."[26] Such policies, to the extent that they slowed the shift of resources from declining sectors to rising sectors, were compatible with industrial modernization only to the extent that the government could assure the latter of capital resources through the medium of credit policy. The French political economy continued to evince the stark contrast between modernizing sectors and stagnating sectors that was characteristic of the 1950s. Lieberman concluded:

Throughout the [1960s, the French economy's] overall output continued to increase at an average annual rate of 5 percent under conditions of quasi-full employment. In spite of the resource drain caused by the French colonial wars, the country succeeded in modernizing and in expanding a number of key industrial sectors to such an extent that its participation in the European Common Market did not bring the economic catastrophe predicted by the old protectionists.... In spite of ... efforts to expand French industry, France in 1970 was still a country characterized by a large degree of economic dualism. Two economic worlds coexisted in the France of M. Pompidou. There was the world of the industrial, progress-minded technocrats.... There was also a separate world made up by large numbers of tradition-loving and protection-urging small farmers, small businessmen, the thousands who had supported Pierre Poujade in the 1950s.[27]

[25]Sima Lieberman, *The Growth of European Mixed Economies, 1945–1970* (New York: John Wiley, 1977), p. 181.
[26]Ibid., pp. 181, 182.
[27]Ibid., p. 193.

The overdraft economy owed its existence to government efforts to prolong the agony of economic decline for certain sectors of the political economy for fear of adverse political repercussions if it allowed modernization to run its redistributive course.

MONETARY STABILIZATION AND POLITICAL POLARIZATION

De Gaulle failed to exploit the immense prestige and power that he brought to government to reimpose monetary and financial discipline on the French political economy. Though he saw himself as the modern-day Poincaré, he stopped short of imposing reforms that would have restored an asset-based economy because such reforms would have deprived the state of much of its institutional control over credit allocation. De Gaulle's reforms thus failed to attack the overdraft economy at its roots. Indeed, de Gaulle left his successor a political economy in which the overdraft structures were reinforced by the reforms (liberalizing in appearance only) of *débudgétisation* and bank deregulation. The outcome was a decade of endemic inflationary pressure that compelled the government to act repeatedly to contain consumer demand and consequently to implement policies that sapped its public support. This was the final element of de Gaulle's legacy: social and political conflict that erupted in the events of May 1968 and caused Georges Pompidou's headlong flight into monetary expansion. Under the presidency of Pompidou, the French overdraft economy functioned very much on the model of its ideal type.

In the beginning, de Gaulle's authority was nourished by mainland impatience with the war in Algeria. It was the overriding desire to find a way out of this quagmire that gave de Gaulle the moral authority to enact the stabilization measures of 1958 and 1959. The end of the Algerian war, René Rémond observed, marked the "absolute" beginning of the Fifth Republic. Raymond Aron remarked tersely, "There is no longer an Algerian war to substitute for a parliamentary majority."[28] Deprived of war, unpopular economic policies gradually undermined de Gaulle's personal popularity and prestige. The erosion of de Gaulle's popular support first became apparent during the legislative elections of 1962 and the simultaneous referendum on a constitutional amendment. The referendum, though a victory for de Gaulle, lacked the triumphal lopsidedness of its predecessors. De Gaulle's support fell from 75 percent (in favor of Algerian self-determination) to 61.7 percent (in favor of the direct election of the president of the Repub-

[28]Both Rémond and Aron are quoted in Chapsal, *La vie politique*, p. 454.

lic). The opposition actually won a majority of votes in a number of *départements,* notably in the Midi, which traditionally voted for the Left. Though the new Gaullist party, the UNR, won 32 percent of the votes (more than any party since 1944) its triumph was nevertheless marred by the fact that abstentions were higher, at 31 percent, than they had been at any time since 1946, and by the progression of the Communist party, which increased its share of the votes from 19 percent to 22 percent.[29]

According to an opinion poll conducted in May 1964, nearly half the population was dissatisfied with the economic and social policies of the government.[30] Discontent was greatest among the farmers and the blue-collar wage-earners. Agriculture, in particular, proved to be an economic headache from the earliest days of the Fifth Republic, a headache for which the liberalizing reforms of Jacques Rueff (which had eliminated a number of price indexations for agricultural goods) were largely responsible. It was estimated that the purchasing power of the French peasantry declined by 6 percent in 1959. That same year the Federation of Milk Producers (Fédération des Producteurs de Lait) demanded an increase of 5 percent in the price of milk, and the National Federation of Farmers' Unions (Fédération Nationale des Syndicats d'Exploitants Agricoles) demanded an overall increase of 5 percent in the prices of all agricultural goods. The economic problems of the countryside were aggravated by mounting overproduction, which in 1960 affected producers of beef, wine, cereals, sugar beets, dairy products, and potatoes.[31]

Economic insecurity on the farm gave rise to numerous and frequently spectacular demonstrations of farmer discontent. In the early months of 1960, farmers stopped traffic on major highways to force the government to call an emergency session of the National Assembly. In June 1961, the artichoke growers of Brittany dumped their produce in front of the town halls of the region and occupied the town hall of Morlaix. In 1961 and again in 1964, agricultural policy nearly brought down the government, which retreated on a number of agricultural issues and took action to prevent further falls in agricultural price levels.

Wage policy, notably in the public sector, gave rise to a second series of social challenges to the new regime. Price inflation during the first five years of the Fifth Republic was 25 percent, threatening the purchasing power of numerous wage-earners. In the public sector, the

[29]See Chapsal, *La vie politique,* pp. 471–81.

[30]Ibid., p. 498.

[31]See *L'année politique, 1959,* pp. xiv, 100–101; *L'année politique, 1960* (Paris: Presses Universitaires de France, 1961), pp. 174–77.

problem was aggravated by the fact that wage concessions had been more parsimonious than in the private sector, where wage concessions had averaged 12 percent annually.[32] The government was master over wage policy in the public sector, which comprises not only the civil service but also a large number of public enterprises, such as the SNCF and the EDF-GDF. The government made the public sector an unwilling partner in its efforts to control inflation by containing wage increases. Disparity in the evolution of public and private sector wages caused discontent, which led in turn to a number of important strike movements. In February 1963, a miner's strike closed down nearly all the mines in the country, rekindling memories of the general strike of 1947. Unlike strikes in some public sectors, such as electricity or the railway, the miners strike hit a resonant chord in public opinion. It was supported publicly by a number of Roman Catholic bishops and even some UNR deputies. During the strike, de Gaulle's popularity plunged to 42 percent, the first time it had fallen below 50 percent. A strike in the EDF-GDF in November 1964 was among the more serious sequels to the miners strike of the preceding year.

Social strife provoked a degree of policy incoherence. The government sought to stabilize the economy and address farmer and worker discontent at the same time. Thus the harsh policy of price stabilization was accompanied in 1963 by a policy that added a fourth week of mandatory paid vacations. Nevertheless, despite its contradictions and acrobatics, the government did manage to meet popular discontent and disapproval with greater resistance than any government of the Fourth Republic, and it was able to maintain the overall rigorous economic course in fiscal and income policy despite agricultural demonstrations, strikes, and public opinion polls which showed that its policies were being supported by only about one-third of the population and opposed by half.[33] Eventually, however, elections—municipal, presidential, and legislative—traced the limits of the public's tolerance for economic rigor.

Political life under the Fifth Republic became increasingly polarized. In the municipal elections of June 1964, the Communist party increased its number of mayors from twenty-five to thirty-four, while the UNR added only one municipal government to its list.[34] In the presidential election of December 1965, de Gaulle was forced into a run-off

[32]Wage increases in the private sector provoked the wrath of the government, causing Michel Debré, while prime minister, to chastise employers for undermining the stabilization policies of the government, which called for annual wage increases of no more than 4 percent.

[33]Chapsal, La vie politique, pp. 508, 511.

[34]See L'année politique économique, sociale et diplomatique en France, 1965 (Paris: Presses Universitaires de France, 1966), pp. 64–70.

election by a vestige of the Fourth Republic, François Mitterrand, who was struggling to unite the Left in opposition to the conservative regime. Although the second round of the election handed the victory to de Gaulle with a massive 55 percent, Mitterrand's score was nevertheless an indication that the Left was overcoming its disunity and that the new institutions of the Fifth Republic, which rewarded bigness and punished smallness, were actually pushing the Left along this path.[35]

Political discontent grew in 1966, which was marked by growing inflation and increasing unemployment, a portent of the "stagflation" of the 1970s, even though it was a good year by GNP growth. The gross national product grew despite stagnation in much of France's industrial sector, which continued to pale under the effects of restrictive credit allocation. Most of the growth was attributable to state-supported activities, such as housing and investments in infrastructure like highways and railway electrification. Economic difficulties, combined with greater unity on the Left, brought together the two major though rival labor unions, the General Confederation of Labor (Confédération Générale du Travail, CGT) and the French Democratic Confederation of Labor (Confédération Française Démocratique du Travail, CFDT) to sign, on January 10, 1966, an agreement to take joint action to oppose government policies. The many coordinated strikes that occurred on May 17 demonstrated the potential power of union collaboration.

The legislative elections of 1967 confirmed the growing strength of the Left and the tendency to bipolarization. The non-Communist parties of the Left—the SFIO, the Federation of the Democratic and Socialist Left (Fédération de la Gauche Démocratique et Socialiste) of François Mitterrand, and a number of Radicals, fielded common candidates. Furthermore, they agreed with the Communist party to withdraw candidates from the second round in order to benefit the candidate of the Left with the highest score. The non-Communist coalition scored nearly 19 percent—not an advance, relative to previous results, but nevertheless demonstrating the electorate's support for a strategy of collaboration with the Communists on a scale that had not been seen since the eviction of the Communist party from government in 1947. As for the Communist party, it increased its electoral score to 22.5 percent. Gaullists, on the other hand, confirmed their domination at the polls by winning nearly 38 percent. The presidential majority, however, barely survived the elections, with 245 seats in the National Assembly—three more than the opposition's 242. As Chapsal writes, the elections guaranteed "neither the government, nor even the re-

[35]See Chapsal, *La vie politique*, pp. 589–92.

gime, the necessary stability to confront the economic and social diffi-culties which were the consequence of a more than dreary economic situation."[36] The stage was set for the events of May.

CONCLUSION

The overdraft economy survived the rise to power of a strong, conservative leader and a constitutional reform that enhanced the power of the government to resist societal pressure for policy. The outcome was a political economy that knew no effective antidote to continued endemic inflationary pressure other than *encadrement du crédit. Encadrement,* in turn, discouraged industrial investment at a time when the salarial and social charges imposed on industry were mount-ing. The government, in order to make more capital available for industrial investment, reformed the banking system in a manner that enhanced the role of *"transformation,"* and thus the dependence of the economy on institutionally allocated credit. This only ratified the finan-cial structures of the overdraft economy. When social and political conflict crescendoed to the point that it broke the bolt that *encadrement* tried to place on monetary growth, the overdraft economy could function according to its ideal type. This occurred after the events of May 1968, until the collapse of the hegemonic order forced the liberal-ization of France's finances.

[36]Ibid., p. 577.

CHAPTER SEVEN

U.S. Hegemonic Decline and Crisis in France

Domestic governmental weakness and a tolerant world economic order conspired to keep the French overdraft economy alive throughout the Fourth Republic and during the early years of the Fifth Republic. That tolerant environment, however, began to change in the early 1960s because of change in the policies of the hegemonic nation that underpinned the international monetary order. The United States became a source of growing international monetary stress rather than stability by refusing to address its own payments disequilibrium. The dollar overhang fed a number of speculative crises during the 1960s while more expansionist monetary policy in the United States began to fuel global inflation. The French overdraft economy was particularly vulnerable to external monetary instability and imperfectly defended against it. French policymakers who were trying to contain inflation through *encadrement* became highly critical of U.S. policy, which they perceived as a principal source of inflation in France.

Growing external stress contributed to internal crisis. In 1968, the Gaullist regime was almost overwhelmed by a prolonged general strike, provoked in large part by impatience with de Gaulle's unceasing efforts to impose monetary stability. The crisis ended in devaluation in 1969, after which the government under Georges Pompidou implemented a highly expansionist economic policy that saw the overdraft economy perform according to its ideal type. Monetary expansion accelerated just as international monetary crisis provoked the collapse of the regime of fixed but adjustable exchange rates in 1971. The crisis left the French burdened with an overdraft economy in which monetary stabilization was particularly difficult to achieve, an increasingly trade-dependent economy that suffered more than most from flexible exchange rates, a rapidly expanding money supply, and the social and political legacy of policies that caused French economic agents to think they were immune from the threat of market-driven processes of economic adjustment. It was in this context that the government sought a way out from this policy conundrum through foreign borrowing and the sophisticated use of *encadrement du crédit* to control monetary growth. It was also in this context that interest in the fundamental reform of the French overdraft economy began to gain ground. In this chapter we look at the effects of U.S. hegemonic decline on French policy in the 1960s and 1970s, beginning with the Franco-American monetary conflict.

INTERNATIONAL MONETARY CONFLICT IN THE 1960S

Charles de Gaulle's France has contributed mightily to the development of theory in the field of international political economy by supplying scholars with the ideal type "spoiler." In the mid-1960s the French, not content with verbal criticism of the Bretton Woods "dollar-exchange standard," began to convert their dollar reserves into gold, which threatened the gold convertibility of the key international currency. Charles Kindleberger had France in mind when he wrote: "The...middle power...possesses insufficient strength to lead the system, and hence is without responsibility, but has enough responsibility to be a spoiler.... Some power, and claims to but not possession of responsibility, may lead the middle power to pursue its own version of the public international interest at one moment, its private national interest at another."[1] The concept of the overdraft economy adds to our understanding of French policy in the 1960s by suggesting that French obstreperousness was not simply the consequence of its economic "size," but was occasioned to a significant degree by real anxieties concerning the inflationary impact of U.S. policy both on the viability of the international monetary order and on the capacity of French officials to contain inflation domestically.

The roots of the U.S.-French monetary conflict go back to the late 1950s, when the first cracks in the hegemonic edifice appeared. The United States began to encounter payments difficulties, causing fear worldwide that the global economy might become threatened by imbalance in the American economy. American payments imbalances incited some governments to make prudent purchases of gold as early as 1957.

[1]Charles P. Kindleberger, "Systems of International Economic Organization," in David P. Calleo, ed., *Money and the Coming World Order* (New York: New York University Press, 1976), pp. 21–22.

During the period 1958–60, Great Britain converted $1.8 billion while France, Belgium, and the Netherlands together converted $1.5 billion. Dollar devaluation scares occurred in the Middle East, the Far East, and Latin America, further undermining central banker confidence in the key currency. Following the rush on gold on the London market in 1960, the French warned the Americans that if they did not take measures to force the London gold price down, the central banks would be forced to convert their dollar reserves. During the fourth quarter of 1960 alone, no less than twenty-six different central banks made precautionary purchases of gold, draining more than $1 billion worth of gold reserve assets from the U.S. economy.

Before 1962, France showed no marked inclination to play the "spoiler." It was indeed one of the countries which, with Germany, Italy, Switzerland, and the Scandinavian countries, showed the greatest reluctance to redeem dollars for gold. As concern for the health of the dollar mounted, France and the Netherlands, in an effort to prevent a rush on gold, proposed that gold specie payments be replaced by gold-guaranteed obligations, a proposal supported by the U.S. treasury but finally rejected by the U.S. government. When crisis erupted on the London gold market in 1960, the French collaborated with the United States and other European countries to create a gold pool, and during the sterling crisis of 1961 it was the Banque de France that advanced the idea of setting up "swap" arrangements to quell speculation.[2] During this period, France's foreign monetary relations were strained with Great Britain rather than with the United States. This was because the British used the dollars that began to reenter their economy after stabilization to restock their reserves with gold bought from the United States rather than repay their debt to the IMF.

The currency crisis of 1961 frightened the French enough that they adopted a policy of gradual conversion of their reserve dollars at the rate of $30 million a month.[3] During the next five years, the French cut their dollar currency reserves from $1.4 billion to $0.5 billion as did the other European countries. The Germans cut their own reserve dollars from $3.3 billion at the end of 1963 to $1.7 billion by the end of March 1965.

The French began to push the idea of international monetary reform in September 1962. At a meeting of the IMF, the young minister of finance, Valéry Giscard d'Estaing, argued that the international economic system was threatened by an inflationary overabundance of

---

[2]Charles A. Coombs, *The Arena of International Finance* (New York: John Wiley, 1976), pp. 74–78.

[3]Ibid., pp. 48–60. See also Fritz Machlup, *Remaking the International Monetary System: The Rio Agreement and Beyond* (Baltimore: Johns Hopkins University Press, 1968).

liquidity, principally because of the dollar overhang. The stabilization of international monetary relations required elimination of the American and British deficits and creation of a sounder international monetary foundation than that currently provided by the structural deficits of key currency countries. Giscard d'Estaing proposed the creation of a new "composite reserve unit" (CRU). This meant a partial return to the gold standard, modified in a way that assured sufficient liquidity to a world that was experiencing rapid growth in international trade. The return to a more classic international monetary order, argued the French, would impose well-defined constraints on policy and thus slow the creation of international liquidity. As Edward Morse explains, "while the Americans were concerned with the world's liquidity needs, French policy was preoccupied with dangers of European inflation that were felt to result from American deficits. This fear of inflation explains much of the French proclivity for balance and equilibrium in international payments."[4] The French government's fear of inflation, to be properly understood, must be put in the context of its own painful and frustrating efforts to put an end to inflation, hampered by a political economy that had amply demonstrated its structural vulnerability both to inflationary pressures and deflationary policies.

While Giscard d'Estaing was promoting international monetary reform, Jacques Rueff was mounting a personal campaign against the creation globally of "false money," caused not only by French credit policy but also by global reliance on a national currency to supply an international monetary standard. Rueff maintained as early as 1959 that instability in the international monetary system was contributing to inflation in France, making Rueff one of the first to ascribe inflationary implications to the net outflow of dollars from the U.S. economy to the rest of the world.[5] Rueff argued that because the international monetary system had become tributary to structural imbalance in the foreign transactions of the United States, only a thoroughgoing reform of the international monetary order could restore stability. Aside from its alarmist rhetoric, Rueff's analysis was not fundamentally different from that advanced about the same time by Robert Triffin, for whom an international monetary system founded on the current account deficit of the key currency country was doomed to instability, either in the form of worldwide inflation or in the form of an international liquidity crisis. Nor was it fundamentally different from that of Giscard d'Estaing, with which it shared the idea of promoting the use of gold in international settlements. But Triffin and Giscard d'Estaing were cognizant of both horns of the international monetary dilemma, that is, inflation

---

[4] Edward L. Morse, *Foreign Policy and Interdependence in Gaullist France* (Princeton: Princeton University Press, 1973), p. 223.

[5] See ibid., p. 217.

and liquidity crisis. Rueff, on the other hand, was hooked by the single horn of inflation. Thus, unlike Giscard d'Estaing, he made no provision for supplementing gold with some unit of account that would assure the world economy of sufficient liquidity to sustain rapid growth in international trade.

Rueff was a tireless pamphletist. He turned to world opinion in a series of articles published simultaneously in France, the United States, and Great Britain and met with members of the Federal Reserve, whom he described in his memoirs as having been "moved and surprised" by the gravity of the problem. Nevertheless, Rueff was viewed as something to a gadfly by mainstream French economists and economic officials, and his radical, pre-Keynesian ideas met with frequent resistance. Giscard d'Estaing was particularly allergic to Rueff's proposals. Though his own CRU scheme was motivated in large part by growing French fears of global monetary inflation, it was also designed to respond to the eventuality that the United States would one day attack its current account deficit seriously and provoke a worldwide liquidity crisis.[6] For this reason, Giscard d'Estaing brushed aside Rueff's proposals as being, as he so delicately put it, "under the dominion of inexactitude in the formulation of the question" (sous le régime de l'inexactitude de la position de la question).[7] Nevertheless, Rueff's views did succeed in winning the support of some influential members of de Gaulle's inner circle, including Étienne Burin des Roziers, de Gaulle's cabinet director, and Maurice Couve de Murville, minister of foreign affairs and Rueff's former collaborator in the Ministry of Finance between 1936 and 1939.

In February 1965, de Gaulle publicly and loudly embraced Rueff's radical proposal for a return to the gold standard, declaring:

> The fact that many states in principle accept dollars on the same basis as gold so as to offset, if need be, the deficits in their favor in the American balance of payments, leads the United States to indebt itself abroad at no cost. Indeed, what it owed abroad, it pays for, at least partially, with dollars which it alone can issue, instead of paying entirely with gold, which has a real value, which must be earned to be possessed, and which cannot be transferred to others without risks and sacrifices. This unilateral facility which is granted to America is serving to cloud the idea that the dollar is an impartial and international medium of exchange, when it is a means of credit belonging to one state.[8]

[6]See Stephen D. Cohen, *International Monetary Reform, 1964–1969* (New York: Praeger, 1970), pp. 39–53.

[7]Quoted in Jacques Rueff, *De l'aube au crépuscule* (Paris: Plon, 1977), pp. 263–64.

[8]*Major Addresses, Statements, and Press Conferences of General Charles de Gaulle, March 17, 1964–May 16, 1967* (New York: Ambassade de France, Service de Presse et d'Information, 1967), quoted in Morse, *Foreign Policy,* p. 224. See also Don Cook, *Charles de Gaulle: A Biography* (New York: G. P. Putnam's Sons, 1983), p. 369.

There is no doubt that de Gaulle's interest in gold was tied to broader foreign policy goals and ambitions.[9] Indeed, his own understanding of and tolerance for economic issues was notably deficient. Fred Hirsch relates de Gaulle's surprise and consternation, for example, when informed by an unfortunate Élysée bureaucrat that France's gold reserves were in fact held and managed by the Federal Reserve Bank of New York, to whom de Gaulle is said to have replied, "If I were the person responsible, I would hardly sleep easily with such an arrangement."[10] De Gaulle's initiative did not have the unanimous support of the French government, however. Giscard declared publicly in June 1965, "I in fact believe that gold is not enough,"[11] and argued that a return to gold, coupled with devaluation of the dollar (as proposed by Rueff) would let the deficit countries off the hook and ultimately have an uneven impact on the world's national economies, most of which did not possess important gold reserves. De Gaulle's victory was not complete until Giscard d'Estaing was removed from the Ministry of Finance and replaced by de Gaulle's most loyal lieutenant, Michel Debré.

There can be no doubt that the Franco-American monetary dispute of the mid-1960s was due in part to the personal initiative of General de Gaulle and was tied to de Gaulle's broader diplomatic ambitions. Nor can there be much dispute that the term "spoiling" captures, at least rhetorically, the thrust of those ambitions quite appropriately. But to make de Gaulle's personal and diplomatic grudge against the United States bear the whole weight of explaining French foreign monetary policy during this period is more than even de Gaulle's ego can bear. To do so is to ignore that French policy during the first four years of de Gaulle's presidency was cooperative and even innovative in its defense of the international monetary order. It is to ignore that not only France but most European countries had, after the currency crisis of 1961, adopted a policy of exchanging their reserve dollars for gold. Above all, it is to ignore that the French had for several years been trying to attack inflation in their own economy vigorously but, because of the overdraft economy, were experiencing real difficulty doing so (see Chapter Six), while the United States had by 1964 charted a new monetary policy course that now embraced inflation as the means to finance both the war in Indochina and programs to end domestic poverty. It is not so difficult to imagine that the French should begrudge the fact that the

[9] See Brian Crozier, *De Gaulle the Statesman* (London: Eyre Methuen, 1973), pp. 569–74.

[10] Fred Hirsch, *Money International* (London: Penguin, 1967), p. 195. In the months that followed, gold reserves were physically relocated to a site considerably closer to the Élysée Palace.

[11] Quoted in Robert Solomon, *The International Monetary System, 1945–1976: An Insider's View* (New York: Harper and Row, 1977), p. 56.

United States would choose this moment to become negligent of its international monetary responsibilities and to become itself a source of global inflationary pressures. If we return to Kindleberger's thesis, it is unclear that there is a theoretically useful place for a "spoiler" in a world ordered by a hegemon that has turned "predatory."

THE CRISIS OF MAY 1968 AND MONETARY POLICY UNDER POMPIDOU

As the external environment that nurtured the overdraft economy began to erode, festering domestic social discontent erupted in crisis. Hegemonic decline, indeed, was not foreign to that crisis, since it fed inflationary pressures that the French government had such difficulty combating. Four years of austerity created the conditions for the general strike of May 1968.

The "events" (*événements*) of 1968 began innocently enough in March as a student protest against educational reforms that limited university enrollments. Student unrest grew until it culminated in the *nuit des barricades* of May 10, during which clashes between students and police turned to riot. The crisis spread to the factories when on May 14 strikes began to erupt spontaneously, taking union leadership by surprise. The unions reacted in disorder. The CFDT, sympathetic to the student movement, sought to use the strikes to press for vague demands for social reform. The CGT, on the other hand, anxious to draw the distinction between the romanticism of the students and the ideologically more "legitimate" material demands of the working class, sought to use the strikes as leverage to procure wage increases and other material benefits. Negotiations ensued, resulting in the Grenelle Accords, which acceded to the CGT's demand for wage hikes but remained non-committal on the CFDT's demands for social reform.

The Grenelle Accords were denounced as treason by student leaders and, much to the consternation of both the government and the CGT, were rejected by a large number of strike committees in the factories. Student and worker unrest, in the eyes of many, began to assume the dimensions of a political revolution. François Mitterrand called for the resignation of de Gaulle and the establishment of a provisional government under Pierre Mendès France. De Gaulle's sudden departure by helicopter from the grounds of the Palais de l'Élysée on May 29 appeared to seal the fate of the Fifth Republic. The next day, however, de Gaulle dissolved the National Assembly and set new elections for June. The elections ended in a tidal wave victory for the Gaullist Union des Démocrates pour la République (UDR), while the parties of the

189

Left were sanctioned by some for their rebellious machinations and by others for their betrayal of the cause. The Communist party fell to 20 percent, the Federation of the Democratic and Socialist Left (Fédération de la Gauche Démocrate at Socialiste, FGDS) to 16.5 percent, the parties of the center, unrecognizable and absent during the crisis, to 10.3 percent, while the UDR climbed to 43.6 percent. The electorate handed the UDR three-fourths of the seats in the National Assembly.[12]

The "événements" influenced the course of economic policy for the next several years. Once order was restored, the government took measures to limit the damage that strikes and large wage increases had inflicted on the French economy. The treasury borrowed heavily from the Banque de France to feed an emergency credit-line that pumped about 3 billion francs of low interest credit into industrial firms. Regulations restricting the lending capacity of the banking system were relaxed. Although the discount rate was increased to 5 percent in July 1968, in order to discourage speculation, credit allocations increased, notably in the form of emergency loans and medium-term credits for exporting and investment. Despite the hike in the discount rate, credit allocation grew rapidly.

Rapid credit growth, coming at a time of equally rapid growth in consumer demand and flagging confidence in the financial foundations of the French economy, hardly helped to stabilize the economy after the strikes. Monetary growth fueled a currency flight that, in the month of June alone, cost the French economy 7.2 billion francs. Patat and Lutfalla observe, however:

> It is easy... to decree what should have been done: contain the growth of credit and the money supply in order to prevent a situation in which excessive internal credit expansion only fueled a currency flight. Such a policy was hardly feasible in the climate of the time, the foremost concern being to start up production and to recoup the wealth that was lost during a month and a half of an almost total shutdown of economic activity. Monetary policy was called on to furnish resources to the treasury and to help French firms get through this difficult period.[13]

By autumn it was obvious that efforts to stimulate investment could not be sustained without threatening the economy with severe monetary

[12]See Jacques Chapsal, *La vie politique en France depuis 1940* (Paris: Presses Universitaires de France, 1969), pp. 592–600. The Fédération de la Gauche Democrate et Socialiste was an electoral coalition of parties and clubs of the non-Communist Left, created after the presidential elections of 1965, which comprised the historic socialist SFIO (Section Française de l'Internationale Ouvrière), the Parti Radical, and the Convention des Institutions Républicaines of François Mitterrand.

[13]Jean-Pierre Patat and Michel Lutfalla, *Histoire monétaire de la France au XXe siècle* (Paris: Economica, 1986), p. 194.

disorder. The government altered its policy, restored exchange controls to slow the currency hemorrhage, and reimposed *encadrement du crédit* to slow the growth of credit to a projected 7 percent between September 1968 and December 1969. Persistent rapid growth in credit allocations, however, forced the government to tighten *encadrement* to 3 percent. This, combined with an increase in the discount rate from 6 percent in June to 8 percent in October 1968, slowed the growth of bank credit from 18.4 percent in 1968 to 12 percent in 1969. Though this figure far exceeded the government's target, it contributed to slow M_2 growth to less than 6 percent. Slower monetary growth, combined with the devaluation of the franc in August 1969 (see below), brought France's balance of payments closer to equilibrium.

The current of discontent that had been undermining de Gaulle's hold on the electorate since 1965 forced de Gaulle to resign after losing a referendum on a rather inconsequential constitutional reform. He was replaced by his former prime minister and negotiator of the Grenelle Accords, Georges Pompidou, in an election marked by the absence of François Mitterrand and by temporary disarray among the parties of the Left.

The challenges that confronted the new president were daunting. Popular discontent still ran high, forcing Pompidou to be conciliatory. Pompidou knew that a rigid conservatism would only threaten political stability, and therefore the institutional achievement of his predecessor. On the other hand, the opportunity and effectiveness of conciliatory rhetoric and policy were weakened by growing bipolarization, which increased Pompidou's dependence on the support of the Gaullist old guard. He was made keenly aware that the stalwarts of Gaullism, and, during the few months that remained to him, the general himself, were watchful of his every move, ready to sanction any deviance from Gaullist orthodoxy.[14] *Ouverture* (opening the government to participation by non-Gaullists) and *fidélité* (loyalty to de Gaulle) were the Charybdis and Scylla of Pompidou's presidency. Pompidou's relationship with his prime minister, Jacques Chaban-Delmas, reveals the difficulty of his political position. Chaban was a "historic Gaullist," a *compagnon de la résistance*, but his politics were to the left of the UDR. Though a member of the UDR, he also counted himself a Radical and had, under the Fourth Republic, been an active supporter of Mendès France. Drawing on Michel Crozier's theme that France was a "société bloquée" (stalled society), Chaban invited the country to break down the three obstacles to a "prosperous, young, generous, and liberated" new society: "a tentacular and inefficient state, archaic and conservative social

[14]Eric Roussel, *Georges Pompidou* (Paris: Éditions Jean-Claude Lattès, 1984), pp. 318, 389.

structures, and a fragile economy."[15] Pompidou's political philosophy was incompatible with his prime minister's policy agenda. During a press conference, Pompidou mused, half-bitterly, "Ah! This 'new society'—I already have enough trouble with the old one!"[16]

Chaban's heterodoxy provoked a not unexpected revolt among the UDR rank-and-file. As the conservative coalition began to erode, the non-Communist Left was reborn as the SFIO merged with smaller parties and clubs to form the new Socialist party (*Parti Socialiste*), whose helm was soon assumed by François Mitterrand. In 1972, the Socialist party signed a governmental program, the "Programme Commun de Gouvernement," with the Communists and some splinter Radicals, giving the Left coherence and unity just as the Right was showing signs of disaggregation.[17] *Poujadisme* resurged as Gérard Nicoud took up the flag of all those who felt neglected or threatened by economic progress, and in particular by the multiplication of large commercial centers, calling on all self-employed workers to withhold their taxes and withdraw their funds from the nationalized banks and public savings institutions. The government showed little conviction in dealing with these challenges. *L'année politique* editorialized: "The state does not know how to react. It makes decisions. These are protested and the protesters erect barriers across the *autoroutes*. The reactions that follow are incoherent, characterized alternately by moments of steadfast resistance, incredible clemency, retreats that no one comprehends, and decisions that are made only to be retracted two days later."[18] Pompidou replaced Chaban-Delmas in June 1972 with the stolidly conservative Pierre Messmer.[19] The more conservative tenor of the new government, however, along with Pompidou's illness and the growing instability in the global economy, caused the final years of Pompidou's presidency to be marked by even greater political torpor.

Pompidou's economic policies reflected his isolation and ambivalence. Like Edgar Faure (who, radical though he was, was supportive of the president), Pompidou sought in economic growth the nostrum for France's social and political ills. Economic policy, he reasoned, had to address the economic frustrations of the citizenry by assuming a more expansionist orientation, even at the cost of inflation. Pompidou eschewed austerity and addressed France's growing trade imbalance through devaluation. An 11 percent devaluation of the franc in August 1969 caused the ratio of exports to imports to climb from 86.4 percent in

[15]Ibid., pp. 349–50. See also Jacques Chapsal, *La vie politique sous la Vᵉ République* (Paris: Presses Universitaires de France, 1984), pp. 443–47.

[16]See Roussel, *Pompidou*, p. 353.

[17]See Chapsal, *La vie politique sous la Vᵉ République*, pp. 457–72.

[18]Quoted in Roussel, *Pompidou*, pp. 393–94.

[19]Chapsal, *La vie politique sous la Vᵉ République*, pp. 482–84.

1968 to 93.8 percent in 1970. The potentially inflationary impact of devaluation, however, required the temporary tightening of monetary and fiscal policy. The discount rate was increased, a surtax was imposed and some sales taxes were increased, and one-sixth of the funds earmarked for public investment were frozen and placed in a special fund, the Conjunctural Action Account (Fonds d'Action Conjoncturelle).[20] *Encadrement du crédit* remained in effect, and the penalties imposed on banks that exceeded their quotas were made more severe.

Nevertheless, these restrictive policies had almost no impact on investment. Devaluation's impact on the economy outweighed austerity's impact, and economic growth during these two years of austerity was very rapid. France's GDP growth remained high at 8 percent in 1969 and 6 percent in 1970, stimulated by investments that increased by 8.8 percent in 1969 and 6.8 percent in 1970 and by an increase in household disposable income of 13.5 percent in 1969 and 13 percent in 1970. Investment was stimulated by increased demand both at home and abroad, while the restrictions on credit allocation acted only very selectively. By 1970, once the balance of payments was restored and the budget was balanced, the government gave up trying to corral the expansionary forces at work within the French economy. Wages were the most visible beneficiaries of this new policy orientation. The real cost of labor, after having increased by 3.5 percent annually between 1963 and 1968, increased by 5.6 percent in 1968 and 6 percent annually between 1970 and 1973. Household disposable income grew by an average 12.6 percent annually between 1969 and 1973, in contrast to an average of 8.2 percent between 1963 and 1968. The expansionist thrust of economic policy was validated by the recommendations of the Sixth Plan, implemented in 1971, which adopted a target for annual industrial growth of 7.5 percent. This represented an acceleration in the rate of industrial growth of one-half percent relative to the preceding decade, even though the capacity of French firms to invest was reduced as a result of the wage settlements of 1968. Pompidou, who personally composed the introduction to the Sixth Plan, argued:

> France cannot renounce the pursuit of rapid growth. No doubt one might think that an evolution that offers some permanent and generously calculated margin of security would better guarantee the maintenance of fundamental equilibria, but such prudence would work against itself. The government is convinced, in fact, that an underemployment of labor, even limited, cannot constitute a means of regulating the economy that would be socially acceptable or technically effective for an economy such as ours.[21]

[20]Peter Coffey, *The Social Economy of France* (New York: St. Martin's Press, 1973), p. 85.
[21]Quoted in Roussel, *Pompidou,* pp. 437–38.

Thus Pompidou sought refuge from political strife in the acceleration of economic growth, paying the bill with the help of a generous credit line. Once balance was restored to France's external accounts, the government decided in October 1970 to lift *encadrement du crédit*. Although the government recommended that banks show moderation and not abuse their new freedom, the banks in fact responded by unleashing a tidal wave of new credit allocations. Whereas during the first nine months of 1970 bank credit had grown by slightly less than 10 percent, credit grew by an equal amount during the remaining three months of the year. The growth of M_2 was held below 9 percent during the first three quarters of 1970, but ended the year with a growth rate of 15 percent.

During the period 1971–73, economic expansion received yet another stimulus in the form of currency depreciation. After the dollar renounced its gold parity in August 1971, the French government acted to combat what it feared would be the negative impact of this de facto devaluation of the dollar on France's foreign trade. It therefore established a double exchange rate for the franc, intervening on the currency market to dissociate the cost of the franc when used for speculative purposes (which was allowed to appreciate) from the cost of the franc when used for commercial purposes (which was not allowed to appreciate relative to the dollar). The stimulus afforded by the depreciation of the franc relative to other European currencies (which floated upward) kept demand for credit high. The government did little to discourage it, and indeed allowed bank credit to grow by 19 percent in 1971 and 23.4 percent in 1972. M_2 growth was greater than 18 percent both years.

The expansionist impact of credit policy was reinforced by an important reform in money market policy. The government, in an effort to raise the dikes before the rising flood of credit, began to encourage banks to buy reserve assets on the interbank "money market" rather than deluge the Banque de France with demands for rediscounts. To do this, it forced the cost of short-term assets bought and sold on the money market to fall below the rediscount rate charged by the Banque de France. The cost of funds bought on the money market fell from 7 percent to 3.5 percent between the end of 1972 and the middle of 1972, while the discount rate fell only from 6.5 percent to 5.75 percent. This preserved the Banque de France from a frontal assault by the banks but did nothing to discourage rapid credit expansion. On the contrary, write Patat and Lutfalla,

> It is certain that the state of mind of neither government officials nor economic agents was deflationary in the least, even up until the final

months of 1973. Thus the French economy was able to benefit from an exceptional opportunity to grow (5.2 percent in 1971, 5.8 percent in 1972, 5.5 percent in 1973). Price inflation increased to 8.5 percent in 1973, but in a context that was inflationary worldwide. Beginning only with the first energy crisis did the potential for imbalance and a deterioration of the situation, contained by this expansionist policy, start to materialize.[22]

The government was not deterred by the inflationary implications of this policy. Roussel relates: "Soon even the specialists were remarking that inflation was being provoked more by credit than by the supply of money in the strict sense of the term.... A former banker, Georges Pompidou, it must be admitted, was not haunted by the inflationary peril."[23]

This vast expansion of bank credit was facilitated by the bank reforms of 1965–67, which therefore, despite the professions of liberalism that accompanied them, had the ironic effect of reinforcing the overdraft structures of the French political economy. Bank resources had grown dramatically in response to efforts to increase their lending capacity. This was especially true of time deposits, which constituted 41.4 percent of bank liabilities in 1973 (49.7 percent in 1979) as opposed to 26.5 percent in 1968. Inversely, sight deposits accounted for 42.8 percent of bank liabilities in 1973 (39.5 percent in 1979), in contrast to 48 percent in 1968. In one sense, the increase in time deposits helped dampen the inflationary impact of increased bank lending. Estimates of the velocity of circulation of M_2 show that it fell from 3.0 in 1960 to 2.1 in 1973. But in another sense it fueled inflation. As the banks' resources grew, so did their share in financing investment, which more than quadrupled between 1970 and 1974 (see Table 15), while the supply of funds from business savings grew only by

Table 15. Gross fixed capital formation and how financed, 1970–1979 (billion francs)

	1970	1974	1979
Gross fixed capital formation	103.7	164.0	263.8
How financed:			
Business savings	67.8	73.7	158.9
Stocks, bond issues, long-term loans	20.3	24.2	41.5
Bank credits	15.6	66.1	63.4

Source: Adapted from Jean-Pierre Patat, *Monnaie, institutions financières, et politique monétaire* (Paris: Economica, 1982), p. 214. Used by permission of the publisher.

[22]Patat and Lutfalla, *Histoire*, p. 202.
[23]Roussel, *Pompidou*, p. 474.

about 10 percent and from the financial market by about 20 percent. Moreover, the banks began to devote a larger proportion of their funds to medium- and long-term loans, the ratio of which climbed from 30 percent of bank credits in 1969 to 35 percent in 1972, setting a trend that continued throughout the decade. Half of bank resources were being used to finance medium- and long-term loans by 1979. Short-term loans, on the other hand, dropped from 55 percent in 1969 to 50 percent in 1972 (40 percent in 1979). The banks accounted for 50 percent of credit allocation in 1962, 53 percent in 1969, and 60 percent in 1973 (and 1979). The semipublic financial institutions were also extending more credit to the economy, but the increase was less rapid: from 25 percent in 1962 to 32 percent in 1969, to 30 percent in 1973 (33 percent in 1979). As for the treasury, its contribution declined dramatically from 25 percent in 1962 to less than 5 percent in 1979.

The banks replaced the state and the semipublic financial institutions as the principal source of credit. The resulting structure better approximated the ideal type overdraft economy in which industry is highly indebted to the banks. Bank credit henceforward accounted for more than 80 percent of growth in the money supply, which (M_2) grew at an average of 16.5 percent between 1970 and 1974, compared with an average growth rate of 12.8 percent in nominal GDP. M_2 as a proportion of GDP rose from 41.2 percent in 1970 to 48.3 percent in 1974. Moreover, and despite the precautions taken by the authors of the 1965–67 reforms, the central bank was being forced to discount an increasing volume of medium-term credit. Bank refinancing accounted for nearly half the central bank's assets in 1972, as opposed to 30 percent a decade earlier (see Table 16). The proportion of central bank credit allocated to the banking system doubled. Efforts to control bank lending through the *coefficient de trésorerie* (which, it will be recalled, required banks to finance a fraction of their rediscountable medium-term credits with their own resources) proved insuffi-

Table 16. Central bank assets, 1962–1972 (%)

	1962	1963	1964	1965	1966	1967	1968	1969	1970	1971	1972
Bank refinancing	30.0	27.7	25.5	27.7	27.4	26.7	45.5	55.0	52.4	61.3	49.7
Treasury financing	30.2	29.2	27.9	23.7	23.2	27.6	30.8	33.0	20.4	18.0	10.1
Reserve operations	39.8	43.1	46.6	48.6	49.4	45.7	32.7	12.0	27.2	40.7	40.2

Source: Adapted from Antoine Coutière, *Le système monétaire français* (Paris: Economica, 1982), p. 40. Used by permission of the publisher.

cient, and in 1973 supplementary measures had to be taken to discourage banks from flooding the Banque de France with rediscountable medium-term loans.[24] The stage was set for the policy dilemma of the 1970s, described in Chapter One, which policymakers addressed by borrowing abroad and by refining the instruments of *encadrement*.

CRISIS AND RESPONSE IN THEIR INTERNATIONAL CONTEXT

The hegemonic edifice that sheltered the French overdraft economy was showing cracks in the early 1960s, and those cracks contributed to the Franco-American monetary dispute of the mid-1960s. Nevertheless, that edifice, crumbling though it was, still stood when internal social and political crisis in France provoked the flight into credit-fed expansion that characterized French policy between 1970 and 1973. Indeed, it was only because that edifice still stood that this flight into growth—the last that would occur in the post-war history of the French political economy—was possible. Without devaluation in 1969, expansionism in 1970 would not have been an option.

De Gaulle surprised the world by refusing to devalue the franc after the "événements" of 1968. Pompidou, in contrast, lost no time and devalued the franc in a swift and quietly executed move effected during the tranquil month of August 1969, defining the franc at its new and final parity of 5.55 francs to the dollar. This was undertaken without IMF aid and consequently without IMF conditionality. Because the possibility of devaluation had already been discussed by the Group of Ten the previous November, Pompidou was able to say that this meeting fulfilled France's legal obligations. "Consultation" notwithstanding, the devaluation came as a complete surprise to everyone.[25] Although the French asked to withdraw $1 billion from the International Monetary Fund in September, requiring meetings between the IMF and the French government, the IMF had little power to amend or police what amounted to a fait accompli. Susan Strange describes the event:

> There is certainly no evidence that the unpublished Letter of Intent, which Finance Minister Giscard-d'Estaing submitted to Working Party

[24] Jean-Pierre Patat, *Monnaie, institutions financières, et politique monétaire* (Paris: Economica, 1982), p. 35.
[25] Susan Strange, *International Monetary Relations*, vol. 2 of Andrew Shonfield, ed., *International Economic Relations of the Western World, 1959–1971* (London: Oxford University Press, 1976), p. 328. For a view of the operation from inside the French government, see Roussel, *Pompidou*, pp. 344–47. Note that Rueff opposed this devaluation.

III, and some days later to the Fund's Executive Board, contained any commitments not already announced in the policy statement at the beginning of the month [of September]—i.e. reduced public spending and a balanced budget for 1970; a balance of trade by mid-1970; credit restrictions and price controls. It was examined at length and, according to *Le Monde* (17 September), accepted without enthusiasm by Working Party III. The Fund drawing, despite the manner of the devaluation, was unanimously approved by the Board.[26]

Robert Solomon questions the magnitude of the French devaluation and even its necessity:

> French prices had risen over the past year, but by little more than in other countries. The deterioration of France's trade balance in the first half of 1969 appears to have reflected in large degree hedge buying of imports in anticipation of rising prices or devaluation or both. Import growth was abruptly reduced in the second half of 1969, though industrial output continued to increase. The quick improvement in France's external position so soon after devaluation seems to fly in the face of all the economic analysis that suggests significant lags in the adjustment of trade to exchange rate changes. One is tempted to conclude that the French authorities were driven to devaluation not by the facts of their economic position but because they felt it imperative to put an end to the expectation that they would devalue.[27]

The *Economist*'s appreciation was less generous: "France devalued when the franc, if overvalued in terms of confidence, was not seriously overvalued in terms of trade. France thus emerged once again with an undervalued currency, an old recipe for success." The United States, as monetary leader, intervened to ensure that France's surprise action did not initiate a spate of retaliatory devaluations, not to influence French policy, either internal or external. Solomon continues: "Again the U.S. concern was to confine the devaluation—to keep other currencies from following the franc down. This effort was successful. The only nations that devalued with France were members of the franc area, mostly African countries." Leadership such as this only made life easier for the overdraft economy.

Global monetary crisis in 1971 threatened to wipe away the commercial benefits of the 1969 devaluation by forcing the franc to float upward. The hegemonic edifice that had sheltered the French overdraft economy behind fixed but adjustable exchange rates collapsed. The French responded by instituting a two-tier exchange rate.[28] A

---

[26]Strange, *International Monetary Relations*, p. 328.

[27]This and the two following passages are found in Solomon, *International Monetary System*, p. 163.

[28]See Chapter Nine.

floating financial franc followed the market upward, while a fixed commercial franc, pegged to the depreciating dollar, defended the booty of the 1969 devaluation. The two-tier exchange rate, however, was only a rear-guard defense, which in 1973 fell to defeat even before the oil crisis erupted. Henceforward, the overdraft economy was left exposed to the world of floating rates, deprived of its Bretton Woods protection.

THE PRESIDENCY OF VALÉRY GISCARD D'ESTAING: ARRESTED REFORM

With the untimely death of Georges Pompidou in 1974 and the election of Valéry Giscard d'Estaing to the presidency, we can return to the period of international crisis and domestic policy predicament with which this study began.[29] Chapter one showed that French efforts to develop policies that dealt with the new international monetary environment had the disadvantage of either accumulating foreign debt or overloading the financial system with regulations that rid the French economy of its dynamism, both financial and industrial, and that did not seem to work very well anyway. Chapter Two argued that the overdraft economy was the source of the predicament. The overdraft economy meant that industrial firms lacked the financial base that would have given them greater flexibility in dealing with the crisis, that they were dependent on lending institutions for the capital they needed not only to promote new investment but to deal with cash-flow problems, that the banks themselves, the source of nearly all money supply growth in the economy, were tightly regulated and scrutinized in their activity, and that the government was saddled with a political economy that was insensitive to incremental adjustments in the supply of credit but that threatened to collapse if the state's control over credit should be used with determination to stabilize prices and currency. This was the political economy with which the French confronted the world of OPEC and floating rates.

As Giscard d'Estaing surveyed this world, he found that his freedom to act was further restricted by the growing bipolarization of French politics. Virtually no important political group now existed outside either the presidential majority or the united opposition of the Left. After the rejuvenation of the Socialist party and the agreement on a joint program of government (Programme Commun) between it and

[29]See Chapter One. On the presidency of Valéry Giscard d'Estaing, see J. R. Frears, *France in the Giscard Presidency* (London: Allen and Unwin, 1981); Olivier Todd, *La marelle de Giscard* (Paris: Robert Laffont, 1977).

the Communist party, the Left grew in strength. The unity of the Rightest coalition, on the other hand, became increasingly fragile and in 1981 finally succumbed to the rivalry between Giscard d'Estaing and the Gaullist leader Jacques Chirac.

Setting aside those constraints and assuming for the sake of argument that it was possible, through argument and rhetoric, to alter economic perceptions and expectations and thus win broad support for monetary rigor and financial reform, Valéry Giscard d'Estaing was nevertheless not one to exercise the type of leadership circumstances required. It is true that he voiced reformist ambitions. He described his vision of an "advanced liberal society" as a "modern, democratic society, liberal in its pluralist power structure, advanced in its high level of economic performance, social unification and cultural development."[30] He was, however, an irresolute reformer, and in philosophy and temperament close to Edgar Faure. Giscard was convinced that political demands bereft of their ideological clothing could be satisfied through finely tuned technocratic adjustments to a healthy, market-driven economy. In the words of Raymond Aron, "the president has an Orléanist philosophy and a Bonapartist temperament."[31] It was one of Giscard's own ministers, Françoise Giroud, who described Giscard's approach to politics as "the art of anesthesia."[32] Jean-Baptiste Duroselle, renowned historian, offered this judgment of the policies of the Giscard presidency in his preface to L'année politique of 1976:

> [He] launched a battle against inflation but moderated it with a series of measures to fight unemployment.... M. Giscard d'Estaing had claimed several times that, between the industrial powers that had succeeded in slowing inflation (Switzerland, Germany, then the United States) and those that had gone beyond the danger point (Great Britain and Italy), the fate of France hung in the balance. Only an act of will would cause the scale to tip in the right direction. Nonetheless, the classical tools [of containing inflation]... were employed by the Chirac government only with moderation.... Salaries continued to climb faster than prices. Direct and indirect subsidies continued to weigh heavily on the budget.[33]

Giscard's hesitations were inspired in part by growing popular unrest, which in turn was the consequence of economic crisis. Though

---

[30]Valéry Giscard d'Estaing. *French Democracy* (Garden City, N.Y.: Doubleday, 1977), Giscard quoted in Chapsal, *La vie politique sous la Ve République*, p. 645. See also Valéry Giscard d'Estaing, *Deux français sur trois* (Paris: Flammarion, 1984).

[31]Aron quoted in Chapsal, *La vie politique sous la Ve République*, p. 645. See also the characterization of Giscard by Jacques Fauvet of *Le Monde* in ibid., p. 648.

[32]Quoted in Chapsal, *La vie politique sous la Ve République*. p. 547.

[33]Jean-Baptiste Duroselle, "L'année politique 1976," *L'année politique, économique, sociale, et diplomatique en France, 1976* (Paris: Presses Universitaires de France, 1977), p. 7. Quoted in Chapsal, *La vie politique sous la Ve République*, p. 561.

Giscard placed a high priority on anchoring the franc to the joint European currency float and thus on aligning French policies on German policies, his Gaullist prime minister, Jacques Chirac, argued that reflation was the only way to stave off a Leftist victory. The cantonal elections of March 1976 gave the Left its first clear national electoral victory, when with relatively few abstentions 52.4 percent of the electorate voted for one of the signatory parties of the Programme Commun. The Socialist party was the principal beneficiary of these elections and made significant advances in *départements* that were traditionally conservative. The perspective of a Leftist victory caused conflict between the two rival factions of the right to intensify, culminating in August 1976 in Chirac's resignation.

Raymond Barre, one of France's principal economists, as well as author of the textbook that nurtured most of the country's technocrats, accepted the office of prime minister with the proviso that he double as minister of finance and be given free rein to combat inflation, restore monetary stability, and balance foreign trade. The *Plan Barre*, as journalists referred to the "Projet de loi rectificative pour 1976," froze prices and wages, introduced money supply growth targets, and encouraged investment with supply-side stimuli, notably restrictions on wage increases. Barre considered unemployment a necessary price to pay to restore equilibrium and growth to the nation's economy. His policies aggravated tensions in the ranks of the majority, forcing him to resort to the small print of the constitution to get his policies passed and implemented and thereby aggravating the government's isolation. Giscard and Barre were given a new lease on life when the Left, despite having won a clear majority in municipal elections in 1977, self-destructed once again in 1978. Unemployment, however, continued to rise, from 400,000 in 1974 to 1,600,000 in 1980. Inflation continued to run high: 10 percent in 1978, 12 percent in 1979, and 13.6 percent in 1980 on the eve of the presidential elections. Social and economic conflict, discouraged in the private sector by high unemployment, continued unabated in the public sector, while enterprises threatened with failure, such as Manufrance, were occupied by their workers. The steel crisis in Lorraine, basically a one-industry region, led to violent incidents and a dramatic "march on Paris" by steelworkers.

Raymond Barre was the overdraft economy's "last chance," but his innovative policies did not succeed in returning the economy to stable growth or in containing mounting discontent. The perception that his policies had failed to procure benefits either in the fight against inflation or even in the fight against endemic trade imbalance was compounded by the perception that his policies were fueling political tensions.

In this context, talk of reform in France's financial structures grew more widespread. There was growing awareness that the reforms of the 1960s were not equal to the challenges of the 1970s, and in fact had somehow caused French finances to go awry. Table 17 shows the growth of bank assets in the 1970s and gives some sense of how bank credit was fueling monetary disorder. Although it is true that bank reserves were consolidated to some degree by bond sales, the continued supply of rediscountable loans, especially export loans to foreign countries, fueled perilously rapid growth in institutional lending.[34] It is during this period (1976–78) that the proportion of rediscounted medium-term loans for exports to total central bank assets grew precipitously. The most striking development, however, was the rapid growth of nonrediscountable medium- and long-term loans. Though such loans accounted for only about one-third of bank assets in 1969, they accounted for more than half of bank assets in 1979. This was due in part to the fact that growth in bank credit was greatest in areas that were relatively new to French banks. Consumer credit grew at an annual rate of 13 percent; credit for housing and real estate, especially mortgages (some of which was eligible for rediscounting), grew at a rate of 23.4 percent; mortgages alone grew at an annual rate of 33 percent between 1969 and 1976. Such growth in lending was not matched by growth in the rate of savings and so contributed to monetary instability.

Table 17. Bank assets, 1969 and 1979 (billion francs)

Assets	1969	1979	Average annual growth (%)
Overdrafts	25.4	78.9	12.0
Short-term credit	96.5	338.4	13.4
Discountable medium-term credit	43.1	123.8	11.1
Nondiscountable medium-term and long-term credit	80.3	569.8	21.6

Source: Antoine Coutière, *Le système monétaire français* (Paris: Economica, 1981), p. 121. Used by permission of the publisher.

The rapid growth of credit aggravated concern about the rate of savings and the form that savings assumed. Such concern was already apparent in the 1960s, when the economic policy orientations of the Gaullist government fomented a marked rise in the demand for capital, due to the fiscal conservatism of the Gaullists, the higher levels of investment following the 1959 devaluation, and the government's en-

[34]See Antoine Coutière, *Le système monétaire français* (Paris: Economica, 1981), pp. 118–22. P. Coupage, "Les banques françaises: Bilan d'une réforme," *Notes et Études Documentaires*, June 9, 1978.

couragement of business mergers (which as a rule required new issues of bonds and stocks).[35] The outcome was banking reform. Now, in the 1970s, the banking reforms of the 1960s seemed to be part of the problem. They had facilitated credit allocation by banks at a dangerously high rate while discouraging the development of the financial market. Preoccupation with the health of the financial market increased in the middle of the decade when radical change in trade patterns aggravated the need for new investment in exporting sectors at a time when the demise of the system of fixed exchange rates exacerbated the inherent monetary instability of the overdraft economy. Moreover, the combined impact of the crisis in oil and money further weakened the financial market. Households were pulling money out of securities in massive amounts. Securities accounted for 14.5 percent of household savings in 1973 but only 2 percent in 1974. Liquid savings, on the other hand, jumped from 44.5 percent of household savings to 58 percent in 1974. The financial market remained depressed for the next several years. Critics argued that the financial market's troubles were not simply conjuntural. They voiced complaints regarding the alleged backwardness of the French market, which they criticized for its technical and fiscal complexity, and called for deregulation.[36]

French officials had been trying to encourage investment in stocks and bonds since the mid-1960s through a number of policies: by creating collective investment funds, *sicavs,* by introducing technical reforms to make the market more efficient and accessible to the public, by instituting the Stock Exchange Commission (Commission des Opérations de Bourse), the equivalent of the American SEC, and above all by stimulating demand for financial assets by multiplying fiscal exemptions and deductions. In 1978, the government gave a significant boost to the financial market by passing the Monory Bill (loi Monory), which accorded new investors in financial assets a 5,000 franc deduction on their taxable income.[37] Because the law applied not only to seasoned investors but also to holders of *sicav* shares, it was an immediate success. In 1978, some 7 billion francs were invested in *sicavs,* 10.6 billion in 1979, and 11.3 billion in 1980. The government gave further

[35]See Paul-Louis Ravier, "Le marché financier," *Bulletin Mensuel de la Chambre de Commerce et d'Industrie de Paris,* November 26, 1972.

[36]See M. Bourgès-Manoury, "La grande pitié de la bourse française," *Nouvelle Revue des Deux Mondes,* January 1, 1977; H. Lévy-Lambert, "Les problèmes actuels de remunération de l'épargne," *Revue des Travaux de l'Académie des Sciences Morales et Politiques,* September 1, 1977.

[37]See G. Guimet, "La loi d'orientation de l'épargne du 13 juillet, 1978: Les sicav-Monory—pari gagné?" *Économie et Finances Agricoles,* July–August 1979. See also "Monory: Recette du succès," *La Vie Française,* November 26, 1979; Bodo Fahlbusch, "Le marché financier français en 1980," *Revue d'Économie Politique 91* (October 1981).

impetus to financial market growth by supplying it with an increasing volume of government bonds. As recession caused the tax base to shrink and the fiscal burden created by unemployment to grow, the Barre government, having committed itself to the fight against inflation, decided to finance the burgeoning budget deficit by issuing securities to the public rather than to the financial system (the banks, the central bank, and the Deposit and Consignment Bank) as in the past, in order to prevent monetary creation. Treasury bond issues increased from 11 billion francs in 1972 and 16 billion in 1976, to 35 billion in 1978 and 48 billion in 1979.[38]

This policy increased yields on the financial market and produced a dramatic rise in bond sales.[39] Unfortunately, the growth in bond issues that these policies encouraged had little impact on the fundamental financial structures of the French overdraft economy. The growth of investment in stocks and bonds, about 14 percent between 1977 and 1979, never outstripped growth in liquid savings. It is even more disturbing that liquid savings grew at about twice the pace of private (as opposed to public) bond issues, suggesting that industry derived little benefit from efforts to strengthen the financial market. Indeed, increased borrowing by the state on a financial market that did not grow in relative terms came at the expense of private borrowing. Though the private sector had laboriously extracted some advantage from such efforts in the previous decade, doubling its share of such bond issues between 1965 and 1975 (see Chapter Six), it suffered from a fiscal crunch in the late 1970s that caused its share of the market to drop from 28.4 percent in 1977 to 24.9 percent in 1979, while that of the state rose from 7.5 percent to 12.1 percent. Despite efforts to stimulate growth in the financial market, industry was being crowded out at a time when *encadrement* was placing greater restrictions on the ability of firms, especially nonexporting firms, to borrow from banks. Industry thus turned to the semipublic financial institutions. Just as the banks were favored during the period of rapid growth of the 1960s, the semipublic financial institutions proved themselves better suited than the banks for the type of financial first aid required by these recessionary times. The Crédit National noted in its 1975 report: "Recent evolution clearly suggests that the newer financial circuits that developed vigorously in years of expansion played a less important role in periods of economic difficulty, while the traditional suppliers of capital, working under the influence of the administration, progressed notably."[40] French

[38]Coutière, *Système*, p. 136.
[39]Ibid.
[40]Quoted in ibid., p. 144. The Crédit National is one of the principal agencies for long-term industrial and commercial credit.

firms were being encouraged to address their financial needs to the semipublic financial institutions, not to a competitive market. Table 18, which shows how the semipublic financial institutions increased their share in financing the French economy at the expense of the financial market, while the share of the banks remained relatively constant, illustrates the persistence of French overdraft financial practices.

Table 18. Credit allocation by source, 1974–1976 (as % of total credit supply)

	1974	1975	1976
Financial market	31.4	35.0	27.7
Semipublic financial institutions	14.0	18.9	19.9
Banks	54.6	46.1	52.4

Source: Antoine Coutière, *Le système monétaire français* (Paris: Economica, 1981), p. 145. Used by permission of the publisher.

Efforts to spark life in the financial market through fiscal policy and thereby enhance its contribution to the financing of the French economy were not enough. It was becoming increasingly apparent that the French economy required nothing short of profound structural reform. The Mayoux Report, commissioned to study ways to decentralize France's financial structures in order to help provincial entrepreneurs find the financing and financial counseling they needed more readily, argued that decentralization would be difficult without "despecializing" the semipublic financial institutions, creating a unified market for credit, and abolishing *encadrement du crédit*. The report advocated greater use of the financial market by firms, even small family-owned firms, which it encouraged to issue stock.[41] The Mayoux Report was only one of a number of studies that called for reforms in the way the French economy was financed, many of which questioned the sagacity of some of France's most venerable interventionist policies, such as the rediscounting of medium-term export credits.[42]

The rising swell of demand for financial reform found expression in the deliberations of the working committees that were preparing the Eighth Plan. Arguing that French policy should be as much concerned with adapting France's financial system to new international constraints

[41]See J. Mayoux, "Le développement des initiatives financières locales et régionales," Rapport au premier ministre (Paris: La Documentation Française, 1979); P. Champion, "Le Rapport Mayoux: De quoi s'agit-il?" *Journal des Caisses d'Épargne 98* (June 1979); L'Association Française des Banques, "Notes de réflexion sur le Rapport Mayoux," *Banque* 388 (October 1979); B. Marguerite, "Le Rapport Mayoux et le redéploiement du système financier," *Issues* (2ᵉ–3ᵉ trimestre 1980).

[42]Commissariat Général du Plan, *Crédit, change, et inflation: Annexes* (Paris: La Documentation Française, 1979), p. 34. See also P. Biacabe, "Quelle réforme pour le système monétaire français?" *Banque* 396 (June 1980).

as it is preoccupied by the adaptation of its industry, the subcommittee on monetary and banking problems stated:

> The adaptation of the financial system should accompany that of the productive system. The action of the financial institutions, in particular the banks, has been very effective during the period of rapid growth, characterized by the great financial needs of the private sector, which lasted until the beginning of the Seventh Plan. This policy allowed France to overcome the late start of the French economy, but it was also a policy of inflation, for which the financial system was no doubt largely responsible. Indeed, the privileged role assigned to financial intermediation and the stagnation of the capital market were the source of excessive growth of the money supply.... These negative aspects [of the French system] had been masked by the growth of indebtedness and inflation. The perspective of reforms can no longer be eluded.[43]

The subcommittee wanted to strengthen the money and capital markets and to diminish the economy's reliance on bank credit. It recommended further deregulation of the banking industry, suppression of a number of specialized privileges and responsibilities, and implementation of a "global business credit" (*crédit d'exploitation global*), one of the reforms proposed by the Mayoux Report. The global business credit was to replace piecemeal short-term discounting of financial paper and medium-term loans, obliging the banks to assume a greater part of the risk of investment and to play a role akin to that of the "universal" bank in Germany. The committee also argued that *encadrement du crédit* be abandoned and that an open market on the American or British model be created that would make possible an effective interest rate policy.[44]

A second subcommittee on monetary policy, after examining ways to improve the system of quantitative credit restrictions and finding none, advocated greater use of interest rate policy and implementation of reforms that would make it work: decompartmentalization of the financial system, remuneration of time deposits at market-determined rates, abolition of privileged discount rates and cheap export credits (to be replaced, presumably, by budget subsidies), reduction of subsidized credit facilities, and greater reliance on the financial market to supply resources to the banks.[45] All the subcommittees were unanimous in their criticisms of *encadrement du crédit*: "The necessity of getting away

---

[43]Report of the finance committee, in Commissariat Général du Plan, *Préparation du Huitième Plan: Annexes* (Paris: La Documentation Française, 1981), p. 100.

[44]Ibid., pp. 99–110.

[45]Ibid., pp. 174–77.

from credit restrictions in order to reestablish a healthy competition has not, a priori, been contested by anyone."[46]

The reports of the working committees of the Eighth Plan were characterized by their advocacy of liberalizing reforms and reduced state intervention. Nevertheless, the planners did not extend their criticism of French credit policy to industrial policy itself, even though credit policy was one of the principal instruments of industrial policy. Indeed, the Eighth Plan defined a new industrial policy for the 1980s, albeit a parsimonious and highly selective one that, it was argued, could accompany and even complement efforts to return the French economy to an asset-based financial structure.[47] Nevertheless, the principal point remains. Planners generally agreed that the state's interventionist power to control the allocation of credit was ill-adapted to the monetary and financial constraints of the times.

Opposition to the plan within the conservative coalition, as well as the electoral defeat of a government that had become unpopular because of its advocacy (more than its practice) of monetary and fiscal rigor, suggest that political conditions did not favor implementation of the financial reforms contained in the preparatory reports of the Eighth Plan.[48] After all, the reforms made clear that creditworthiness and competitiveness were to replace administrative criteria in determining who was given credit. They made clear that the state would be less willing to assume the risk associated with indebtedness and investment. Finally, they made clear that the expectations of French economic agents had to be revised downward at a time when the Left was holding forth the promise of higher growth and greater prosperity.

---

[46]Ibid., p. 89. The importance of a thorough structural reform was perceived unequally by members of the working committees. Many placed great trust in the continuation of a trend (observed in the 1970s and forecast to continue through 1985) of diminishing dependence on credit. The need for financial intermediation, or *"transformation,"* was projected to decline as the level of investment remained moderate and the level of savings remained constant, largely as a result of the restrictive monetary policies adopted in 1976. Firms, households, and local government were projected to reduce their levels of indebtedness, the liquidity of the economy was projected to fall, the financial market was projected to develop strongly (though more under the stimulus of public borrowing than private borrowing), and the importance of the banking system in gathering savings and in allocating credit was projected to diminish (though the great gainers were seen to be semipublic financial institutions, such as the Deposit and Consignment Bank). Though some planners did not foresee the spontaneous development of an asset-based liberal economy, they did see the excesses of the overdraft economy receding on the horizon and believed it would be sufficient to accompany that evolution with gradual liberalizing reforms.

[47]See *L'année politique, économique, et sociale en France, 1979* (Paris: Éditions du Moniteur, 1980), p. 385.

[48]Ibid., p. 148. See also *L'année politique, économique, et sociale en France, 1980* (Paris: Éditions du Moniteur, 1981), pp. 108, 128, 468, 617.

THE FRENCH INDUSTRIAL FIRM IN 1980

The French industrial firm's high level of indebtedness and dependence on institutional financing confronted monetary policymakers with sizable difficulties, primarily because of the firm's relative insensitivity to incremental changes in interest rates and great vulnerability to policies that placed effective restrictions on the supply of credit. By the late 1970s that challenge was compounded by the fact that industrial firms had over the last fifteen years assumed a strategic position within the overall structure of the French welfare economy.

In 1983, some 45.4 percent of France's gross domestic product was being appropriated and redistributed by the state, placing France in the company of the welfare states of northern Europe, such as the Scandinavian countries, the Netherlands, and Belgium, which typically redistribute about half their GDP. The figures for other advanced industrialized democracies vary from 40.6 percent in Italy to 27.7 percent in Japan, between which one finds Great Britain (37.8 percent), Germany (37.4 percent) and the United States (29 percent). The proportion of the GDP appropriated and redistributed by the state had been growing for several decades. From 26.7 percent in 1949, it grew to 35 percent in 1965, eight percentage points higher than the OECD average and 5.5 points higher than the European Community average.[49] France, however, because of de Gaulle's policy of *débudgétisation*, was unusual to the extent that a large part of the welfare bill was paid directly by workers and firms. In 1982, 18.9 percent of the GDP was appropriated by various welfare programs directly from firms and households without passing through the general budget. This figure compares with 9.2 percent for the OECD and 11.9 percent for the European Community. Moreover, direct social levies grew rapidly in the 1960s and 1970s, reaching 16 percent in 1974. In contrast, the percentage of GDP appropriated by the state in the form of taxation remained fairly stable throughout the 1960s and 1970s.[50] Consequent-

[49]See David R. Cameron, "The Colors of a Rose: On the Ambiguous Record of French Socialism" (1988, Typescript), pp. 7–8 and n. 11 (available from the Center for European Studies Working Papers, Harvard University); OECD, *OECD Economic Studies: The Role of the Public Sector* (Paris: OECD, 1985), p. 51; David Cameron, "Public Expenditure and Economic Performance in International Perspective," in Rudolf Klein and Michael O'Higgins, eds., *The Future of Welfare* (Oxford: Basil Blackwell, 1985), p. 17. Welfare expenditures in France failed to introduce greater equality into income distribution because transfer payments were distributed proportionately across all households rather than directed disproportionately to poorer households. See Cameron, "Colors," p. 8, and "Colors," n. 12: OECD, *Economic Outlook, Occasional Studies: Income Distribution in OECD Countries* (Paris: OECD, 1976).

[50]Michel Pébereau, *La politique économique de la France: Les instruments* (Paris: Armand Colin, 1985), pp. 8–16.

ly, the industrial firm came to occupy a sensitive position in the French welfare economy. In 1974, some 263 billion francs were appropriated for welfare expenditures, including health care (184 billion francs), family allowances (47 billion), housing allowances (13 billion), work-related injury insurance (12 billion), adult education (*formation permanente*) (6 billion), accident insurance (8 billion), and administration (11 billion). Of the 263 billion francs, 166 billion was contributed by employers, 48 billion by employees, and 49 billion by the state budget. And because the employer was expected to secure the purchasing power of a paycheck from which were extracted individual welfare contributions that also tended to rise, the finances of France's industrial firms were placed under mounting pressure. Those pressures contributed to inflation.[51]

Wage policy compounded the financial burden assumed by the industrial firm. After the "événements" of 1968, the state began to index wages for the first time since the practice was eliminated by the Rueff reforms of 1959. The first manifestation of this new wage policy came in 1968, when the minimum wage was increased by 35 percent and indexed to the evolution of the average wage rather than to that of prices (previously readjustment in the minimum wage occurred only when prices rose by 2 percent or more during two consecutive months). The new sliding scale promised more frequent and more substantial increases in the minimum wage. From there, indexation worked its way into wage policy in the public sector. In 1969, a sliding wage scale, which indexed minimum wage increases to inflation, was introduced into the contracts of Électricité de France (EDF), and that sliding scale was subsequently adopted by most public enterprises and many private firms.[52]

Price policy added to the financial burdens of welfare and wage policy. Prices in France have come under some form of government control throughout almost the entire history of postwar France. Only during the government of Raymond Barre, between 1978 and 1981, was there any sustained effort to eliminate price regulation and allow market mechanisms to adjust supply and demand of goods and services. The government's powers to regulate prices were as great as they were varied. *Taxation*, whereby the government actually determined prices, constituted the most powerful regulatory tool. It was employed immediately after the war (and, more recently, during the economic crisis of 1983). More typically, however, the government subjected prices to a *blocage des prix*, or price freeze, whereby prices were prohibited from

[51]See Jean Chardonnet, *L'économie française*, vol. 3: *La politique économique intérieure française* (Paris: Dalloz, 1976), pp. 88–98.

[52]Ibid., pp. 134–38; Pébereau, *La politique économique*, pp. 258–72, esp. pp. 265–71.

surpassing a level attained at some given point in time. *Blocages* were the typical companion of monetary stabilization plans, such as those of August 1952, February 1954, June 1956, July 1957, September 1963, November 1968, and September 1976 (and most recently, June 1982). In 1947, the French government subjected prices to what it termed "controlled freedom," or *liberté contrôlée*, which gave the government veto power over price hikes. During the mid-1960s the government defined a form of control called "supervised freedom," or *liberté surveillée*, according to which an enterprise could increase the prices on some of its goods on the condition that it compensate by lowering them on others. The "stable price contracts" (*contrats de stabilité*) adopted this principle in 1965 and again in 1973, 1974, and 1977. Finally, the government negotiated a form of price control with major enterprises which it termed "contractual freedom," or *liberté conventionnelle*, whereby the enterprise committed itself to contain prices and consent to certain investments (for example, decentralizing investments) in exchange for state financial support.

As explained in Chapter Two, the history of the government's efforts to regulate prices reveals the inefficacy of such efforts over time. Price controls were insufficient to halt inflation during the last years of the Fourth Republic, insufficient to contain the "stepladder" evolution of prices during the first decade of the Fifth Republic, and powerless to overcome the price and monetary instability introduced into the French economy by the monetary and energy crisis of the 1970s. The negative effects of price regulation on the financial health of France's industrial enterprises, on the other hand, were great. Price controls reduced profit margins because they affected the price of the enterprise's product while doing little to contain production costs as determined by labor and the cost of imported raw materials. Thus, government policy diminished the capacity of French firms to finance their investments out of business savings and increased their dependence on credit. Jean Chardonnet writes:

> The reduction in profits that results from the application of price controls...reduces the firm's capacity for self-financing. Thus, the rate of self-financing has fallen from more than 70 percent in 1971...to less than 60 percent in 1974, giving rise either to excessive indebtedness, the financial costs of which in turn place pressure on prices, or to a reduction in investment, which can be all the more dramatic when, during periods of inflation, price policy is reinforced by restrictive credit policies.

Chardonnet continues by citing the macro-economic implications of such policies:

The lack of continuity is apparent. By increasing the burden of fiscal and social appropriations, and by restricting the availability of credit and the level of aggregate demand, the state tends to "freeze" the economy. By applying such measures and by repeating them in time, it provokes crises or recessions. Then it adopts measures to restore expansion by loosening the constraints, and then, fearing inflation—the causes of which it has, curiously, failed to understand—it returns to the application of more restrictive policies.

He concludes by describing the self-defeating impact of such policies on the industrial firm:

[The state] adopts certain measures to improve self-financing, but they are of only temporary application and are not sufficient to address the permanent causes of the reduction of self-financing, which are to be found in the state's policies of appropriating business funds through taxation and social levies and in *its* price policy.[53]

The strategic role of French firms in the overall structure of the French welfare state placed added pressure on the firms' finances, reinforced their dependence on institutional lenders, and reinforced the state's concern for the financial health of French industrial firms. In sum, welfare policy combined with price regulation to strengthen the hold of the overdraft economy in France. The burdens borne by the monetary policymaker thus assumed overwhelming proportions just as international support for the French overdraft economy had effectively crumbled, rendering imperative the need for domestic structural reform.

CONCLUSION

The concept of hegemonic decline continues to feed a lively debate among students of international political economy, not only because there is disagreement about what its consequences might be, but also because there is disagreement even about whether it is actually taking place.[54] Fortunately, this second debate does not intrude into the arena of First World monetary relations, where there can be no doubt that the United States once assumed burdens of leadership that it since has cast off. The United States took the lead after the war to recreate a world economy based on monetary convertibility. That effort, which ended with the establishment of the European Payments Union, provides a clear instance of self-discrimination on the part of a United

---

[53]Chardonnet, *L'économie française*, pp. 132, 168, 169 (emphasis in the original).
[54]See Introduction, n. 7.

States willing to sacrifice its immediate commercial interests to the higher task of promoting greater economic and political integration among the capitalist democracies. Moreover, during this time and up to the mid-1960s, the United States did more than the International Monetary Fund to provide adjustment assistance to the Europeans. After the return of European currencies to convertibility in 1958, the United States persisted in its self-discriminatory leadership role by facilitating currency devaluation by European governments caught in payments imbalance, both by accepting to absorb—through devaluation— the inflationary pressures generated by European policies and by actively coordinating efforts to dispel the danger of competitive retaliatory devaluations by other countries.

In the mid-1960s, however, the United States, beset by payments problems of its own, began to shed the burden of self-discrimination in monetary affairs. It failed to address the threat that its own growing payments deficit created for the world economy, and, with the advent of the Johnson administration, even allowed policy to turn inflationary. It cast its internationalist garb aside and exploited the dollar's status as key currency to expand the money supply while avoiding the onus of devaluation. The United States became a "predatory hegemon,"[55] one that used its power to exploit its advantage through self-indulgence, not to create order through self-discrimination. Certainly the word *hégémonie*, as it laboriously forced a passage through the lips of Charles de Gaulle, had only this meaning. Finally, in 1971, when devaluation could no longer be forestalled, the United States gutted the system of fixed exchange rates altogether rather than submit to international discipline. The responsibilities of hegemonic leadership in monetary affairs, endured since 1947, were jettisoned de jure.

The French overdraft economy was viable only within the framework of the hegemonic monetary order. If the French had been able to stay their expansionist, *volontariste* course so long, it was only because that course was validated by the hegemonic order. The overdraft economy depended on that order for support when its own internal control mechanisms, weakened both by the institutional structures and by the patterns of economic behavior it had fostered, failed to restore balance to external transactions. The monetary leadership of the United States supplied a type of "insurance" to French policymakers which "covered"

---

[55]The term is found in John Conybeare, *Trade Wars* (New York: Columbia University Press, 1987). See also Riccardo Parboni, "The Dollar Standard," in Jeffry A. Frieden and David A. Lake, eds., *International Political Economy* (New York: St. Martin's Press, 1987); Robert Gilpin, *The Political Economy of International Relations* (Princeton: Princeton University Press, 1987), chap. 4.

the commitment of the latter to supply in turn a type of economic insurance to whole sectors of the French political economy.

America's withdrawal from its role as leader in international monetary relations affected the capacity of the French to conduct monetary policy as early as the mid-1960s. Neglect of the dollar overhang, aggravated by the adoption of inflationary policy, compounded the difficulties confronting the French in their efforts to promote noninflationary growth in their own economy, the source of which was in the overdraft economy's peculiar institutional structures and patterns of economic behavior. The first reaction of the French in the mid-1960s was to seek reform in the monetary regime such that the United States would be constrained to abandon its inflationary course. It is true that those reforms would have similarly constrained the French to exorcise the inflationary demon from their own economy. It was assumed, however, that reforms enacted in 1958 were sufficient to accomplish this, provided the international environment was amenable. When the campaign for international reform collapsed, the French were forced to turn inward to adapt their political economy to new external realities. Compelling political constraints stood in the way of those efforts throughout the rest of the 1970s. Only under the Socialists did external stress become such that the need for deep structural reform could no longer be ignored.

CHAPTER EIGHT

Socialist Government and Capitalist Reform

In 1981, François Mitterrand became the first Socialist to assume the office of president of the Fifth Republic. When he sought to consolidate his victory by dissolving the National Assembly and calling for new parliamentary elections, the electorate responded by giving the Socialist party an absolute majority in the assembly. Mitterrand assumed the office of president with even greater institutional power than de Gaulle had. Now he could use that power to force a radical departure from policy orientations of the past, as called for in his program. Within eighteen months, however, it had become apparent that the power wielded by the Socialists was insufficient to assure the success of their program. Renewed monetary disorder forced the Socialist government to implement policies of monetary rigor beside which the policies of Raymond Barre paled. Surprised by the scope of monetary disorder, the Socialists in 1983 began blowing the dust off plans for financial reform that were shelved and forgotten after the 1981 elections. In 1984, the government began to subject financial structures and practices to a battery of liberalizing reforms that owed little or nothing to the Socialist platform.

The turnabout in policy was nothing short of spectacular and caused considerable confusion among students of French politics. Though some observers claimed outright that the laws of the marketplace and the constraints of international economic interdependence had disabused the Socialists of their ideological naiveté, others argued that the turnabout was not imposed from without, for it was clear that it was embraced from within Socialist ranks by those on the right wing of the party who preferred rigor and liberalization to other options that would have reformed the French political economy from the left.

214

Hence, argued some, the cause of the turnabout had to be sought in the conflictual alliance of the diverse ideological currents that made up the Socialist party.[1] In a third interpretation, occupying the middle ground, reform was seen as a more or less mercantilist effort to adapt the tools of state interventionism to a world economy that had achieved a very high level of financial interdependence, and so render more effective the efforts of the state to ensure the competitiveness of the French economy.[2]

This book argues that the root cause of both the policy turnabout and the reforms was the incompatibility of the post-hegemonic international monetary regime of floating exchange rates and the domestic legacy of that hegemonic order, France's overdraft economy. In this chapter, I recount the turnabout in monetary policy that occurred in 1983 and the implementation of structural reforms after 1984, and then I analyze the forces and constraints that explain the implementation of capitalist reforms by a Socialist government.

Economic Policy under the Socialists

Socialist economic policy came in two varieties. The first, implemented during the Socialists' first year in power, was euphoric, explosive, and short-lived. The second, inaugurated in 1982, was morose, dull, and seemingly unending. In their first year in power, the Socialists pursued what Peter Hall calls a policy of "redistributive Keynesianism."[3] Family allowances were raised by as much as 81 percent, housing allocations were increased by as much as 25 percent, health benefits were extended, old-age pensions were increased, the purchasing power of social transfers was augmented by 12 percent over two years, and the minimum wage was raised by 15 percent in real terms. Simultaneously, the government enacted measures to reduce unemployment. The work week was shortened, new programs were created that lowered the

---

[1]David R. Cameron, "The Colors of a Rose: On the Ambiguous Record of French Socialism" (1988 Typescript) (available from the Center for European Studies Working Papers, Harvard University).

[2]Philip G. Cerny, "From Dirigisme to Deregulation? The Case of Financial Markets" (Paper presented at the International Conference on Thirty Years of the Fifth Republic, Paris, June 1988); and idem, "Financial Market Deregulation and the Competition State" (Paper presented at the annual meeting of the American Political Science Association, Washington, D.C., August 1988).

[3]Peter Hall, *Governing the Economy: The Politics of State Intervention in Britain and France* (New York: Oxford University Press, 1986), p. 194. See also Pierre-Alain Muet, "Economic Management and the International Environment, 1981–1983," in Howard Machin and Vincent Wright, eds., *Economic Policy and Policy-making under the Mitterrand Presidency, 1981–1984* (New York: St. Martin's Press, 1985), pp. 73–81.

retirement age from sixty to fifty-five and that encouraged older employees to work half time, and employers were given fiscal incentives to hire. Such measures not only promoted the redistribution of wealth in favor of the aged and the less well off, but also helped slow the growth of unemployment and sustain economic growth during a period of global recession. Hall writes: "Although 140,000 formerly illegal immigrants joined the labor force under a government amnesty, unemployment rose only 4 percent in France during 1982, against a rise of 29 percent in Germany and 22 percent in the U.S. No other Western nation had been able to reduce the growth of unemployment so significantly. The French economy grew by 2 percent over two years, while growth in most other European nations was stagnant."[4]

Unfortunately, policies of aggressive Keynesian reflation could not be sustained in a highly open economy surrounded on all sides by recession. They caused public expenditures to rise 11.4 percent during 1981 and 1982, which in turn caused the budget deficit to climb from 0.4 to 3.0 percent of the gross domestic product in 1982. To finance its policies, the government launched a six-year tax-free "solidarity bond" at 16.75 percent interest, but the bond failed to procure sufficient revenues to finance the government's programs, thus opening the door to increased inflation.[5] Inflation, already reinforced by the 1979 oil crisis, remained high at 12.5 percent in 1981, 11.0 percent in 1982, and 9.3 percent in 1983, significantly higher than in neighboring countries, in which inflation was falling rapidly.[6] Meanwhile, redistributive policies, which were largely financed directly by industrial firms, caused *prélèvements obligatoires* (government levies) to increase by 34 billion francs. Conversely, business investment declined by 10 percent in 1981. Janice McCormick writes: "Available capital for investment had ... been eroded by rising social security payments and taxes on business. Taxes and social security charges were 36.3 percent of GNP in 1976, 42.5 percent in 1980, and expected to be above 44 percent in 1982. Wages had also risen dramatically. With profit margins down, credit expensive, and growth less certain, business had little to be optimistic about."[7]

Higher social levies, in conjunction with a growing inflationary differential that favored imports, prohibited France's industry from responding to the increase in aggregate demand produced by the injection of new money into the economy and thus occasioned a rapid deterioration in France's trade balance. Though private consumption

[4]Hall, *Governing the Economy*, p. 195.
[5]See Janice McCormick, "Apprenticeship for Governing: An Assessment of French Socialism in Power," in Machin and Wright, eds., *Economic Policy*, p. 50.
[6]Hall, *Governing the Economy*, p. 198.
[7]McCormick, "Apprenticeship," p. 51.

grew by 2.7 percent in 1981 after a decline of 2 percent in 1980, its benefits accrued disproportionately to foreign exporters.[8] Hall notes: "Imports of autos rose 40 percent, electrical appliances 27 percent and consumer goods 20 percent during 1982. As a consequence the trade deficit ballooned from 56 billion francs in 1981 to 93 billion francs in 1982."[9] French industry was caught between rising financial burdens and a shrinking global market. In 1982, foreign demand for French products was compressed by a 3 percent drop in world trade, but German exports to France rose by 29 percent.[10] The government, to spur investment, increased employee contributions to welfare programs in an effort to ease the financial burden on French industry. Business taxes were cut and, to compensate, value-added taxes were increased from 17.6 percent to 18.6 percent.[11] Though household tax increases seemed to augur austerity, such measures were provoked more by the decline in investment than by the fear of inflation. Meanwhile, inflation grew apace. Wages rose at a nominal annual rate of 18 percent, and economists began to predict price inflation of 15 percent.

The French economy soon found itself so rapidly and profoundly ensnared in crisis that the government's critics were charging incompetence. The government's best defense was to recall that no one expected recession in the U.S. economy, produced by the Federal Reserve Board's refusal to monetize a growing U.S. budget deficit.[12] France was caught off guard more than others, however, and that can be attributed only to the dizzying emotional impact of a long-awaited and hard-won electoral victory. Mitterrand acknowledged in 1983, "I was carried away by our victory; we were intoxicated. Everyone... predicted the return of growth by 1983. Honestly, I lacked the necessary knowledge to say they were wrong."[13] Mitterrand's first-year dash for growth recalled the Pompidou years in its excess and also in its ultimate fate as, between October 1981 and March 1983, the franc was devalued three times.[14]

The hope that devaluation would suffice to correct the trade imbalance was disappointed, and this emboldened critics in and out of government who were calling for a radical change in policy. The second

---

[8]Ibid.

[9]Hall, *Governing the Economy*, p. 198.

[10]Jean-Paul Fitoussi, "Comment" on McCormick's essay "Apprenticeship," in Machin and Wright, eds., *Economic Policy*, p. 65.

[11]Although it was lowered from 7 percent to 5.5 percent on food items.

[12]See Hall, *Governing the Economy*, pp. 193–94; Muet, "Economic Management," pp. 71–76, 80–83.

[13]*Le Témoignage Chrétien*, July 11, 1983, quoted in Hall, *Governing the Economy*, p. 195.

[14]Devalued, that is, within the framework of the EMS. See Chapter Nine. See also Henri-François Henner and Jean-Jacques Yvernault, "Les dévaluations du franc depuis 1981," *Revue d'Économie Politique* 93 (October 1983).

devaluation, in June 1982, brought that change of course. In order to contain inflation, the devaluation was accompanied by a four-month wage (except the minimum wage) and price (except milk) freeze and a commitment to hold the budget deficit to 3 percent of GDP. Although the low rate of economic growth—0.6 percent by the end of 1982 and throughout 1983—warranted a less deflationary fiscal policy, inaccurate growth estimates by the government (which predicted 2 percent growth), coupled with the commitment to keep deficits to 3 percent of GDP, incited the government to reduce projected expenditures and thus to reduce deficit spending to a level that perpetuated low growth and worsened unemployment.[15]

The screw was tightened the following year when, after the third devaluation, the government implemented a program of economic "rigueur."[16] Public spending was cut by 24 billion francs; wages were limited to 8 percent growth, less than the 10 percent target for price inflation; taxes were raised by 40 billion francs, in part through imposition of a 1 percent surtax (the "solidarity contribution," designed to support the social security funds) and in part through imposition of a compulsory loan on the wealthiest taxpayers (those who paid more than 5,000 francs), in fact, a 10 percent surtax deductible in subsequent years; sales taxes were increased on tobacco, alcohol, and gasoline; and the prices of public services (gas, electricity, transportation) were increased. Finally, strict controls were imposed on foreign financial transactions, with dire consequences for the annual August migration of Parisians to sunnier climates. The measures were severe enough to provoke street demonstrations. A long and bitter strike occurred in health services; large demonstrations brought together artisans, small shopkeepers, and the *patrons* of small businesses; a dockers' strike paralyzed foreign trade; and student unrest awakened fears of a "mai '68 à l'envers"—a "May '68" turned around and directed against a government of the Left.[17]

Fiscal policy was held to this parsimonious course in 1984 when expenditures were increased by only 6 percent, compared with increases of 28 percent and 12 percent in previous years.[18] Revenues, on the other hand, were increased by 6.3 percent, thereby achieving some reduction in the deficit's size compared with the GDP. Of particular interest in the 1984 budget was the government's effort to stimulate investment by raising industrial assistance grants by 11 billion francs,

[15]Cameron, "Colors," p. 36.
[16]*L'année politique, économique, et sociale en France, 1983* (Paris: Éditions du Moniteur, 1984), p. 387.
[17]Ibid., p. 409. See also Hall, *Governing the Economy*, p. 201.
[18]See Cameron, "Colors." See also *L'année politique, 1983*, p. 444.

the funds for which were generated by cutting other programs. Moreover, efforts were made to increase state financial aid to research, to education, and to programs that fought unemployment.[19] In the same vein, the government created an income tax exemption for investors in mutual risk venture funds, modified the capital gains tax in a manner that benefited investors, and created a new savings instrument, the corporate passbook account. This supply-side logic extended to wage policy. In an effort to alter inflationary expectations, Jacques Delors set the target rate for salary growth at 4.9 percent, just below the anticipated inflation rate of 5.0 percent.[20]

The budgets for 1985 and 1986 adhered to this deflationary course, but in order to stimulate investment the 1985 budget reduced government levies from 44.7 percent of the gross domestic product to 43.7 percent. Expenditures were reduced in order to honor the commitment to keep the deficit below the threshold of 3 percent of GDP. In the budget proposal for 1986, the last to be submitted to the Socialist-dominated legislature, growth in expenditures was limited to less than 4 percent, well below the anticipated increase in nominal GDP. Personal income taxes were reduced by 3 percent, and further reductions were implemented in business taxes. The government's fiscal policy was by now hardly distinguishable from the "supply-side" policies of various conservative parties in other countries.

Monetary policy, like fiscal policy, continued on the restrictive path assigned to it after the devaluation of 1982. This was in marked contrast to the policy orientation adopted by the Socialists in their first year in power, when despite a 14 percent inflation rate inherited from the previous government, it raised the ceiling on credit allocations permitted under *encadrement* by 1 percent in July 1981 and by another 2 percent in September. Following the second devaluation, in July 1982, however, the government reversed course and decreased the credit ceiling imposed by *encadrement* by a hefty 3 percent. With the adoption of a more restrictive target of 10 percent for M_2 growth in 1983 (lowered to 9 percent in May), *encadrement* was tightened again to a paltry 2.5 percent for the rest of the year, while privileged credit arrangements that benefited certain sectors, such as steel, refining, or the Électricité de France, were reduced or suppressed. Only export credits were allowed to grow.[21]

[19]*L'année politique, 1983*, p. 65.

[20]Ibid., p. 453.

[21]See ibid., p. 419; Patrice Charra, "Vaincre l'inflation à la française," *Échange et Projets* 37 (March 1984); Conseil National du Patronat Français, "Lutter contre les vraies causes de l'inflation," *La Revue des Entreprises* 452 (December 1983); Jean Marchand, "Dévaluation et chasse à l'inflation," *Revue Politique et Parlementaire* 84 (June 1982); Jean-Pierre Sereni, "Inflation: Le 'Delorisme' à l'épreuve," *Le Nouvel Économiste*, October 12, 1981.

The government adhered to this restrictive monetary course in 1984 when it reduced the M_2 growth target to between 5.5 and 6.5 percent, well below the anticipated inflation rate of more than 9 percent. Bank lending was held to an 8 percent increase by *encadrement* in 1984, down from 11 percent (for the year) in 1983 and 15.7 percent in 1982.[22] The government targeted M_2 growth within a range of 4 to 6 percent in 1985 and 3 to 5 percent in 1986. It reinforced this restrictive policy by negotiating or mandating ceilings on wage and price increases, beginning with the mandatory wage and price freeze that followed the 1982 devaluation. As one bemused observer noted, the Socialist party outperformed its conservative predecessor in its efforts to impose price stability and to contain the growth of wages.[23] By 1985, the Socialists had brought inflation to under 6 percent, compared with an average in excess of 10 percent under the government of Raymond Barre. Real wages, which grew by an average of 2 to 3 percent a year under the Barre government, stagnated under the Socialists. On the other hand, unemployment exceeded 10 percent during the last year of the Socialist-dominated legislature, compared with 6 percent under the regime's conservative predecessors. Jacques Riboud, an opponent of austerity, broke majority ranks by calling the new policy orientation a return to capitalism and a rejection of the goals of nationalization.[24] Many of Mitterrand's supporters dared to ask aloud if the French Socialist government was in fact socialist at all, or even social democratic.[25]

LIBERALIZING REFORMS

Turning from macro-economic policy to the area of structural reform, one can observe the same turnabout in policy. The Socialists came to power intending to restore the state to a more firmly interventionist posture. As they were forced to bite the bullet of monetary stabilization, they tried to use the state's enhanced control over economic life to allay the deflationary impact of stabilization. Beginning in 1983, however, the government began to reverse course and to impose substantial liberalizing reforms on financial institutions and practices.

The nationalizations brought twelve industrial firms into the public sector, which, added to those already in it, gave the state ownership of

[22]*L'année politique, 1983*, p. 477.
[23]Cameron, "Colors," p. 45.
[24]Jacques Riboud, "Les ambiguités de la politique bancaire," *Revue Politique et Parlementaire* 87 (February 1985).
[25]See Cameron, "Colors," p. 45.

thirteen of the twenty largest firms in France, accounting for 24 percent of industrial employment, 32 percent of turnover, 60 percent of investment, and 30 percent of exports.[26] In addition to nationalizing large industrial firms, the Socialists assumed ownership of thirty-eight banks in February 1982.[27] Moreover, by nationalizing "parent" or holding companies, the state acquired a controlling interest in a number of banks that nominally remained in the private sector. Consequently, among the 197 banks that were not nationalized, only 116 remained independent of direct or indirect state control, representing merely 1.6 percent of total deposits (including in the denominator the cooperative and Crédit Agricole sector) and 1.2 percent of total credits to domestic clients.[28]

Although politicians and observers debate whether nationalization was worth the expense (nearly 90 billion francs in capital and interest payments over fifteen years), given the fact that it did not appreciably increase the state's control over investment decisions, some observers contend nevertheless that it produced two real benefits. First, as Peter Hall argues, it allowed the state to "accelerate the pace of rationalization in several industries, notably chemicals," and second, it assured continued investment in several key industrial sectors in spite of world recession.[29] The state signed three-to-five-year "planning contracts" with the nationalized firms, which received thereby the assurance of adequate funds for investment. Thus, in 1983, during a period of growing austerity, the nationalized industries received 20 billion francs, of which 12.6 billion came from the budget and the rest from the banking sector. Other funds were raised on the capital market or through specialized programs to support regional development or research. In return, the nationalized industries were required to invest 31 billion francs in nationalized industries in 1983, "equivalent to 50

[26]The twelve were: Compagnie Générale d'Électricité (electrical construction, heavy engineering, shipbuilding, telecommunications, electronics), Thomson-Brandt (electronics, telecommunications, domestic appliances), St.-Gobain-Pont-à-Mousson (glass, building and insulating materials, castings, paper, electronics, computers), Péchiney-Ugine-Kuhlman (aluminum, copper, basic and refined chemicals, pharmaceuticals), Rhône-Poulenc (fertilizers, chemicals, pharmaceuticals), Usinor (steel), Sacilor (steel), Dassault (aeronautical construction, professional electronics), Matra (aerospace, electronics), CCI-Honeywell-Bull (computers), Compagnie Générale de Constructions Téléphoniques, and Roussel-Uclaf (refined chemicals and pharmaceuticals).

[27]See Paul Fabra, "Banking Policy under the Socialists," in Machin and Wright, eds., *Economic Policy*, p. 174; Hall, *Governing the Economy*, pp. 203–6; Christian Stoffaës, "The Nationalizations: An Initial Assessment, 1981–1984," in Machin and Wright, eds., *Economic Policy*.

[28]Fabra, "Banking Policy," p. 177.

[29]Hall, *Governing the Economy*, p. 205; David Cobham, "The Nationalization of the Banks in Mitterrand's France: Rationalisations and Reasons," *Journal of Public Policy* 4 (November 1984).

percent of total industrial investment in France and roughly 20 percent more than the firms had otherwise planned."[30] The impact of this policy on the financial structures of the French political economy was one of enhancing dependence on institutionally allocated credit and aggravating the need for direct state intervention to control the flow of that credit to the economy. Peter Hall recounts:

> Three months after the banks were supposedly guaranteed operating autonomy, they were instructed to lend 6 billion francs to the nationalized industries, purchase 7 billion in state debt during 1983, and maintain their industrial lending rates at 14 percent. Small and medium-sized enterprises were also expected to benefit from such loans. In order to use the banks as an instrument of policy their *tutelle,* or traditional superviso-ry responsibility, was transferred to a new monitoring unit at the Ministry of Economics and Finance, and the National Credit Council was reorgan-ized. The French banks had been subject to the *encadrement du crédit* . . . since 1972, but loan recipients were now more carefully scrutinized and some banks were expected to supervise the rationalization of entire industrial sectors.[31]

Writing more than a year after nationalization, Paul Fabra concluded that the "general framework within which the banks operate has not been changed,"[32] and that judgment was carried further by Alan Philip:

> Greater pressures have been put on the banks and the *Caisse des Dépôts* to support firms in trouble and to lend to the nationalized industries. The central bank's rediscounting facilities have been greatly revived and expanded. . . . The system of *encadrement du crédit* has been preserved, thus frustrating competition between the banks for business, reducing the dynamism of the financial sector and channelling the efforts of bankers into exploiting concessions offered by rediscounting loans with the cen-tral bank. . . . Some of the post-1981 developments in the banking sector look more like regressions to the 1950s than moves to modernize and make the financial system fit for the competitive 1980s.[33]

This reinforcement of state control over credit was welcomed by some Socialist theorists who had been anticipating a return to a finan-cial *volontarisme* of the most ingenuous kind. One group of Socialist economists, writing just prior to the elections of 1981, advocated not only nationalization but also abolition of the money market, forced

---

[30]Quotations and 1983 figures from Hall, *Governing the Economy*, p. 205.

[31]Ibid., p. 205–6.

[32]Fabra, "Banking Policy," p. 182.

[33]Alan Philip, "Comment" on Fabra's essay "Banking Policy," in Machin and Wright, eds., *Economic Policy*, p. 185.

bank mergers that would reduce the number of credit institutions to ten (a number, they reasoned, more easily managed by public authorities), and a "'selective' credit policy...to promote national industry through the active intervention of specialized establishments and reduced-rate long-term loans."[34] Sharing power with the partisans of such *volontarisme*, however, were advocates of more market-oriented policies, such as Jacques Delors, who as finance minister worked hard to combat the *volontarisme* of the left wing of the party. Delors was not a strong supporter of nationalization, and he went so far as to pledge that the *compagnies financières*—that is, the large business banks such as Paribas—would either not be nationalized or would be subject to a nationalization of only 51 percent of their stock.[35]

Delors lost that battle, but his hand was strengthened by the monetary crisis that provoked the two devaluations of June 1982 and March 1983. Economic austerity prompted efforts to liberalize the economy.[36] New savings instruments were introduced, such as the "titres participatifs," a new hybrid debenture stock that allowed private capital to participate in public sector enterprises, and the "certificats d'investissements," nonpriority nonvoting capital shares. A "second market" (second marché) for unlisted securities was created to facilitate access to the financial market by small and medium-sized firms.[37] "Rules were simplified for new flotations, new financial instruments authorised, the 'monthly settlement' market reformed, securities 'dematerialized'—no more bond and share certificates by the end of 1984, only computerized records—and financial market authorities' powers strengthened."[38] Moreover, private banking was allowed to make a discreet reappearance. Writing in 1983 (a year after nationalization), Paul Fabra captured the irony of these developments:

> P.O. Gestion, an investment bank created by David de Rothschild, is now being considered for recognition as a bank with affiliation to the French Banking Association. M. Jean-Marc Vernes, Marcel Dassault, Edmond de Rothschild and others have bought the Banque Industrielle et Commerciale du Marais. The former head of Crédit Lyonnais, dismissed by the Mauroy Government..., is today managing director of a small bank (Stern) that has been employed to assist a newly nationalized industrial group.[39]

[34]Fabra, "Banking Policy," p. 177.
[35]See ibid., pp. 176–77.
[36]*L'année politique, 1983*, p. 386.
[37]See François de Witt, "Nouvelle vague à la bourse: Voici les entreprises qui vont pouvoir profiter de l'ouverture du 'second marché,'" *L'Expansion*, February 17, 1983; *L'année politique, 1983*, p. 362.
[38]Cerny, "From Dirigisme to Deregulation?" p. 20.
[39]Fabra, "Banking Policy," p. 179.

Though another observer lamented, "For every step forward taken in a 'liberal' direction, there seems also to have been a step backwards,"[40] subsequent events amply demonstrated the determination of the liberal reformers. Financial liberalization took a "quantum leap forward"[41] after July 1984 when Laurent Fabius was asked to form a new and more pragmatic government, which included Pierre Bérégovoy as minister of finance, the first finance minister to visit the Paris Stock Exchange since 1962.[42] Negotiable bank certificates of deposit were introduced, which encouraged banks to raise capital beyond their deposit base and to lessen their dependence on central bank discounting and quasi-discounting through the interbank market.[43] In addition, new public short-term instruments were introduced, demand for which rose rapidly from 31 billion francs in December 1985 to 255 billion francs a year later. New instruments for interest rate and currency hedging were copied on models supplied by the international markets. New institutions were created: a fund (caisse) for mortgage refinancing, the capital banks (banques de trésorerie), transaction banks (banques de marchés), and arbitrage banks (banques d'arbitrage), which all operated in the reformed money market. The Paris financial futures market, the *Marché à Terme des Instruments Financiers*, opened in 1986 to the amusement of journalists, who exclaimed, "Under a Socialist government... Paris sees the opening of a futures market: the last word in capitalism."[44] Other reforms liberalized and strengthened the securities market by reducing commissions, rendering commissions on bond issues freely negotiable, and reinforcing the powers of the main regulatory body, the Stock Exchange Commission (Commission des Opérations de Bourse). As the financial market was modernized, foreign companies like Citicorp brought about further change in the financial landscape by introducing the French to venture capital.[45]

Other liberalizing reforms were introduced into financial structures and practices.[46] In a reform that attacked the very structural foundations of the overdraft economy, Pierre Bérégovoy announced on November 5, 1985, that large enterprises would be given access to the money

[40]Philip, "Comment," in Machin and Wright, eds., *Economic Policy*, p. 185.

[41]Cerny, "From Dirigisme to Deregulation?" p. 11.

[42]Ibid., pp. 24–31.

[43]*L'année politique, économique, et sociale en France, 1984* (Paris: Éditions du Moniteur, 1985), p. 407.

[44]"When Pierre Bérégovoy Gets His Inspiration from Chicago," *Journal des Finances*, February 22–28, 1986, quoted in Cerny, "From Dirigisme to Deregulation?" p. 25.

[45]See Chantal Bialobos, "La finance française découvre le capital-risque," *L'Expansion*, April 19, 1984.

[46]See Jean-Charles Naouri, "La réforme du financement de l'économie," *Banque* 459 (March 1986).

market, which thus lost its interbank exclusiveness.[47] With this reform, an enterprise could issue 10 million francs worth of short-term (ten days to six months) paper on the money market. In theory, this encouraged enterprises to lend and borrow on the market rather than at the bank window. The finance minister also announced that the market for negotiable treasury bonds would be opened progressively to nonbanks, allowing any type of investor—bank, household, or industrial firm—to bid for bonds (in 10 million franc, ten-day coupons).[48] By decompartmentalizing the money market and rendering it accessible to all, the reforms of 1985 were a step forward in the creation of a more unified financial market, capable of handling the supply and demand of very short-term capital and long-term capital. Some of these reforms had already been proposed in earlier reform projects, such as the Marjolin-Sadrin-Wormser Report of 1968 and the Mayoux Report of 1978, but were rejected—either in part or in whole—by the governments of the time.

In order to feed this new market, the government created three new savings instruments: the certificate of deposit (*certificat de dépôt*: six-to-twenty-four-month maturity, at a rate freely negotiated, sold in coupons of 5 million francs); capital bills (*billets de trésorerie* which filled a similar function for industrial firms and were made available in maturities varying from 10 to 120 days and also in minimum amounts of 5 million francs); and negotiable treasury bonds (*bons du Trésor négociables*, similar to the above but benefiting the treasury and, unlike previous bonds, purchasable by the public and short-term, generally one to three months, also in coupons of 5 million francs). The capital bill appears to have been the result of the government's desire to help the industrial enterprise free itself from its overdraft account, and it is tempting to recognize in the negotiable treasury bond a belated acceptance of Jacques Rueff's ban on long-term bond issues by the state and state agencies.[49]

As structures were reformed, new policy instruments were created and old ones abandoned. In 1985, steps were taken to phase out *encadrement du crédit*[50] (a process that was completed in 1987 under the conservative successors of the Socialists), and the principal locus of monetary control was shifted from the banks to the new reformed

[47]Philippe Jaffre, "L'unification du marché des capitaux," *Banque* 460 (April 1986).

[48]*L'année politique, économique, et sociale en France, 1985* (Paris: Éditions du Moniteur, 1986), p. 460.

[49]Ibid., p. 461. Creation of the certificate of deposit led the government to redefine the monetary target in terms of M_3 plus all issues of certificates of deposit by banks.

[50]Jean Cheval, "Les innovations dans la conduite monétaire en France: Perspectives monétaires 1986," *Chroniques d'Actualité de la SEDEIS* 34 (April 1986).

open market. This made it possible to control interest rates and monetary growth through intervention by the central bank. Henceforward, monetary control was to be based "on a better control of credit by the banks, which [were] incited to issue bonds in order to avoid monetary creation, which in turn should allow monetary regulation through interest rates beginning in 1986."[51] Finally, exchange controls, reintroduced in 1982, were all but abolished.[52]

Just as the government imposed liberalizing reforms on financial structures, so it reduced direct credit allocations by the state. Three-quarters of all loans to business in 1979 came from state or semipublic financial institutions, including nationalized banks and subsidiaries. Some 43 percent of all loans were subsidized by the state, either directly or through the medium of privileged refinancing arrangements enjoyed by such institutions as the Crédit Agricole or the French Bank for Foreign Trade. As interest rates fell, however, the government began to "banaliser" such loans, that is, to render them more uniform. The government replaced the institutionally specialized loan subsidy programs managed by the National Credit Fund, the Small Business Investment Fund (Crédit d'Équipement des Petites et Moyennes Entreprises) the Cooperative Fund (Crédit Coopératif) and the Regional Development Companies (Sociétés de Développement Régional) with a single special investment loan (prêt spécial à l'investissement).[53] Philip Cerny informs us: "Total subsidised loans dropped by about a quarter from 1983–86, while budget costs fell from 45 billion francs in 1985 to only 16 [billion] in 1986. Support for exports ... shifted from subsidised loans to direct subsidies and pure guarantees."[54]

By 1985, the financial structures of the French political economy were looking distinctly different not only from what the Socialists had envisoned in 1980 but also from what they had looked like for the past forty years. Although industry was still highly indebted and dependent on institutional support, it was given freedom and encouragement to raise funds on an open money market. At the same time, it was being nudged away from reliance on more-or-less specialized semipublic financial institutions, each with its peculiar credit program, and made to deal with a more homogeneous banking system. The banking system, in turn, was invited to take a more active and entrepreneurial

[51]*L'année politique, économique, et sociale en France, 1986* (Paris: Éditions du Moniteur, 1987), p. 392.
[52]See "Assouplissement du contrôle des changes," *Actualités BFCE* 189 (February 1984); "France: De nouveaux assouplissements au contrôle des changes," *Actualités BFCE* 209 (February 1986); "France: Importante libéralisation du contrôle des changes," *Actualités BFCE* 211 (April 1986).
[53]*L'année politique, 1985*, p. 370.
[54]Cerny, "From Dirigisme to Deregulation?" p. 31.

role in financing industry. Rather than serving as the simple conduit between industry and state institutions, such as the Banque de France (through medium-term rediscountable loans), or the semipublic financial institutions, banks were decisively encouraged to assume the role of intermediary between industry and a reinvigorated financial market, to which they were henceforth considered to be answerable. In sum, the Socialist reforms created the conditions for an evolution of French financial structures toward the "German model" (so overtly scorned by many Socialists in the early days of their government), according to which large banks assumed an active role in industrial investment decisions by virtue of their strategic position between the financial market on the one hand and indebted industrial borrowers on the other.

REFORM: CHOICE OR CONSTRAINT?

The Socialists neither intended nor expected to become the champions of liberalization and the "German model," and observers have been hard put to make sense of it. Peter Hall and Jack Hayward[55] argued that developments in the international political economy invalidated policy patterns developed over the past several decades. In the beginning, Hall argues, economic planning and industrial policy served two basic purposes: the "modernization and reorganization of the nation's productive apparatus" and the legitimation of the redistributive consequences of this process through appeal to the national interest. The plan, however, could not be held to the redistributive agenda because it was subject to predation by industrial interests. Moreover, after the victory of de Gaulle, the ascendant Right was unwilling to sustain a process of economic reorganization that undermined electoral support concentrated among the "farmers, pensioners, shopkeepers and others sympathetic to the traditional sectors."[56] In Lowi's terminology, policy for both authors became distributive rather than redistributive. As distributive policy collided with resource scarcity, however, it produced a "state divided against itself," which found in inflation a temporary nostrum to its self-inflicted schizophrenia:

> Conventional wisdom holds that a state divided against itself cannot stand; but there is a sense in which precisely the opposite is true. A state faced with multiple tasks and well-defined conflicts of interest among the

[55]For the purpose of the argument developed here, the two interpretations are sufficiently compatible that Hall's is made to represent both.
[56]See Hall, *Governing the Economy*, p. 163.

social classes it governs...may find it useful to maintain a degree of deliberate malintegration among its various policy-making arms. In this way each arm can mobilize consent among its particular constituencies by pursuing policies which, even if never fully implemented, appear to address the needs of those groups. In many cases, the pursuit of incompatible policies renders most of them ineffective, but this technique prevents any one group from claiming that the state has come down on the side of its opponents. Such has been the behavior of the French state within the economic sphere in recent years.[57]

The capacity of such a state to live with itself, however, was contingent on the existence of a buoyant and supportive international environment. As global economic growth slowed after the energy crisis, and as the international monetary environment became intolerant of inflation in open economies, the French government, now Socialist, was made to bite the bullet of economic redistribution once again. Though international constraints created the political, if not economic, opportunity to reinvigorate French *dirigisme* and to direct it to its rightful purpose—the redistribution of wealth and the modernization of the economy—that effort, Hall concludes, was frustrated by slow growth, disagreement within the governing party, and (echoing Hayward) the legacy of "quasi-corporatist arrangements between the state and producer groups."[58]

Hall's and Hayward's accounts are at odds with the interpretation of Socialist policy proposed by other observers, who underscore the importance of domestic political factors. David Cameron, for instance, has argued that the existence of international constraints cannot suffice to explain Socialist policy because those constraints were not ineluctable. The Socialists had a viable choice between giving priority to balancing international accounts or promoting domestic growth and employment,[59] and they chose the former. Their decision was the child of preference, not constraint, for by leaving the European Monetary System (EMS) the Socialist government could have found the freedom it needed to pursue the reflationary track that it chose when it assumed power. By remaining within the EMS, the Socialist government shouldered an international burden it could just as well have shed. Seen together, the radical leftism of 1981 and the equally radical embrace of monetary and fiscal rigor in 1983 reflect a deeply embedded ambivalence over the meaning of socialism and the political mission of the Socialist party in France. That ambivalence, in turn, reflects the party's check-

[57]Ibid., p. 176.

[58]Ibid., p. 221; see ibid., pp. 213–26. Hayward is more circumspect than Hall concerning the likelihood that France can adapt its *dirigiste* structures to new international realities.

[59]Cameron, "Colors," p. 65.

ered history, its divers composition, and an electoral strategy that left unresolved glaring incompatibilities between widely divergent ideological commitments.

In a third interpretation, Philip Cerny traces the liberalization of France's financial structures and processes to the existence of a global "financial revolution" that obliged Europeans to work to improve the international competitiveness of their financial institutions. For Cerny, financial liberalization can be understood without reference to factors that are specifically Socialist or even specifically French. On the contrary, the root cause of French liberalization is located in the United States, where an ideologically driven program of financial deregulation and the need to finance a ballooning budget deficit both conspired with the system of floating rates (which permitted the rapid rise of the dollar relative to other currencies) to lure European capital to the United States. Europeans "saw their lack of sufficient investment capital as the main obstacle to recovery.... Capital market deregulation was necessary to compete with the U.S. for international funds."[60] Great Britain took the lead in 1983. France followed soon thereafter.

Each of these rival interpretations adds to our understanding of a baffling event. Cameron's reminds us that the explanation must account for Socialist openness to the idea of reform, Cerny's points to events occurring beyond France's borders, and Hall's and Hayward's explores the domestic institutional and structural constraints that affected French policy. Each, however, has weaknesses that are the converse of its strengths. Cameron's account, for example, underestimates the force of external constraint on French policy. It will be recalled that floating rates created real problems for the economies of Europe, both because of their high level of trade openness and because of growing inelasticities in demand for imported goods, such as oil and other resources priced in dollars. Depreciation under the regime of floating exchange rates did not proffer the same benefits that devaluation used to bring under fixed rates. On the contrary, by increasing import prices, depreciation fed domestic inflation and exposed the economy to intolerable levels of monetary instability and to vicious circles of depreciation and inflation. One contemporary study concluded that the impact of depreciation on domestic inflation in France had actually increased since the late 1960s.[61] Evidence of this constraint

[60]Cerny, "From Dirigisme to Deregulation?" p. 22.
[61]Michel Castinat et al., "Les incidences d'une dévaluation du franc ont-elles varié depuis vingt ans?" *Économie et Statistique* 178 (June 1985). See also Henri Sempé, "Le phénomène économique et financier des variations monétaires: Contribution à l'étude de l'inflation," *Annales de l'Université des Sciences Sociales de Toulouse* 31 (1983), 205–7; Pierre Salama, "France: Le taux de change et sa manipulation," *Critique de l'Économie Politique* 29 (December 1984). See also Chapter One.

abounds in accounts of policy-making during that period. Peter Hall cites a report that argued "it was no longer possible to rectify a balance of payments deficit by devaluing the exchange rate. For every 10 centimes that the franc fell against the dollar, the French import bill rose by 2.5 billion francs. That was almost enough to cancel out its beneficial effect on exports." Drawing on the calculations of Raymond Courbis and André Keller, Hall continues:

> The French state was desperate to maintain the high level of the franc against the dollar in order to cut the import bill. Mitterrand tried to persuade the Reagan administration to lower its interest rates. Instead, rising interest rates in America and speculation against the franc carried the currency from 4.30 against the dollar in 1980 to 5.35 in April 1981 and 8.60 by 1984. The effects on the French economy were catastrophic. It has been estimated that the rise in the dollar reduced the French growth rate by 1 percent in 1982, raised unemployment by 24,000, inflation by 3–5 percent, and the public sector deficit by 36 billion francs. Its effect on import prices alone lifted the trade deficit by 57 billion francs in 1982. This, in turn, renewed speculation against the franc. The Mitterrand Government found itself in a vicious circle not entirely of its own making.[62]

Thierry Pfister and Philippe Bauchard, in their account of the first years of the Socialist government, also underscore the importance of external constraints for policy choices.[63] A number of high-level officials representing a broad range of ideological positions were originally in favor of leaving the European Monetary System in order to let the franc depreciate, but they became hostile to the idea when the costs and dangers implicit in such a radical course of action became clear. Early on, Pierre Bérégovoy (the same who was destined to become the first minister of finance to visit the Paris Stock Exchange), Michel Rocard, and Michel Jobert, on the conservative end of the governmental spectrum, sided with Pierre Chévènement, on the radical end of the spectrum, and Laurent Fabius, who leaned to the left, in advocating a more radical foreign monetary policy. They were supported (outside of government) by Jean-Jacques Servan-Schreiber, a confirmed advocate of European integration. The move was resisted principally by Finance Minister Jacques Delors on the right and Pierre Mauroy, a centrist. Considerable debate and vacillation prevailed throughout the first two years of the Socialist era. Mitterrand's own position on the question

[62]Hall, *Governing the Economy*, p. 196, 199.

[63]Thierry Pfister, *La vie quotidienne à Matignon au temps de l'union de la gauche* (Paris: Hachette, 1985); Philippe Bauchard, *La guerre des deux roses: Du rêve à la réalité, 1981–1985* (Paris: Bernard Grasset, 1986).

changed frequently. He resisted the idea when it was first discussed after taking office, but he came close to accepting it at the time of the second devaluation of the franc in June 1982. Only determined resistance on the part of some members of the government dissuaded him.[64]

The debate resurfaced when the franc was forced to devalue a third time. This time, however, former supporters of the idea of leaving the European Monetary System crossed the aisle to join the advocates of prudence. Chief among these was Laurent Fabius, who had been a vocal advocate of the government's original expansionist and redistributive policy course. Fabius requested a detailed summary of France's international financial position from the treasury, which responded by informing him that the reserves, despite two large international loans in the fall of 1982, were desperately low:

> Delors, supported by most of the government's economists and key advisers at the Élysée, produced a continual series of memoranda on the precarious state of French finances. Budget Minister Laurent Fabius, a proponent of the "other policy," was briefed by Treasury chief Michel Camdessus that French monetary reserves were only thirty billion francs, not enough to survive the hammering of speculators once the franc was allowed to float. A devaluation of twenty percent would automatically send the foreign debt from 330 billion francs to 400 billion. Close presidential advisor Jacques Attali had rallied to the camp of caution, as did many of the president's technicians. They warned him that if the franc were set free to float it would immediately sink by twenty and perhaps thirty percent. No one would lend to France. The effect of higher prices on imports would be immediate, while any positive effect on exports would be much slower in coming. Once out of the European Monetary System, France could expect no support from its European ex-partners. The only defense of the franc would then be to hike interest rates from the prevailing fourteen percent to twenty percent or higher. No one would invest at such rates.[65]

Fabius's "conversion" was followed by that of such key figures as Jean Auroux and Jacques Riboud, a former critic of austerity. Though a more radically nationalist foreign monetary policy was still supported by Bérégovoy and Gaston Defferre (even though both were of the right wing of the party), Fabius's shift sufficed to lay to rest the idea of leaving the EMS. The claim that the Socialists had options they chose to ignore loses much of its power when the costs of those options are assessed. The external constraint operating on the monetary policies of France and its European neighbors was a compelling one.

[64]See Julius Friend, *Seven Years in France: François Mitterrand and the Unintended Revolution, 1981–1988* (Boulder, Colo.: Westview Press, 1989), pp. 64–66.
[65]Ibid., p. 66.

Analysis of the external constraint exposes the limitations of Cerny's interpretation of financial liberalization as well. Although financial deregulation in the United States and the deficits of the Reagan years undoubtedly militated in favor of deregulating the stock exchange, they fail to explain why interest in such reform had been mounting for a decade and why state ownership of the banking system (not to mention industry) and relatively tight state control over credit allocation proved insufficient to shelter the French economy from the global impact of Reaganomics. The answer to this question is to be found not in the United States but in France. The French political economy suffered increasingly from its inadaptation to an international monetary environment that was hostile to inflation (at least in the trade-dependent economies of Europe). The state, whatever its control over the allocation of credit, simply lacked the power to regulate and control monetary growth in a sustained fashion. Although monetary authorities continued to employ with address their power to promote investment through subsidized loans and other specialized programs, thus effectively disconnecting interest rate policy (which was assigned the task of supporting the external value of the franc) from domestic credit policy, that power only reinforced the structural weaknesses of the overdraft economy by validating industry's dependence on institutionally supplied credit.[66] Industrial indebtedness, in turn, was such that inflation had become a necessary component of industrial solvency.[67]

During the 1970s, industrial dependence on institutionally supplied credit grew as the ability of French firms to finance their own investments fell. The rate of *autofinancement,* the contribution of business savings to productive investment, fell from a typical figure of 70 percent in the 1970s to only 51 percent in 1981 and 40.3 percent during the first quarter of 1982. Corresponding figures for Great Britain, the United States, and Germany were 108 percent, 88 percent and 80 percent respectively.[68] Inversely, industry's need for external funding grew by 17 percent in 1981. The National Institute for Statistics and Economic Studies (INSEE) calculated that industrial borrowing amounted to nearly 6 percent of the gross domestic product in 1982, up from 4.5 percent a year earlier.[69] Industry's failing

[66]Antoine Cachin, "La politique française de déconnexion des taux d'intérêt," *Revue d'Économie Politique* 93 (October 1983).

[67]Thierry Chauveau, "L'inflation et les entreprises," *Revue Économique* 36 (September 1983).

[68]"Banking on Recovery: A Survey of International Banking," *The Economist*, March 26, 1983.

[69]Ministère du Plan et de l'Aménagement du Territoire, *Le financement des entreprises*, Rapports de missions au ministère d'État (Paris: La Documentation Française, 1983), p. 17.

financial health was caused in part by the tendency of the share of value added going both to wages and to taxes to rise (wages from 6.8 percent to 7.5 percent and taxes from 2.7 percent to 4.3 percent), while the share going to profits fell from 17 percent to 9.6 percent.[70] The report of the study commission on industrial finance for the Ninth Plan revealed that "if one eliminates public investment, the growth of which contributed positively...up until 1976, it is necessary to speak of a veritable collapse of private sector capital expenditures, which has accelerated the process of deindustrialization in the French economy."[71] Industrial investment diminished by 12 percent in 1981 and by 7 percent in 1982, after having responded weakly but favorably to monetary stimulus in 1979 and 1980 (growing by 2 percent and 4 percent respectively).[72] Although ten years of economic crisis had, according to André de Lattre, resulted in a more rational affectation of financial resources, the secular decline in productive investment was nevertheless a source of preoccupation.[73] According to a second observer, it had become essential to devise ways to allocate at least an additional 1 percent of GDP to industrial investment, drawing on whatever financial resources were available, internal or external.[74]

The redistributive policies enacted during the first months of the Socialist government increased industrial dependence on institutionally allocated credit, and the banking system was enrolled in the effort to satisfy that need. "Since May 1981," Paul Fabra observed, "the banks have been obliged to participate in financing the public sector deficit on a large scale and in a more systematic way than ever before."[75] Although the government had assured the recently nationalized banks that they would remain autonomous in their operations, the government was obliged in January 1983 to come to the aid of ailing industries by injecting 45 billion francs of capital. It did so by asking the semipublic financial institutions to provide 26 billion francs worth of long-term loans at low rates, 7 billion francs in "participatory loans" ("prêts participatifs"), and 7 billion in risk insurance, and finally, by asking the banking system to provide another 7 billion francs worth of low-interest loans.[76] The latter had already been instructed to lend 6

---

[70]Hall, *Governing the Economy*, p. 197.

[71]*Le financement des entreprises*, p. 15.

[72]Ibid. See also Michel Fried, "L'investissement industriel et son financement," *Bulletin du Crédit National* 10 (4ᵉ trimestre 1982).

[73]André de Lattre, "Investment and Outlook for the French Economy," *Isveiner Bulletin* 43 (October 1982).

[74]Alain Cotta, "Investissement industriel et croissance de l'économie française," *Revue Économique* 34 (July 1983).

[75]Fabra, "Banking Policy," p. 182.

[76]*L'année politique, 1983*, p. 351; see also pp. 363–65.

billion francs to the nationalized industries and to maintain their industrial lending rates at 14 percent.[77] Growth in credit allocation was rapid during the early years of the Socialist period: 18.8 percent between June 1981 and June 1982, which, in an economy in which credit accounts for most of the growth in the money supply, explains a rate of money supply growth of 12.3 percent over the same period.[78] The inflationary impact of monetary growth was compounded by the higher cost of credit to nonprivileged borrowers: "the cost of providing long-term loans at reduced rates to industry is that ordinary non-privileged borrowers face higher interest charges."[79]

To the extent that firms (especially public firms) borrowed abroad, French industry's financial situation was weakened further by its having to reimburse loans in foreign currencies, especially dollars, at a time when the franc was weak. France had become one of the principal borrowers on the international market for capital. According to the OECD, France borrowed $14.5 billion on international markets in 1982. Other observers placed the amount borrowed on foreign markets closer to $23 billion (compared with the United States' $26.5 billion).[80] In 1983, according to the OECD, France, at $13.3 billion, was the world's second largest international borrower—behind the United States ($14.9 billion) but ahead of Japan ($11.6 billion) and Canada ($8.5 billion). Although, by the end of 1983, austerity had begun to reduce the need to borrow, France nevertheless borrowed nearly $13 billion on foreign markets in 1984, bringing total foreign indebtedness to nearly $70 billion (not counting debts incurred by large public enterprises such as EDF and the SNCF).[81] Total foreign debt amounted to 9 percent of the GDP and imposed an annual servicing burden estimated at $10 billion in 1984, $11.5 billion in 1985, and $21 billion in 1988. Foreign indebtedness alone justified a policy of austerity.[82]

In this context, *encadrement* was powerless to repress inflationary pressures. Despite the drastic tightening of *encadrement*, credit in 1983 was continuing to grow at a fast pace, and though money supply growth seemed to be slowing, this was less the effect of credit control than it was of France's external payments position.[83] Observers detected no link between the evolution of the money supply, inflation, and the

---

[77]Hall, *Governing the Economy*, p. 206.

[78]Alain Redslob, "Un système bancaire socialisé," in Michel Massenet, ed., *La France socialiste* (Paris: Hachette, 1983), p. 151.

[79]Fabra, "Banking Policy," p. 182.

[80]*L'année politique, 1983*, pp. 380–81.

[81]Ibid., p. 494.

[82]*L'année politique, 1984*, pp. 512–13.

[83]P. Biacabe, "La politique monétaire en France," *Revue d'Économie Politique* 94 (October 1984).

restrictive character of monetary policy. The system of *encadrement* itself was showing signs of inefficiency resulting from bureaucratic sclerosis. By increasing the administrative cost of supplying credit, which costs were relayed to the economy, *encadrement* actually fed inflation.[84]

In sum, in 1983, France's industry was caught in a vise of decreasing profitability and increasing indebtedness: "the growth of indebtedness and the reduction, even the disappearance of profit margins is putting a large number of French firms in danger."[85] A report commissioned by the Senate, made public in June 1984, maintained that the nationalization of the banking sector, which was supposed to facilitate control of monetary growth while increasing the state's power over the allocation of resources to industry, had failed after two years to make good on its promise. It had instead aggravated the sector's characteristic lack of dynamism. *Encadrement du crédit* (a "profoundly conservative" policy tool encouraging "lazy solutions" on the part of banks, according to a report submitted in preparation of the Ninth Plan)[86] had to be tightened rather than loosened, exceptional tax levies had to be multiplied, interest rate policy was more deflationary than before, and the banks were forced to extend loans to industry while being insufficiently capitalized by the state (now the principle "stockholder") forcing the banks to offer new issues of "titres participatifs" or nonvoting stock. Bank profitability dropped dramatically in 1982, and by 1983 it had barely regained the level attained in 1981. In reaction to the situation in France, banks reduced their domestic activities and sought compensation abroad. In 1980, foreign activity accounted for 22 percent of bank profits, and in 1982 for 95 percent.[87] By September 1984, the banking system joined industry as one of the government's major preoccupations. The new minister of finance, Pierre Bérégovoy, met with bank directors to develop policies that would restore profitability and dynamism to the banks. These included reductions in employment, the introduction of new technologies, and coordination of activities designed to achieve economies of scale. Though modest, the minister's recommendations prefigured the more thoroughgoing liberalization of the financial sector that was soon to follow.[88]

Powerless to use its extensive controls over the allocation of credit to promote noninflationary growth, the government acquiesced in the

[84]Henri Sterdyniak and Christian Vasseur, "Encadrement du crédit et politique monétaire," *Observations et diagnostiques économiques* 11 (April 1985).

[85]Michel Massenet, "Préface," in *La France socialiste*, p. 31. See also in the same volume, Bertrand Abtey, "Les entreprises en péril," pp. 254–70.

[86]*Le financement des entreprises*, p. 92.

[87]*L'année politique, 1984*, p. 447; Alain Chetaille, "L'activité internationale des banques françaises," *Issues* 20 (4ᵉ trimestre 1984).

[88]*L'année politique, 1984*, pp. 471–72.

ineluctability of structural reform. France, in the words of its prime minister, Pierre Mauroy, had to rid itself of "this inflationary disease."[89] Hall is correct in underscoring the importance of the government's decision to "tame the inflationary habits of a nation that had always depended on them in order to generate growth."[90] The Socialists were aware of the link between France's financial structure and the "inflationary disease" that weakened the economy's ability to adjust to external shocks and market shifts. There is a critique of these structures and practices in a June 1983 report by the Credit Information and Study Center (Centre d'Information et d'Etude du Crédit), a government research institute, significantly entitled "After the Welfare State, Welfare Credit Is Questioned":

> With the arrival of hard times, welfare credit...grew in favor because it provided solutions to the problem of financing the welfare state by allocating short-term financial aid to this or that economic sector as needed. That very facility gave rise to the risk of excessive use. It contributed to the rise after 1974 in the proportion of preferential credits in the total financing of the economy which remained thereafter at a high level. Welfare credit is a financial tranquilizer that becomes addictive if used too much. The symptoms of the crisis are the same as in the case of the welfare state: each sector that benefits becomes a lobby that opposes any withdrawal of financial aid. Aid increases and uses up a growing portion of resources..., reducing the maneuvering room of the state and economic actors.[91]

Combating the inflationary disease meant that the government had to reclaim the power to regulate money supply growth in a sustained fashion. This in turn required the abolition of the preferential credit lines that were the source of the "presumption of assured borrowing power" that perpetuated the overdraft economy. For this reason, the path to the recovery of monetary policy-making power passed through deregulation of the banking system and the financial market generally. Though reformers had known this for nearly a decade and suspected it for a decade more, the lesson was forgotten in the euphoria of the electoral victory of the Left and had to be painfully relearned by the Socialist government.

Financial deregulation, therefore, was intended to accomplish several tasks. First, by abolishing privileged credit lines it was to discourage the allocation of resources to unproductive uses. Many French firms in the late 1970s and early 1980s were borrowing to cover cash-flow shortages

---

[89]*L'Express*, April 8, 1983, quoted in Hall, *Governing the Economy*, p. 201.
[90]Ibid.
[91]Centre d'Information et d'Étude du Crédit, "Après l'État providence, le crédit providence en question," *Bulletin Mensuel* 52 (June 1983).

rather than to finance investment, and so were investing less just as they were increasing their level of indebtedness. Second, deregulation was intended in the long run to despecialize a number of well-endowed, sectionally specific financial institutions, such as the Crédit Agricole and the Deposit and Consignment Bank, in order to make their resources more broadly available to the French economy. (Hitherto, the resources of such institutions were made available to the broader economy only to the extent that they bought assets on the interbank market.) Finally, by abolishing privileged lending programs that rested ultimately on generous support from the Banque de France, deregulation was intended to cause interest rates charged to nonprivileged borrowers, among which were many small but nevertheless dynamic firms, to fall as inflationary financing was discontinued.[92]

Deregulation ran deeper than this, however, reaching to the heart of the overdraft economy. By deregulating the banking industry, the government sought to lessen the costs of disinflation both to banks and to industrial firms. Deregulation encouraged the banks to consolidate their financial base by increasing their capitalization through more active appeal to the financial market (hence the certificates of deposit) and to regulate their lending activity by relying more heavily on their bank reserves rather than on the money market or central bank refinancing of privileged credits. Though large industrial firms would initially suffer from the subsequent restriction to bank credit resources, the initial cost was compensated by greater direct access to the financial market through the creation of the capital bill and by the greater competition that deregulation imposed on the banking industry. This move was intended to encourage greater bank efficiency, market sensitivity, and—it was theorized—lower borrowing costs.[93] Because the situation of France's industrial firms was such that it could not be hoped that French industry would become an asset-based rather than an overdraft sector, it was proposed that the French political economy evolve toward the German model, based on the "universal bank," according to which an asset-based banking sector provided for the financial needs of a dependent industrial sector.[94] The banks, in turn, would intervene more actively in industrial affairs but would regulate their own activity by basing it on the financial market.[95] Accompanying

---

[92]Fabra, "Banking Policy."

[93]Étienne Bertier, "Pauvres banquiers," *L'Expansion*, July 3, 1986; Olivier Pastre, "La modernisation des banques françaises: Incertitudes et enjeux," *Banque* 461 (May 1986).

[94]Bernard Prudhon, "Intermédiation financière française et intermédiation financière ouest-allemande: Perspectives pour une réforme," *Revue d'Économie Industrielle* 30 (4ᵉ trimestre 1984).

[95]See Commissariat Général du Plan, "Quels intermédiaires financiers pour demain?" Rapport de la Commission (Paris: La Documentation Française, September 1984,) p. 9.

this reorientation was a change in attitude toward industry, characterized by the minister for industry, Laurent Fabius, as one of new respect for private enterprise and private initiative. The government henceforth placed a premium on building a constructive arm's-length relationship with industrial leaders.[96]

The report of the financial commission of the Ninth Plan provides intriguing support for this thesis. Because it was written by the Socialists in 1983 (and therefore before the more active embrace of liberal reformism in 1984), it confronts the reader with a curious amalgam of proposals designed both to enhance the role of the market and to devise ways to put the state's newly acquired institutional power over the nationalized banking system to good use. It states clearly the ambitions of bank reform, though those ambitions are placed within the context of a more state-led, interventionist policy orientation:

> By progressively improving the structure of credit establishments, the institutional environment, and banking techniques, it will become possible *to reduce the tensions and the perverse effects produced by conjunctural regulatory measures.* As our country confronts an unstable international environment, it is important that it dispose of a financial system endowed with great flexibility.
>
> To reach this goal, the first task is to reduce the banking system's heterogeneity, which means more than simply attacking the disparity between establishments that are structurally in debt and others that are structurally in surplus. This task is so important that the state (*les Pouvoirs Publics*) must use all the tools at its disposal in the area of [structural reform], bank regulations, and monetary policy....
>
> The second task consists of reinforcing the financial structures of the credit institutions so as to enable them to accompany the needs of newly created enterprises or those being developed. Besides reinforcing bank reserves and increasing productivity, this objective also assumes that the advantage for the depositor of working through a financial intermediary does not completely hide the fact that the composition and remuneration of savings cannot be dissociated from the manner in which funds are employed and remunerated on the financial market.[97]

This document and others suggest that more was involved in financial deregulation than the simple ambition of competing with the markets of London, Tokyo, and New York. On the contrary, financial deregulation was perceived as the sine qua non of the French policymaker's ability to recover monetary policy-making powers of which he had been deprived by the overdraft economy. By liberalizing finances, the Socialists were not simply complying with or submitting to the dictates of the market, but were trying to regain control over the economy.

[96]*L'année politique, 1983*, pp. 402–3.
[97]"Quels intermédiaires financiers pour demain?" p. 112 (emphasis added).

Seen in this light, financial liberalization was not wholly incompatible with the broader social and economic ambitions of the Socialists. The legacy of Mendès France—advocate of hard decisions, decisive leadership, and government unfettered by privilege—was evoked to help square Socialist ideology with capitalist reform. One observer of early Socialist efforts to rethink the financial system documents the existence of "a wave of anticorporatism (vague anti-corporatiste) that, evident as early as 1982, antedated liberalization by two years."[98] The *Mendésisme* inherent in the reformism of Bérégovoy did not go unnoticed by observers. Wrote the editorialist of *L'année politique*, "Like Pierre Mendès France, M. Pierre Bérégovoy justified rigor by defining the conditions for a return to healthy growth," which were "financial stabilization by fighting inflation and reducing the budget deficit, and economic modernization, both in industry and in the services [notably the financial services]."[99]

CONCLUSION

Three rival explanations of financial liberalization in France have been considered here, and all have their merits. There can be no denying that the pursuit of growth through inflationary policy collided with the more hostile world of slower growth and greater competition for markets. The precise link between this observation and the liberalizing financial reforms, however, is less obvious. It leaves unanswered the question why the French could not use *encadrement* and other state interventionist tools to overcome their addiction to inflationary policy. It also does not answer the question why *dirigisme* in financial matters, if not in industrial affairs too, was seen to be the problem rather than the solution. The explanation according to which such reforms were undertaken in order to make France more competitive in a world economy characterized by a very high degree of financial interdependence, though similarly incontrovertible, also leaves key questions unanswered. The link between efforts to revive the French financial market and efforts to reform the tools and the practices of monetary policy is not obvious. The documents themselves suggest that the government was more concerned with its inability to formulate and implement monetary policy than with growing international competition in financial markets. The third explanation, that the Socialists were not "really Socialists," is also incontrovertible, and it is not particularly enlightening

[98]Danièle Granet, "Caisses d'épargne: La fin des sinécures," *Nouvel Économiste*, June 14, 1982.
[99]*L'année politique, 1984*, p. 457.

either. For example, it does not explain why the Socialists—though not really socialist—should be more "capitalist" than either Barre or Giscard d'Estaing.

No explanation of the liberal financial reforms can elude the observation that the French were no longer the masters of their monetary policy. They had lost the power to be deflationary when leaders of a conservative stripe thought it appropriate to be deflationary, and they had lost the power to be expansionist when leaders of any stripe thought it necessary to be expansionist. They lost the former in the late 1940s and early 1950s, when their preference for highly leveraged policies of rapid growth (or growth without the redistributive consequences of growth, as characterized in an earlier chapter) left the political economy with a fragile financial base that rendered it both more resistant and more vulnerable to deflation than most economies. They lost the latter when change in the international monetary system, occasioned by change in U.S. policy, deprived them of the possibility of achieving monetary adjustment through devaluation.

If, then, the Socialist government embraced the cause of liberal reformism and thus caused a state characterized by its interventionist power to surrender much of that power to a market that the Socialists themselves had never much liked or much trusted, it was because the government, ironically, found in that surrender the only means by which to retrieve the power to dictate monetary policy. In an earlier chapter we reasoned that as states multiply insurance programs for their populations they become ensnared in a vicious circle that diminishes their control over outcomes. Something very much like this took place in France. The government, to free itself from this vicious circle and so to reaffirm its control over the evolution of monetary aggregates, reneged on an unspoken promise that French industry had long ago built into its economic expectations: assured credit through one lending institution or another, controlled or regulated by the state.

CHAPTER NINE

France and the European Monetary System

Financial reform was a quest for greater monetary control, an attempt to break out of the vicious circle in which the domestic political economy had become mired because of moral hazard. France's diplomatic efforts to promote reform in international monetary relations were the external correspondent to domestic reform. France's advocacy since 1973 of more binding international monetary arrangements, problematic when viewed in the light of its reputed nationalism, embodied its efforts to retrieve control over monetary policy through external reform, just as internal liberalization embodied the effort to retrieve control through domestic reform. France's foreign monetary policy, especially its efforts to help create the European Monetary System, lends salience to the concept of "second image reversed," according to which external factors shape domestic political outcomes, which in turn shape international outcomes.

The European Coal and Steel Community was portrayed as something of a greenhouse for the Monnet Plan of industrial modernization, but by 1973 Europe had long since ceased to be that greenhouse. The liberalization of trade and the subsequent change in trade patterns challenged the French economy to adapt. Tariff barriers were decreased by 10 percent in compliance with the Treaty of Rome. Exchange controls were almost entirely abolished as France reluctantly followed Great Britain's lead in leaving the European Payments Union and restoring its currency to full convertibility. Within ten years after signing the Treaty of Rome, European Community (EC) countries had nearly abolished tariffs on trade between themselves, while the existence of common trade barriers between the European Community and the rest of the world was threatened by negotiations between the EC and the European Free Trade Association, as with such non-EC countries as Greece, Turkey, and Austria. Finally, the "Kennedy round" negotiations pressed the issue of trade liberalization on a global scale.

For the French economy, the impact of trade liberalization was dramatic. In the early 1960s France's economy was still relatively sheltered. Exports amounted to 12 percent of GDP in 1960 but grew to 19 percent in 1969 and to 20 percent in 1973. In 1960, more than one-third of French exports went to the countries of "l'Union Française," France's former colonial empire, and only 22 percent went to the European Community. By 1968, those proportions were reversed: 13 percent and 43 percent respectively, and 5 percent and 48 percent in 1973.

There has always been a "high" politics and a "low" politics to France's policy toward European integration. The high politics was driven by the fear that "Anglo-Saxon meddling" would revive a security threat on France's eastern frontier. The low politics, on the other hand, was driven by the ambition to exploit American and German desire for reintegration in order to press for international institutional arrangements which facilitated the voluntarist economic policies that, it was believed, would speed France's economic modernization. The two goals were not unrelated, because it was felt that a modern economic base would assure France's economic equality with Germany and secure for France greater say in the shaping of postwar Europe.

In the case of the European Coal and Steel Community (ECSC), the high and low politics of France's European policy found an acceptable solution, but in general the high and low politics of European integration were not so easily reconciled. Such was the case with the Treaty of Rome. After the Berlin Blockade in 1949, when the United States began to push for German rearmament within the framework of some common security arrangement—a proposal that was favorably received by the government of Konrad Adenauer—France put up stiff resistance and was subjected to strong American pressure to abandon its objections. In response to that pressure, France produced, in October 1950, its own plan for German remilitarization, the European Defense Community (EDC). Jean-Pierre Rioux writes, "This was the twin of the Schuman Plan (its elaboration was once again supervised by Jean Monnet), and it applied to the problem of arms the same principles being tried for coal and steel."[1] Domestic opposition to the plan was intense, however, and in August 1954, after two years of acrimonious debate, government inaction, and change in the international political situation (the Korean War came to an end and the death of Stalin eased

[1]Jean-Pierre Rioux, *The Fourth Republic, 1944–1958* (Cambridge: Cambridge University Press, 1987), p. 144.

tensions in Europe), the National Assembly allowed the EDC to die "an ignominious death."[2]

The United States, still intent on anchoring West Germany to a unified and pro-Atlantic foundation, moved swiftly to orchestrate its admission to NATO, as it had threatened to do since 1949. By October 1955 it was done. Threatened with a loss of influence over the solution to the "German question," the usually pragmatic and cautious Edgar Faure accepted with alacrity the call made by the governments of Belgium and Luxembourg in 1955 to embark on a new phase in the construction of Europe. French interest in the idea of European integration was reinforced by the Suez crisis, which "attested the impotence of Europe and gave added impetus to efforts at integration."[3]

French support for the Common Market owed little to economic interest at this time. This is not to say that the French found the idea economically uninteresting or that discussion of the economic consequences of market integration did not figure predominantly in the negotiations. Rather, it is to observe that the economics of the Common Market were profoundly different from those of the European Coal and Steel Community. The ECSC promoted and facilitated French *volontarisme*, as embodied in the Monnet Plan, and validated France's mercantilist policy orientation. The Common Market, on the other hand, threatened practices and habits that had become ensconced in the structures of the French political economy in the decade since World War II. Indeed, if market integration appealed to some, it was precisely because it challenged practices that were held responsible for what many perceived to be the *malthusianisme* of the French political economy. Interest in the Treaty of Rome, however, was inspired principally by the fear of losing influence over the German question. Indeed, after the treaty was signed, the French opened discussions with the West Germans in November 1957, "in the hope of forming some sort of continental front against the Anglo-American domination of the Alliance."[4] De Gaulle met with Chancellor Adenauer at his residence in Colombey-les-Deux-Églises as early as September 1958, and again at Bad Kreuznach in November. Despite having been the most vociferous critic of the EDC, de Gaulle now acted to hasten commercial integration within the framework of the European Community, often freeing up protected sectors for free trade ahead of schedule, occasionally by shifting quotas to non-EC countries, such as Great Britain.[5] Although

[2]Michael M. Harrison, *The Reluctant Ally: France and Atlantic Security* (Baltimore: Johns Hopkins University Press, 1981), p. 30. See also Rioux, *Fourth Republic*, pp. 201–8.

[3]Guy de Carmoy, *The Foreign Policies of France, 1944–1968* (Chicago: University of Chicago Press, 1970), pp. 92, 97.

[4]Harrison, *Reluctant Ally*, p. 44.

[5]See de Carmoy, *Foreign Policies*, chap. 15.

de Gaulle's ambitions seemed fulfilled with the signing of the Franco-German treaty of 1963, Germany's strong allegiance to its U.S. ties proved disappointing. When de Gaulle realized he could not build on Franco-German reconciliation a European regional bloc capable of providing him with the kind of leverage he was seeking in his relations with the United States, his relations with Germany turned more instrumental and exploitative, and his appetite for the economic benefits the community might be made to surrender increased. In 1965 De Gaulle provoked a major crisis that threatened the very existence of the community but won a major concession in the form of the Common Agricultural Policy.[6]

This overview brings us to the late 1960s, when European Community leaders began discussing the issue of monetary integration, where we find the same uneasy mix of high and low politics. Diplomatic ambition explains France's initial interest in monetary integration. When the change in the international monetary order deprived the French overdraft economy of its international support, however, the low politics of finding ways to deal with the crisis supplanted the high politics of using monetary integration as a means to promote broader diplomatic goals. Floating rates bared France's powerlessness to control monetary growth in a sustained fashion. That powerlessness, in turn, exacerbated France's vulnerability to German and American monetary policy and diminished France's power to influence the course of economic policy in Europe. Decline in power, both domestic and external, fueled France's internal and international reform efforts. In external reform, France sought the means to restore its domestic power over monetary growth, just as it sought in internal reform the means to reduce its vulnerability to and dependence on policy choices made in Germany and the United States. In this chapter we explore the history of European monetary integration, noting the change in French policy that occurred after the demise of the Bretton Woods world of fixed but adjustable rates.

THE WERNER PLAN

France's decision to participate in a joint European float in 1973 generated considerable surprise among foreign observers who remembered de Gaulle's skeptical and exploitative attitude toward European integration. Nicholas Kaldor spoke for many when he exclaimed:

> I know of course that M. Pompidou, M. Giscard d'Estaing, M. Barre and other prominent Frenchmen are in the very forefront of the drive toward

[6]Ibid., p. 373; Harrison, *Reluctant Ally*, pp. 111–12.

European monetary integration. The Hague Summit and the Werner Report were largely the result of French initiatives. All I can say is that I find it very difficult to understand what they are after—because I cannot believe that they have ceased to be Frenchmen, and that they are indifferent to the question whether France as France—as part of Europe no doubt, but still as France—will ensure prosperity and full employment [within] her own territory, or only as part of the wider territory of Europe.[7]

The motives that prompted the French to support the idea of monetary integration in 1969 had little to do with money and much to do with the desire to break out of the semi-isolation that was the legacy of Gaullist foreign policy. The need for fence-mending was great indeed as France found itself relatively isolated from its European neighbors as a result of its actions during the negotiations on the Common Agricultural Policy, the failure of its efforts to impose devaluation on the United States, and its isolation during the IMF negotiations on Special Drawing Rights. Above and beyond strictly economic relations, de Gaulle's whole ambition of enhancing the position of France by being the intermediary between East and West was shattered by the Warsaw Pact invasion of Czechoslovakia and by Willy Brandt's and Richard Nixon's initiatives to improve relations with the Soviet Union. "France's hoped-for role as a broker in detente was bypassed," writes Anton De Porte.[8] The French faced once again the secular threat of being "odd man out" in a Europe ordered by German-American co-action.

Pompidou's foreign policy sought to back France out of the dead end in which events had left it. This required fence-mending not only vis-à-vis the Europeans but also vis-à-vis the Americans and the British.[9] Pompidou rejected de Gaulle's stubborn refusal to admit Great Britain into the European Community, "because he understood," De Porte continues, "that France could not achieve its goals in Europe unless it ended its alienation of the Five, centered most specifically on the veto." Subsequently, Pompidou's European policy was very active, "more like [that] of the Gaullist first phase than [that] pursued between 1964 and 1968."[10] When, therefore, in early 1968, Pierre Werner, prime minister of Luxembourg, proposed that monetary solidarity among EC members be tightened by irrevocably fixing exchange rates

---

[7]Intervention by Kaldor during the ninth colloquium of the List Society, in *Floating—Realignment—Integration: Ninth Colloquium of the List Society*, ed. B. Schefold (Basel: Kyklos-Verlag, 1972), p. 57.

[8]A. W. De Porte, "The Fifth Republic in Europe," in William Andrews and Stanley Hoffman, eds., *The Fifth Republic at Twenty* (Albany: SUNY Press, 1981), p. 406.

[9]See Harrison, *Reluctant Ally*, pp. 169–70.

[10]De Porte, "Fifth Republic," pp. 406, 407.

between community currencies, by creating a European unit of account, and by establishing a European Monetary Fund, Pompidou seized on the plan in much the same way that Edgar Faure seized on the common market proposal in 1955. When the Werner Plan was sent to the European commission for further study, it came back as the Barre Plan (Raymond Barre was then the European Community Commission's vice-president). Some of the more ambitious proposals advanced in the Werner Plan were modified, but the basic theme was confirmed that the community needed a system of balance-of-payments adjustment assistance, stricter rules concerning adjustments of parity, and tighter fluctuation margins between their currencies. The time for tighter monetary cooperation had come, it was argued, because of increasing levels of financial interdependence which were placing real constraints on the capacity of governments to implement monetary policy autonomously. The currency crisis of the mid-1960s had drawn attention to the existence of the Eurodollar market, while the recent devaluation of the franc had severely tested the viability of the European Community's new Common Agricultural Policy. Therefore, when Willy Brandt brought up the subject of monetary integration at the European Summit of The Hague in December 1969, he found, perhaps to his own surprise, that the idea had support—even from the French.[11] Indeed, Pompidou went beyond the proposals contained in the Barre Plan and proposed a common EC policy vis-à-vis the International Monetary Fund.[12] It is important to bear in mind, however, that this cooperative attitude was not particularly costly at the time. Germany had only recently, in 1966, stabilized its currency, and the position of the franc was very strong in the wake of the 1969 devaluation. Under these circumstances, the prospect of tighter bands of currency fluctuation was not onerous.

Pompidou's attempt to secure a rapprochement with the members of the European Community through monetary integration was soon put to the test by the currency crises of the early 1970s. In the final years of the decade, confidence in the dollar fell dramatically and massive amounts of capital flowed into French and German currencies and securities. Germany, preoccupied by the inflationary effects of this capital inflow, responded with currency controls and in May 1971 ceased to intervene on the currency exchange in order to allow the mark to appreciate upward. The Dutch, in a similar move, floated the guilder. The French, on the other hand, were fearful of losing the

---

[11]See Jacques van Ypersele and Jean-Claude Koeune, *The European Monetary System* (Luxembourg: Office for Official Publications of the European Communities, 1985), pp. 37–38.

[12]Eric Roussel, *Georges Pompidou* (Paris: J.-C. Lattès, 1984), p. 375.

commercial benefits of the 1969 devaluation and consequently refused to float the franc despite a massive inflow of speculative funds: $2 billion in net foreign assets in July and August 1971.[13] The French, their position dictated both by commercial interest and principle (Europeans should not be made to pay for America's balance-of-payments deficit), maintained that the dollar should be devalued and opposed the revaluation of European currencies. The Americans, of course, refused to consider devaluation. They argued that, given America's defense commitments toward the other industrialized democracies, the latter should adopt a more sympathetic attitude toward its payments problems.

When the United States suspended convertibility in August 1971, the French moved energetically to prevent the franc from appreciating against the dollar. Like the Belgians several months before, they instituted a two-tier exchange system. For the purposes of trade, the exchange rate of the franc was fixed; for the purposes of currency and financial transactions, the franc was allowed to float. Strict exchange controls were imposed in order to prevent arbitrage between the two markets. This policy was remarkably successful. Over the next several weeks, the dollar actually appreciated by 0.4 percent relative to the commercial franc and by 10 percent relative to the mark.[14] During this period, Franco-German relations turned quite bitter. Germany found virtue in the float, and the German minister of finance, Karl Schiller, worked hard to organize a joint float of EC currencies. The French, on the other hand, were seeking to enlist German aid in their efforts to block the disguised devaluation of the dollar and the demonetization of gold.[15] The storm did not subside until fixed rates were restored (albeit within enlarged margins and moreover without gold convertibility) by the Smithsonian agreements of December 1971.[16] Only then did the implementation of a plan for a European Monetary Union again become feasible. By the resolution of March 22, 1972, European governments agreed to reinforce economic policy coordination, to diminish the margins of fluctuation, and to create a European Monetary Cooperation Fund. They also agreed to intervene on the market primarily with European currencies rather than with dollars. This obviated the need to agree on a common value for the dollar and

---

[13]William Wiseley, *A Tool of Power: The Political History of Money* (New York: John Wiley and Sons, 1977), p. 274; Leland B. Yeager, *International Monetary Relations: Theory, History, and Policy* (New York: Irwin Press, 1976), p. 484.

[14]Wiseley, *Tool of Power*, p. 295.

[15]Roussel, *Pompidou*, pp. 446–53.

[16]Wiseley, *Tool of Power*, p. 299.

sidestepped a key issue on which the French and German points of view greatly diverged.[17]

THE EUROPEAN CURRENCY FLOAT, 1973–1978

A gradual change in France's position began to occur in the summer of 1972. First, the commercial advantages of the 1969 devaluation were diminishing. France's balance-of-payments surplus fell from 10 billion francs in 1970 and 1971 to 1.5 billion in 1972, and finally to a 3 billion franc deficit in 1973. The dwindling commercial advantage, already largely offset by foreign transfers by immigrant labor, was further diminished by inflation. Meanwhile, long-term capital flows went from surplus to substantial deficit, and short-term inflows, though heavy in the summer of 1972 during the speculative attack on sterling, fell off sharply in subsequent months.[18] The Smithsonian parities and with them the European Monetary Union, could no longer be defended. The pound dropped out in 1972, and the Swiss floated the Swiss franc in January 1973. Renewed speculation rocked the currency market in February 1973. But unlike the speculative crisis of 1971, during which the dollar fell relative to European currencies, it was now the mark that was being pushed up relative to European currencies and most notably relative to the franc, which was beset both by inflation and by payments imbalances.[19] Speculation threatened France with the collapse of its two-tier system and threatened the world with a second float of the mark. On March 4, the Germans informed the French that they would soon float the mark again, preferably with the franc in a joint European float, but without it if need be. Faced with this ultimatum, the French acquiesced. Within a week, the European Community arranged a joint float, dubbed the currency "snake" by journalists, which included the franc but not the pound or the lira.[20]

By participating in the joint European float against the dollar in 1973, the French agreed to something they had vehemently opposed in 1971. The turnabout in policy was motivated not only by the speculative pressures that were being placed on the franc, but also by preoccupation

[17]Daniel Deguen, La politique économique de la France (Paris: Les Cours de Droit, 1982), part 2, pp. 310–14. Conflict continued over the issue of exchange controls and the issue of economic policy coordination. The Germans adopted exchange controls themselves during the summer of 1972. See Wiseley, Tool of Power, p. 314.

[18]Yeager, International Monetary Relations, p. 484; Deguen, La politique économique, pp. 133–35.

[19]Deguen, La politique économique, pp. 325–30.

[20]Wiseley, Tool of Power, p. 324. Upon joining the European joint currency float, the French abolished the two-tier market for the franc in March 1974.

with the growing contrast between French problems and German successes. As the French economy sank into trade imbalance within three years of a currency devaluation that many observers already believed was unnecessary, Germany absorbed external shocks, pursued rigorous monetary policies, and ran trade surpluses. One official recalls:

> I worked with the Comité Interministériel des Affaires Extérieures. I was a great partisan of Schiller but found myself in a minority. The majority refused to float [in 1971] and sought to promote a return to the system of fixed parities. In reality, however, what we were refusing was the appreciation of the franc. We chose a policy of facility, believing that currency devaluation brought commercial advantages.... [During the period 1973–74, however] in the Ministry of Finance, discussions and debates about the "German model" recurred like a leitmotif.[21]

This leitmotif became a dominant theme under the Giscard d'Estaing presidency. Giscard gave voice to the ambition, explicitly inspired by the German model, to make the franc a strong currency within the joint float, declaring at the Franco-German summit of July 1974: "Action engaged in France will be executed with all necessary determination. It should allow us by the end of this year, to see our inflation rate approach that of Federal Germany, and our objective would be, within a year from now, to assure true parallelism in our policies."[22]

Unfortunately, the ambition to imitate German policy was embraced at a time when change in the international political economy was just beginning to unmask the structural weaknesses of the overdraft economy in France. By August 1973, persistent inflation was already threatening to push the franc through the snake floor. The oil crisis of October 1973 provided the final blow, forcing the franc out of the snake in January, 1974.[23] However disappointing this setback may have been for Giscard, it failed to weaken his conviction that France required a strong currency. Indeed, leaving the snake exposed the franc to the threat of a vicious cycle of currency depreciation and domestic price inflation. The value of the French franc against the snake initially fell lower (at times by 15 percent) than was desirable for reasons of stability. This, combined with the visible contrast offered by the economic vitality of countries that remained in the snake, confirmed Giscard's strong currency convictions. In the words of one observer: "The cohesion and vitality demonstrated by the minisnake [the snake without the franc],

---

[21]Personal interview, Paris, June 1983.

[22]Quoted in *Le Monde*, July 1, 1974, p. 13. See also Marcel Linden, "L'Allemagne n'est plus un modèle," *Documents* 36 (September 1981).

[23]Jean-Yves Habérer, *La monnaie et la politique monétaire* (Paris: Les Cours de Droit, 1979), p. 184.

despite adverse forecasts, made an early return of the franc to the snake seem desirable for political reasons as well."[24]

The growing threat of serious monetary instability caused the French to press for reforms in international monetary arrangements while, domestically, they took measures to stabilize the franc. Finance Minister Jean-Pierre Fourcade proposed a plan that called for coordinated community interventions in the exchange market to maintain a community parity for the dollar (and thereby control the appreciation of the mark), greater flexibility in intra-EC exchange rate adjustments, greater EC credit facilities, and a new unit of account.[25] Fourcade's proposals were rejected, not only because the Germans saw currency appreciation as a way of containing inflation but also because they feared that the French proposals would oblige Germany to absorb part of the inflation generated by the economies of their less virtuous European partners.[26] Beyond the frontiers of the European Community, France proposed at the summit conferences of Rambouillet and Jamaica that Europe's currencies be revalued in exchange for some coordination of policy among advanced industrialized countries. Domestically, meanwhile, austerity measures strengthened the franc to the point that, by 1975, it was able to rejoin the snake at the same parity at which it had left in 1974. This underscored the seriousness of Giscard's monetary ambitions, but it provoked objections on the part of the governor of the Banque de France, the employer's union, and even Giscard's own finance minister.[27]

Once again the franc's foundational weakness made participation in the joint float problematic. When Prime Minister Jacques Chirac became alarmed at the possible political repercussions of prolonged austerity and decided to reflate, prices shot up by 12 percent, enlarging the inflation differential with Germany, where inflation was running at 6 percent, and sending the franc once again to the snake floor. The franc was in a vulnerable position when renewed speculation in the spring of 1976 caused investors to flee the sinking currencies of Italy and Great Britain and seek refuge in the mark. This pulled the snake

[24]Deguen, *La politique économique*, p. 335.

[25]Loukas Tsoukalis, *The Politics and Economics of European Monetary Integration* (London: George Allen and Unwin, 1977), p. 156. See also Deguen, *La politique économique*, pp. 330–34; *Agence Europe/Documents*, September 17, 1974; van Ypersele and Koeune, *European Monetary System*, p. 44.

[26]A short account of the evolution of German monetary interests can be found in Peter Ludlow, *The Making of the European Monetary System* (London: Butterworth Scientific, 1982), pp. 4–12.

[27]Rainer Hellmann, *Gold, the Dollar, and the European Currency System: The Seven-Year Monetary War* (New York: Praeger, 1979), pp. 49–50. See also Habérer, *La monnaie*, pp. 192–94.

upward, forcing the French to ask for a realignment. When Belgium refused to devalue and the Netherlands refused to revalue, France was left either to devalue unilaterally or to pull out of the snake a second time. Not wanting to compound electoral defeat with monetary devaluation—the government had just suffered a setback in local elections—Giscard decided in March to pull out of the snake.

Though the franc depreciated by 20 percent in the weeks that followed, the government was firmly resolved to avoid a destabilizing spiral of inflation and depreciation. "At this point," writes Rainer Hellmann, "President Giscard d'Estaing was convinced that only a drastic stabilization program, conceived and implemented by an economist of international reputation and high esteem in France, could spare the country a disastrous decline like the one experienced by the Italian economy."[28] It was under these circumstances that Raymond Barre was named prime minister.

Raymond Barre subjected the French economy to an austerity program that was so successful, at least in the short term, that by 1978 the French were again contemplating joining the joint European float. Giscard, however, was not willing to risk a third forced exit. Exploiting Germany's exasperation with the Carter administration, Giscard pressed the issue of reforming the snake in a manner that facilitated participation by the franc.[29] This time, in contrast to the failed effort of 1974, the French were successful. The informal snake was jettisoned, and France and Germany established a much more elaborate monetary arrangement, the European Monetary System (EMS). Compared with the snake, the EMS made French participation easier in four ways. First, it established rules governing currency realignments and discouraged unilateral withdrawal from the snake, thus reducing the chances that the 1976 crisis would reoccur. Second, it spread the burden of

[28]Hellmann, *Gold*, p. 64.

[29]Germany was also motivated by a desire to put a stop to the growing tendency of other countries to hold marks as a reserve currency. They were afraid that if the deutschmark continued to be used as a reserve currency, "economic policy would either have to allow the exchange rate of the deutschmark to rise constantly and more rapidly than the inflation differential would justify, and thus accept the structural modifications that would result for the national economy, or it would have to halt this evolution of exchange rates which no longer corresponds to the basic givens of the economy. In that case, the Bundesbank would absorb the dollars offered for exchange by intervening on the currency exchange, an operation that would risk an inflationary expansion of the internal money supply. Given the present circumstances, it seems absolutely necessary, as the Council of Experts indicated in its 1978 report, that the American dollar return to its role as key currency, forsaken for the present, and fill it in a more effective manner" (André Grjébine, "Le deutschmark menacé par sa prospérité," in *Le Système Monétaire Européen, Cahiers Français* 196 [May–June 1980]). See also Lemineur-Toumson, "Les choix monétaires européens, 1950–1980," *Études Internationales* 12 (September 1981).

realignment more equitably across strong and weak currencies. Because parities were defined relative to a basket currency, the European Currency Unit (ECU), in which each participant's money was weighted according to its gross domestic product, a change in the exchange rate of any given currency redefined the value of the ECU and therefore of the parities of the other currencies. For this reason, realignment required multilateral negotiation.[30] Third, the European Monetary System conferred tighter bands on countries with large economies. Though the EMS obliged participant countries to intervene when their currency reached the official margin of 2.25 percent above or below parity, it "expected" steps to be taken when the currency reached its "divergence indicator," which lay inside the 2.25 percent margin. The band defined by the divergence indicator varies inversely with the size of the country's economy. For Germany, the divergence indicator was set at 1.51 percent, for France, at 1.8 percent.[31] Though France also has a "large economy," and is therefore also constrained by a narrow band, it nevertheless pressed the idea of the divergence indicator as a way to place fetters on the ever-ascending mark. Fourth, the EMS lightened the burden on the franc by strengthening certain multilateral aid mechanisms instituted back in 1972. Short-term European Monetary Fund quotas were raised from 5.8 billion ECUs to 14 billion, and special drawing rights from 3.6 billion ECUs to 8.8 billion. Total quotas available for medium-term loans were increased from 4.25 billion ECUs to 11 billion. Short-term (three-month) loans, which formerly could be renewed only once, could now be renewed twice. Finally, participants were allowed to borrow without limit for up to forty-five days.

EXPLAINING FRENCH SUPPORT FOR THE EUROPEAN MONETARY SYSTEM

Though the European Monetary System appears to embody French interests by facilitating French participation in a joint European float, the motives that incited the French to assume such a constructive role in the EMS are still not entirely clear. The French were wedded to the goal of making the franc a strong currency, but they promoted external

[30]The basket can be revised. To avoid manipulation, however, revision is permitted only once every five years, or when the weight of one of the currencies varies by 25 percent or more.

[31]Since the mark in 1978 accounted for 33 percent of the ECU basket, Germany's divergence indicator was set at $(100\% - 33\% = 67\%)$ of the legal fluctuation margin of 2.25 percent, or 1.51 percent. German reticence about the divergence indicator explains the absence of any clear obligation.

reforms that facilitated participation in the snake by weak currency countries. The two types of explanations usually encountered emphasize either the strong currency motivation or the weak currency motivation and, on the face of things, are much at loggerheads with one another.

The first family of explanations shares the claim that France looked to the European Monetary System to help strengthen its currency. France was compelled to do so by at least three factors. First, growing trade interdependence increased the need all across Europe to stabilize currencies. This is the reason most often and most readily given by French officials. The day the agreement was signed, Giscard d'Estaing declared, "The establishment of this zone of stability will mean stable prices for about half France's foreign trade. This will be a factor of confidence and encouragement to invest, and so a positive factor for employment."[32] The compatibility of the diverse national economies of Europe, and notably the great diversity of output, make it a natural zone for monetary union. "Many of its members have wide industrial bases, and the result of a monetary union would be a large, vibrant currency area with a highly diversified output. It is difficult to imagine a shift in demand or supply for any one commodity that would cause such disequilibria within the EEC as to force an individual country to alter its exchange rate."[33]

A second factor was the need for external allies to help fight inflation. When Giscard introduced the European Monetary System to the public, he made it clear that inflation in France had to be brought down because European integration would benefit the French economy only if it evolved in a manner compatible with economic evolution in its neighbors.[34] This apparent readiness of the French to accept the rigors of monetary discipline was shared by other countries, especially the smaller ones, which had learned the advantages of pegging their currencies to the mark. Benjamin Cohen writes: "A genuine change of attitude has occurred, proponents argue, especially in the system's more inflation-prone members." Cohen cites Niels Thygesen: "Past attitudes to the role of exchange-rate changes as an instrument or as an escape route to reach a more satisfactory combination of balance on current external account and higher levels of employment and investment have been increasingly questioned.'"[35]

[32]Quoted in *L'Aurore*, December 7, 1978.
[33]John R. Presley and E. S. Dennis, *Currency Areas: Theory and Practice* (London: Macmillan, 1976), pp. 99–100.
[34]*L'Aurore*, December 7, 1978.
[35]Niels Thygesen, "The Emerging EMS: Precursors, First Steps, and Policy Options," in Robert Triffin, ed., *EMS: The Emerging European Monetary System* (Brussels: National Bank of Belgium, 1979), p. 106, quoted in Benjamin J. Cohen, *The EMS: An Outsider's*

The third factor was Giscard's desire to regain a position of prestige within Europe. French leaders feared that France's mediocre performance was causing it to lose influence to Germany and argued that France had to adopt economic policies broadly comparable to those of Germany to make France Germany's equal. "It would not be a good idea for Europe to be dominated by one country," argued Giscard d'Estaing. "What I want France to achieve is to make sure that there are in Europe at least two countries of comparable influence...Germany and France."[36]

All three factors are well documented and all three appeal to intuition, but all have problems and inadequacies. For example, Europe's high level of trade interdependence unquestionably made currency stability desirable, but it is less certain that the European Monetary System was needed to supply that stability.[37] Critics of the EMS were quick to argue that the whole institutional and regulatory setup of the system was actually designed to avoid the costs of an authentic monetary integration. A first step toward true monetary union, they argued, would have consisted in aligning inflation rates on that of Germany, the least inflationary country. As Pascal Salin argued, if Europe's governments really wanted to align their currencies, the question of regime would have been superfluous: "From the point of view of real internal and external adjustment, the choice of an exchange rate regime is not essential for European monetary union. In particular, if the inflation rates continue to diverge between member countries, floating exchange rates are absolutely necessary."[38] Other critics argued that the EMS actually threatened to exacerbate exchange rate instability because it restored the possibility of riskless speculation, as it existed under Bretton Woods.[39] The threat was aggravated by the fact that the EMS lacked a common policy vis-à-vis the dollar.[40]

In sum, critics argued, the stable currency argument reverses cause and effect. There was nothing in the European Monetary System that

View, Essays in International Finance 142 (Princeton: Princeton University Press, June 1981), p. 14.

[36]Giscard d'Estaing, quoted in Peter Ludlow, "The Political and Diplomatic Origins of the European Monetary System" (Report to the Conference on The Political Economy of the European Monetary System, Bologna, 1979, Mimeographed), p. 22. See also Ludlow, *The Making of the EMS*, pp. 31–33.

[37]Koichi Hamada, "On the Political Economy of Monetary Integration: A Public Economics Approach," in Robert Z. Aliber, *The Political Economy of Monetary Reform* (Montclair, N. J.: Allanheld, Osmun, 1977).

[38]Pierre Salin, *L'ordre monétaire mondial* (Paris: Presses Universitaires de France, 1982), p. 129.

[39]L. Yves Fortin and Martin Perrot, "Un point de vue Nord-Americain," *Études Internationales* 12 (September 1981), 517–18, 525.

[40]Jean Denizet, *Monnaie et financement international* (Paris: Dunod, 1982), p. 263.

imposed currency stabilization on any member country. Indeed, the reverse was true. The EMS was made possible because most countries, above all France, had already embarked on a course of domestic price stabilization.[41] Hence, the decision to create an international monetary arrangement is puzzling. It was not needed if Europe's governments were serious about attacking inflation, and it was not adequate if it was designed to give member-states both the incentive and the means to get serious about fighting inflation.

Was prestige, then, the principal factor that motivated the French to collaborate in the construction of the European Monetary System? If so, Giscard d'Estaing lost his wager. The initial success of the EMS was so dependent on a turnabout in German policy that it highlighted the quasi-hegemonic role Germany was soon to play. Ludlow writes of the Bremen meeting of the European Council, held July 6 and 7, 1978: "In some respects...the most significant result of the Council as a whole was the public proof that it gave of the German chancellor's emergence as the dominant leader in the European Community. Only a few days before the Council, the *Economist* had still seen M. Giscard d'Estaing in the role. From Bremen onwards, the French president became increasingly the 'brilliant second'."[42]

According to the second family of explanations, the French were driven principally by the desire to facilitate the pursuit of mercantilist policies. William Wiseley has claimed that the French were motivated primarily by the desire to preserve the Common Agricultural Policy (CAP). There is no doubt that floating rates complicated CAP arrangements, CAP prices being administered prices. When the Common Agricultural Policy was first created, prices were established in a common accounting unit defined relative to gold (the Agricultural Accounting Unit of 1962, later the European Unit of Account [EUA]). Fixed exchange rates allowed European officials to translate CAP prices into national currencies easily. Trouble arose, however, when exchange rates were revised. When the franc was devalued, for example, French agricultural goods, priced in francs, became cheaper in EUAs, giving them an advantage on foreign markets. On the other hand, if the French, under pressure from their partners, increased agricultural prices in order to offset the price advantage obtained through devaluation, they exacerbated domestic price inflation. The solution to the dilemma came after the devaluation of the franc in 1969, when it was decided to leave agricultural prices, expressed in their national currencies, unchanged but to tax (or subsidize) agricultural exports so that their price, expressed in other community currencies, would also

[41]Ludlow, *Making of the EMS*, p. 44.
[42]Ibid., p. 139. See also A. W. De Porte, "Fifth Republic," p. 408.

remain unchanged. The name of this tax was the Monetary Compensatory Amount (MCA).[43] While MCAs were in effect, the devaluing or revaluing country was expected to take steps to restore domestic agricultural prices to their European price levels, as expressed in EUAs. For France, this transitional period was set at two years, during which period MCAs were renegotiated and readjusted in meetings of the European agriculture ministers.

Floating exchange rates naturally placed severe strains on this system. After 1973, therefore, it was decided to maintain a theoretical common price for agricultural goods which would continue to be expressed in Agricultural Accounting Units. Each currency was accordingly given a theoretical parity against the accounting unit, called the "green exchange rate." Discrepancies between the actual exchange rate and the "green rate" were adjusted using MCAs. Under this system, MCAs became a permanent feature of the CAP and were recalculated weekly.[44] There were three distinct drawbacks to this arrangement. First, it was extremely complex, causing the meetings of Europe's agricultural ministers, at which both agricultural prices and green currency rates were negotiated, to become the marathon struggles that so amused the rest of the world. Second, they increased the weight of agricultural expenditures within the EC budget. MCAs became a financial burden and a target for critics who claimed that agriculture loomed too large in community affairs. Third, it gave farmers in weak currency countries the impression that they were being discriminated against. Farmers in strong currency countries saw their buying power increase without any loss of foreign markets when their currency appreciated, but farmers in weak currency countries suffered a loss in buying power when their currencies depreciated without any compensating gain in market share. Critics argued, moreover, that the strong-currency country farmers were able to use their improved buying power to improve farm productivity and to increase their competitive edge. Hence, the argument goes, the French were in a position to benefit from a European monetary arrangement that restored agricultural price unity. By restoring a system of fixed parities between the EC currencies, MCAs—expensive, complex, and unfair—could be phased out. This was the ambition of the European Council, which in its own words "underscored the importance it attaches to avoiding any further creation of durable MCAs, reducing existing MCAs in order to restore unity to common agricultural prices."[45] When agreement on the EMS

[43]See Christine Verger, "Les montants compensatoires monétaires," in *Le Système Monétaire Européen, Cahiers Français* 196 (May–June 1980).

[44]See ibid.

[45]Giscard d'Estaing quoted in R. Hellmann, "Les dessous de l'accord," in *Le Système Monétaire Européen, Cahiers Francais* 196 (May/June 1980), 35.

was achieved, Giscard argued that it contained "good news for French farmers, for our partners have accepted the return to price unity for agricultural goods in Europe by progressively dismantling the MCAs."[46]

Whatever the apparent strengths of the CAP argument, it also contains weaknesses. As a historical matter, the Common Agricultural Policy quite simply did not figure predominantly in EMS negotiations. In fact, those negotiations almost failed because of last-minute misunderstandings concerning CAP. Negotiators agreed that the European Monetary System would begin functioning on December 29, 1978. As late as December 19, however, the European Community's agricultural ministers had not reached an agreement on how CAP was to be amended in order to comply with the new monetary system, having been furnished with only vague recommendations about phasing out MCAs. The Germans, in particular, resisted any attempt to limit future MCAs and turned a deaf ear to talk of eliminating them. As one French diplomat stated, "The CAP was present, but was not a driving force in creating the EMS. If anything, it created an obstacle. The CAP was not really threatened by floating rates. We could have gone on negotiating and renegotiating MCAs almost indefinitely. However, when we had to come up with some definitive solution to CAP's problems as part of the EMS negotiations, things became rather difficult."[47]

In the end, the European Monetary System failed to solve the difficulties CAP had to contend with. In the words of Jacques van Ypersele and Jean-Claude Koeune, "the advent of the EMS has both simplified the calculation of the MCAs and introduced a new complication," to the extent that Great Britain did not join the EMS and that Italy joined with a broader band of currency fluctuation.[48] For countries that chose to adhere to the EMS, the European Community's agricultural ministers agreed in March 1979 that future MCAs should not become permanent but should be phased out within two years of their creation, as agreed in 1969. On the other hand, because the EMS restored some practical significance to the "green rates" by linking them to a rejuvenated currency basket, the ECU, rather than to the outdated Agricultural Accounting Unit, it was decided that green rates would be manipulated more energetically in order to avoid the creation of MCAs. Finally, the ministers agreed not to press the divisive issue of what to do with MCAs created in the past that were still being applied. Having thus swept most of the divisive agricultural issues under the rug, the European Monetary System could become operational.[49]

---

[46]Quoted in *L'Aurore*, December 1, 1978.

[47]Personal interview, Paris, July 1983.

[48]Van Ypersele and Koeune, *European Monetary System*, p. 65.

[49]It was later agreed that suppression of MCAs would take place at a time when it would not result in a drop in German farm prices.

A second version of the mercantilist argument underscores what some critics of the European Monetary System have perceived to be its inflationary bias: "The present system implies a convergence toward the 'mean' inflation rate rather than toward the lowest inflation rate, thus contradicting the claim of the leaders to have created a system of monetary stability."[50] Drawing on this criticism, some scholars have argued that France's true interest in the EMS was to re-create a more tolerant international environment for its inflationary industrial policies. Far from applauding the creation of the EMS, advocates of radical monetary integration expressed keen disappointment. The ECU was not the common currency they were calling for, but merely a refurbished EUA bolstered by the vague commitment that it would be used for currency market interventions. The EMS, moreover, established neither a European central bank with some say over national policies, nor an independent bank endowed with the right to issue a parallel money. On the contrary, it established a lender of last resort that had even less say over national policy than the International Monetary Fund. "We are thus left with an adjustable peg arrangement supported by more liberal credit facilities," according to which, argued critics, "central bank interventions in the foreign exchange markets will be interrupted by periodic parity realignments."[51]

The adjustable peg, because it allows states to adjust trade deficits by devaluing the currency, is implicitly tolerant of the inflation that provokes those trade deficits.[52] If the past were to provide a guide to the future, critics could reasonably predict that the European Monetary System would facilitate numerous currency readjustments. Between April 1972 and March 1979, parities were defined or redefined an average of two-and-a-half times a year. Even among the five currencies that participated in the snake without interruption, there was considerable exchange rate variation. The mark appreciated against the Danish krone, for example, at an average rate of 4 percent per year.[53] Nothing in the refurbished snake that was the EMS suggested that it would perform better. Moreover, the sizable expansion of the European Community's mutual credit facilities and the inclusion of gold as well as dollars in the reserve pool backing the ECU, which increased the

[50]See Pascal Salin, *Union monétaire européen: Au profit de qui?* (Paris: Economica, 1980), p. 67.

[51]Michèle Fratianni, "The EMS: A Return to an Adjustable Peg Arrangement," in Karl Brunner and Alan H. Meltzer, eds., *Monetary Institutions and the Policy Process*, Carnegie-Rochester Conference Series on Public Policy 13 (Amsterdam: North Holland, Autumn 1980), p. 158.

[52]See Fratianni, "The EMS"; and Cohen, "The EMS," pp. 19–21.

[53]Roland Vaubel, "The Return to the New EMS: Objectives, Incentives, Perspectives," in Brunner and Meltzer, *Monetary Institutions*.

amount of usable reserves held by member central banks, made it easier rather than more difficult for member governments to avoid deflationary policies.[54]

Another target of criticism was the divergence indicator, the object of which, critics feared, was to constrain Germany's restrictive monetary policy by obliging it to reflate:[55]

> A divergence indicator which assigns a "moral" responsibility for economic policy adjustment to the most deviant country, regardless of the direction in which it deviates, is inconsistent with the declared aim of reducing inflation rates in the Community. As, for example, the German Council of Economic Advisers... has emphasized, a reduction of inflation rates would require [asymmetrical] rules for policy adjustment, and it has offered various suggestions for such rules. The divergence indicator, on the other hand, favors assimilation of inflation rates toward the Community average. It is designed to punish excellence in the fight against inflation and to reward mediocrity.[56]

As with the strong currency argument, there is much truth in mercantilist interpretations of the European Monetary System. But just as the strong currency thesis cannot dismiss mercantilist objections, neither can the mercantilists dismiss objections raised by the supporters of the strong currency thesis. First, mercantilist ambitions were not highly visible in French actions. In fact, the EMS owed its existence largely to German confidence in the domestic stabilization program of Raymond Barre. In the words of Peter Ludlow, "with Raymond Barre confirmed as prime minister, there seemed solid hope that France would pursue not only a non-Gaullist, pro-European foreign policy, but also domestic policies that would enable the French, if no other nonsnake government, to remain within and prosper inside a zone of monetary stability."[57] Governments that were more reluctant to tackle inflation, such as Italy and Great Britain, showed little enthusiasm for the European Monetary System. Great Britain refused to join, and Italy, after a last-minute crisis, joined only when offered a larger currency fluctuation band of 6 percent.[58] Second, exchange rates within the EMS were remarkably stable during the first two years of its existence (though the franc was looking ripe for devaluation by the end of 1980). In sum, there is no clear indication of either virtue or vice in France's

---

[54]Cohen, "The EMS," p. 20. See also Roland Vaubel, *Strategies for Currency Unification* Kieler Studien 156 (Tübingen: Mohr, 1978).

[55]See Fratianni, "The EMS," pp. 145, 158.

[56]Vaubel, *Strategies*, pp. 182–83. See also Hellmann, "Les dessous de l'accord," pp. 33–35.

[57]Ludlow, *Making of the EMS*, pp. 84–85.

[58]Ibid., pp. 81–84.

attitude toward the EMS. On the one hand, it is unlikely that France could have forgone devaluation even in the absence of the Socialist victory in 1981. On the other hand, there was no notable rush on the part of the French to profit from the supposed inflationary bias of the system.[59] Finally, the divergence indicator was not used. The EMS, in fact, has functioned fundamentally like a currency snake, as Jean Denizet has observed: "It is striking in this regard to observe that not a single study of the EMS over the past three years has ever revealed any deviation relative to the ECU—it would have been astonishing that a country had not sought proof of its 'innocence' and that no one had been accused as an alleged 'perturber.' On the contrary, one must notice that publications on the EMS all rely on a different indicator—that of a divergence relative to the strongest currency."[60]

Both the "strong currency" and mercantilist interpretations of the European Monetary System rest on good evidence, yet neither can dismiss the other. When one recalls the constraints placed on policymakers by the overdraft economy, however, it becomes apparent that there is no real need to choose between them. It matters little whether the French wanted a strong currency or whether they wanted to pursue inflationary policy. The combination of an overdraft economy at home and floating rates abroad deprived them of the ability to do either in any controlled fashion. The French pushed for reform of the snake because they sought to regain *control* over their monetary policy. The overdraft economy was the source of constraints that were more easily managed within the framework of a system such as the EMS than within the framework of a system such as floating rates or a rigid currency snake. Because of the overdraft economy, the franc was an endemically weak currency that needed external constraints. In the absence of such constraints, depreciation aggravated inflationary pressures against which the economy was poorly defended. The snake, though it provided constraints, brought little benefit to the French economy because it discriminated against weak currencies. When hot money fled the dollar and flowed into marks, it generally bypassed the franc. This imposed the need for restrictive measures to defend the franc's parity against the mark, which meant restricting the flow of credit. The EMS proved advantageous, at least when compared with other available options, because it provided the constraints of a system of fixed parities and thereby diminished the threat that currency depreciation would aggravate domestic inflation, but allowed France to

[59]See also Ralph C. Bryant, "The Viability of the EMS: A Comment on the Papers by Vaubel and Fratianni," in Brunner and Meltzer, *Monetary Institutions*.

[60]Denizet, *Monnaies*, p. 258. Divergence relative to the strongest currency is the indicator that appears daily in the pages of *Le Monde*.

share some of the costs of stabilization with its neighbors, if only by spreading the burden of currency realignment across both strong and weak currency countries.[61]

The EMS appeared to provide the external constraint of fixed rates yet promised to be more congenial toward weak currencies than the snake was. It provided more multilateral aid to deficit countries and greater constraints on German monetary policy by making currency realignment a multilateral affair, thus placing some pressure on Germany to align its policies on those of its less virtuous neighbors. Henceforward, France belonged to a joint currency float in which it could hope to remain.

THE EUROPEAN MONETARY SYSTEM SINCE 1978

The European Monetary System has surprised skeptics with its staying power and its ability to withstand monetary crisis.[62] Despite realignments within the system, exchange rate volatility between the EMS currencies is less than it was before the system was created, with regard not only to nominal exchange rates but also to real, inflation-adjusted exchange rates. Moreover, volatility has decreased over both the short term and the medium term.[63] But the injustice that the EMS was designed to correct persists. The task of adjustment still seems to fall disproportionately on the weak currency countries, which are typically obliged to impose policies of monetary rigor on their economies in order to slow the depreciation of their currencies relative to the perennially strong mark. Indeed, in the eyes of some partisans of monetary rigor, it is the European Monetary System's single most impressive virtue to have fostered a significant degree of policy conversion around the "German standard." "Convergence," however, is distinct from the ideal of monetary "cooperation" that seemed initially to animate the creators of the system.[64] German officials have more than once made acquiescence in deutschmark revaluation conditional on

[61]Although it performed this task very imperfectly because the dollar continued to float.

[62]Tommaso Padoa-Schioppa, "The European Monetary System: A Long-term View," in Francesco Giavazzi, Stefano Micossi, and Marcus Miller, eds., *The European Monetary System* (Cambridge: Cambridge University Press, 1988).

[63]J. Williamson, *The Exchange Rate System*, Policy Analyses in International Economics 5, 2nd ed. (Washington, D.C.: Institute for International Economics, June 1985). See also van Yersele and Koeune, *European Monetary System*, p. 74; Giavazzi et al., eds., *European Monetary System*.

[64]M. J. Artis, "The European Monetary System: An Evaluation," *Journal of Policy Modelling* 9 (Spring 1987), 186–92.

implementation of acceptable policies—that is, anti-inflationary policies by the devaluing country. For example, as part of the 1981 realignment Germany insisted that France eliminate 15 billion francs worth of expenditures from its 1982 budget, accounting for the first "pause" in Socialist reforms.[65] The 1983 devaluation found the Germans requiring that France reduce its budget deficit by increasing worker contributions to social security, by imposing a compulsory loan on taxpayers, and by reducing expenditures by 20 billion francs. Though members of the French government balked at the "unacceptable diktat" and complained of the creation of a "DM zone," German conditionality was accepted.[66]

If the European Monetary System did not work as planned, part of the explanation is that monetary conditions in the early 1980s were quite different from what they were in the 1970s, when the EMS was put together. In 1978, the dollar was a weak currency. Speculators besieged the market with orders for marks. German monetary officials needed their neighbors' help to quell speculative demand for the mark, which threatened either to bid the mark up to levels that threatened economic activity or to unleash inflationary pressures in the economy as foreign currencies swelled the monetary base. During the early 1980s, on the other hand, it was the dollar that was rising, compelling German monetary authorities to increase interest rates in order to slow the emigration of German capital to the new world. This militated against meeting the French halfway. Unilateral measures to strengthen the mark sufficed; indeed, the prospect of luring capital to Germany by making the mark more attractive than other European currencies may have been a tempting one. In short, the situation worked against the spirit of burden-sharing that the EMS embodied. When, after 1985, the dollar began to decline, the situation resembled that of the 1970s once again, making for greater equality between the French and the Germans. The monetary readjustment of April 1986, whereby the franc was devalued 3 percent and the mark was revalued by 3 percent, was obtained without conditions.[67]

Nevertheless, the history of Franco-German relations in the 1980s demonstrates, if demonstration is required, that the European Monetary System did not resolve France's monetary difficulties—indeed, the persistence of such difficulties has whetted France's appetite for a more

[65]Peter Hall, *Governing the Economy: The Politics of State Intervention in Britain and France* (New York: Oxford University Press, 1986), p. 199.

[66]David R. Cameron, "The Colors of a Rose: On the Ambiguous Record of French Socialism" (1988, Typescript), pp. 82–83 (available from the Center for European Studies Working Papers, Harvard University).

[67]*L'année politique, économique, et sociale en France, 1986* (Paris: Editions du Moniteur, 1987), pp. 424, 460, 492.

global monetary reform. When the OECD nations met in Paris in May 1983 to prepare for the Williamsburg summit, Mitterrand proposed that a new international monetary conference be organized "at the highest level" within the framework of the International Monetary Fund in order to define the rules of a new international system. He claimed, moreover, that monetary disorder, on the increase since 1971, was putting the world economy "at the mercy of a panic." Mitterrand argued further that a return to "sustained and healthy growth" required reconstruction of a "new global economic order" that would stabilize international monetary and commercial relations as well as the market for raw materials.[68] This was not mere bravado on Mitterrand's part. Since the appearance of the first cracks in the hegemonic edifice that structured international monetary relations, France's interest in international cooperation in the monetary sphere, even in the heady days of bank nationalization, has been quite intense. Before Socialist policy took a turn to the right, the Mauroy government was among the most active supporters of a reform of the EMS that would have instituted regular consultations between European, American, and Japanese monetary authorities and created a single credit line between the Federal Reserve Bank and the European Monetary Cooperation Fund (Fonds Européen de Coopération Monétaire, or FECOM).[69] By donning the garb of Don Quixote and tilting at the windmills of international monetary disorder, Mitterrand championed French monetary interests that have not changed substantively since de Gaulle's early crusade against the dollar overhang. The custom of annual or biannual summit meetings among OECD countries goes back to Valéry Giscard d'Estaing's efforts to stir interest in international monetary reform by hosting the first such summit meeting at Rambouillet in 1975. At that meeting Giscard defended the thesis that the crisis confronting the global capitalist economy was first and foremost a monetary crisis (a thesis vehemently opposed at the time by Mitterrand).[70] Successive calls for a new international monetary system formulated by de Gaulle in the mid-1960s (and by Giscard d'Estaing even prior to that time) provide further testimony to the continuity of France's position on this question of international monetary reform. In the light of the analysis of this volume, such continuity reflects the inadaptation of the

[68]*L'année politique, économique, et sociale en France, 1983* (Paris: Éditions du Moniteur, 1984), p. 413.
[69]See van Ypersele and Koeune, *European Monetary System*, pp. 108–09; *L'année politique, économique, et sociale en France, 1982* (Paris: Éditions du Moniteur, 1983), pp. 505–8; *L'année politique, 1983*, p. 414.
[70]*L'année politique, economique, sociale et diplomatique en France, 1975* (Paris: Presses Universitaires de France, 1976), pp. 168–70.

French overdraft economy to the post-hegemonic monetary world of floating rates. Such diplomatic efforts are the external counterpart to domestic reform.

Twenty years of efforts to reform the international monetary system have met with only polite refusal. As the French have three times broken their lance against international, especially American, resistance to monetary reform, so have they turned three times to Europe to approximate at the regional level the sort of order they advocate at the global level. After failing in the SDR negotiations, the French pressed the idea of a European monetary union a mere four years after de Gaulle's characterization of the European Community as a *volapük,* a "thingamajig" (though French interest in European monetary integration had at that time more to do with "high politics" than with "low politics"). In similar fashion, once the Jamaica agreements buried proposals advanced by the French at Rambouillet, the French spearheaded efforts to reinforce European monetary solidarity, giving birth to the European Monetary System. Finally, in the 1980s, U.S. President Ronald Reagan's refusal to consider monetary reform[71] caused the French to turn once again to Europe with a spate of proposals to reinforce European cooperation and solidarity.[72] As the world asks whether the global economy in the wake of U.S. hegemony is threatened with collapse into rival regional blocs, it would do well to recall how the divergence of U.S. and French monetary interests has driven the French to impart a distinctly regionalist touch to their European policy.[73]

CONCLUSION

French attitudes toward European integration have undergone significant change since the creation of the European Coal and Steel Community. Prior to the mid-1970s, French interest in the construction of Europe typically had its source in "high politics" rather than in the "low politics" of economic relations. After 1974, international monetary instability, because of its impact on policy-making in an overdraft economy, prompted French interest in European monetary integration for its own sake rather than for broader diplomatic goals that might be attached to it. French acquiescence in the Barre Plan had been more

[71]See Édouard Balladur's proposal that the international community create a "world EMS" in "Rebuilding an International Monetary System," *Wall Street Journal,* February 23, 1988.

[72]*New York Times,* January 17, 1988.

[73]See Robert Gilpin, *The Political Economy of International Relations* (Princeton: Princeton University Press, 1987), pp. 373–76.

symbolic than real, and more a function of overall diplomatic goals than of specifically monetary goals. By 1974, however, the French were displaying a keen interest in collaborating with the Germans to construct a more elaborate and institutionally more constraining monetary system than the snake. Pompidou's interest in reform was largely symbolic politics, but Fourcade's was not.

Domestic reform and the commitment to European monetary integration went hand in hand. Rather than end in France's withdrawal from the European Monetary System, the crisis of 1983 gave the final impetus to domestic financial reform. The complementarity of domestic and external reform efforts becomes clear in light of the analysis in Chapter Three, where France's problems were attributed to the spread of moral hazard through the domestic political economy, the effect of economic insurance largely underwritten by monetary and credit policy. That policy orientation was viable only because the international monetary order facilitated monetary expansion and trade adjustment through exchange rate manipulation. That order, in turn, depended on the willingness and ability of the hegemonic United States to share the cost of insuring French economic agents, both directly with financial aid and indirectly through self-discriminating international monetary (and trade) arrangements. When that willingness began to fade in the mid-1960s and disappeared altogether in 1971 (at least where Europe was concerned), the French were left saddled with a political economy mired in moral hazard that deprived policymakers of a significant degree of control over monetary and economic outcomes. Such control was defined as power in Chapter Three. Thus, one can argue that the liberalizing reforms of the 1980s were designed to increase French power, as were the reforms the French sought to introduce into international monetary relations. But because international reforms required that other countries—above all the United States and Germany—relinquish some portion of their own power (still defined as control over international monetary and economic outcomes), French diplomacy was not particularly successful despite the achievements of the European Monetary System. Consequently, most of the burden of France's effort to restore the power it lost was placed on domestic reform.

Conclusion

The cause of financial liberalization in France (and of France's interest in European monetary integration) can be traced to the withdrawal of U.S. support for the international monetary order of fixed but adjustable exchange rates. Floating rates exposed the existence of moral hazard in the French economy, which manifested itself in the form of an overdraft economy that was resistant yet highly vulnerable to policy efforts to stabilize the currency. In this concluding chapter, I summarize the argument, discuss the success of France's efforts to purge its political economy of moral hazard, and then exploit the history of French monetary policy to address theoretical debates concerning, first, the link between domestic political and economic structures and foreign economic policy and, second, the nature and evolution of the hegemonic order.

THE ARGUMENT

The argument began with the observation that, though the system of floating rates helped France overcome the initial impact of the supply shocks of the mid-1970s, it also generated a new policy challenge, that of vicious circles of inflation and currency depreciation. The threat of a destabilizing spiral of depreciation and inflation incited the French to pursue a strong currency policy. Deep-rooted rigidities within the domestic political economy, however, inclined officials to seek ways to avoid the deflationary consequences of this new orientation in monetary policy, first by borrowing heavily on international financial markets and, once that option began to reveal its limitations, by using the state's discretionary control over the allocation of credit to slow money supply

266

growth while assuring the flow of credit to export industries. A policy of "delayed adjustment," it was hoped, would "prolong" the process of adjustment until French industry—rationalized with the aid of an activist credit policy—could increase the economy's export capability and render it more resistant to the effects of monetary rigor. Despite such efforts, when the second oil crisis occurred in 1979 the French economy proved more fragile and more vulnerable than in 1973. By the end of the decade, growing awareness of the need to uproot the economy's deeply embedded rigidities was spurring interest in aggressive liberalizing reforms.

In Chapter Two, the economic rigidities unmasked by the global economic crisis were traced to the existence in France of an "overdraft economy." The financial market was narrow and industry depended to a high degree on bank credit to supply its liquidity needs. This explains the fact that bank credit accounted for the quasi-totality of money supply growth throughout the 1970s. The high degree of dependence on bank credit placed significant constraints on monetary policy by rendering firms insensitive to incremental changes in the supply and price of money, yet highly vulnerable to more abrupt changes. Moreover, the institutional structures that sustained this credit-driven political economy deprived the Banque de France of a number of tools of monetary regulation that were being used effectively in other advanced industrialized countries. Consequently, monetary discipline was difficult to impose at a time when floating rates required a strong currency, which is why the government of the relatively liberal Raymond Barre was forced to rely on more interventionist policy instruments to control the growth of credit. Financial constraint, more than administrative ambition, explains the persistence of financial interventionism at a time when both the president of the Republic and the prime minister were advocating greater liberalism.

In Chapter Three, I argued that the French overdraft economy manifested the existence of moral hazard—that is, a condition whereby the capacity of economic agents to foresee and to prepare for economic shocks is impaired by their imperfect perception of risk. The diminished perception of risk is, in turn, the consequence of the agent's perception that he or she is guarded or insured against it. In France, moral hazard manifested itself as the presumption of assured borrowing power, which encouraged firms to reject financial investment for precautionary purposes and to increase their level of institutional indebtedness. The financial fragility that resulted from such behavior placed pressure on monetary officials to sustain that presumption or confront the very real possibility of financial crisis, and so hampered their ability to combat inflation through monetary rigor.

For this reason, the French political economy was particularly vulnerable to inflation, and payments imbalances provoked by inflation could generally be addressed only by devaluing the franc. Under the monetary regime of fixed but adjustable exchange rates, of course, as supported by U.S. hegemonic leadership, devaluation was a viable option. Indeed, the U.S. hegemonic order was expressly constructed in a way that facilitated efforts to diminish social unrest in smaller countries that might threaten American influence and interests. American foreign economic policy thus facilitated French efforts to protect the expected incomes of French economic agents against the hazards of the marketplace. The United States provided "coverage" for whatever adjustment problems moral hazard might spawn in foreign accounts by granting the deficit country the power to achieve adjustment at its expense and at that of the international community.

This thesis was explored historically in Chapter Four through Chapter Eight, where I showed that the seeds of the overdraft economy were sown in the years immediately following World War II, when France rejected financial consolidation in favor of policies that forced the pace of industrial recovery and modernization through a *volontariste* program of industrial investment. One justification for *volontarisme* was that of promoting modernization while mitigating the stress of economic change on distress sectors. This policy orientation was facilitated by American financial support and diplomatic support for French claims regarding German economic reconstruction. The latter allowed the French to play a major role in determining the rules of European economic integration and gave France the opportunity to design community institutions that were consonant with its economic policy orientations. This was particularly evident in the case of the European Coal and Steel Community, which, Alan Milward observed, provided external validation and support for France's first plan of economic modernization.

In promoting the cause of *volontarisme* both at home and abroad, however, the French financed industrial modernization by transforming liquid assets into long-term investment capital. The result was industrial dependence on institutionally supplied credit, atrophy in the financial market, a marked bias toward excessive monetary creation, and growing recourse to direct state control over the evolution of credit, wages, and prices. The Bank of International Settlements, as early as 1949, drew attention to the peculiar way in which the financial structures of the French political economy were evolving and urged reform. Successive French governments tried to stabilize prices but did little to alter the economy's financial foundations. The structures of the overdraft economy were repeatedly ratified, and breaches in the edifice were repeatedly plugged. Three events stand out in this regard: the development of the treasury circuit in the mid-1950s, de Gaulle's refusal to restore financial orthodoxy in the early years of the Fifth Republic, and the banking reforms of 1967.

The ratification of the overdraft economy was the ineluctable consequence of policies that pursued three goals. The first goal was the promotion of political stability at home, particularly during the mid-1950s, when, during a time of colonial war, political life was marked by growing discontent on the part of farmers, small businessmen, and civil servants. Such was the preoccupation also of the Pompidou regime when, in the aftermath of the events of May 1968, continued unrest in the factories fed growing political polarization. The second goal was the promotion of productive investment to assure the competitiveness of the French economy as it reoriented its foreign trade away from its empire and toward the European Community. The final goal was to ensure that the government had some degree of mercantilist control over investment decisions in pursuit of the preceding goals as well as in pursuit of Gaullist *grandeur*.

Ironically, the overdraft economy evolved in part in response to social, economic, and political problems of which it was itself the source. The bank reforms of 1967, which set the stage for the rapid monetary growth of the Pompidou years, were enacted to overcome the French economy's lack of investment capital, which in turn was the consequence of policies that had discouraged investment in financial assets since the days of the Liberation. In like manner, the fear of successive governments to subject the French economy to a market-driven shift of resources was aggravated by the militant resistance of certain social categories, such as small businessmen and farmers, the prosperity and power of which, as well as the economic expectations of which, had their source in policies that had eschewed, again since the days of the Liberation, the redistributive implications of monetary rigor. The economic and political challenges that confronted successive French governments reflected the existence of the political vicious circle spawned by moral hazard, analyzed in Chapter Three.

In the early 1960s, however, the hegemonic monetary order, which validated French financial structures and practices by making monetary adjustment possible through devaluation, was transfigured in a manner that signaled its impending dissipation. Growing trade and financial interdependence, together with the inflationary reorientation of U.S. monetary policy, spawned an international monetary environment that was less congenial to France's overdraft economy. U.S. policy became itself a source of monetary growth and inflation in France. French policymakers were hampered in their efforts to defend their economy against imported inflation by financial structures and practices that were adapted to a very different kind of orientation in U.S. monetary policy. The French responded to the challenge by demanding reforms in the international monetary system, thus setting the stage for the Franco-American monetary conflicts of the mid-1960s.

Global monetary crisis in the early 1970s finally provoked the collapse of the monetary system of fixed but adjustable exchange rates and exposed the French economy to the danger of destabilizing spirals of inflation and currency depreciation. As indicated above, the overdraft economy was ill-defended against this danger. This gave rise to the policy experiments with foreign borrowing and selective credit restrictions with which this study began. Because, however, those policy responses seemed only further to debilitate the French political economy and to increase its vulnerability to external shocks, the French government under Raymond Barre began to take a serious look at more radical liberalizing reforms. Electoral constraints frustrated that effort, leaving the task of reform to the Socialists who assumed power in 1981. After experimenting with a reinvigorated policy of state intervention, external monetary constraint forced the Socialists to implement profound liberalizing financial reforms in 1984 and 1985. The Socialists embraced liberalization not because of ideological preference but because of the imperative need to restore the state's power to exercise control over the evolution of fundamental monetary quantities: monetary growth, prices, credit, and the value of the currency.

In the final chapter, I examined the impact of international change on France's foreign monetary policy, notably with reference to France's involvement in the construction of the European Monetary System. Prior to the demise of the system of fixed but adjustable exchange rates, France was attracted by the prospect of European monetary integration chiefly for reasons of high diplomacy. When the demise of the regime of fixed exchange rates revealed France's vulnerability to vicious circles of depreciation and inflation, however, France warmed to the idea of monetary integration for the more strictly economic benefits it could provide. The weakness of the franc, due in large part to the overdraft economy's low tolerance for policies of stabilization, precluded any lasting participation in the primitive European joint float. The European Monetary System, on the other hand, by placing some constraints on German policy, constituted a more supportive system for the franc. Nevertheless, because the dollar remains wholly outside the system and thus undisciplined (the Louvre Accord notwithstanding), the EMS still does not provide the franc with the international support system it has required historically. Dollar instability aggravated the difficulties encountered by the franc in the 1980s and has continued to nourish French demands for international monetary reform.

THE FRENCH OVERDRAFT ECONOMY TODAY

Where do the French stand today in their efforts to reform the overdraft economy and to purge the French political economy of moral hazard? To answer this, I must pick up the story where it was left in Chapter Eight—that is, at the end of the first Socialist legislature. The legislative elections of March 1986 awarded a narrow victory of two seats in the National Assembly to the conservative parties, the UDF and the RPR. Jacques Chirac, prime minister under Valéry Giscard d'Estaing, was chosen to head the government under the Fifth Republic's first experiment with a government that included a president of the Left and government of the Right—an experiment which politicians demurely referred to as *cohabitation*. The Right, having rediscovered liberalism during its years in opposition, returned to power with a program that was no less ideologically pronounced than that of the Socialists in 1981. Liberalization, especially denationalization of the banking and industrial sectors, dominated the agenda.

The finance portfolio was given to Édouard Balladur, who inaugurated his term with a 6 percent devaluation relative to the mark, accompanied by cuts in budget expenditures and measures designed to restrict money supply growth.[1] Structural reforms were not introduced until May, but went far to complete the task of financial liberalization begun by the Socialists. Reforms included the abolition of exchange controls, the abolition of *encadrement du crédit* (the preconditions for which were created by the Socialist reforms), the abolition of regulations governing the timing of new bond issues, the opening of the money market to all borrowers and lenders, the authorization of short-term (ten-day) certificates of deposit, and finally, the abolition of interest rate controls on bonds and long-term deposits. In September, the government began reprivatizing—*festinans lente*—state-owned industrial firms.[2]

This first battery of reforms was followed in November by a second reform package, the principal objective of which was to modernize and liberalize the banking sector by facilitating issuance of certificates of deposit, by granting banks freedom to create or shut down branch offices, and by abolishing an old and ineffective reserve requirement and replacing it with a new one, the *coefficient de ressources permanentes*, which was calculated relative both to long-term (five-year) bank assets

---

[1] *L'année politique, économique, et sociale en France, 1986* (Paris: Éditions du Moniteur, 1987), pp. 424–25.
[2] Ibid., pp. 438–40, 486–87.

and to liabilities.[3] In December, interest rate policy, as determined by interventions of the Banque de France on the open market, became the principal tool of monetary policy, thus bringing the tools of monetary policy in France in line with practices that were current in other advanced capitalist nations.[4] Finally, the government created yet a new series of instruments designed to encourage savings, the rate of which had fallen from a typical figure of 18 percent in the mid-1970s to 12 percent a decade later. These included individual investment retirement accounts, fiscal stimuli, and changes in regulations that facilitated household purchases of stocks and bonds.[5]

By introducing this battery of reforms, the government pursued the same goals as its Socialist predecessor. First, it sought to increase the volume of long-term savings available for industrial investment by unifying the financial market and according investors competitive rates. Second, it sought to assure "the regulation of the money supply by [controlling] interest rates rather than by controlling credit." It was said of this reform: "The creation of a unified capital market now finally endows the Banque de France with a modern instrument with which to control the money market through interventions on the open market. . . . In the end, this important reform aims at modernizing the financial system and French monetary policy in order to put an end to the rigidities from which the economy is suffering."[6]

To assess the impact of these reforms on the French political economy, let us begin by examining the state of the economy at the end of the Socialist legislature in March 1986. At the time of the elections, the Socialists could boast that they had reduced inflation to 4.7 percent, the lowest rate on record since 1967 (though still nearly 3 percent above the German rate), improved the financial situation of France's industry, which in turn helped to spur a 20 percent increase in industrial investment since 1984, and achieved balance in the current accounts for the first time since 1979. Moreover, the Socialist years saw a strong resurgence of the Paris Stock Exchange. Initially victimized by investor panic following the Socialist victory and the nationalizations of 1982, the Paris market, following the policy turnabout of 1983, became the scene of a spectacular increase in the value of stocks and bonds from a base index of 100 in December 1981 to an index of 265.8 in 1985 and

---

[3]On reserve requirements, see p. 72, n. 35; p. 150, n. 31; p, 170, n. 14.

[4]The Banque de France, however, taking no chances with this reform, set up a backstop in the form of a new regulatory mechanism that allowed it to vary the percentage of *réserves obligatoires* that individual banks were required to deposit in their central bank accounts.

[5]*L'année politique, 1986*, pp. 497–501.

[6]Ibid., p. 439.

460.4 in 1987. The volume of transactions rose from 26 billion francs in 1976 to 411.2 billion francs in 1986; bond transactions rose from 28.2 billion francs in 1976 to 1,673 billion in 1986. Stock market capitalization rose from 9 percent of the GDP in 1978 to 25 percent in 1986, "putting [France] in the same league as other major industrial economies."[7]

France's rediscovery of the stock market was not merely the product of new legislation and the creation of new savings instruments. Industry was nudged toward the market by greater parsimony in state support. In similar fashion, banks were forced to move into securities, not only because bank capitalization (in the case of certain banks at any rate) was insufficient but also because restrictions on the allocation of credit limited opportunities to earn income on interest, thus obliging banks to seek new sources of income in the form of brokerage commissions.[8] The shift of France's industries and banks toward the financial market was buoyed by investor confidence in the profitability of industry, which in turn was fortified by the slowdown in inflation and the corresponding decrease in industry's debt burden.[9]

There are, therefore, indications that financial reform has created the foundations for a stronger, asset-based political economy. The rate of *autofinancement*—that is, the financing of investment through business savings—rose dramatically after 1984.[10] The rate of self-financing, traditionally low (typically 70 percent), dropped to about 60 percent after the energy crisis of 1974. It climbed to 65 percent again in response to Raymond Barre's supply-side policies, but following the energy crisis of 1979 it fell again to 50 percent. It remained unusually low over the next three years, reflecting the impact of the "dollar shock" as well as the Socialist policy of pumping aid to industry through the banks and other financial institutions. The rate of self-financing picked up in 1982, however, and by the time of the 1986 elections it reached an unprecedented 90 percent. This trend was facilitated by the increase in business profits (before taxes), which in turn was facilitated by a drop in interest rates and by price deregulation.[11]

[7]Philip G. Cerny, "From Dirigisme to Deregulation? The Case of Financial Markets" (Paper presented at the International Conference on Thirty Years of the Fifth Republic, Paris, June 1988), p. 16. Cerny cites the *Financial Times*, March 11, 1987. See also *L'année politique, économique, et sociale en France. 1985* (Paris: Éditions du Moniteur, 1986), p. 490.

[8]See Cerny, "From Dirigisme to Deregulation?" p. 30.

[9]Philippe Durupt, "La bourse de cristal," *Perspectives 1982* 16 (February 1984).

[10]See *L'année politique, 1986*, p. 539.

[11]It was also facilitated, however, by a drop in gross fixed capital formation—that is, a drop in investment—occasioned by austerity after mid-1982. On the other hand, gross fixed capital formation rose vertiginously again after 1984. See also Conseil National du Crédit, *Rapport Annuel, 1981*, p. 117.

Changes in the structure of savings provide a second sign that the reform effort has been effective. Investors have tended to desert traditional savings instruments, such as accounts held in savings banks (*caisses d'épargne*), in favor of less liquid forms of savings that offer a greater return. In mid-1985, the direction of the Deposit and Consignment Bank noted a three-month drop of 7 billion francs in liquid savings and a surplus in newly created accounts, such as the "industrial development accounts" (*Codevi*) or the "people's savings accounts" (*livrets d'épargne populaire*), that funneled household savings toward the market for financial assets.[12] This reorientation was not entirely new since it had already been inaugurated by the Monory laws of 1978. But renewed activity on the financial market gave the trend toward less liquid savings instruments a visible boost. Savings, which had fallen to 12 percent of the GDP in previous years, climbed to 13.4 percent in early 1985 and was showing a strong tendency to climb higher as stocks and bonds rose to historic highs.[13]

There were still, however, reasons to be skeptical about the ability of the French political economy to sustain the rigors of greater financial liberalism. The French were unable to exploit an expanding international economy, made buoyant by rapid growth in the United States after 1982, to rekindle domestic growth. Between 1983 and 1986, the gross domestic product grew by about 1 percent per year, making the economy of France the weakest among the major industrial powers. The rapid rates of industrial growth that were characteristic of the French economy before 1974 had all but disappeared. Industrial production had remained flat since 1974 and showed only a cautious trend upward after the Socialist policy reversal of 1982.[14] Economists worried that there was a structural explanation behind industrial stagnation which weakened the chances for successful reform. A decade of state efforts to use its financial power to spur growth had left France with an industry excessively specialized in trade with less developed countries, and subsequently ill-adapted to competing in the more consumer-

---

[12]*L'année politique, 1985*, p. 425.

[13]*L'année politique, économique, et sociale en France, 1984* (Paris: Éditions du Moniteur, 1985), p. 479; *L'année politique, économique, et sociale en France, 1983* (Paris: Éditions du Moniteur, 1984), pp. 457–58, and, on the stock exchange, p. 493. However, one must remain cautious in drawing conclusions, because much of the impetus behind the regeneration of the stock exchange came from bank-managed investment clubs, especially *sicavs*, which retain a certain liquidity and thus do not necessarily denote a reorientation toward long-term savings on the part of French households. See Frédéric Bompaire, "Les sicav de trésorerie," *Banque* 447 (February 1985); Jacques Riboud, "Sicav et FCP: Des artifices monétaires et bancaires à découvrir," *Revue Politique et Parlementaire* 88 (April 1986).

[14]*L'année politique, 1986*, p. 535.

oriented markets of the industrialized countries. According to one study, the structural sclerosis of French industry was such that it was unable to respond to an increase in domestic demand of 3 percent or more.[15] French industry revealed its weaknesses even in times of good performance. One observer, describing the improvement in France's foreign trade during 1984, added:

> The turnabout in foreign transactions should not mask the structural weaknesses of French foreign trade. Its fragility is the result of excessive specialization in a small number of highly specialized sectors: cereals, automobiles, engineering, and above all, arms. In 1984, the sale of arms reached a record level of 61.8 billion francs that is, 7.3 percent of total exports; the fact that such exports have doubled in the last year is making French industry dependent on a small number of Middle Eastern clients (Abu Dhabi and Saudi Arabia alone purchase more than 20 percent of [France's] production of arms).[16]

The same observer was not surprised that improving export performance had not prevented a downward trend in France's share of the world market from 10.4 percent in 1979 to 8.3 percent in 1984.[17]

Moreover, whatever the fortunes of the French financial market, which in GDP terms now compared favorably with the markets of other advanced industrialized countries, the financial needs of French firms continued to dictate reliance on institutional borrowing, if only because of the unusually high burden of welfare levies that were imposed on French firms. Thus, while ostensibly elevating the role of the financial market in allocating capital, the government nevertheless increased subsidized loans to industry from 14.35 billion francs in 1984 to 18 billion in 1986, and increased subsidized loans to artisans by 14.3 percent to 8.4 billion francs. Although the government, in a spirit of economic realism, abstained from coming to the aid of steel and the metallurgical firm of Creusot-Loire, it still intervened to bail out other industries threatened by financial failure, such as the paperworks of La Chapelle–Darblay and the naval yards.[18] The cost of such interventions was covered in part by public borrowing, which reached record levels by the time the Socialists left office. By April 1986, the national debt stood at 1,200 billion francs, of which 500 billion was medium- and long-term. The annual cost of servicing the debt climbed from 26 billion francs in 1980 to an estimated 89 billion francs in 1986—that is, from 5 to 10 percent of the budget.

[15]Ibid., p. 407.
[16]*L'année politique, 1985*, p. 342.
[17]See ibid.
[18]Ibid., pp. 370, 410. Note that the total of all subsidized loans fell. See p. 226.

Since 1987, optimism has returned, though no clear reversal of fortunes has occurred. Growth has been much higher, nearly 4 percent, but trade in manufactured goods other than arms, traditionally in surplus, has fallen into deficit since 1987, despite continued rapid growth in world trade. Moreover, France's export troubles can no longer be laid at the door of inflation. On the contrary, France's waning presence on international markets seemed to be due quite simply to an inadequate supply of French goods. A recent study by Patrick Artus and Eric Bleuze suggests that investment in certain sectors has not been sufficient to meet demand.[19] And that insufficiency undoubtedly has roots in the comparative financial weakness of French firms, especially when compared with their American, German, or Japanese counterparts.[20] France's persistent difficulties selling manufactured goods on foreign markets suggests that its capacity to survive outside the financial cocoon that the overdraft economy once provided remains uncertain.

In assessing the likelihood that reform will succeed in relieving France of its overdraft economy, two questions remain. The first concerns the role of the banks; the second concerns the tolerance of the political system. The French overdraft economy will not be replaced by one in which well-capitalized firms manage well-endowed financial portfolios according to the needs and opportunities of the moment. In other words, it is exceedingly unlikely that the French political economy will come at any time soon to resemble that of the United States or even Japan. The French firm will continue to rely heavily on institutional lenders—banks and semipublic financial institutions. The object of reform has been to make these institutional lenders, rather than the industrial firms, more answerable to the financial market. Up to now, the financial system duplicated its relationship toward industry by entering into a comparable state of dependence vis-à-vis the Banque de France. The object of reform has been to break that dependence, render the financial institutions responsible for their own financial strategies, and in so doing relay via the banks the dictates of the marketplace to the industrial firms that continue to depend on them. In sum, though the French political economy will not come to resemble that of the United States, there is some hope that it might come to resemble that of Germany. Banks would exercise greater power within the enterprise, and the state would assume an arm's-length relationship with regard to both the enterprise and the financial institution.

[19]See Alain Vernholes, "Des investissements insuffisants à l'origine des mauvais résultats du commerce extérieur," *Le Monde*, February 10, 1990. Vernholes refers to Patrick Artus and Eric Bleuze, "Déficit du commerce industriel de la France et capacités de production: Un examen sectoriel," *Économie et Statistique* 228 (January 1990).

[20]Vernholes surmises that it may also have to do with uninspired management.

It is too early to speculate on the chances for success of such a program, or to recognize any indicators in events that have occurred since the reform. Skepticism is warranted, however, concerning the government's power to discipline itself. John Goodman, in a comparative study of central banking in France, Germany, and Italy, demonstrates how the degree of central bank independence from government is reflected in monetary policy. "Dependent central banks enable political parties, electoral pressures, and labor to influence policy. Independent central banks dampen the effect of those variables on the monetary policymaking process."[21] The Banque de France is the most dependent of the three banks that Goodman studies, and the sensitivity of monetary policy to political ambitions is the greatest. There has been no change in the statutes of the Banque de France that would shelter the central bank from the whims of an incumbent who might wish to manipulate monetary policy for political gain.[22] The political challenges of reforming the overdraft economy are such that a government of any political stripe will continue to confront the temptation of using whatever institutional power it might be able to wield—especially that which comes from the institutional subordination of the central bank—to assure the supply of capital resources to sensitive sectors and firms. Liberal financial reform has weakened but not eliminated the "interventionist temptation."

Second, because of the perpetual deadlock between Left and Right, the French political system is not one that facilitates economic reform—and above all, reform that deprives the French citizen of economic security. The Socialist experience bears this out. Brought to power by elections that were marked principally by division and abstention among their conservative adversaries, the Socialists, despite their overwhelming parliamentary majority, actually had little maneuvering room with which to chart a policy course. Within seven months of their overwhelming electoral victory, off-year elections held in January 1982 favored candidates of the conservative opposition. The "accidental" character of the Socialist victory margin was underscored by the results of local (cantonal) elections in March 1982, which deprived the Left of its electoral supremacy and actually increased the local representation of opposition parties. The opposition reclaimed a sizable electoral majority a year

---

[21]John B. Goodman, "Monetary Politics in France, Italy, and Germany: 1973–1985," in P. Guerrieri and P. C. Padoan, *The Political Economy of European Integration* (Brighton: Harvester Wheatsheaf, 1989), p. 191. Goodman, however, does suggest that the room for maneuver of countries (even those with dependent central banks) has been circumscribed by financial integration.

[22]See "La réforme du pouvoir monétaire en France," *Commentaire* 31 (August 1985).

later at the municipal elections of March 1983.[23] The parliamentary elections of March 1986, though they gave a narrow victory to the conservative coalition, were characterized nevertheless by a fundamental immobility on the part of the French electorate, as seen in Table 19. With the fate of governments hanging by such a perennially narrow margin, the temptation to use the state's tools of economic intervention to dope the economy is engraved in the structural givens of French party policies.

Table 19. Electoral cleavage: Percentage of registered votes won by Left and Right, 1974–1981

	Left	Right
1974 presidential election, 2d round	42.78	43.43
1978 legislative elections, decisive round[a]	40.05	42.20
1981 presidential election, 2d round	43.83	40.05
1981 legislative elections, decisive round[a]	40.08	32.28
1986 legislative elections[b]	41.40	40.09

Source: Jacques Chapsal, *La vie politique sous la Ve République* (Paris: Presses Universitaires de France, 1984), pp. 731–32; *L'année politique, économique, et sociale en France, 1986* (Paris: Éditions du Moniteur, 1987), pp. 34–35.
[a]Varies by electoral district.
[b]One round, proportional.

THE OVERDRAFT ECONOMY AND THEORIES OF THE STATE

Theoretical debate in the 1980s has centered on the power of the state and state institutions to determine the contours of foreign economic policy. The history of the French overdraft economy both sustains and challenges theoretical conceptualizations of the relationship between domestic political structures and external policy behavior.

In 1978, Peter Katzenstein attributed differences in both the objectives of foreign economic strategies and the instruments with which governments pursued those strategies to differences in domestic institutional structure, as characterized by the degree of centralization in state and society, on the one hand, and the degree of differentiation between state and society on the other.[24] When the advanced industrial

[23]Jacques Chapsal, *La vie politique sous la Ve République* (Paris: Presses Universitaires de France, 1984), pp. 707–13, 724–34, 793–97, 843–46.
[24]Peter Katzenstein, "Introduction: Domestic and International Forces and Strategies of Foreign Economic Policy" and "Conclusion: Domestic Structures and Strategies of Foreign Economic Policy," in Peter Katzenstein, ed., *Between Power and Plenty: Foreign Economic Policies of Advanced Industrial States* (Madison: University of Wisconsin Press, 1978).

countries were subjected to the external economic shocks of the mid-1970s, states that exhibited centralization in both societal and state structures inclined toward neo-mercantilist responses, while states that exhibited greater decentralization inclined toward liberal responses. With regard to France, a high degree of centralization in state structures and a low degree of centralization in societal structures explain a strategy that combined liberal and neo-mercantilist elements.[25]

John Zysman pursued this line of inquiry by examining the influence of financial structure on policy. He distinguished three models of finance. The first, found in the United States and Great Britain, is based on the capital market. Security issues are the predominant source of long-term industrial funds. Banks, firms, and governments are placed in "distinct spheres, from which they venture forth to meet as autonomous bargaining partners." The second model is the credit-based system found in France, in which the weakness of capital markets obliges firms to turn to lending institutions. In this system, institutionally allocated credit becomes a linchpin and the government is compelled to intervene to bolster the system and to make administrative choices concerning allocation. Thus the "borderline between public and private blurs, not simply because of political arrangements, but because of the very structure of the financial markets." The third model, represented by Germany, is a credit-based system dominated by a small number of credit institutions that themselves are not dependent on state assistance. "Government does not have the apparatus to dictate allocative choices to the financial institutions and consequently it has no independent instruments in the financial system with which to influence companies. Banks, however, can serve as policy allies for government, on terms negotiated between the government and finance."[26]

Zysman reasons that "by knowing the financial system one [can] predict the nature of the process of adjustment." Thus, "a capital market-based financial system would be linked to company-led growth, a credit-based system with administered prices would be linked to state-led growth, and a credit-based system with bank domination would be linked to negotiated change." The French-style credit-based system allowed the government bureaucracy to attempt "to orient the adjustment of the economy by explicitly influencing the position of particular sectors, even of individual companies, and by imposing the solutions on the weakest groups in the polity." The credit-based system assured the success of French economic planning; it allowed the gov-

[25]See also John Zysman, "The French State in the International Economy," in Katzenstein, ed., *Between Power and Plenty*.

[26]See John Zysman, *Governments, Markets, and Growth: Financial Systems and the Politics of Industrial Change* (Ithaca: Cornell University Press, 1983), pp. 69–72.

ernment to subject certain sectors to a market-induced process of decline while assuring investment funds to sectors whose expansion was essential for development; and finally, it gave the state the power to serve "as crutch and prod in the transformation of French industry away from an insular world in which small-scale production and intercompany connections slowed change toward an international marketplace in which a more modern industry composed of hierarchically managed giant corporations could compete with its counterparts."[27]

Financial reform has, of course, drastically altered the France that Zysman so thoroughly analyzed. Although, as claimed above, the state has not relinquished tools with which to promote certain types of industrial investment, selective control over credit allocation no longer is one of those tools. The state is still master of its subsidies and can influence credit policy by awarding interest rate subsidies for certain types of investment. Otherwise, however, the French system has aligned itself on Zysman's third model, the credit-based system in which the state intervenes as a negotiating party rather than as a more activist director of activity.

Zysman identified weaknesses within the French system that might account for its reform. Because the state exercised significant control over the allocation of credit, it determined which groups would be compensated and which would be allowed to confront the market unassisted. Traditional industry and agriculture were protected, Zysman claimed, and labor was squeezed. "An imposed solution that excludes some groups is like a tightly wound spring: the tighter it is turned, the more likely it is to snap."[28] The spring did snap, Zysman argues, when electors awarded the presidency to François Mitterrand in 1981.

The political history of French credit policy attempted here seeks to complement and prolong Zysman's analysis by paying greater respect to the political weakness that lay at the origins of the French system, by analyzing the constraints on policy that credit dependence spawned, and by replacing the system within the broader historical context of the international political economy as it evolved under U.S. hegemony, and showing how the development of French credit structures was contingent on certain features of that hegemonic order. The outcome is an appreciation of state capacity that is more historically contingent and dynamic. In the decade since students of international and comparative politics first directed their attention to the role of state institutions and institutional structures in fashioning policy and behavior, our understanding of the relationship between structure and policy has gained in sophistication, and our willingness to associate centralism with state

[27]Ibid., pp. 286, 91, 168–69.
[28]Ibid., p. 310.

autonomy and the power to pursue coherent, interventionist policy has grown more hesitant. John Ikenberry, for example, argues for a more dynamic conceptualization of the role of state and societal institutions. Institutions "can influence the way that the actors involved perceive *interests*, domestic and international," as well as "influence the *capacities* of government officials to carry out policy."[29] The institutional setting, however, is itself the object of an unending process of construction and reform:

> That institutional setting is the outcome of a confluence of historical forces that shape and reshape the state's organizational structure. From this "institutional" perspective, the challenge for scholars is to uncover the historical dynamics—both domestic and international—that shape the organizational structures of state and society, and the way that these structures shape, constrain, inhibit, and enable societal and governmental actors. The assumption behind this approach is that the relative importance of specific variables is time-bound, and theories of foreign economic policy must therefore be placed within a larger historical and institutional framework.[30]

Surveying research on the state, Peter Evans, Dietrich Rueschemeyer, and Theda Skocpol conclude that the state's ability to formulate policy *autonomously* from societal influence should not be confused with the state's *capacity* to undertake given tasks, notably in the face of societal resistance. Autonomy and capacity are two distinct dimensions of state strength that are not even covariant. A state that enjoys great autonomy in policy-making may enjoy little capacity to implement its policies, while a state that enjoys little autonomy may have great capacity to implement its policies. Moreover, autonomy and capacity are subject to change over time. Ironically, both can suffer from efforts to enhance them: "Whether originally autonomous or not, state interventions in socioeconomic life can, over time, lead to a diminution of state autonomy and a reduction of any capacities the state may have for coherent action."[31]

Recent research on France sustains this more cautious assessment of the state's ability to act as "a corporate actor." Harvey Feigenbaum's

[29]G. John Ikenberry, "An Institutional Approach to American Foreign Economic Policy," in David Lake and Michael Mastanduno, eds., *The State and American Foreign Economic Policy*, special issue of *International Organization* 42 (Winter 1988), p. 235.

[30]Ibid., p. 223.

[31]Peter B. Evans, Dietrich Rueschemeyer, and Theda Skocpol, "On the Road toward a More Adequate Understanding of the State," in their co-edited volume *Bringing the State Back In* (Cambridge: Cambridge University Press, 1985), p. 354. See also, in same volume, Rueschemeyer and Evans, "The State and Economic Transformation: Toward an Analysis of the Conditions Underlying Effective Intervention."

study of the French state's relationship with the oil industry evokes the image of a state that has become immersed in the imbroglio of societal conflict and become a tool of group interest.[32] The state is "captured," according to Feigenbaum's imagery, by dominant class and group interests. It retains its interventionist capacity, but rather than act autonomously to stifle social conflict, the state becomes part of Lenin's "who-whom" dichotomy. Feigenbaum writes: "The French state is strong, but it is not autonomous. It has had little trouble imposing high prices on French consumers while demanding sacrifices from those least able to resist. It has done nothing to extract concessions from the oil industry.... Thus the state's management of the economy ultimately reflects and reinforces the fragmentation of society.[33]

Peter Hall's conceptualization of state-society relations is more pluralist than Feigenbaum's. But although the state attains to greater autonomy in Hall's account, it "appears as a network of institutions, deeply embedded within a constellation of ancillary institutions associated with society and the economic system." As such, the fortunes of the state as "autonomous actor" rise and fall. The French state sowed the seeds of its own debilitation by assuming an activist role in modernizing the French economy. "Precisely because institutions are ultimately human artifacts,... it takes positive action to sustain or reproduce them; and incremental adjustments of behavior, in response to new challenges, can bring about broader shifts in the state-society relationship. In this case the evolution of French planning gradually began to erode the *étatisme* [stated-centeredness] of the French state."[34]

Jack Hayward's examination of economic policy-making and Ezra Suleiman's study of efforts to deregulate the profession of the *notaire* confirm the observations of Evans, Rueschemeyer, and Skocpol. According to them, the state, in its efforts to enhance its autonomy and its capacity, generated forces that ultimately circumscribed both by creating, legitimating, and reinforcing clientele groups that had privileged access to state institutions and that used this access to resist government efforts to curtail their privileges. Suleiman describes a phenomenon that assumes the form of a vicious circle:

> Emphasis needs to be placed on the state's role in encouraging the development of a societal group which leads to a clientelistic relationship and which in the end leads to severe constraints on the power of the state to effect changes in the group's position in the society. State capacities are

[32]There is some resemblance between Feigenbaum's interpretation of interest group liberalism and Lowi's conceptualization of it.

[33]Harvey B. Feigenbaum, *The Politics of Public Enterprise: Oil and the French State* (Princeton: Princeton University Press, 1985), p. 173.

[34]Peter Hall, *Governing the Economy* (New York: Oxford University Press), pp. 17, 180.

therefore greater when the state seeks to strengthen societal groups than when it seeks to reform them after it has endowed them with strong organizational capacities and granted them privileges.[35]

It is certainly not insignificant that one encounters this view frequently in the writings of French observers of French politics. Suleiman quotes Jean-Noël Jeanneney, for whom "too much state is not a problem here, but rather its excessive timidity."[36] For many French observers, the state is a Leviathan that cannot say no. Chardonnet, for example, wrote in the mid-1970s:

> The State,... in spite of its apparent force, reveals sensitivity to pressures that are placed upon it. A small minority within the university goes on strike in 1968 for purely political reasons? The state capitulates, creating the absurdity of autonomous universities, multiplying the number of new teaching and administrative positions.... Is there dissatisfaction among the magistrates, are there revolts in the prisons in 1974? The state increases the budget of the Ministry of Justice. The post office goes on strike in the autumn of 1974? The state...creates new jobs, apparently without having studied beforehand whether the greater volume of mail could not be handled by automating certain services. A certain demagogy should not be excluded a priori.[37]

A Leviathan that is incapable of saying no is fated to become, in the words of one former high French official, "*kafkaesque* in its complexity and *ubuesque* in its omnipresence."[38]

This vision of a state that has "forged the shackles that bind it" is the one I defend in this book.[39] More precisely, I advance no claims with respect to the "autonomy" of the French state vis-à-vis societal actors,

[35]Ezra N. Suleiman, *Private Power and Centralization in France: The Notaires and the State* (Princeton: Princeton University Press, 1987), p. 325. Suleiman cites research that comes to similar conclusions: Jean G. Padioloeau, *L'État au concret* (Paris: Presses Universitaires de France, 1982); idem, *Quand la France s'enferre* (Paris: Presses Universitaires de France, 1981); Douglas Ashford, *Policy and Politics in France: Living with Uncertainty* (Philadelphia: Temple University Press, 1982); Jean-Pierre Worms, "Le préfet et ses notables," *Sociologie du Travail* 8, no. 3 (1966), 247–75; Jacques Rondin, *Le sacre des notables* (Paris: Fayard, 1985); Elliot J. Feldman, *Concorde and Dissent: Explaining High Technology Failures in Britain and France* (New York: Cambridge University Press, 1985); Feigenbaum, *Politics of Public Enterprise*; John Ambler, "Equality and the Politics of Education," in John Ambler, ed., *The French Socialist Experiment* (Philadelphia: Institute for the Study of Human Issues, 1985), pp. 116–44; John T. S. Keeler, "Agriculture Reform in Mitterrand's France," in Ambler, *French Socialist Experiment*; Valerie Rubsamen, "The Media and the State in France," Ph.D. diss., Princeton University, 1985.

[36]Quoted in Suleiman, p. 326.

[37]Jean Chardonnet, *La politique économique intérieure française* (Paris: Dalloz, 1976), p. 50.

[38]Lionel Stoléru, *La France à deux vitesses* (Paris: Flammarion, 1982), p. 180.

[39]See also Michael Loriaux, "States and Markets: French Financial Interventionism in the Seventies," *Comparative Politics* 20 (January 1988).

given this book's focus on the external constraint that monetary policymakers had to confront. On the other hand, the history of financial reform in France does provide evidence that the state, in its efforts to strengthen its capacity to intervene in economic life, does generate forces that in time weaken that capacity. This happens not only because the state, in its interventions, gives birth and nourishment to new societal counterparts that subsequently make claims on policy, as Suleiman and Hayward discovered, but also economic expectations and patterns of economic and political behavior are generated that, though diffused through society, nevertheless place effective fetters on policy. A large part of the task of liberalization is precisely to alter expectations that in France assumed the form of "moral hazard." Thus, the history of financial reform in France contributes to a better understanding of the state by revealing the importance of such expectations. It also contributes to a better understanding of the state by attributing the development of state capacity to a tolerant and even supportive international environment. Let us examine these two contributions in greater detail.

MORAL HAZARD AND ECONOMIC LIBERALIZATION

The state placed fetters on itself by generating economic expectations that affected the market rationality and political behavior of broad sectors of the French political economy. It encouraged individuals to prefer liquid and semiliquid savings accounts to financial investment, and firms to neglect investment in financial assets as a precaution against economic uncertainty. It allowed firms to assume that their power to borrow was assured, and thus to fall into a situation of utter dependence on the supply of capital through lending institutions. The state generated organized opposition to economic modernization among small businessmen and farmers, not only by entering into clientelistic and corporatist arrangements with them but also by pursuing monetary and credit policies that kept them alive as a class and gave new life to their obsolescent economic expectations. The state's freedom to act autonomously thus became constrained by the legacy of policies that had in the beginning allowed the French government to overcome political weakness and isolation by providing a type of insurance in the form of quasi-assured (though regulated) credit lines to industrial firms, inflationary rents to small businessmen, and administered prices to farmers.

The history of French policy encounters an intriguing echo in the history of policymaking in Eastern Europe. Ellen Comisso, in her comparative study of the member states of the Council of Mutual

Economic Assistance (CMEA), which had the characteristic of being uniformly centralized and therefore "strong," argued that the effect of centralization alone is not sufficient to explain the policy response of socialist bloc countries to the crises of the 1970s. Comisso is led to underscore the importance of the degree of differentiation between the state and the economy (a variable that was originally identified by Katzenstein but that has received little specific attention except by Zysman). Differentiation "measures the degree to which the activities of producers, consumers, and labor suppliers depend on the decisions of . . . state authorities." Low differentiation, such as one found in Soviet bloc countries, has a decisive impact on a nation's economic behavior and policy because it means that "producing units bear neither the costs nor the risks of their activities." Comisso borrows the term "soft constraints" from Janos Kornai, according to whom the development of close ties between the state and industrial firms weakened the power of the market to constrain economic activity: "Budget constraints are 'soft,' and adjustment costs, benefits, and strategies of individual economic units can . . . be shifted to the higher-level authorities whose decisions determine them."[40]

The notion of "soft constraints" helps explain why the initial response of CMEA countries to the supply shocks was expansionist: "Adverse changes in oil prices and availability in the 1970s were widely perceived as shortage constraints, thus limiting output, while both enterprises and planners largely discounted the potential demand constraints stemming from recession in Western markets."[41] Moreover, and more important for our purposes, it explains why state strength often coexisted with economic weakness. As Laura Tyson writes:

> Because [firms] are ultimately owned by the state and because the state is ultimately responsible for their welfare and performance, enterprises act in the correct expectation that if they run into financial difficulties, the state will bail them out. . . . [The] resulting softness of budget constraints considerably weakens incentives to respond to changing prices. Consequently, . . . if the state wishes to change the behavior of enterprises, it must do more than simply "get the prices right"—and getting the prices right often proves very difficult for state officials unaccustomed to interpreting and responding to changing world-market conditions.[42]

[40]Ellen Comisso, "Introduction: State Structures, Political Processes, and Collective Choice in CMEA States," in Ellen Comisso and Laura D'Andrea Tyson, eds., *Power, Purpose, and Collective Choice: Economic Strategy in the Socialist States* (Ithaca: Cornell University Press, 1986), p. 32; I thank Peter Katzenstein for drawing my attention to this parallel.

[41]Laura D'Andrea Tyson, "The Debt Crisis and Adjustment Responses in Eastern Europe: A Comparative Perspective," in Comisso and Tyson, eds., *Power, Purpose, and Collective Choice*, pp. 69–70.

[42]Ibid., p. 70. As in France, protection was the incumbent's response to political

The notion of "soft constraints" obviously squares with many of the phenomena we have encountered in our analysis of the French over-draft economy. Though the degree of differentiation between the state and societal actors is greater than in the CMEA countries, it is smaller than that encountered in most OECD countries. This is particularly true of relations between the state and credit institutions. Not only were many lending institutions managed by civil servants, but they operated under specific licensing arrangements that gave them certain privileges and sectoral responsibilities. As for the banks proper, they were regulated in such a way that certain activities sponsored by the state received some form of state guarantee.[43] The most notorious arrangement of this sort was the rediscountable medium-term loan, used to promote exports. Credit institutions, in other words, acted under a type of "soft constraint" identified by Kornai, since the costs and risks of their activities were ultimately born by the state, notably the Banque de France. Moreover, as in Eastern Europe, soft constraints typically gave rise to the perception that the principal threat to economic activity was the bottleneck of essential inputs. Whereas in Eastern Europe this fear applied to real goods, it applied principally to capital in France. The French state acted very much according to the same logic as its erstwhile socialist bloc counterparts when it began to experiment with institutional reforms that were designed primarily to overcome such shortages. The reforms of 1966–67, which tried to tame the practice of *"transformation"* in order to tap France's vast reservoir of liquid savings to finance industrial investment, are an example of the logic of "soft constraints." France's response to the supply shocks of the 1970s, when it borrowed heavily on foreign financial markets in a manner similar to certain eastern bloc countries and newly industrialized countries, provides a second example.

Finally, the notion of soft constraints explains the difficulties the French experienced in responding to the challenges of the 1970s and 1980s. Because state control over institutional lending had dominated the financial environment in which French industrial firms had to operate, firms began to believe they were immune to financial distress or, in the terms of overdraft economy theorists, that their power to borrow from some lending institution was assured. Subsequently, because French firms never learned to invest in financial assets as a

weakness. See Valerie Bunce, "The Empire Strikes Back: The Evolution of the Eastern Bloc from a Soviet Asset to a Soviet Liability," *International Organization* 39 (Winter 1985). As the eastern bloc countries liberalize, not one at the time of this writing has yet eliminated subsidies.

[43] In the CMEA states, by contrast, the ministries were the "banks" and the "bankers."

precaution against economic uncertainty they were at the mercy of policies that tried to place restrictions on the supply of credit. As a result, French firms became both insensitive to incremental adjustments in the supply of credit and yet highly vulnerable to more radical adjustments in the supply of credit. Government policy had to allow for the fact that the financial fragility of French firms was uncommonly high. Moreover, the government's sensitivity to the firms' position was enhanced by the role that individual firms had come to assume in the financing of France's social policies. In brief, the French lost control of their monetary policy. When change in the international monetary system made that loss palpable, the French were obliged to reform the overdraft economy and to restore market constraints.

"Soft constraints," in more abstract terms, generate moral hazard. Moral hazard obstructs the government's efforts to adjust economic activity to altered external circumstances or to adapt economic structures to new economic conditions. Whether the economy is socialist or capitalist matters little. Moral hazard hampered the efforts of Valéry Giscard d'Estaing and Raymond Barre to find and implement responses to change in the international monetary regime. Interpreting the studies of Comisso and Tyson in the light of the analytical framework advanced here, we can see that moral hazard too hampered the efforts of a number of CMEA leaders to find and to implement responses to the debt crisis provoked by the change in U.S. monetary policy that occurred in the early 1980s.[44]

The ultimate response to moral hazard—in the socialist bloc countries, including the Soviet Union, as in France—was market deregulation. This is the second way in which the history of the French overdraft economy enriches our understanding of the political role of the state. Because moral hazard places constraints on policy and subjects incumbent to a vicious circle of growing societal demand for protection and growing incapacity to respond to economic shocks, incumbents seek to restore their power to formulate policy responses to such shocks by attacking moral hazard itself. In the case of France, financial reform was designed to force banks and lending institutions to regulate their activity by obliging them to finance it with capital raised on the financial market. Banks and lending institutions, in turn, were to relay market constraints to the industrial enterprises that continued to depend on them.

John Ikenberry, in his provocative study of American petroleum policy, identifies a similar effort to restore political power to the state

[44]Bulgaria did formulate a successful response, but for other socialist countries to respond would have meant the dismantling of political society—party, plan, and state—as it was structured.

through market liberalization. He concludes that state interventionism, though undertaken in pursuit of the national interest, "may provide a mechanism for private claims on state resources" and thus place constraints on policymakers by depriving them of policy choices. Flexibility—that is, "the ability of executive officials to provide themselves with the broadest array of options as they anticipate the next socioeconomic crisis"—can, Ikenberry argues, weigh in as heavily as interventionist power when it comes to assessing the state's capacity to formulate and pursue policy with autonomy. Ikenberry concludes, "Thus a fuller appreciation of state capacity must entertain the possibility that the imposition, extension, or maintenance of market processes in specific circumstances does not simply ratify the interests of societal actors but may be intimately associated with the state's pursuit of its own goals. Strategic abstention, withdrawal, and the reshaping of previous interventions are aspects of state capacity, just as much as strategic intervention—aspects we must appreciate analytically and be able to predict historically."[45]

GLOBAL LIBERALIZATION AND U.S. HEGEMONIC DECLINE

The history of French monetary and credit policy also supplements our understanding of the role of the state in economic life by directing our attention to the international conditions that hamper or facilitate state intervention in the economy. In particular, it alerts us to the possibility that U.S. leadership in the world economy during the first decade-and-a-half following World War II facilitated interventionism, as well as to the possibility that the dissipation of the hegemonic order is a principal factor behind liberalization in our time.

The hegemonic order created the conditions for the propagation of moral hazard in national economies. It follows, then, that the increasingly nationalist orientation one can observe in U.S. policy since the mid-1960s, and above all since the mid-1970s, would force nations to adopt reforms that rid their economies of moral hazard.[46] Comparisons with such countries as Japan, Korea, and Finland—which, like France, once had overdraft economies[47]—sustain this observation. The challenges produced by hegemonic decline, however, and the precise

---

[45]Quoted in G. John Ikenberry, *Reasons of State: Oil Politics and the Capacities of American Government* (Ithaca: Cornell University Press, 1988), p. 206.

[46]A similar statement can be made for the eastern bloc. See Bunce, "Empire Strikes Back," for a provocative account of Soviet policy in Eastern Europe, the relevance of which has been underscored by recent events.

[47]Jean-Pierre Patat, *Monnaie, institutions financières, et politique monétaire* (Paris: Economica, 1982), pp. 235–37; Jean Bouysset and Christiane Dossé, "L'intermédiation financière au Japon," Commissariat Général du Plan, *Préparation du Huitième Plan: Annexes* (Paris: La Documentation Française, 1981), pp. 245–94. On Finland, see R. Airikkala and T. R. G.

manner in which different states responded to it, varied significantly from country to country and defy easy generalization. Despite our tendency to conceive of the "international system" as a coherent whole—as an "ether-like" entity—nations insert themselves in the international political economy in a great variety of ways.

Japan, like France, earned a reputation for mercantilism in foreign economic policy. As in the case of France, however, one must be cautious in assigning labels. In the first decades of the twentieth century, the Japanese government interfered little in financial affairs, and between World War I and 1928 Japanese corporations relied heavily on the bond market for investment capital.[48] Only beginning in the late 1920s did the Japanese begin to erect a system of control over the allocation of credit, in pursuit first of military strength, then of postwar reconstruction, and finally of sustained economic growth. Thus, financial structures evolved that mirrored those of France: a relatively concentrated system of banks, a relatively complicated set of credit regulations, and a proliferation of government financial institutions.[49] Though U.S. occupation forces attempted to dismantle wartime economic structures, reform efforts failed to reorient the system decisively toward the market. The Supreme Commander for Allied Powers (SCAP) succeeded in abolishing most government financial institutions, but the Industrial Bank of Japan, which had been the largest lender of all to wartime industrial firms, remained intact. In what Kent Calder calls "perhaps the most portentous failure of the Occupation period, SCAP failed to reorient Japanese corporations from their newly developed system of indirect finance toward the pattern of direct finance, based on capital markets, that was prevailing in the United States."[50] Nor did the Occupation succeed in dismantling the major banks, which had been one of the most central elements of the prewar *zaibatsu* that U.S. occupation officials were intent on disassembling.[51] As in the case of France, the United States acquiesced

---

Bingham, "The Formulation and Control of Monetary Policy in an Open Overdraft Economy: The Case of Finland," Actes du Séminaire des Banques Centrales et des Institutions Internationales, *Cahiers Économiques et Monétaires* 6 (Paris: Banque de France, Direction Générale des Études, April 1977).

[48]Kent Calder, "The State and Selective Credit Programs in Japan, 1946–1986" (1986, Manuscript), chap. 1, p. 12.

[49]The government institutions did not survive the war.

[50]Calder, "State," chap. 1, p. 42.

[51]See "U.S. Initial Post-Surrender Policy for Japan," September 22, 1945, in *Documents Concerning the Allied Occupation and Control of Japan*, vol. 1: *Basic Documents*, compiled by the Ministry of Foreign Affairs, Division of Special Records (1949), part 4: "Economic": "To this end it shall be the policy of the Supreme Commander to favor a program for the dissolution of Zaibatsu, the large industrial and banking combinations that have exercised control over a great part of Japan's trade and industry."

in the mercantilist preferences of the Japanese as U.S.-Soviet tensions mounted.[52]

American tolerance and support for the preservation of certain mercantilist features of the pre-war political economy facilitated the subsequent elaboration of financial structures that T. J. Pempel described in 1977 as "among the most centralized and controllable in the world."[53] Calder, however, invests much effort in qualifying this statist interpretation and offers the reader a vision of a more pluralist and chaotic Japanese political economy. He makes the contrast stark between Japan and France, which he makes fill the role of the ideal type "strong state" in much the same way that students of French politics use Japan to provide a statist foil against which to highlight French policy incoherence. He describes financial structures that evolved more under the constraint of a chronic capital shortage than under the direction of strategically rational state actors. Credit policy, in general, encouraged bank activity. Bank of Japan discount rates were lower than short-term rates offered by banks, creating for the latter the opportunity to borrow from the central bank and lend elsewhere. The power of the Bank of Japan to control credit allocation applied principally to short-term finance. Regulations accorded certain categories of borrower assured rediscount at privileged rates and regulated bank activity by imposing penalty discount rates, much like the Banque de France in the 1950s and 1960s. A "Loan Mediation Bureau" oversaw the transformation of liquid savings deposited in banks into long-term loans for industry. The Bank of Japan's lack of leverage vis-à-vis the banks, however, limited its role to one of mediation. It could only make "markets to replace banker-industry connections dislocated by the war" rather than pursue any "abstract, autonomous norms of its own choosing." Calder continues, "An examination of Loan Mediation Bureau decision making... confirms the image of *ad hoc* decisions oriented more toward bailing out distressed firms than establishing consistent, long-term-oriented guidelines for credit allocation." As for the Ministry of Finance, it comes off looking appreciably less coherent than its French counterpart, further undermining the received view of Japanese mercantilism. Indeed, in the early 1960s, the Japanese Ministry of International Trade and

[52]See George F. Kennan, *Memoirs: 1925–1950* (Boston: Little, Brown, 1967), pp. 375–76: "If one was to regard the protection of Japan against Communist pressures as a legitimate concern of the United States government, then it was simply madness to think of abandoning Japan to her own devices. She had been totally disarmed and demilitarized, rendering Japanese society vulnerable to Communist political pressures and paving the way for the Communist takeover."

[53]T. J. Pempel, "Japanese Foreign Economic Policy: The Domestic Bases for International Behavior," *International Organization*, Autumn 1977, esp. p. 736, quoted in Calder, "State," chap. 1, p. 39.

Industry (MITI) looked—unsuccessfully—to the French example "to integrate financial-sector and industrial policy approaches to the distribution of credit."[54]

The consequence of an institutionally mediated, highly leveraged growth strategy in both France and Japan was the emergence of an overdraft economy. Industry in Japan, as in France, was allowed to become highly dependent on the allocation of credit by banks. Frances Rosenbluth writes: "The demand for funds to finance profitable domestic investment was very high. Banks were heavily indebted to the Bank of Japan during the recovery and rapid growth years and overcommitted to corporate borrowers."[55] Furthermore, as in France, the need for capital supplied by financial intermediaries fostered the development of a highly compartmentalized financial structure as specialized financial institutions were assigned to particular economic sectors and given privileged charters to facilitate their activities. In Japan, as in France, credit policy was progressively assigned an "industrial welfare" function:

> "Industrial welfare," defined primarily by private-sector firms themselves in terms of their common organizational interests in uncertainty avoidance, global market share expansion, employment maintenance, and returns to share-holders, has been the principal function of Japanese government involvement in finance, through relatively inefficient uses of credit, such as massive support to industries of the past and to inefficient distributors.[56]

Similar structures in France and Japan explain similar performances. Economic growth in both countries proceeded at a high rate. The average rate of GDP growth for France between 1947 and 1976 was 5.5 percent, while that of Japan was 9.7 percent. During the same period, the money supply grew at an annual rate of 15 percent in France and 20.9 percent in Japan. And, though savings in both Japan and France remained abundant, they also remained highly liquid—between 1970 and 1978 only 28 percent of Japanese savings was held in long-term assets. Subsequent rapid growth in the money supply and the preference for liquidity fueled inflation in Japan, just as in France. During the period 1947–76, inflation averaged 6.1 percent in France and 8 percent in Japan.

Despite similarities in financial practice and structure in the post-war era, international change affected the two political economies in dis-

[54]Calder, "State," chap. 1, pp. 29, 59, 56–58, 15.
[55]Frances McCall Rosenbluth, *Financial Politics in Contemporary Japan* (Ithaca: Cornell University Press, 1989), p. 54.
[56]Calder, "State," Introduction, pp. 16–17.

tinctly different ways. Although it is true that Japan, like France, also liberalized its financial structures and practices in response to international change, liberalization followed a different logic, such that Frances Rosenbluth, in her analysis of Japanese financial reform, can ignore the change that took place in the international monetary system and can in fact refer to international factors only to the extent that growing financial interdependence created new interests and opportunities for certain Japanese actors. As analyzed by Rosenbluth, Japanese financial liberalization was not driven by the stress provoked by the breakdown in the machinery of economic governance, itself induced by change in the international economic environment. Rather, it was driven by change in domestic sectoral interests as Japan's position in the world economy evolved from that of deficit country in trade and debtor country in finance to that of a surplus and creditor country. The impetus for reform came not from state officials or government incumbents, as in France, but from societal actors: "Deregulation [was] propelled by financial institutions, acting in cooperation with the Ministry of Finance and sometimes politicians, to construct a new set of rules they need to compete in a changing economic environment."[57]

To conceive of financial reform in France in the terms Rosenbluth uses for Japan would be nonsensical. We would have to believe that financial actors, for the most part belonging to the public sector and members of the *grands corps*, prevailed on the state (of which they were part) and the Socialist government to diminish the power of the state and the government over capital allocation in order to strengthen the capitalist structures of the French political economy through deregulation. At the risk of oversimplifying, we can say that the comparison of reform in Japan and France suggests that the former was driven by opportunity while the latter was driven by constraint. Japan did not suffer from the demise of the Bretton Woods regime of fixed but adjustable exchange rates to nearly the same extent that France did. Indeed, Japan's ascendence through the ranks of the world's economic powers seemed to accelerate in the 1970s and 1980s. Reform for Japan meant adjusting to that ascendance rather than, as for France, preventing precipitous decline.

It is true that domestic factors help account for the difference in the nature of reform in France and Japan. Among such factors one can cite a typical rate of savings in Japan which was not only higher (at 19.6 percent in 1970) than France's (15.4 percent) but also characterized by greater stability. A greater proportion of liquid savings was held in currency and sight deposits in France, whereas time deposits were

[57]Rosenbluth, *Financial Politics*, p. 5.

more predominant in Japan.[58] Greater stability in savings, in turn, had its source in a social policy that lagged considerably behind that of France for quite a long time. Retirement plans and pension funds benefited only a small number of workers, and higher education is not free, as it is in France. Other domestic factors, such as the shorter gestation time between investment and output, historically low in Japan, and such as wages that historically were lower and more flexible, conspired to enhance the competitiveness of Japanese goods on export markets. Stable and ample liquid savings were thus able to combine with accumulated foreign export earnings to blunt any shock that change in the international monetary system might have generated.

Of greater importance to Japan's ability to foster monetary stability, however, was Japan's mode of insertion in the international political economy. First, Japan is, contrary to popular wisdom, significantly less dependent on foreign trade than France. Lower trade dependence (12 percent of GDP in 1979, compared with 22 percent for France) aided by stricter trade protection had the effect of mitigating the threat of a destabilizing spiral of inflation and currency depreciation which so preoccupied the French during the 1970s. Second, Japan was able to construct a more favorable and more asymmetrical trade relationship with the hegemonic United States than were the Europeans. Robert Gilpin writes:

> For the sake of rebuilding Japanese power and maintaining its strategic position in the Pacific, the United States tolerated not only Japanese restrictions on American direct investment but Japanese barriers against American exports as well, and what Americans would come to regard as Japanese "dumping" on the American market. In the larger interest of Pacific security, the United States in effect encouraged the Japanese export-led growth drive. The United States demanded no economic quid pro quo, as it did in the case of the Common Market.[59]

Asymmetry in trade, combined with internal features of the Japanese political economy that facilitated export-led growth, helped foster a virtuous circle of growth, success in foreign trade, and reinforcement of the capital base of Japan's principal industrial firms. As Calder describes it, capital growth meant that by the late 1970s "any firm which wanted to borrow funds in Japan could do so on the basis of market criteria, without reference to state priorities." Government control over the allocation of credit became weak. Simultaneously, the growing supply of capital cut the cost of borrowing on the market or

---

[58]See Patat, *Monnaie*, p. 235.

[59]Robert Gilpin, *U.S. Power and the Multinational Corporation: The Political Economy of Foreign Investment* (New York: Basic Books, 1975), p. 111.

through unregulated institutional channels and thus decreased dependence on government financial institutions, such as the Japan Development Bank. Inversely, government institutional lenders grew "more and more conservative—more and more like the private investment bankers, with whom they continually associated—and less interested in the socialization of risk." Calder continues:

> This seeming irrelevance of the government financial system to industrial strategy was, ironically enough, the product of its success. The ability of [state allocated] policy finance to foster heavy industry in the 1950s and 1960s had created a complex of industries—steel, shipbuilding, shipping, and indirectly even machine tools and autos—which had succeeded massively in international competition. This success had generated the trade surpluses and excess liquidity which finally undermined the structure of credit controls during the early 1970s.[60]

Japanese firms never experienced the cash-flow problems that plagued French firms in the 1970s and that prevented the latter from taking better advantage of the recession and the drop in investment to decrease their indebtedness vis-à-vis lending institutions. In contrast, Japanese firms, increasingly better capitalized and progressively less indebted, were able to profit from the deflationary 1970s to decrease their dependence on credit. Japanese industry ceased to be an overdraft sector by gradual evolution, not by precipitate reform. Japanese industry climbed out of its dependence on institutionally supplied credit and indeed was soon supplying capital to the rest of the Japanese economy. Banks, which traditionally were heavier borrowers on the money market than their French counterparts, began to borrow short-term from industrial firms, using bonds as collateral. In 1979, certificates of deposit were introduced as a way to facilitate business lending to banks.

In a word, the success and the expansion of Japanese export industries, combined with the conservatism of the banking sector, gradually transformed Japan's overdraft economy into one in which an overdraft sector coexisted with a well-capitalized and economically robust asset-based industrial sector. The *Economist*, describing how Japanese firms were "escaping—albeit slowly—from the tutelage of the banks," quotes a director of a shipping firm: "Ten years ago, we had to invite our bankers to dinner, so they sat in the *tokonama* (the privileged position in a Japanese dining room)...but now the banks ask us to dinner, so we sit in the *tokonama*."[61]

[60]See Calder, "State," chap. 9, pp. 6, 13, 17.
[61]*The Economist*, August 22, 1987, p. 65.

294

Finland provides an example of an overdraft economy whose mode of insertion in the international political economy failed to generate levels of stress sufficient to provoke structural reform. Finland's financial market during the decades following the war was, like that of France, very narrow. Government policy was partly responsible for this. Like their Gaullist counterparts in France, successive Finnish governments failed to provide the market with a significant volume of public debt, preferring to keep the public accounts balanced and frequently in surplus. Finnish firms, like those of France, held monetary assets primarily for transaction purposes rather than as a precaution against unforeseeable liquidity crises. The Finnish economy also tended to be inflationary. Inflation ran at an average of 5.1 percent between 1960 and 1967, climbed to 6.4 percent between 1968 and 1973, and remained at about 12.5 percent throughout the 1970s. The corresponding figures for the OECD as a whole were 2.7 percent, 5.4 percent, and 10.4 percent. As in France, the structure of the financial system inclined the central bank to exercise direct administrative control over the operations of the banking system. The banking system was highly concentrated and highly indebted to the central bank, enabling monetary officials to control the expansion of credit by setting rediscount ceilings and credit expansion limits for individual banks. Finally, as in France, the central bank's power over the allocation of credit was used to pursue specific industrial and economic goals, such as export promotion.

There are differences, however. The Bank of Finland, unlike the Banque de France, never had to rely systematically on credit restrictions to achieve its goals, but rather was able to regulate credit expansion successfully simply through the use of rediscount policy. In effect, the two most important instruments of central bank policy were its power to affect the cost and availability of central bank credit to the commercial banks and its control over international capital movements. They were easily targeted and fluctuated considerably over the course of the business cycle.[62] Finland's ability to use instruments that the French found inadequate can be explained by the simple fact that there was no substantial international market for Finland's currency, and hence little speculative movement in and out of it. Finnish authorities found exchange controls sufficient for dealing with foreign capital movements and were never tempted, like their French counterparts, to implement an active and flexible exchange rate policy based on monetary growth targets and interest rate policy. Finland's immunity from movements of "hot money" spared Finnish officials many of the headaches suffered by the French.

[62]See Airikkala and Bingham, "Formulation and Control," p. 96.

Jung-en Woo has written an arresting analysis of financial policy and reform in the Republic of Korea, whose similarities with France are striking.[63] "Repression of finance" characterized the development of the postwar political economy in Korea as in France. Throughout its history, the state insulated its financial market from the world and regulated the flow of foreign capital. Banks were nationalized, and the state used its resultant power over financial policy to provide loans to industrial investors, notably the monopoly firms, or *chaebôl*, at interest rates that were frequently negative in real terms. Credit policy in Korea, as in France, was designed to speed industrial development.

Like the French, Koreans concocted numerous specialized financial programs, like the Machinery Industry Promotion Fund, the National Investment Fund, or the export loan program, from which industrial borrowers could benefit, but the attractiveness of such programs far exceeded anything observed in France. Special export loans were offered at real interest rates of − 14 percent in 1975, − 12 percent in 1976, 1977, and 1979 and − 10 percent in 1980. The predictable outcome was a rate of inflation that frequently exceeded 20 percent in the 1970s, and a cheap-credit inflationary boom that gave rise to an unregulated "curb market" for capital on which interest rates frequently exceeded a usurious 40 percent (between 15 percent and 20 percent in real terms).

As in the case of France, domestic financial fragility meant vulnerability to external shock. In the case of both oil shocks, however, Korea was able to respond with wage restraint, devaluation, export promotion, and foreign borrowing. Woo writes, "[What] happened in 1979–1980 could easily be, and was, corrected with the tools and habits of this same flawed economy: industrial reorganization by fiat, labor repression, foreign loans to ride out the bad times—and then simply a wait for the end of global recession, when the factories would run at full capacity." Korea's external debt after the second oil shock climbed from $20.3 billion in 1979 to $46.7 billion in 1985. By this time, of course, devaluation and foreign borrowing had lost their usefulness as far as the French were concerned.

As in the case of Japan, certain features of Korea's domestic political system explain the temporary success of strategies that were no longer operative in France, not the least of which was the facility of labor repression under a dictatorship. Real wages dropped by 1 percent in 1981 while labor productivity jumped 18 percent. "Wage restraints," writes Woo, "were an artifact of sheer political terror.[64] Again, howev-

[63]Jung-en Woo, *Race to the Swift: State and Finance in Korean Industrialization* (New York: Columbia University Press, 1990).
[64]Ibid., pp. 182, 180–81.

er, one must look at Korea's peculiar mode of insertion in the international political economy to understand fully why it could respond to external shock with tools that the French had long forgone. First, Korea's trade relations were highly regulated until the mid-1980s. Average tariff rates exceeded 30 percent as late as 1982. Tariff rates exceeding 50 percent were applied to 15.5 percent of total imports in 1983. Second, a "front-line" state, Korea was made the object of much financial solicitude by the United States and, at the insistence of the latter, by Japan. "Korea was allowed the luxury of deviation [from the canons of capitalism], a state-led and late development, as long as it remained in the interstices of global capitalism and on the forefront of the Cold War."[65]

Eventually, however, in Korea as in France, the issue of reform could no longer be dodged. Domestic constraints combined with severe external political pressures to force the issue of liberalization in trade and finance. Domestically, the "desire to reduce the burden of socializing risk—the problem of default—in a system where the state was creditor" gradually became "an imperative as the amount of non-performing loans skyrocketed in the 1980s, making extremely credible the threat of massive financial collapse."[66] High levels of inflation goaded grudging domestic support for liberalization in trade and created the need for a rigorous stabilization plan that caused domestic credit expansion to fall from a staggering 41 percent in 1980 to 30 percent in 1982 and finally to 13 percent in 1984. Again, however, one must pay particular attention to external factors. International (especially American) pressure to liberalize the market had become very great. The number of antidumping and countervailing charges brought against Korea under General Agreement on Tariffs and Trade (GATT) legislation climbed from thirteen in 1981 to thirty in 1984, jeopardizing nearly 18 percent of the volume of Korean exports.

In response to such pressures, both internal and external, trade barriers were all but eliminated. "By the summer of 1989, the average tariff in Korea was among the lowest for the non-OECD countries, enabling it to dodge the new crowbar of super 301."[67] More relevant to the present study is the fact that financial structures and practices were deregulated. Banks were privatized, ceilings on interest rates were lifted, and specialized credit programs were abolished. Interest rates on loans, which had been negative in real terms, now climbed to 10 percent at a time when inflation was disappearing. Banks were allowed to buy stock in Korean firms and to expand into a wide variety of

[65]Ibid., p. 202.
[66]Ibid., p. 192.
[67]Ibid., p. 188.

financial services, while ceilings were lifted on commercial paper and unsecured corporate bonds. Moreover, barriers to foreign banks and financial institutions were lifted.

The speed as well as the success with which the Koreans liberalized their political economy in response to internal and external pressures is striking. Korea's mode of insertion in the international political economy is not foreign to such success, because its asymmetrical trade relations with the United States helped its industrial firms, like those of Japan, to realize foreign earnings, to increase their capital base, and thus to evolve from an overdraft sector to an asset-based sector. Unlike the gradual process that occurred in Japan, however, the transformation was sudden and violent, propelled by the threat of imminent financial collapse and irresistible foreign pressures.

Finland, France, Korea, and Japan all experienced the overdraft economy, yet policy orientations in the 1970s differed significantly from one country to the other, as did the evolution of economic structures. Finland experienced little need to alter its policy orientations. Japan, through a gradual series of incremental reforms, was able to stabilize its currency and its internal monetary situation. The French attempted first to use the state's control over borrowing and lending to prolong the process of adjustment to change in international payments patterns. Then, as their efforts encountered little success, they conceived of and ultimately implemented a number of financial reforms designed to rid France of the constraints of the overdraft economy altogether. Korea's liberalization was the most revolutionary of all. The opportunity to pursue a strategy of export-led growth, access to Japanese and American capital, and the military dictatorship's power of repression prolonged the overdraft economy's viability throughout the 1970s. In the 1980s, however, growing financial instability and the destruction of the asymmetries of Korea's relationship with a country which in its particular case had remained hegemonic, provoked rapid reform.

One cannot fully understand such differences without paying attention to the unique mode of insertion of each of the four national economies in the international political economy. Finland, because of its low degree of vulnerability to exchange rate fluctuations, was able to avoid the need to concoct innovative policies or structural reforms to deal with the overdraft economy's inability to foster the sort of monetary discipline that the world of floating rates generally demands of small, open economies. The task of reform in both Japan and Korea was facilitated by asymmetry in their commercial relations with a hegemonic power, facilitating the evolution of their industry from overdraft to asset-based sectors. France, however, combined a high degree of trade openness, a heavily traded currency, and the absence of a strong asset-based export sector. This diversity in the mode of insertion in the international political economy makes it difficult to arrive at generalizable conclusions. One is obliged to reject Keohane's claim that "without a conception of the *common* external problems, pressures, and challenges . . . we lack an analytic basis for identifying the role played by domestic interests and pressures. . . . Understanding the constraints imposed by the world political economy allows us to distinguish the effects of common international forces from those of distinctive national ones."[68] The distinction between the "internal" and the "external" is not so clear. Though the sorting out of variables, disembodied from their historical context, is a necessary activity for nomothetic theory-building, it is far from certain that the real world makes this kind of sorting possible. As I argue elsewhere, the complexity of the phenomena we must deal with inclines scholarship toward the comparison of idiosyncratic national histories rather than toward a science composed of covering laws that can be lifted from historical contexts. John Ikenberry arrives at similar conclusions: "This claim of causal complexity complicates the theoretical enterprise, and leads to a final methodological claim of the primacy of contingent historical analysis. The institutional structures of countries emerge from distinctive national experiences. Consequently, theory must remain historically grounded and sufficiently contingent to allow for the variations in institutional structures."[69]

U.S. HEGEMONY THROUGH THE LENS OF FINANCIAL REFORM IN FRANCE

In the case of the four countries examined above, U.S. policy played an important part in creating the conditions for structural change in the domestic political economy and even in determining the direction of that change. The United States established an asymmetrical trade relationship with Japan that enabled Japanese firms to export their way out of their dependence on institutionally allocated credit. On the other hand, America's repudiation of its asymmetrical monetary relationship with the Europeans laid bare the vulnerability of the overdraft

---

[68]Robert Keohane, "The World Political Economy and the Crisis of Embedded Liberalism," in John H. Goldthorpe, ed., *Order and Conflict in Contemporary Capitalism* (Oxford: Clarendon Press, 1984), p. 16, quoted in Ikenberry and Mastanduno, "Introduction: Approaches to Explaining American Foreign Economic Policy," *The State*, p. 4 (italics added).

[69]Ikenberry, "Institutional Approach," pp. 225–26. See also the Introduction to the present book and Michael Loriaux, "Comparative Political Economy as Comparative History," *Comparative Politics*, April 1989.

economy in France. The history of French financial development can inform our understanding of what U.S. hegemony meant and how it worked.

International trade liberalization has imposed itself on the discipline as the principal characteristic of the American hegemonic order. That characterization, however, owes much to the "hegemony" of Stephen Krasner's elegantly argued structural realist rendition of the thesis.[70] John Conybeare, however, is persuasive when he asks what economic benefit the hegemon, in an international liberal trading order, could possibly derive from its hegemony.[71] For Robert Gilpin, on the other hand, the imposition of hegemonic order gives rise to an international trading system the laws of which are politically determined and therefore capable of being endowed with a greater or lesser dose of liberalism.[72] With respect to the U.S. hegemonic order, liberalism in trade was no more or less the defining characteristic than was the implementation of industrial policies by participant countries that controverted the power of the market to foster national specialization in keeping with the doctrine of comparative advantage. The principal characteristic of the U.S. hegemonic order was indeed its "embedded liberalism."[73] To grasp the nature of that order, it does not suffice to point to the spectacular expansion of international trade and the equally spectacular dismantling of tariff barriers. One must also point to the multiplication of policy tools that empowered participating governments to intervene in their domestic economies.

More specifically, the hegemonic order was born of efforts on the part of the United States to shore up Western European governments against what American policymakers perceived as a threat of growing Soviet and Communist influence. That policy prompted the United States to shelve its liberal reformist ambitions, as embodied above all in the Bretton Woods agreements, and to assign priority to European political and economic integration. The immediate consequence of that policy was to shift bargaining power to the Europeans. This enabled

[70]Stephen Krasner, "State Power and the Structure of International Trade," *World Politics* 28 (April 1976). See also Timothy McKeown, "The Limitations of 'Structural' Theories of Commercial Policy," *International Organization* 40 (Winter 1986); Stephen Haggard and Beth Simmons, "Theories of International Regimes," *International Organization* 41 (Summer 1987).

[71]John Conybeare, *Trade Wars: The Theory and Practice of International Commercial Rivalry* (New York: Columbia University Press, 1987).

[72]See Robert Gilpin, *War and Change in World Politics* (Cambridge: Cambridge University Press, 1981), pp. 127–44.

[73]See John Gerard Ruggie, "International Regimes, Transactions, and Change: Embedded Liberalism in the Postwar Economic Order," in Stephen Krasner, ed., *International Regimes* (Ithaca: Cornell University Press, 1983).

the Europeans to dilute America's liberal interpretation of what integration meant. Bretton Woods, the Organization for European Economic Cooperation (OEEC), not to mention the stillborn International Trade Organization, all failed to play a determining role in the actual structuring of the hegemonic order. Unable to secure acceptance of the American vision of an integrated and liberal European Community, held together by strong supranational institutions, the United States had to settle for a Europe brokered by the French and the British. The resultant European structures, embodied in the European Coal and Steel Community and the European Payments Union, made ample room for the pursuit of economic policy orientations, embraced at war's end, that deviated significantly from the ideal types that informed American policy. This is not to belittle the multilateral achievements of this period,[74] but such achievements fell well short of the ambitions of American officials and were made possible only after compromise with the governments of Europe.

For the French, the outcome was an international economic order that prolonged the viability of their postwar interventionist and *volontariste* policy orientation. It was that policy orientation, in turn, that ultimately generated the overdraft economy, as the French continued to finance modernization through monetary creation and the *"transformation"* of liquid assets rather than through the market remuneration of real savings. French policy illustrates the coexistence of international economic integration and persistent economic interventionism by national governments that characterizes the "embedded liberalism" of the postwar economic order.

Marxian or Marxian-derived interpretations of the hegemonic order also encounter difficulties when confronted with the evidence. For historians such as Joyce and Gabriel Kolko and Fred Block, the postwar policies of the United States were inspired chiefly by the need to preserve trade and investment opportunities in Europe that were threatened by the economic nationalism of frequently left-leaning postwar governments. Marshall aid was designed to shore up political forces in Europe that would defend international capitalism. The success of American policy signified decline in the living standards of the European working class as governments set out to prop up the capitalist system by restoring conditions of capitalist profitability. "The economies of Europe were *intentionally* manipulated to *lower* living standards, create new unemployment, and sharpen inequality—a time-

---

[74]For a more conservative estimate of achievement in trade relations, see Alan S. Milward, *The Reconstruction of Western Europe, 1945–1951* (London: Methuen, 1984), pp. 421–25.

tested capitalist cure for an inflationary economy and an essential aspect of their concept of 'recovery.' "[75]

The French case bears out this interpretation in certain points, but on the whole suggests that it is unwarranted. It is true that the United States acted to preserve investment opportunities in Europe in general and in France in particular, and it is true that it did try to use its aid to foster stabilization policies. On the other hand, the history of French-American relations during the period 1947–52 is one of acquiescence by the United States in the *volontarisme* of a France that was determined to purge the French economy of the *malthusianisme* of its capitalist past, be it at the expense of capitalist orthodoxy. Although efforts were made to slow inflation in 1949 and 1950, and although the government opposed the demands of workers during the strikes of 1947 and 1948, the pattern of French policy was, and would remain for the next decade, one of nonconfrontation with societal actors and one of preference for policies that sustained societal expectations of economic betterment and security. Such preferences were only imperfectly mirrored by political life under the Fourth Republic, which remained characterized by the legacy of deep-rooted cultural and social cleavages, but are expressed well in the monetary policies of successive French governments, which generally remained uniformly expansionist.

Nor were French policies excessively idiosyncratic when compared with those of other European countries. Italy stood out in OEEC negotiations concerning the distribution of Marshall Aid funds because of its rigorous monetary policy orientation and was, significantly, roundly criticized by the other European participants who accused it of fostering trade imbalances in Europe.[76] In addition, though the German Federal Republic declared allegiance to the principles of economic liberalism from the first years of its existence, recent research suggests that Germany's liberal reputation is not entirely faithful to the facts. Indeed, its attitude in trade negotiations revealed real hesitation regarding the prospect of trade liberalization. In bilateral negotiations with the French, both sides agreed on the legitimacy of recourse to quotas in the event of severe trade imbalances, and both agreed that industrial and agricultural groups of both countries would meet regularly in order to assess whether adjustments to the trade agreement were

---

[75]Joyce Kolko and Gabriel Kolko, *The Limits of Power: The World and United States Foreign Policy, 1945–1954* (New York: Harper and Row, 1972), p. 382, quoted in Robert A. Pollard, *Economic Security and the Origins of the Cold War, 1945–1950* (New York: Columbia University Press, 1985), p. 156. See also Fred Block, *The Origins of International Economic Disorder* (Berkeley and Los Angeles: University of California Press, 1977), pp. 30–31, 90.

[76]See Milward, *Reconstruction*, pp. 205–6.

necessary, and finally, both were quite determined to protect their agriculture.[77]

In sum, little in the historical record warrants the interpretation according to which the United States sought to use its economic superiority to create conditions that favored the growth and expansion of American capitalism by combating economic nationalism in Europe. The United States did fight that battle, but it lost. The chief characteristic of the hegemonic order was the element of compromise that rendered economic nationalism in Europe compatible with European economic integration and the development of world trade. The hegemonic order, like the temple of Concord, was erected on the site of factional strife.

Nor should "liberalization" be chalked up solely to the credit of the hegemonic order. On the contrary, the multilateral trade negotiations of the 1960s and 1970s can be interpreted as efforts on the part of the United States to undo the asymmetrical trading order it had patched together at the onset of the cold war. Trade liberalization, to the extent that it characterizes international economic relations today, originated from efforts to dismantle the hegemonic order, not from efforts to construct it. That the United States brought its enormous economic power to the bargaining table should not confuse us as to the deconstructionist nature of the enterprise. It is, moreover, the partial failure of those efforts that explains the "new protectionism" of the 1970s.

The postwar history of economic policy in France is relevant to another contention that one encounters in the literature: that a community of views or of ideology preceded the construction of the hegemonic order.[78] The presumed community of values explains "the willingness of the partners of a hegemon to defer to hegemonial leadership.... Hegemony rests on the subjective awareness by elites in secondary states that they are benefiting, as well as on the willingness of the hegemon itself to sacrifice tangible short-term benefits for intangible long-term gains."[79] The history of the French overdraft economy does not support this claim. Looking at the domestic politics of France, only the MRP seems to have wholeheartedly shared America's vision of an integrated Europe and to have sympathized with America's ambition of global political reform. It is, however, less than certain that the MRP could have durably shared America's vision of a liberal, capitalistic

---

[77]Ibid., pp. 425–27.

[78]See Robert Keohane, *After Hegemony* (Princeton: Princeton University Press, 1984), pp. 43–46; Ruggie, "International Regimes."

[79]Keohane, *After Hegemony*, p. 45.

world economic order, given its Catholic social ideals. Nevertheless, even this "ideological" convergence between the MRP and American policymakers was fashioned by American policies that sustained the MRP's influence in French politics by facilitating the French government's leveraged modernization policies. In other words, hegemony was clearly prior to ideological convergence and, indeed, made ideological convergence possible. In the words of Alan Milward, "The intention was that values would follow aid, rather as in previous centuries trade had been thought to follow the flag, and that these values would deeply influence the political development of the European countries in a favourable direction."[80]

AFTER HEGEMONY: THE PROSPECTS FOR GLOBAL LIBERALIZATION

The hegemonic order began to unravel in the mid-1960s. In 1971, the United States expressly relinquished its commitment to a monetary order of fixed exchange rates which facilitated adjustment through devaluation by states that relied on inflationary policy to promote social peace. The pursuit of more nationalistic economic policies by both the Carter and Reagan administrations continued to chip away at the asymmetries that once characterized the *Pax Americana*.

The world that U.S. hegemony has left behind, however, is not a world that hegemonic theory would have predicted. Greater nationalism, or, more appropriately, less internationalism in the United States, has not provoked a return to nationalism across the globe. World trade continues to increase at a faster pace than world aggregate GNP. Financial markets are deprived of protectionist regulations. In Europe, governments project that all nontariff barriers to the exchange of goods, capital, and labor will be eliminated by the end of 1992. France, once the most skeptical of EC nations, is now at the forefront of integration. In the area of monetary relations, the French have, since 1983, been one of the driving powers behind the continued development of the European Monetary System. In January 1988, Édouard Balladur, minister of finance in the government of Jacques Chirac, declared, "The moment has come to examine the possibility of creating a European central bank that would manage common currency."[81] Looking beyond the confines of the European Community, the French have consistently championed the elaboration of more binding international monetary arrangements and rules. Balladur, again, suggested

---

[80]Milward, *Reconstruction*, p. 123.
[81]*New York Times*, January 17, 1988.

that global monetary relations be structured by an international regime based on the EMS model.[82] France's Europeanism and its dismantling of the statist controls and regulations that once governed its foreign economic relations, not to mention its newfound internationalism, have provoked observers to claim that we are now witnessing the end of French "exceptionalism."

Analytical frameworks and theories that currently dominate the field of international political economy do not offer an entirely satisfactory grasp of how international economic structures are responding to the withdrawal of the United States from the hegemonic role it assumed in the 1950s and early 1960s. The simple force model, according to which hegemonic decline should lead to the resurgence of a multiplicity of conflictual nationalisms, clearly explains neither the current movement toward greater European integration nor France's insistent and repeated call for a new Bretton Woods. It is the inability of the simple force model to account for the evolution of the post-hegemonic international political economy that enabled Keohane to reject it in favor of a theory that posits the existence of a suppressed though rational demand for policy coordination on the part of national governments, which can now be satisfied because of the facilitating role played by international organizations. There is no denying the logical force of Keohane's argument, or the fact that high levels of cooperation apparently continue to characterize international economic relations. It is less than clear, however, that Keohane's account explains "real" events. Restricting ourselves to the monetary realm examined in this volume, the absence of "beggar-thy-neighbor" policies of currency depreciation is most expeditiously explained, at least in the case of the open economies of Europe, by the threat of destabilizing spirals of depreciation and inflation, which effectively deprives the Europeans of the opportunity to exploit the regime of floating rates for commercial gain.[83]

---

[82]See Édouard Balladur, "Rebuilding an International Monetary System," *Wall Street Journal*, February 23, 1988.

[83]See Keohane, *After Hegemony*, p. 210: "The United States did not have to persuade its partners not to follow beggar-thy-neighbor policies in response to dilemmas of collective action: the persistence of a regime provided reassurance about others' intentions and practices." The resilience of the open trading order may also be best explained by dropping the neo-realist assumption of the unit-like national and strategically rational actor and by adopting a sectoral approach. See McKeown, "Limitations"; idem, "Tariffs and Hegemonic Stability Theory," *International Organization* 37 (Winter 1983); Stephen D. Krasner, "The Tokyo Round: Particularistic Interest and Prospects for Stability in the Global Trading System," in Jeffry A. Frieden and David A. Lake, eds., *International Political Economy: Perspectives on Global Power and Wealth* (New York: St. Martin's Press, 1987). Providing interesting insights are Charles Lipson, "The Transformation of Trade: The Sources and Effects of Regimes Change," in Krasner, ed., *International Regimes*; and Helen Milner, *Resisting Protectionism: Global Industries and the Politics of International Trade* (Princeton: Princeton University Press, 1988).

Louis Pauly, on the other hand, has supplied us with an informative and enlightening analysis of financial market deregulation in the United States, Canada, Australia, and Japan which suggests that internationalist norms, supportive of economic openness, are indeed gaining adherence in the OECD world: "Market access policies have in recent years been converging in the direction of increasingly common regulatory standards." As banks have sought to establish footholds in foreign markets, national governments have reacted both by opposing or by seeking to control foreign bank access, and by promoting efforts on the part of their own banks to penetrate foreign markets of other countries. States have thus entered into a process of communication with other states, giving rise to expectations of reciprocity. "External expectations and actual domestic policies moved toward greater conformity, and those policies were thereby endowed with an intersubjective sense of legitimacy. A customarily accepted set of coordinating norms was emerging." Pauly concludes:

> After three decades of policy development, the institutional interpenetration of national banking markets in the advanced industrial world is now well developed. Convergent domestic laws and practices are creating a basic normative foundation for necessary interstate coordination on market access issues. Increasingly accepted regulatory standards, embedded in unique domestic structures, are important elements in an evolving process through which competition in one sector of modern capitalism is broadened and equilibrated by the interaction of the states at its core.[84]

Pauly supports his thesis with evidence from Europe, which he found to be generally consistent with the process observed on the Pacific rim.

Pauly's attention to the evolution of international custom provides a welcome challenge to scholarship that has tended to assume anarchy unproblematically. This applies, of course, to hegemonic theory itself, which is a derivative of the realist paradigm. Nonetheless, customs and norms emerge from interactions that are themselves, to a greater or lesser extent, governed by uneven growth and by the impact of uneven growth on an international political economy that was once more hegemonic than it is at present. The link between uneven growth and policy is apparent in the Canadian and Australian cases, which Pauly analyzes. In the Australian case, as in the French case, efforts to shelter the Australian currency from the effects of floating rates through exchange controls proved futile. And in both the Australian and Canadian cases, the issue of bank deregulation was pressed hard when the Reagan administration implemented fiscal and monetary policies

---

[84]For Pauly's analysis, see Louis W. Pauly, *Opening Financial Markets: Banking Politics on the Pacific Rim* (Ithaca: Cornell University Press, 1988), pp. 2, 7, 182, 184–85.

that addressed the effects of uneven growth through massive foreign borrowing, thus inciting the migration of the world's capital to the United States that demanded either more oppressive regulation or reforms that enhanced the attractiveness of domestic capital markets.[85] Although the gradual acceptance of the norm of reciprocal national treatment ensured the prevalence of the second solution, it is still an open and urgent question for students of international political economy whether the norm will prove robust in the face of continued uneven growth, or whether uneven growth will overwhelm such norms and cause them to collapse.

It is tempting to view the liberalization of international financial relations with optimism. One should not, however, forget that there is a reason why markets were regulated in the first place. Incumbents are assailed with demands for protection from markets, demands that can be made to feed the coffers and the ranks of the political opposition. Market regulation has typically been the incumbent's response to such demands. For liberalism to succeed, incumbents must repress or dispel demands for protection. This has not been immediately difficult because of the widespread perception that Keynesian or social democratic regulatory policy has failed. Nevertheless, restricting our attention to France, where liberalization effectively buried the enthusiasm provoked by Mitterrand's electoral victory of 1981, one cannot help but be aware of a sentiment of alienation and powerlessness, the political repercussions of which may be seen in rising rates of abstention and the rebirth of a nationalist and even racist Right. The economic nationalism of the Center Left has been vanquished. But what of the future nationalism of the Right? Is it so difficult to imagine a French Right campaigning against the European Community, against international capital, and against American *"hégémonie"*?[86]

This is not a prediction, but it is a justification for skepticism, a justification for remaining loyal to Rousseau in a world that appears to incline toward Kant. It is clear that one cannot go beyond mere speculation on the basis of observations of one country. Nevertheless, the history of the overdraft economy suggests that the task of reading the future of the post-hegemonic world will not be accomplished by assuming away the contextual and idiosyncratic features of domestic political life. It is, after all, at the nexus of the domestic and the international that the incumbent must govern.

---

[85]Ibid., pp. 124–34, 112, 136, 141.
[86]In French, the term refers principally to the predatory variety.

Index

Cornell Studies in Political Economy

EDITED BY PETER J. KATZENSTEIN

The Fruits of Fascism: Postwar Prosperity in Historical Perspective, by Simon Reich

The Business of the Japanese State: Energy Markets in Comparative and Historical Perspective, by Richard J. Samuels

In the Dominions of Debt: Historical Perspectives on Dependent Development, by Herman M. Schwartz

Europe and the New Technologies, edited by Margaret Sharp

Europe's Industries: Public and Private Strategies for Change, edited by Geoffrey Shepherd, François Duchêne, and Christopher Saunders

Ideas and Institutions: Developmentalism in Brazil and Argentina, by Kathryn Sikkink

Fair Shares: Unions, Pay, and Politics in Sweden and West Germany, by Peter Swenson

National Styles of Regulation: Environmental Policy in Great Britain and the United States, by David Vogel

International Cooperation: Building Regimes for National Resources and the Environment, by Oran R. Young

Governments, Markets, and Growth: Financial Systems and the Politics of Industrial Change, by John Zysman

American Industry in International Competition: Government Policies and Corporate Strategies, edited by John Zysman and Laura Tyson

Library of Congress Cataloging-in-Publication Data

Loriaux, Michael Maurice
 France after hegemony: international change and financial reform
Michael Loriaux.
  p. cm. — (Cornell studies in political economy)
  Includes index.
  ISBN 0–8014–2483–6 (alk. paper)
  1. Monetary policy—France. 2. Credit control—France.
 3. Foreign exchange administration—France. 4. Deregulation—France.
 5. Monetary policy—United States. I. Title.
  II. Series.
  HG979.5.L67 1991
  332'.0944—dc20